THE BOOK OF MARRIAGE

A NEW INTERPRETATION BY TWENTY-FOUR LEADERS OF CONTEMPORARY THOUGHT

ARRANGED AND EDITED BY

COUNT HERMANN KEYSERLING

NEW YORK
HARCOURT, BRACE & COMPANY

Published, October, 1926
Second Printing, November, 1926
Third Printing, January, 1927
Fourth Printing, March, 1927

PRINTED IN THE U. S. A. BY
QUINN & BODEN COMPANY, INC.
RAHWAY, N. J.

Introduction

To my invitation to contribute to *The Book of Marriage,* Bernard Shaw replied: "No man dare write the truth about marriage while his wife lives. Unless, that is, he hates her, like Strindberg; and I don't. I shall read the volume with interest, knowing that it will consist chiefly of evasions; but I will not contribute to it."

This is one of Shaw's famous *boutades.* No one has written more openly on marriage, and yet without causing offence, than he. However, I gladly make use of the Irish sage's witty sally as preface to this book, because in a humorous form it cautions simultaneously against two very serious dangers when treating of marriage problems: the danger of cowardly concealment and the danger of indiscretion. In fact, no one can hope to assist in dealing with this most intimate of all questions whose fearlessness does not empower him to speak of all without causing injury, and whose very nobility of character would make it quite impossible to divulge private matters, so that an unprejudiced person could never even think of interpreting his statements as disclosures. The first and last aim of *The Book of Marriage* is *to help.* Consequently courage and purity are the twin sources of its inspiration.

The Book of Marriage means to help all who are about to enter on marriage; all who are personally distressed by this problem; all who have impartially realized what a terribly serious crisis marriage is passing through today, and that the entire ameliorative future of humanity depends on a favourable settlement. For there can be no doubt of this: since no problem, without exception, concerns everybody more closely than this relationship, which from its very origin determines the bodily and spiritual character of every human being, and which, due to the constancy and intimacy of its influence, continues to assist in determining the character of each partner, the ruin of marriage signifies general ruin, whereas improvement and perfection in it denotes general progress. The appeal of *The Book of Marriage* is, thus, literally to each and all.

But how can a book of pure cognition assist in solving the highly practical problem of marriage? The reader will find nothing that resembles a sermon, nothing didactic in the customary sense of the term; nothing, in a word, savouring of an attempt to influence another's will. Only that form of assistance can possibly help the individual which refrains from giving him direct aid and does not deprive him of responsibility, but teaches him to find his way by himself, independently of others. This can be accomplished in the following manner: Realized truths evolve creative powers in the individual who is really willing to let himself be transformed by their influence. The most wonderful thing in psychic life is that ideas clearly comprehended succeed, in the long run, by means of subconscious processes, in creating actual realities which correspond to them. Thus pure cognition is the one thing essential wherever defectiveness due to miscomprehension is found to exist in the field of realities. And this is so in the case of marriage. The primary cause of its present critical condition is the misconception of its meaning. It is because hardly any one knows what marriage signifies that almost every one woos the wrong person, that hardly one in a thousand knows how to lead a proper married life. Consequently the realization of true significance will lead in the case of marriage, if anywhere, to a radical cure. In order that realization should alter facts, only two conditions are indispensable: first, that the knowledge in question should be properly formulated, and secondly, accepted in such a manner as to prove efficacious.

The first condition depends on the precision of the formulas adopted, the evidence conveyed by the "style," the strictly logical concatenation, and the psychological treatment. In the case of a book, this effect depends on the author's art. In the present case the collaborators are twenty-four in number. But they collaborate in exactly the same sense as do the different players of a well-trained orchestra, or, more accurately, as the various tones of a single harmony. *The Book of Marriage* is an organic whole. The first part deals with the general outlines of the problem. The different sections of the ensuing parts bring into clear relief its particular aspects. As these aspects are limited in number, and since they can appear in only one way when adequate reasoning and clear visualization are brought to bear on them, it is precisely the diversity of authorship which insures the required unity of meaning. For the treatment of each particular aspect of the problem was entrusted strictly to the individual who, by reason of his or her special aptitude, was pre-eminently capable of apprehending and expressing it. If the book had been written by a single author, however paradoxical this may seem, it could never have attained the same degree of unity; for no individual is equally well endowed in all respects. I did not give definite instructions to any of the collaborators. All I did was to formulate clearly the requisite questions and arguments and to seek the persons best suited to deal with them adequately. Having found them, I had no reason to worry about possible contradictions; for it was out of the question that the various authors should fail to complement each other like the tones of a harmony. Naturally they think differently on different questions, and these divergencies occasionally amount to contradictions. But when taken thus in concert, contradictions act contrapuntally. The Buddhist Paul Dahlke, for example, writes as an opponent of marriage. The effect of his treatise, within the symphonic whole, is such that the meaning of asceticism, its justifiable range and the limits of its usefulness, becomes clearly evident.

The Book of Marriage thus states the problem in the full completeness of all its essential aspects. It treats solely of marriage, ignoring the other possible relations between the sexes. The starting-point is marriage, not love, propagation, national welfare, morals, or any similar subject. Each question with its answer is worked out with the utmost precision, clearness, and pregnancy.

So much then for the logical aspect of the book. But in order to produce a creative effect it was necessary to present questions and answers in such sequence as would suit the psychological requirements of interest, attention, and other conditions of understanding. Thus again *The Book of Marriage* appears as a living entity, as it discloses its full meaning only when read in this order. The same rules that apply to the movements of a symphony obtain for the composition of this book. It was conceived and arranged throughout from the standpoint of a pre-existing unity; it does not contain a single item that was not premeditated from the point of view of the whole. And since it answers all fundamental questions relating to matrimony, *it also contains the key to the solution of every individual problem arising in married life.*

We have thus reverted to the original intention of the book, which is to help, and are at the same time confronted with the question of the possibility of rendering practical assistance. I said that cognitive realization can alter actual conditions, provided the insight obtained be formulated and accepted in such a manner as to insure its practical efficacy. The reader will not be long in finding out that the first of these requirements is fulfilled. He will, apart from the precision of the formulation and the evidence of the method of presentation, as well as from the strictly logical concatenations, become fully aware of the fact by the effect the pregnancy and conciseness of the essays will have on his mind. Involuntarily, he will feel the need of continuing the line of thought by himself; for many things that the authors had personal knowledge of and alluded to, without fully expressing, will now impel the reader to seek his own adequate expression. What the reader should do to acquire full benefit from the experience of others is simplicity itself: *Let him, while reading the book, give himself up entirely, mind and soul, to the ideas revealed therein.* Let him read the entire series from beginning to end, and then read, for a second time, the first part which contains the general outlines of the problem in its entirety; finally he should allow the ideas he has received to continue active in his mind. He will not be long in discovering that what made the most vivid impression on his mind was just what concerns him personally. He will realize that he has been applying, as a matter of course, the particular form of his individual problem to the general problems placed before him. At the same time he will become conscious of the general significance of his individual position, in its true relationship to the meaning of marriage in general. He should meditate on what he has realized, and the word, if he be truly willing, cannot fail to be made flesh in his mind. Thus knowledge may here also lead to salvation and deliverance.

COUNT HERMANN KEYSERLING

SCHOOL OF WISDOM
Paradeplatz 2., Darmstadt, July, 1925.

Contents

PART ONE

The Correct Statement of the Marriage Problem

COUNT HERMANN KEYSERLING

The Correct Statement of the Marriage Problem

THE fundamental problems of life cannot be solved according to a schedule, because they are both in reality and intrinsically individual problems; on every occasion when they arise the individual character of each affords the only starting-point for its solution, and consequently in every single case the solution must be unique also. To infer from these facts that the statement and solution of the problems in question is a matter of subjective arbitrariness, however, is to fall into a gross misunderstanding: the unique nature of the concrete situation is the manifestation of universal significance which is inherent in the problem as such and independent of its particular expression. This universal significance is, taken formally, just as strictly determined by the mere formulation of the problem as an equation is by its terms; it comprises exact possibilities and limits which neither opinion nor arbitrary considerations can change. Further, the formal possibilities and limits prove to be substantial entities wherever the problem expresses a necessity of life. Here, incorrect statement and solution give rise, not only to nonsense, but to actual disaster. That it must be so is evident when the problem arises with the fact of life itself, which is *a priori* to all suppositions and desires. The significance of birth and death,[1] for example, is inde-

[1] For the significance of death, see the cycle entitled *Werden und Vergehen* in my book *Wiedergeburt,* published by Otto Reichl, Darmstadt, 1926.

pendent of any personal interpretation; it insists on being understood and endured. A false notion here, in one way or another, leads to an *ad absurdum*. The state of affairs is less clear where the problems, in their given form, are not by nature inevitable and prescribed by destiny, but created by man; this especially applies to such problems as find their solution in cultural forms. However, the same is true here also, as the problems of the intellect and spirit, in contrast to those considered above, have in the same sense to presuppose creative man, as the other problems presuppose organic life. Here again, the starting-point determines strictly definite possibilities and limits; the formal statement corresponds to actual conditions and facts wherever the problem is universally felt to be essential to life. Only in this case not actuality is substantial, but what ought to be. Whereas natural forms signify for humanity "given facts" (*Gegebenheiten*), cultural forms represent results to achieve (*Aufgaben*). But as such, these also possess a significance independent of any opinion or arbitrary consideration; only such a person can satisfy and solve them as has understood this significance. Consequently the most personal of problems dealing with life can only be solved by acquiring an insight into its universal nature. On the other hand, if this insight is acquired, it suffices to show the only right method of solution in each individual case. This applies especially to the problem of marriage. Marriage is neither an outcome of natural laws nor the play of destiny; and it is only possible in a pure form when a definite level of consciousness has been attained, being altogether a creation of the spirit. Nevertheless it is not an arbitrary production, as all savage peoples who possess tradition—and these are fundamentally more bound by their traditions than are later civilized peoples—are acquainted with marriage in one form or another; the more social consciousness is developed, the deeper becomes the significance of marriage. Neither adverse opinion nor practical refutation has ever succeeded in undermining the esteem in which it is held: and whenever its true significance has been fully realized, it has aided any person who felt the vocation to the highest form of self-development. Neither is marriage an empty form that can acquire any meaning: its conception is determined by strictly definite possibilities and limits. It possesses from the outset a specific meaning. To make this relevant is the aim of this book.[2]

WHAT is marriage? In the first place it is not the self-evident fact that most people take it for who are not induced by personal misadventure to oppose or repudiate its true significance. It is not the generally valid solution of all problems dealing with love, nor yet the natural fulfilment of every human craving; primarily because man is complex and too little integrated to permit of all his impulses being brought under one head without coercion. Primarily, every one is by nature polygamous, and woman

[2] Readers of my books will have already recognized from this introduction that *The Book of Marriage* is a special manifestation of the spirit and impulse of the School of Wisdom. In fact I have conceived and arranged it similarly to one of the Darmstadt sessions. The sole aim of the School of Wisdom is the reconstruction of life on the basis of fully realized significance. It can only accomplish this general purpose by giving the right solution to each specific problem. The principal publications up till now have been my books *Schöpferische Erkenntnis* and *Wiedergeburt,* which are being published by Otto Reichl in the autumn of this year (1926). At the annual sessions at Darmstadt, world problems are given a new adjustment and symphonic treatment, exactly as with marriage in this book. The results are then printed in the annual publication entitled *Der Leuchter* (up to 1926, seven volumes have appeared). The School of Wisdom deals with special problems bearing on life, in its proceedings *Der Weg zur Vollendung* (up to 1926, eleven numbers). Further details are given in the prospectus, which can be obtained from the offices of the School of Wisdom, Darmstadt, Paradeplatz 2.

more so than man, as her eroticism is more delicately graded. One consideration will suffice to make this clear, namely that the natural goal of love is, for the differentiated woman, only in exceptional cases the goal of her erotic needs; the latter being already satisfied by flirtation. As marriage partners, both man and wife think primarily of their progeny; neither the father nor, especially, the mother sees anything more in the other partner than a means to an end; this accounts for the disregard in which women are held by all primitive men and explains the typical experience that woman as the mother-animal—and how many are only this!—sees in her mate, on the one hand, a necessary evil, and on the other, the impersonal protector and supporter. These two points readily explain why marriage so rarely satisfies the demands of people who possess a highly personal consciousness, and it is just on this basis that most marriages among civilized races are built. When entering on marriage most people suppose that their choice represents the one and only person possible in each case, while later experience only too often proves that the person selected appeared to be the "only possible one" merely because the racial problem only arises for the individual as a personal problem; or else they appeared only for a short time to be made for each other. Unfortunately no form of marriage is wrecked so easily as that which is based solely on personal attraction, whereas, on the contrary, the latter has the best chances of survival if love does not turn to marriage. In the same way, only in very exceptional cases does the wife preserve her potential character as sibyl and muse. And here we touch on the third reason why marriage is not the self-evident fulfilment of all aspirations. That which primarily constitutes a person's idiosyncrasy is essentially solitary; it is incapable of any communion that would impede its solitariness. Far beyond the remotest solitude complete consciousness of unity can be attained: this is the consciousness of metaphysical unity, which remains valid whether one interprets it from the standpoint of monism, as a theory stating the essential solidarity of separate units, or as a substantial entity preserving its own identity. Metaphysical unity, however, is not what is sought after by a man desiring to escape from isolation. The empirically single entity remains to itself the last resort, and consequently to break down this isolation and to communicate with others is impossible, except on the principle of polarization.[3] These three points readily account for the fact that so few happy marriages are to be found among cultured human beings. If people marry, as is usually the case, only for erotic or generative purposes, or to still the inward sense of loneliness, this fails to lead one to disappointment only when the sense of a separate ego is not highly developed, the eroticism not differentiated, and personal consciousness only reflects racial aspirations.

Nevertheless, the frequency of unhappy marriages in all ages has not in the least impaired the spiritual ideal of marriage for any succeeding generation; in fact each new generation has merely inferred from the mischance of its predecessors that it must learn to do better. Consequently the true significance of marriage cannot be fully contained in what marriage fails, entirely or completely, to achieve. For whatever man continues repeatedly to set himself as a task is just as truly essential to his spiritual and intellectual life as mere existence proves a natural necessity. Actually the marriage problem has to be treated in a different way from the method usually employed. Love alone does not lend marriage significance, nor do self-preserva-

[3] In this connection, see my essay, *Von der Grenze der Gemeinschaft,* in Volume III of my *Weg zur Vollendung* (published by Otto Reichl).

tion and propagation; since, according to its very idea, marriage is, notwithstanding all the usual definitions which the expectation of each person belies, not merely a racial question, but primarily a personal matter. On the other hand, the real ego as essentially a solitary entity does not allow of communion. Further, marriage can only be conceived as a durable life-companionship between man and wife when it is both a sexual and personal bond. This is the case not merely on account of its particular significance, but also for sociological reasons. And in fact, it was never differently contemplated even where polygamy, either as the maintenance of several wives or in the shape of permissible divorce and remarriage, destroyed this idea from a practical point of view. Under these circumstances the life-form of marriage must possess a special and independent significance. Love, propagation, and self-preservation can only act as components. Within its domain the isolation of the ego must be fundamentally secured. Such a conception of higher unity is actually realizable: *it corresponds exactly with an elliptical field of force.* The latter has two foci which are fixed and never can be merged in one another; its interpolar tension cannot be abolished if the field is to remain intact. The interpolar tension is at the same time an independent unit created by the field of force itself. This unit cannot be deduced from the specific character of each pole, taken separately or together, or from any other possible relation existing between the two. In the very same sense marriage represents an independent unit over and above each partner and his particular impulses. Marriage, taken formally, is an independent category of reality, which according to Kant's usage of the term (i.e., independently of all empirical causation of its content) has an *a priori* value. If a marriage relationship is once established, no matter how it originated, it represents pictorially an elliptical field of force.

In marriage, sexual, propagative, economic and social bonds acquire a new and special significance; the same applies to personal and joint destiny. That this significance is not merely the same everywhere—otherwise marriage would not always have remained an ideal for all normal young people—but is actually valid and active wherever marriage relations exist, is proved by the common experience of how greatly marriage alters the character of the partners, and in quite another manner from any other form of partnership. New qualities arise, new dominants determine life, and most important of all, the motives which led up to marriage are soon relegated to the background. No matter how great and enduring the love, the sexual element soon assumes a secondary rôle—just as in the case of liaisons, the chief drawback consists in the exaggerated importance attached to this element—also the subjective pretensions to happiness lose much of their force. In place of these, intimate ties relating to mutual destiny are formed which, for any one who is not too superficial, are far more valuable than any passion or selfish happiness, for by means of these ties deeper-rooted powers and aspirations of the human spirit are able to work themselves out. This special consciousness of unity is the immediate creation of the marriage relation. It is the best illustration of the truth that to a great extent "significance" creates the facts, and not vice versa.[4] The elevation of character and assimilation that takes place in the case of married couples never reaches down to the individual nucleus—and this accounts for the typical *réveil de la veuve,* which in its vehemence is often comparable to

[4] This is the main thesis of my *Schöpferische Erkenntnis.*

the *réveil du lion,* the reverting of a widow, no matter how much she was formerly merged in her husband's character, to her original family type—it rests largely on the fact that both partners assimilate more of the particular spirit of their union, the longer marriage lasts. In the same manner, the defective type of bachelor or old maid is essentially a psychic manifestation; it is in fact much more the want of a specific spiritual reality, which marriage creates, than the lack of erotic and generative experience. Even if this has been plentiful, the defective type still appears wherever the consciousness of unity mentioned above has remained undeveloped, just as, on the contrary, the psychological type of married woman develops under favourable intellectual and spiritual conditions, even in a *mariage blanc.* These few examples should suffice to show that marriage rests first and last on the particular state of tension which it creates. The tensile state reacts creatively by means of suggestion on the mental and spiritual as well as on the physical plane and creates a corresponding new reality. For it seems proved beyond doubt that sexual intercourse not only operates productively as regards the birth of children, but also in the case of the parents themselves.

But how can this special condition, which is unknown to Nature, and which from a selfish point of view represents for each more of a bond than a satisfaction, be recognized as a vehicle of the ideal, so that all ethical systems will require it and every religion admit its sacramental character? Now we are approaching the substantial foundation of what up till now has only been worked out in a categorical form. *Because of this state of tension which constitutes marriage, first the non-individual and suprapersonal elements which are the basis of each person's individuality are given the requisite focus, which enables man to order his personal life in accordance with the universal whole of life. And at the same time the uniqueness of his individuality, which remains for him the ultimate entity, receives the necessary adjustment to insure its freedom within this correlation.* Man not only possesses a unique personality but is primarily a representative of the race, a social being and a part of the cosmos. This fact is difficult for the mind to comprehend because of its subjective limitations and preconceptions. Its reality is nevertheless certain. Not merely as seen from the outward perception of life as a whole, where intuition distinctly shows that isolated independence is a rare and incidental flower growing on the superindividual stem, but also from the point of view of each separate entity, and that without contradicting its metaphysical uniqueness. Life as a collective whole actually requires, for the realization of its highest expression, a dual cooperation. Social instinct precedes self-consciousness. Every religious and ethical system and all intellectual and spiritual ideals have their foundation in the primary reality of the superindividual state. All ideals, which are nothing else than the exponents and symbols of an inner reality, attest to a state beyond isolation. That these are actual realities is shown again and again by the practical consequences of their neglect. Here we have in mind especially such conditions as bring about the isolation and retrogression of social instinct and consequently introduce disease. This state of affairs can be remedied by resuscitating social instinct.[5] Consequently the empirical ego

[5] I fully explain in my book *Unsterblichkeit* how superindividual consciousness precedes individual in importance, and how every ethical system depends on this. The reality of a human cosmos (*Menschheits-kosmos*) as a premise based on psychic personality is dealt with in an essay entitled *Weltanschauung und Lebensgestaltung* in my *Wiedergeburt.* The principal merit of the school of "individual psychology" (*Individual-psychologie*), founded by Alfred Adler, is to have demonstrated the pathological character of isolation and of defective social instinct.

is from the outset bound to a correlative "thou." Now marriage represents the archetype of this interpersonal tension, taken in its widest sense. In marriage, cosmic conditionality and personal freedom, which sets its own tasks, form an indissoluble synthesis. In it the world of facts and the world of values are merged. It is clear that the synthesis of marriage is not the only condition under which this is achieved. Whoever has outgrown racial bonds and is above egotism, and whose consciousness reflects metaphysical unity, can find his proper adjustment in the cosmos as an outwardly separated entity. But the vast majority of people have not outgrown racial bonds, nor are they above egotism or metaphysically conscious. In the great majority of cases, the will to live in the natural sense predominates. For all such persons, marriage offers the best means to perfection. Marriage is the only way, or at least the most easy, by which they can merge their natural instincts with their spiritual nature, to form a higher union. Under these conditions, is it surprising that marriage is generally recognized as fulfilment of a higher degree than any gratification of particular inclinations, or any performance of special duties? In marriage all particulars are drawn into a higher correlation, in which state it first receives its full personal and cosmic significance. That is why marriage is considered a religious duty in India. That is why the Chinese, with their sense for the correlation of the cosmos, see in the unmarried state something inferior to human status. And that is why marriage is looked upon as a sacrament by the Christian religion, and its ethics as a paradigm for all moral problems. For the same reason illicit sexual intercourse is considered immoral. Physiology is in itself ethically indifferent. But the fulfilment of humanity certainly requires that particular impulses should be lived out in proper relation to their cosmic association; to shift the accent or break away from this principle is directly to convert the most beautiful to the most foul; this is apparent with terrible clearness in the case of love. Here is the explanation why generation after generation, though personally unhappy and disappointed, has always held up to youth a picture of marriage as the estate of bliss; this is why even match-making mothers pay only slight attention to forebodings of unhappiness that may affect their children, as against their precept to marry: for marriage must prevail. The end justifies the means. A wise woman once laughingly commended a marriage, the unhappy termination of which I had predicted, with these words: "Then they will be unhappy, and out of that they will make something." The foolish act similarly, but without the courage to grasp the truth.

We have here reached a conclusion of paramount importance: that marriage, as a solution of the problem of happiness, is misconceived from the outset. A happy marriage, in an egotistic sense, such as infatuated lovers expect, is just as rare as love-children who turn out well, in spite of all existing prejudices. The essential difficulties of life do not end, but rather begin, with marriage. The conscious acceptance of responsibility in life means *ipso facto* the acceptance of suffering.[6] It thus becomes evident to what a great extent selfish expectation of happiness, in the case of engaged couples, depends on a "trick of nature," according to Schopenhauer's usage of the term. Nor should one forget here the special circumstance that fulfilment results in the disappearance of the craving. The happiness of being betrothed consists in

[6] Compare the cycle *Werden und Vergehen,* especially the part entitled *Geschichte als Tragödie,* in *Wiedergeburt* (Darmstadt, 1926).

the vitalizing feeling of the "as yet untouched," and this is terminated by marriage. One may even say that the current conception of conjugal happiness is dependent on the point of view of those who do not possess one another; the same is true, owing to a process of identification, of all such outsiders as invariably rejoice at every wedding. Every one should make up his mind to this once and for all. Then he is ripe for the reconciliatory truth that happiness, as such, can never constitute a problem. Happiness comes from a sense of achievement; its significance, however, is always dependent on definite assumptions. There is the happiness of love, of motherhood, of creation, and many other varieties. In order to experience these, one must have one's object clearly in view; then happiness comes as the result of achievement. From this it will be clear to what extent conjugal happiness can exist, without contradicting what has gone before. At its lowest stage it signifies an assured routine. Nature is full of routine, and man, as Dostoevsky teaches us, is the one animal that adapts himself simply to every condition. Consequently, on this plane a gratified existence is always assured. A problem that is not set does not exist. Even a slave would not murmur continually against a destiny that he accepted as legitimate. Thus the marriages of primitive people, as long as natural impulses are satisfied, are seldom unhappy, of whatever kind the special circumstances may be. These impulses rarely remain unsatisfied. Hence a state similar to marriage exists even among animals. For this reason, under normal conditions, where the type dominates the individual, marriages arranged by experienced relatives, who take both non-individual and universal considerations into account, are usually happier than love-matches, unless love happens to express the needs of the race and type.[7] Personal affection is more often subsequently awakened in the latter case than it is enduring in the former. At a more individualized stage, conjugal happiness is only possible if the significance of marriage has been truly comprehended, and if there is the good will to carry it out. Unless the question is put in the right way, the answer respecting happiness must be in the negative. It was just in order to lighten the task of thoughtless and impulsive youth in acquiring self-restraint, and to minimize the conscious perception of disappointment due to selfish desires, that the sages of former times attached to marriage, even in its primitive form, so much abstruse metaphysic. The ethics of matrimonial and parental duty have the same object in view when claiming that duty and happiness go hand in hand. The beginning in marriage is always difficult. Even the instinctive practice on the part of all married people of defending the prestige and bliss of the honeymoon is primarily the result of a wise wish to suggest to each newly married couple that it is the happiest time of life, in order to withhold from them the truth, until their souls are ripe for it. For marriage is above all the acceptance of responsibility. And this is exactly what the impulsive nature will not consent to.

This also explains why married couples who are permanently happy never bear in mind the difficulties experienced at the commencement. These do not outweigh positive considerations, any more than a true mother ever resents the travail of childbed. This also accounts for the fact that the cares and difficulties that accompany responsibility and so harshly contradict the fairy-tale of

[7] See my views on marriage in the East and West, in the section on Peking in my *Travel Diary of a Philosopher*.

happiness can never undermine true conjugal felicity. If the significance of marriage is rightly understood, and here the correct adjustment of the unconscious is considerably more important than a clearly formulated view, then the highest conceivable fulfilment of earthly existence is made possible. *For the fulfilment of marriage and its happiness entail the acceptance of the suffering pertaining to life. It gives the latter a new and deeper meaning.* For it lifts conscious man to the heights where the equation of life can be solved. Thus it really proves a shield against suffering. Life and suffering are one, inasmuch as there can be no construction without simultaneous destruction, and as harmony only passes as such as a liberation from dissonance. I will give a brief summary of the conclusions arrived at in the cycle *Werden und Vergehen,* in *Wiedergeburt.* If man wishes to live, he must also be prepared to suffer; if he seeks for joy and happiness in the ordinary sense, he will obtain only partial fulfilment, and that this does not correspond to the true significance of life is evidenced by the feeling of emptiness which inevitably follows every purely selfish gratification. But whoever accepts suffering from the outset places himself in the very centre of the meaning of Life. For him there is a stage beyond joy and suffering, in the same sense as melody is a stage beyond the death and birth of the single notes. For him, no unhappiness can rob life of its meaning. Thus, in so-called happy marriages, the problem of happiness is not solved, in the usual sense of the word, but properly speaking it is dismissed.[8] Dismissed, inasmuch as it is accepted as a part of the tragedy of life. And now we are prepared for another truth, which at first sounds paradoxical: Marriage is not

[8] In what sense most problems of life cannot be solved, but can only be dismissed, is shown in my lecture, *Spannung und Rhythmus,* in *Wiedergeburt.*

by nature a condition of happiness, but a tragic one. We term tragic the conflict for which there is no conceivable solution. In this sense all conscious life is plainly tragic, for its entire course depends on the interruption and destruction of existing equilibria, and consequently, the constant formation of new states of tension. It is impossible to live without ever and ever again incurring guilt, as is shown by the commonplace fact that each creature unavoidably lives at the expense of others, and that children cannot help proving themselves ungrateful from the standpoint of their parents. Not to mention the fact that no radical change on the plane of history is possible without crime.

But if we consider life in another dimension, that of its solidarity, in which each individual lives just as much for the rest as in the struggle for existence he lives at their cost, the same tragic quality will be recognized, for mutual aid can never lead to that unity which love demands. Of this class of tragedy, marriage represents the archetype. Let us keep in mind its fundamental definition: marriage sets up an indissoluble state of tension, and its very existence depends on the preservation of this state. Man and woman, both as individuals and as types, are fundamentally different, incompatible and essentially solitary. In marriage they form an indissoluble unit of life, based upon fixed distance. But every impulse tends on its own account to overcome the latter. Love requires a blending, a merging in one another, ranging from physical intercourse right up to intellectual and spiritual comprehension. The desire for power, whether active or passive, requires the submission of one person to another; the desire for happiness means peace, the cessation of tension. All these problems are insoluble, because the very existence of marriage depends both on their not being solved and on their insolubility; an ellipse can never become a circle. The aspirations of love and power originate in the urge of primordial cells to become parts of some higher state. The desire to abolish tension amounts to a desire for death. All higher forms of life are built up of unrelieved lower tensions. The higher it rises, the more tragic is its character. In the animal kingdom the tension between the sexes is subjectively discharged as soon as copulation has taken place. In the case of man it is perpetual, and ever in vain do man and woman attempt to unite, to understand one another. The constant practice of sexual intercourse is symbolic of this, for when it is not due to affection, it is considered a conjugal duty, regardless of a desire for progeny. Another illustration of this is the fact that primitive couples see nothing contrary to happiness in their quarrels and discords; at this level, as tension cannot be abolished, they actually function as harmless safety-valves. Neither can the conflict which each feels to exist between self-interest and duty to the other partner and the children be avoided; the conflict between personal ambition and social obligations is absolutely inevitable, for ultimately each person is a completely separate entity. But the very significance of marriage is contained in this paradox of two separate entities, interdependent and bound to one another, who do not, however, mingle or lose their identity. In marriage, man becomes aware of the tragedy essential to life, in the form of a personal problem, a problem in the sense that tragedy cannot be abolished. Human life, inasmuch as it is superior to that of plants and animals, starts only with the perception of the inevitability of tragedy and its willing acceptance. From this it is evident in what sense a perfect marriage must represent for man the highest achievement of his purpose. In marriage tragic tension is instinctively accepted as the basis of life. In marriage, from the very outset each individual finds his correct adjustment to the cosmic purpose. And henceforth the problems of life are set beyond the plane of tragedy. They are set in accordance with their universal and ultimate significance. Thus suffering can mean happiness just as much as satisfaction can; and the most poignant pain can be joyously accepted if it is recognized as the fulfilment of man's destiny. Thus creative responsibility becomes the ultimate aim of all cravings for happiness.

And now we are in a position to understand why the true significance of the marriage problem can be comprehended only in its highest expression, and why it can be solved only by highly developed people: marriage acquires its true meaning only when partnership is based on the realization of its tragic significance. All relations between man and woman where this is not the case are either preliminary stages or retrogressions. Under the latter conditions, it is certainly easier to find banal satisfaction; for neither cabbages nor cows know anything of tragedy. On the other hand, every one, even the most primitive, has an inkling that marriage begins to achieve its purpose only at the tragic stage. All marriages which have served humanity as symbols or models were examples of austere destiny joyously met. There can be no thought of conjugal happiness until this is no longer endangered by unhappiness. This consideration gives rise to several points of interest. First, it explains why at a low level of development domestic partnership based on a proper division of labour and responsibility has always proved the only durable form of conjugal felicity. Secondly, all models of ideal married life which have found general acceptance represent the highest expression of "conventional marriage" (*Standesehe*). [By "conventional marriage" (*Standesehe*), I mean, in accordance with its original and correct sense, marriage as the body of a specific ethos, the ethos of a definite cultural order, of a definite "standing" in the cosmos. As a corollary, it also sets the blood-limits within which the choice of partners is in each case permissible. Heredity is only incidentally a decisive factor, because marriage as opposed to monachism aims at the perpetuation and raising of stock to a standard determined by spiritual ideals.] Up till now, when a general high level did not exist, the significance of marriage could be realized exclusively on the heights of human attainment. For realization presupposes the subordination of all particular impulses. There must be the will to harmonize all the components on which the marriage relation is based. Consequently, if marriage is contracted or annulled merely on grounds of passion, this can never be taken as a sign of superior character, but of inferior status. Marriage is essentially responsibility. Thirdly and principally, the above considerations account for the fact that matrimonial happiness on a lower plane is detrimental to a person who has otherwise reached a higher. Today the satiety of the bourgeois conception of happiness awakens nothing but disgust in every intelligent and aspiring youth, and the hostility felt toward the marriage order is chiefly due to its being identified with this conception. Fully developed man must never feel satiated, as his entire value depends on the illimitableness of his aspirations. Satiety is only possible wherever aspiration has given place to some form of routine. And this proves derogatory in proportion to the man's abilities. Thus the intellectual woman, as opposed to the primitive female, appears repugnant as a mere creature of sex or maternal animal; and the man completely submerged in conjugal life seems abject. From this one can judge how pernicious is the Christian idea which sees an ideal in the mere fact of marriage. It is absolute nonsense to regard marriage as the legitimate gratification of animal passion and an opportunity of letting oneself go. This ideal is unworthy of mankind, and wherever it is upheld, it causes more harm than any Astarte cult. Marriage is essentially an ideal common to all humanity, for, if properly understood and carried out, it *precludes* the possibility of attaining satisfaction on a low plane, and consequently establishes a higher one. Its intention is not to slacken but to intensify conditions. That is why unhappily married people more rarely do harm to their souls than those who are happily married. Not only does an unhappy marriage promote self-development more positively than does a state of ease due to lack of experience, but it leads more readily to that inward happiness which is the necessary consequence of achievement than any harmony can hope to do which fails to make life more intense. Naturally I do not wish to imply that marriages in which one member irritates the other possess in consequence a positive virtue. I refer exclusively to suffering that intensifies. But this much remains true, in spite of demur: very few people can stand conditions of life that are too happy; the great majority become stultified by them. Life is only felt to be real when it is creatively active. Thus people who appear to outsiders to be exceptionally happy, because of their freedom from care, are as a rule the least satisfied. Man does not notice the fact of his state as such; he only becomes aware of such problems as are set by the existence of his particular state. For this reason the will to adventure is the primary phenomenon of human life. The pauper aspires to wealth, the obscure person to recognition, not actually for the thing in itself, but because he wishes to widen his range, to proceed beyond his present state. That is why the rich so often envy the poor. That is why a young girl desires to leave the protection and security of her home; in reality she wishes to experience the very opposite of what constitutes an ideal for parental forethought. It is just the risk that she instinctively looks for in marriage. Yes, Nietzsche was right in stating that human life can never be understood statically but only dynamically, as the will to fuller life; that is to say, intensification. Man desires to be free, not in order to be spared tribulation—this is more liable to increase in proportion to the degree of self-determination attained—but in order to grow. So he accepts the tensile state of marriage chiefly for the reason that, by its means, regeneration and new growth are made possible. On the physical plane this is represented by the birth of children. On the spiritual and mental plane it is exemplified by the partners' inner development, as a result of their fully accepting and discharging the obligations of life as laid down by marriage. Not only are parents educated just as much by their children as vice versa, but it is characteristic of the marriage tension, as a relation between two persons capable of development, that the desire to resolve the tension becomes sublimated in the sense that one partner either lifts the other to a higher plane, or wishes to be lifted by him. This accounts for the ineradicable worship of the eternal feminine, on the part of man. This explains the desire of every woman to reverence her lover. The deepest significance of marriage, from the standpoint of the individual, is the intensified life it gives rise to. Consequently, it is clearly evident how senseless it is to look on marriage as a safe haven, or on satiety as a conjugal ideal.

LET us summarize before proceeding further, and at the same time place our lights somewhat differently, in order to illuminate certain points better. Marriage is not primarily an erotic union. If it implies merely this to the great majority of Westerners, it is due to the reflex action of inherited Christian asceticism, producing unconsciously an idea of marriage as the legitimate fulfilment of otherwise sinful desires. No unprejudiced nations and times ever felt like this. The erotic element occupies in every psycho-physical organism a prominent position, but erotic gratification signifies, under normal conditions, the alpha and omega of the purpose of life only for certain phases of life and for a few inferior types. (In this connection, one has only to remember that it is exclusively in the sphere of western Christendom that love is looked upon as a decisive factor.) But neither is the begetting of children the real purpose of marriage, as it can be accepted by developed man. Children are merely the outcome or aim of the procreative impulse, that is to say, of the race; and no conscious person feels inwardly identical with this. In fact, he only feels himself identical with the unique part of his personal entity. Consequently marriage must mean to him something intrinsically personal, if he is to regard it as a means to perfection. It thereby appears how erroneous must be any conception which takes things as a model merely because they are "natural." Nature is the basis of man's life, and its claims should never be despised. But the truly human stage in life always commences above this natural order; this latter is only a means for him to realize his soul.[9] This is most clearly seen in regard to propagation, the most natural function of his life. Nature only knows of racial preservation and cares nothing for progress and

[9] Compare the chapter *Das Ziel,* in my *Schöpferische Erkenntnis.*

evolution; whereas the human aspect of propagation is contained in the idea of breeding, that is to say, in attaining cultivation and refinement. This, however, depends principally on spiritual motives and not on natural impulses, and the fact in itself is sufficient to account for marriage as a problem quite apart from that of racial preservation. Man can only transcend the limits of the physiological nature he was born with when living under the influence of a particular mental and emotional atmosphere. Tradition signifies on the cultural plane the very same thing that heredity does on the natural plane. From this it follows incontrovertibly that it is contrary to the very essence of marriage to attempt to divorce it from motives that transcend natural desires and have always been ascribed to it by ethics and religion. Further, this consideration definitely controverts the theory which holds that the entire purpose of marriage consists in love and propagation. These non-natural motives are not incidental or artificial accessions, but an essential part of it. Thus religion and ethics are shown to be fundamentally correct in regard to this matter. We will not, however, enter into details here. If, in the meantime, we examine the significance of traditional ideas and laws of marriage, we find that they one and all purpose to express theoretically and demonstrate practically what we recognize to be the essential quality of marriage: that it is an independent category over and above sexual union as well as racial considerations, and possesses, besides a generic and cosmic sense, a unique metaphysical significance, the realization of which is the ultimate aim of marriage. In fact, the true meaning of marriage was already correctly understood in the earliest times. Thus, all primitive laws which have been handed down to posterity are valid as regards their significance. The first of these relates to the equality of birth of the partners. From a purely formal point of view, a bi-polar relation is only tenable if the poles are situated, at the level of the higher component, on the same plane. Should this not be the case, a readjustment will take place in the direction of the lower member. Since the object and aim of all breeding is the evolution of a higher type, it stands to reason that equality of birth is, from the point of view of posterity, the first condition for a successful marriage. Therefore, without any doubt, as mankind becomes more fully developed mentally it will adhere even more strictly to this principle than the primitive peoples. This certainly must not be interpreted as referring to that narrow conception of the term which only takes name and station into account and only too frequently contradicts the real meaning of equality of birth. But it should be taken as referring to true equality, which will be increasingly dependent on mental and spiritual coordinates, the higher mankind evolves. The second law deals with monogamy. It is quite impossible for any person to enter into a state of bi-polar tension with more than one other. From an intellectual point of view, a polygamous marriage relation is even inconceivable, whereas practically it cannot be realized, because exactly that which constitutes the essence of marriage cannot develop in a harem (to cite from the outset the most extreme expression of polygamy). The harem means, from a man's point of view, a manifold liaison, a breeding institution, or a private brothel, according to the particular circumstances; while for the women, it is something similar to an Amazonian state. In both cases, the women inhabit a kingdom of their own, and in both they are veritable sovereigns, in spite of their outward apparance of weakness. This accounts for the fact that harem women, as soon as circumstances are favourable, attain a high degree of individual development in a remarkably short time, and as experience shows, very quickly find their way to the emancipated state of modern woman. The third law in question prescribes the indissoluble nature of marriage. When a relation consists essentially of an indissoluble unity existing between two poles situated in space and time, divorce becomes a real contradiction in terms. Of course from a practical point of view, this third law becomes increasingly difficult to carry out, but not on account of its inappropriateness, but because under complex conditions of life it is increasingly difficult to contract a marriage worthy of the name. If one is in fairness bound to admit that, in accordance with the modern state of developed consciousness, divorce in the case of a wrong marriage is frequently a lesser evil than its continuance, then every form of frivolous wooing must also be condemned all the more strictly. Under the new circumstances, to marry the wrong man or woman should be accounted immoral, in the same sense as up to the present free love has been condemned. The possibility of remarrying every year ruins marriage much more fundamentally than even the most frequent practice of adultery, for the latter does not at all affect marriage as such, but only offends against certain of its components, whereas divorce lays an axe at its roots. If the poles are continually changed, a durable state of tension cannot develop or endure. Consequently such American women as possess this characteristic are, as types, either Amazons or courtesans, and the men, as husbands, appear subjugated to such an extent as is otherwise found only in polyandrous communities. This shows with particular clearness how overstressing one component of a complex relation—in the United States, the "moral idea"—destroys the balance of the whole system. It would be reasonable to regard as breaches of conjugal faith only cases in which an offence is committed against the particular character of marriage. This does not imply any leniency toward what is customarily looked upon as betrayal. But the latter is not an offence against the marriage relation proper. It can destroy an erotic union, it can endanger society, it can signify disloyalty to others or to oneself; but it does not endanger marriage, properly speaking. Adultery existed all through the ages and was never looked upon as a real danger to marriage, in spite of the stringent protective and deterrent measures that were continually in force, for good reasons of their own; whereas facilitating divorce does seriously threaten marriage.

The time has come to make a clear statement of actual facts so as to purge them of a common theological misconception, for marriage is not a concession to the weakness and sins of the flesh, but a means of attaining the highest spiritual development. Consequently it can be predicted that marriage, far from being "eclipsed," will continue to grow in importance as mankind proceeds to develop. And this is not primarily due to the greater measure of individualization on which a higher state of development is dependent, which in turn implies that the general is expressed more and more exclusively in the image of the particular—"the noblest dedicates himself to one alone" (Goethe)—but because the essential quality of marriage, as opposed to sexual union and propagation, will be recognized to an ever greater extent as a personal problem. At the same time the capacity will increase for building up this particular form of union in the true way. Taking this into account, it becomes evident that the present attempts at marriage reform, far from constituting a danger, will lead to a truer conception of its real significance than was hitherto possible.

Every spiritualized state grows out of what was originally a non-spiritual one. Its evolution is slow, and only at the end of the process is it clearly seen what was intended from the beginning. The normal path toward spiritualization does not lead away from Nature; this is the most notable error of all the doctrines which see in the monastic state an ideal for humanity. As long as the human race persists, there will be need of birth and upbringing. As long as the human race persists, polarization will be the road to advancement; and the polarization of man and woman will in every respect remain the most fruitful condition. As long as the human race persists, the ego of normal man will have to bind itself outwardly to another entity in order to attain its own perfection. Where there can and should be change is here: Nature must always become less and less determinative, ever less of an end in itself, and ever more a direct means to spiritual realization.

We are now in a position to approach the practical problem which marriage posits in every single case. Marriage, as we have seen, is not a fixed state, arbitrarily established, to which each person is forced to comply, but should be looked upon as a problem that has to be solved ever anew. For marriage is not a natural condition capable of self-realization, but a cultural state whose essential meaning, however much it exists by itself, can only be realized by such as are free to make their own decisions.[10] This alone implies that each particular case requires particular expression. The unique character of the particular problem which arises in each case will be-

[10] My *Schöpferische Erkenntnis* (Darmstadt, 1922) shows how in every case the development of significance into appearance is a process working from within toward the outside, through the medium of a free subject.

come finally evident when one recalls what marriage strictly means; namely, an indissoluble relationship of bipolar tension. To realize this fundamentally, each case requires special conditions, depending on the character of the poles; nor can every pair of poles compose this unity of a higher order. To treat the last point first: in a primitive state of society it is not difficult to make a proper choice of partners; the nearer the society is to Nature, the less importance is attached to individual characteristics, and the easier everything goes "by itself," because instinct has free play and is sure of attaining its goal. Under such conditions there is practically no restriction of choice, and almost any person may marry any other, as long as they harmonize as regards type. Here also married life requires practically no skilful handling. This accounts for what so many cultured people fail to understand, the happiness of marriages in which the man is a creature of brute strength and the woman a mere masochistic, sexual, and maternal animal—a condition which is unfortunately still frequently met with in the so-called cultural circles of Europe—this is indeed a case of harmony. The problem always becomes more difficult to solve as differentiation and spiritualization increase, and in an extreme case it assumes such a highly individual character that the conception of the "one and only possible mate" (*Einzig-Mögliche*) is no longer imaginary, but the result of actual necessity. As regards the particular character which the marriage relation has to adopt in accordance with the nature of the poles, this important point arises from its fundamental definition: *that no concrete aspect or expression is conceivable which would not, under certain circumstances, correspond with the significance of marriage,* as here everything depends on the real individuality of the partners. Their relation to one another is to a certain extent predetermined by their type characteristics. In a matriarchal community marriage means something different from what it means in a patriarchal state, since in the former case family associations are given prominence, and in the latter case man and his ideals (for particulars, see Frobenius). In England, where on principle the individual takes precedence of the family, marriage must, if for no other reason, have a different meaning from what it has in Italy, where the *casa* or "house" constitutes a vital association extending from the paterfamilias to the domestic servants and ever since Etruscan times has comprised the real unit beyond which no individual is permitted to go: under these conditions a marriage can never represent more than a part of the communal life of a "house," and consequently it can attain only by way of exception the same high degree of development as where the two partners are looked upon as the principal factors. Now as regards individual choice: the particular nature of an appropriate marriage always depends on the characteristics and impulses which are actually predominant in the partners. Where this is a desire for power and authority, as it appears, in a refined form, in royal families, only a marriage that has this for its dominant factor can be regarded as adequate. Where the main object of life is economic, as in the case of peasants and merchants, a money marriage is fundamentally more suitable than a love match. That is why what is known as marriages of discretion are so often successful, as property means so much more to the majority of people than anything else, and gratitude binds many people more permanently and durably than any type of affection could. Real love marriages—I refer only to such, for it is well known that every marriage is proclaimed to be a love match—are doubtful undertakings, because only highly cultured people are capable of attaching any real importance to a purely personal sentiment. The same considerations account for the fact that in some marriages the typical respective rôles played by the partners, which are supposed to be the only ones possible, appear interchanged, just as every race and age determines them differently to a slight degree. The modern movement for marriage reform is principally based on this: when the character of one of the poles has undergone a change, and this is the case with the woman of today, the particular expression of the marriage relation must alter accordingly, *precisely in order that the relationship may continue unimpaired.* This is the main point. Marriage in itself is a system of eternal validity. In order to achieve its eternal significance, a new particular content must be given it, from time to time, and from man to man.

AND this requires both understanding and artistic skill. This brings us to the central point of the marriage problem. Above the natural plane, fulfilment of its significance never occurs automatically. Let us for a moment consider the most elementary problem relating to marriage, that of choosing partners, because by means of it we find the key to the solution of all further problems. Why are most people of culture unsuitably married? Because they are too differentiated to feel themselves from the outset such unified beings as under favourable conditions are subsequently created by the marriage tension; and yet they are not sufficiently developed mentally to correct the deficiency of instinct by conscious means. Marriage, as we have seen, means something superior to the erotic, propagative, and personal desires, as it brings these together as components of a higher order of integration. They do not constitute this higher union by nature nor by any law of their own being, as lovers always like to imagine. Consequently marriage can only achieve the desired realization if all these components were taken into account when the choice of partners was made. The differentiated man or woman of today is guided almost exclusively by erotic impulse and self-interest. If the entire personality is not made the decisive factor when choosing partners, then it is more reasonable that the motives which lie both above and below the personal plane should decide, as the social factor is actually the most prominent and important, even from an individual standpoint. For man's constitution includes over seventy per cent of racial and social attributes. This fact fully accounts for "conventional marriages" (*Standesehe*), arranged by others, being in general more satisfactory than any love marriages, which take into account individual inclination only. Instinct proves its reliability in the case of marriage by the fact that both man and woman feel themselves attracted with their entire beings to the woman or man who really suits them. This is not the rule with peasants, where the economic aspect dominates, but it does apply to the not over-intellectualized nobleman (in the widest sense of the word, e. g., the typical Englishman, who contracts less bad marriages than any other European). The latter is not swayed by particular allurements, but his entire being is directly attracted by people of his own social and personal standing. Intellectualized man can only acquire requisite integration by "realization of significance" and the subsequent new adjustment of intellect and soul.[11] Where this is wanting, the choice of partners will seldom prove satisfactory. In the latter case the necessary art consists in the person being integrated

[11] Compare the chapter, *Was uns Not tut,* in my *Schöpferische Erkenntnis.*

to such an extent by the aid of creative recognition, prior to marriage, that his consciousness reflects the desire of his entire being and not merely a portion of it. For this reason the differentiated modern man should be warned against marrying before thirty, and the modern girl before thought and experience enable her to regain virginal simplicity. Later generations, being the product of a more favourable intellectual and spiritual atmosphere, will, by nature, again possess sufficient instinct to permit of their marrying earlier.

That is all that need be said concerning the art of choosing the right partner. But just as great an art is "being married" itself. We must deal with this more fully, as up till now its importance has been completely neglected. Under primitive conditions there is hardly a question of this art. The reason is the same here as makes the entire problem of marriage appear simple under such circumstances; so there is no need for me to return to this aspect of the subject. But at higher stages of development this profound art is a fundamental requirement, for wherever, by some means or other, marriage is realized to be a tragic state of tension, it cannot be maintained as a state of happiness and progress without constant care and skilful vigilance. No doubt the requisite faculty is inborn with woman. As a type, she has to bear with life. Consequently she is more realistic than man, and her whole psychology is so adjusted as not to sweep aside difficulties, but to master them. Further, as she is the primarily altruistic element in humanity, she experiences no difficulty in sacrificing her personal will; neither is her starting-point in marriage ever altogether unfavourable, as she chooses the man and not vice versa, except where rape, trafficking, and other forms of coercion are still prevalent; but in modern life this hardly comes into consideration. In this respect, it may be said that civilization has minimized the difference between the patriarchal and matriarchal state, in favour of the latter. Just as in Nature it is the female who determines whom she will permit to approach her as mate, so in civilized communities also it is the woman with whom the final decision rests; coercion very seldom takes place, and seduction without latent acquiescence is hardly possible. This is proved by the fact that no woman believes another was led astray unless she really desired it.[12] At any rate, today the woman has freedom of choice, and standing as she does close to Nature, and also on account of her maternal instinct, she rarely makes a decision entirely false from her own standpoint. Furthermore, she is the born ruler, for one really does not govern others by coercion, but by suggestion; and this is based on instinctive consideration for others and thus presupposes a maternal feeling. Thus it is just her passive mode of life that makes woman a predestined regent, and this explains why most of the queens in history were great queens. This is one more reason why the art of marriage seems inborn in most women. Lastly, marriage is a part of their own urgent, personal interest. By nature, the opposite is true of man. He has no direct interest in marriage, for he is seldom aware of his paternal instinct, and scarcely ever as early as when he usually marries. He represents the adventuresome and irresponsible element in humanity, and since there are lacking in him just those motives which make woman a predestined artist in this sphere, he may be said to have no natural capacity for marriage. This is why marriage more frequently

[12] In this connection, it is a striking fact that Mathilde von Kemnitz, who is at present the best authority on the psychology of women, has advocated the protection of youths against the seductive wiles of woman and finds the protection of girls superfluous. See her *Erotische Wiedergeburt*, Verlag "Die Heimkehr," Pasing vor München.

harms a man's spirit and soul than it does a woman's; unaware of what marriage signifies, he does not raise himself by its agency, but deteriorates inasmuch as he identifies himself more and more with such impulses as find in marriage their natural gratification. He also lets himself go; that is to say, he relapses to the condition of a spoilt child; whereas the whole significance of marriage is the maintenance of a state of tension. Thus the problem of being married is by nature a masculine problem. But as two persons are required for marriage, the more talented one has the mission of teaching the other. Here, however, no inherent instinct is of avail. Besides, on a higher plane of consciousness, the difference between man and woman in this respect is vanishing. If woman becomes differentiated, she loses proportionately so much more of her instinctive faculties than he does that the problem of "being married" is, on a higher plane, an almost equally difficult art for both man and woman. This state of affairs is the normal condition with all developed people in the modern West, and soon it will become so all over the world.

THEREFORE let the final part of this essay be devoted to the art of marriage as such, apart from the particular problems of man and woman. We will, as far as possible, keep clear, in doing so, of all fortuitous and casual conditions, and only treat of such aspects of the question as are of general significance. And I shall only deal with the highest expression that marriage is capable of, because spiritual problems can only be solved in this, their loftiest aspect.

GRANTED that the very existence of marriage depends on a durable state of tension between two distinct poles, and that this state is by no means a matter of course; then it follows that the fundamental principle of the art of marriage rests on the precept of keeping an appropriate "distance"—in fact, the very opposite of that condition which lovers dream of as ideal. The validity of this fundamental principle is indisputable; a relation that is essentially contingent upon tension, if it is not self-sustaining, can be maintained only by means of a consciously practised reserve. And this applies more especially, the more intimate the relation on which the state of tension is based. Goethe once expressed himself somewhat as follows: People who are very intimate must have secrets to withhold from one another, because they are not secrets to each other's eyes. He meant exactly what has been more definitely formulated above. Man and woman should never endeavour to be completely merged in one another; on the contrary, the more intimate they are, the more strictly should they cherish their own individuality, and it should be the unwritten law that neither must encroach on the rights of the other. In the case of highly differentiated people, conjugal happiness wholly depends on this sound principle of keeping one's distance; and in this respect, a by no means unimportant art is to sense the right time for separating for a short while. But in reality this principle is equally valid everywhere. Its application is obvious as regards the maintenance and preservation of passion; in this case, if no restrictions are imposed, allurements soon fade, just as a loose string yields no musical tone. In this respect, the new fashion of cultivating the nude indicates the very opposite of a demoralized state; it may rather be said to cancel the result of the "first fall," and its ideal goal seems to be the disposal of the problem of love. The same, however, applies to intellectual and spiritual interests, and the more intimate the relation is, the more the partners should cultivate reserve. On this account, at the height of French culture husband and wife addressed one another as "you" and not by the familiar "thou." The instinctive knowledge of this requirement has led from the earliest times to the use of separate apartments for men and women. For the same reason, the separate life of each has been made a taboo for the other party. I instance this and the reverencing of the father as absolute master and the mother as supreme goddess, because by nature both man and woman only too readily fail to hold that distance which alone can keep the marriage relation alive. If this is essentially so and always was so, then it will apply all the more in the future, as mankind continues to develop. Consequently in the future marriage will possess this characteristic of reserve even more than it formerly did.

The second fundamental principle of the art of marriage requires that the state of polar attraction should rest on the proper recognition of the qualities peculiar to the two poles and their absolute equality of rights. As regards the latter point, which is already implied in the definition of marriage as a unitary field of force, this does not in any sense mean equalization. Aristotle was right when he said that equality is the right relation among equals and inequality among unequals. On account of the great primary differences between man and woman, and the usual inequality in the development of the partners, as well as the particular differences which external conditions and capacities give rise to, the claim for equal rights can only have one meaning: that each plays his corresponding part, and that the one who is more advanced should help the other forward. It is difficult to make generalizations here, as in each case the solution of a special concrete problem is called for; and the only general advice one may safely give is this: that every youth and girl should be informed respecting the entirely different psychology of the opposite sex.[13] Let it then suffice to make this statement: Woman is by nature the responsible, altruistic, and working part of humanity. This truth, which is recognized by all savages, cultured Europe had very largely forgotten, and only thanks to the feminist movement is the nonsense likely to cease. In a sensible marriage as much responsibility as possible should be allotted to the woman, and not the contrary; this is the only real way to make her truly happy. On the other hand, the entire value of the man's part consists in what he performs "alone," and thus outside the sphere of marriage. A movement toward a return to primitive conditions will therefore assist all parties to attain a higher development. Secondly, it should be the man's self-evident duty to nurture the woman's intellectual interests and to raise her intellectual status, or where this is not possible, to promote her mental development as much as he can, instead of checking it. It has been asserted that mental energy reacts on women as a sexual stimulus. The truth of the matter is that on account of woman's greater proximity to Nature, she yearns all the more ardently for the spiritual; that is why she has always been the pioneer of new religious movements. Man can commit no greater folly than to keep woman in a state of cow-like animality. In this respect, nearly all the so-called good marriages require reform; for every marriage which degrades even one of the partners, or keeps him from rising, is bad. Thirdly, it should be the noblest duty of every married man, wherever affection exists between the couple, to awaken passion in the woman and to lead her accordingly.

[13] The best works dealing with this subject that have so far appeared are those of our two collaborators, Mathilde von Kemnitz and Beatrice M. Hinkle.

Only in exceptional cases does a woman's passionate nature awaken of itself. But the marriage relation requires that it should be complete also in this respect. Its natural foundation is the gratification of natural cravings; and if it fails to accomplish this, it will lead, in spite of all the ideal theories, to pernicious repressions and corresponding counter-reactions. Here the man must take the initiative. He must prepare himself specially. It is hardly possible to estimate how many marriages fail to prosper or are actually ruined because the man lacks any inkling of the art of love. If man supposes that he has the right to expect the pleasures of passion, so has woman. For on the plane of modern consciousness, the conception of woman as man's chattel has lost its psychological hold. Today it is an absolute crime to see in woman merely an object, instead of a person possessing, in every respect, equal rights. But it is also the duty of the woman to show the way, where she is superior. She should never acquiesce, for reasons of convenience or indolence, where marriage, as the tensile relation between two equivalent poles, requires her to act as an educator. This especially applies in the affective sphere. That the man should lead where he is the less developed is irrational, and very many of the defects in all former civilizations rested on this fact. But enough of details. Let us proceed directly to the third principle of the art of marriage, which was already implied in the second: that marriage, as a way toward ascension and fulfilment, must always be regarded as a dynamic relation and never as static. This has applied in regard to posterity. The more mankind becomes intellectualized, the more this must apply to the partners themselves. Mankind is essentially evolutionary. Consequently, two people who are joined together must either grow together or become stunted; there is no other possibility. The marriage relation, however, requires unity, which in this case is only possible on the basis of equality of birth and conscious plane. Consequently the one who is further developed must continually strive to elevate the other, if the relation is not to lose the very significance of marriage. Naturally I refer to the proper training of the other partner to independence on a higher plane, which must not be confused with the customary censorious displays or "scenes." This real training can be accomplished only by supreme tactfulness and respect for the other's personality. At this point the *dignity* of marriage in comparison with all other possible relationships becomes patently manifest. How absurd is the conception that sees in marriage a haven or a legitimate opportunity for letting oneself go, whereas in reality it requires for its very existence the continuous development of both parties! Thus matrimonial polarization is by nature both intellectually and spiritually creative. And this again benefits posterity, for, as I have shown in my book, *Die neuentstehende Welt,* the inner disposition of the parents is not only transmitted by means of psychic influences in education, but by the influence of the milieu on the protoplasm and embryo. It is this third principle of marriage which gives the second its full significance. The latter stipulates that the relation of the two poles should be based on the proper recognition of the specific character of each and their equality of rights. Only that aspect of the relation between the sexes can be taken as static which applies to the differences in nature, unchangeable by time or evolution. Everything beyond this is essentially movement and flux. Everything beyond this already lies in the dimension of what I call "realization of significance," whose normal path leads upward and not downward. Here it becomes finally evident to what an extent the very purpose of marriage is misunderstood if one takes it to be a realm of sanctioned indolence. The majority of conjugal infelicities are principally attributable to this misconception. Whatever he may think superficially, man can forgive himself everything except the sin of self-detention, nor can he ever forgive another for checking his highest aspirations; whereas every one will accept, in his inmost being, the most severe suffering, if he feels assured that it is necessary for his proper development. For all these reasons there is no better warrant for conjugal happiness than to observe the third principle strictly.

Now we are in a position to consider the fourth principle. This requires that the marriage relation should in every detail be self-consistent. Let us keep in mind that the marriage relation is essentially independent, self-founded. The communion it inspires is neither identical with sexual nor with social association. The only other generic term which corresponds with its nature is unity of destiny. If this particular relation is easy to realize on a lower plane, where woman's destiny corresponds closely with the idea of propagation and man's individual freedom of movement is not contested, then just the contrary is true of higher stages of development. Nothing appears more difficult than to achieve a synthesis by means of differentiated entities, a synthesis that has two integrated persons as necessary components. On the other hand, it is now possible to achieve a synthesis only on the basis of what mathematicians call the integral. For the differentiated person the instincts of love and propagation have become independent forces. His individualization does not permit him any longer to renounce his personality, and ethical refinement of feeling, when present, makes it impossible for him to countenance the subjugation of one partner by the other. Under these conditions a durable marriage relation between man and woman is only tenable on a higher plane, in fact on the actual plane which marriage signifies, and only by means of its purely independent character. Of course, from a theoretical standpoint it is also possible to find here complete contentment in the other partner. And since higher development brings individualization in its train, whereby it becomes always more difficult to devise a general form of gratification for particularized impulses, the problem of the right choice of partners is the more acute and serious, the higher the stage of development. On the other hand, at higher stages of development, "equivocation" is no longer effective; if a thing is not actually ideal, it cannot hold its position as such. Consequently, in principle, the art of marriage may be said to amount to the following: that is, if millions are not to be condemned for the sake of a single exception. Marriage, thanks to this art, can lead, in spite of its incomplete gratification of individual cravings, to the perfection of that specific form which in every case brings with it, for the individual irrespective of the conditions, the desired beneficial results. But let us at once warn the reader against a fatal misconception. Marriage is not every man's vocation. The more highly a person is developed, the more he must experience a real calling for it. The artist who is entirely absorbed in his work, and the God-seeker who lives completely for the development of his individual self, are fit for marriage as great exceptions only. And it would be less to be condemned if the former were to form a free liaison, and the latter to retire as a monk from the obligations of social life, than for both to contract worthless marriages. On account of the unique nature of the marriage relation, it will not tend more and more to become the only possible relation between the sexes, but on the contrary, as evolution proceeds, it will always become less so.[14] On the other hand, in future always fewer people who could legally marry will choose other forms of union. The legal aspect, which is to many so repulsive, represents one more co-ordinate for determining its cosmic centre, and consequently implies in itself the fulfilment of its purpose. What is already essentially marriage need not shrink from the traditional form. Furthermore, it should be remembered that marriage as an artistic creation necessitates a strict observance of the laws of form. On the other hand, the tendency will grow for only those men and women to marry between whom love arises, as a consequence of their relation's finding its best possible fulfilment in marriage. That this relation is the best under all possible conditions is a prejudice which must at length also be publicly dropped. It has already been shown that in spite of the essential indissolubility of the marriage relation, divorce is preferable to a bond which only stifles the two persons tied by it. Similarly, the disadvantages connected with illicit unions are less than those of bad marriages, if only the participants' sense of responsibility is sufficiently well developed to take all the consequences upon themselves. The claims of birth control seem imperative here. Unfortunately, on account of the tragic character of life, a solution of the problem that does not entail any disadvantages at all is impossible. As it will never do to place illegitimate children on the same footing as legitimate, or entirely to prevent the former from being born, the solution of the problem which the future will probably arrive at will consist in the legal assumption that the child lives entirely by his own right; this would be quite in keeping with Nature, for as regards the child's origin,

[14] In this connection, compare the section *Kyoto* in my *Travel Diary of a Philosopher*.

the parents *are* merely agents. This course of evolution is all the more probable as life in an industrial era is in many respects nomadic, and must at first occasion, since it lacks the inner sustentation of a traditional faith, a general loss of prestige for marriage, and accordingly a decrease in the number of marriages contracted. In so far as marriage means the life-form of a past age, it will endure only inasmuch as it corresponds with man's eternal wants as well as with his personal desires. Consequently it is of the greatest importance to comprehend truly the meaning of matrimony, and to establish this special relation in accordance with the fourth principle of the art of marriage, on an entirely self-contained and independent basis.

It is evident that the more complex the conditions, the greater will be the demand for artistic handling. The more talented the partners, the greater the necessity for tact and discretion if marriage is to run smoothly. This skill in adjustment is an art, in the same sense as that whereby a poet selects special words to fit his metres and discards others in order to attain a unity of diction. The more manifold a man's nature, the greater will be his desire for manifold relationships. This the marriage bond must not hinder. On the other hand, neither must the latter be injured. This dilemma, in itself, calls for wisdom and art for its solution. Here it is a question of understanding and paying proper attention to deeply rooted emotions and impulses, primitive by nature, but on this account all the more demoniacal. First of all it is necessary to practise silence and reticence. Just a few obvious examples will suffice: If one partner speaks of everything without reticence and shows his feelings without restriction to the other, he is not open-minded, but ill-bred and even barbaric. The person who does something that would cause another to suffer, if he or she became aware of it, and has not even the courage to carry his guilt alone, deserves to be despised. According to an old French custom, a husband was required to leave the room when his wife received a visit from another man. This was an admirable way of protecting marriage from certain kinds of conflict and misunderstanding. Every one is naturally jealous of the person he loves; women even look upon it as an elementary form of politeness that their lovers should exhibit jealousy. To demand that a lover should be entirely free from jealousy is therefore simply brutal. The possibility of its growing beyond control must be guarded against; this is exemplified by the French custom cited above. The precept regarding conjugal loyalty can be properly understood only from the same point of view. The more gifted and developed a man is, the greater the variety of emotions he is capable of feeling, and the more numerous the persons and things he has a right to come in contact with—but on condition that he does not injure one at the expense of the other. How many women, however, consider themselves free from reproach if they can show that they have been true to their husbands in the usual narrow sense of the word! Here clear and unprejudiced thought is required. Loyalty respecting matters of sex counts for much less as regards the real significance of marriage than does loyalty in matters touching mutual destiny. Whoever compromises the harmony of the souls has already committed a serious offence. Whoever destroys mutual destiny for the sake of some love-affair—whether, as a man, he deserts his wife, or, as a woman, petitions for divorce on account of her husband's misdemeanour—uproots marriage in a far worse sense than Messalina did, who, while remaining empress and true consort of an emperor, spent her nights in brothels. It is the particular form or content of marriage that counts, and not primarily any one of its components. This particular content should be ever more clearly realized, as consciousness develops, as a form of life which exists primarily in its own right. Thus marriage progresses from a semi-natural state, which it originally was, ever more and more to a pure work of art. And it is continually demanding more of those who dare to approach it. Now we are in a position to deal with Kierkegaard's doctrine (I cite him because he happens to be an extreme exponent of the views in question), according to which marriage belongs exclusively to the sphere of ethics, and at the same time transcends it. In fact, the formative laws of marriage from an individual standpoint are primarily ethical principles. Marriage duties, as far as the individual is concerned, can only be based on a super-empirical "imperative" and are not deducible from any natural necessity or inclination. For the erotic man or woman, nothing exists beyond sexual attraction; for the aesthete, a mere repetition is an abomination. As such, both are unfit to comprehend the majesty invested in the commonplace. The words loyalty and faithfulness are divested of meaning in their sphere. As an ethical being, man introduces values into the world which are valid only for his spiritual nature, but which correspond as closely and as necessarily to the latter as natural laws do to Nature. And this he is bound to do, if he desires to attain self-realization. But in this as in all other cases, the ethical claims are the outcome of the minimum and not the maximum standard of the autonomous spirit. Here as everywhere "duty" is merely a projection, and consequently a dead rule, which man is called upon to obey only until he is sufficiently developed spiritually to take the right course, guided by inner necessity and not because of a sense of duty.[15] The latter is a rudimentary or embryonic form of keeping man straight. This accounts for the fact that the man who always talks of his duty is the most soulless of all creatures. What can be projected on the surface of moral rules as duty really represents the mere skeleton of a full moral life. Only when man has learned to realize the integrated totality of his nature in marriage, only when he can experience in it simultaneously fulfilment (biology), commandment (ethics), art (aesthetics), and a sacrament (religion), does he begin to achieve the full meaning of marriage. Let us look back from the heights we have reached to the difficulties and suffering inherent in matrimony. Marriage, apart from all its advantages, demands daily and hourly self-sacrifice, renunciation, and the shouldering of responsibility and blame. It requires this at every stage, but the difficulties are proportional to the degree of development attained. Why should man in his present undeveloped state desire to accomplish this difficult art? Is the risk not too great? Is it worth the effort?

Well, it is just this hazardous venture which is a part of marriage that causes every one for whom marriage can at all mean a personal problem to strive after its accomplishment. In it man seeks his highest responsibility. In it he takes upon himself cosmic destiny, inasmuch as it concerns him as a part of creation. As consciousness evolves, it becomes increasingly difficult to bear the burden of responsibility. But then just the capacity to bear it gives the measure of man's dignity. Illustrative of this is the mere fact that on higher planes, marriage is impossible without discipline and art. This is

[15] See the last section of the chapter on America in my *Travel Diary of a Philosopher.*

certainly displeasing to the vegetable and animal which are parts of every man's character, and abhorrent to his indolent and sentimental nature with its cowardliness and fear of thinking. People find it vexatious, even scandalous, that marriage is not an ideal in itself, and that all the problems of life are not solved immediately two lovers, or even two merely suitable persons, find one another. It is also counted an offence that the recognition of the ethical and religious-sacramental nature of marriage should not also legalize and sanctify the meanness and baseness which are more widespread in it than anywhere else. All this does not help. The true significance of marriage does not allow itself to be disregarded. Its true nature will always come further to the front, and if this does not manifest itself at first in the actual establishment of a new and better order, then it will do so all the more clearly in the destruction of the irrational and nonsensical. From an empirical point of view, marriage is essentially a tragic state of tension. Just for this reason it can realize the purpose of life as a whole better than any other form can do. For the whole of life is nothing else but a tragic state of tension; and marriage embraces, as parts of its own constitution, all the specialized forms of tension found in life. These range from the natural right up to the spiritual. But life is not a tragedy in the last resort, and for this reason, in spite of all its drawbacks, it is beautiful; and consequently, where conjugal happiness is achieved, it outweighs all possible suffering. Although the life of spiritually conscious and self-governing man appears at first to comprise more suffering than the instinctive stages of his development do, yet on this plane the tragic character of life can finally be overcome. For it then plays the part for man that a tuned instrument does for a musician. One can play only on tightened strings. The fulfilment of that life which is the life of free, creative man is related to these problems, which seem to contradict the idea of a cosmic order ruled by the spirit of goodness and beauty, much in the same way as melody is related to the violin.

PART TWO

Marriage in Space and Time

A. W. NIEUWENHUIS

The Genesis of Marriage

SUCH an important feature of civilization as marriage naturally possesses a different character according to the race, age, and country under consideration. It is, however, found to exist among all peoples, and has since the earliest times constituted the legal bond between man and woman. Whereas it was formerly believed that a pre-marriage period could be proved in the case of some of the savage races extant today, this has now been shown to be a mistake. Sexual intercourse takes place outside of marriage, and the latter can be suspended and cancelled; but then the former is only permissible before marriage, unless it is a form of degeneration or a part of a religious cult.

In this introductory essay, for the sake of clarity, I will term every form of durable and legitimate intercourse between man and woman marriage, thus deviating somewhat from Count Keyserling's definition. In the course of evolution the original form has only become purer. Further, to illustrate the genesis of marriage, I will treat of living primitive races, as their condition reflects in every way that of the prehistoric ones; by this means it is possible to give a much more graphic description. Lastly, I will not deal with marriage alone, but with communal life as a whole, because under primitive conditions this largely influences marriage itself.

The investigator soon recognizes that the manifold phenomena can be reduced to a few fundamental conceptions. All primitive peoples, whether they reside in America, Africa, Asia, or Australia, possess similar ideas concerning consanguinity or relationship, which can be accounted for by one of three systems; namely, the matriarchal, patriarchal, and parental or cognate. The investigator also finds that there are everywhere three motives that lead to marriage: mutual sympathy, the desire for progeny, and the necessity for mutual aid in the struggle for existence. However, the generic motive plays the prominent part, which is increased the more primitive the conditions.

Consequently, when discussing the genesis of marriage, one must start out from the conception of relationship. An aversion to marrying close relatives, much as it still persists with us today, is found to exist among all races. Only the conception of relationship varies greatly within the above mentioned three systems. The differences are indeed so great that our ideas of blood-relationship can be applied only with great caution to foreign races. Even expressions which have quite a definite meaning for us, such as father, mother, sister, brother, signify for all the Malay races, for example, that the men and women belong to two consecutive generations. And on this classification depends whether marriage is permissible or not.

Instead of further theorizing, I will cite concrete examples. The best place for studying primitive conditions is Australia. For centuries the aborigines of that continent have lived under various climatic conditions and environment without mixing with more highly developed tribes. Taken generally, they have reached that cultural level which expresses itself in a nomadic life. Although these conditions hold good throughout the continent, one comes across a great variety of the simplest forms of marriage. In order to acquire a proper idea of these forms and their significance to the various communities, a short description may serve best. Spencer and Gillen inform us, in their *Native Tribes of Central Australia:* "The aborigines lived and still live in a great number of small groups dispersed over a very wide area. It appears that each group has assigned to it for its wanderings a definite district which is named after the special hunting-ground and place of assemblage. The single migratory groups consist generally of one or two families, e. g., one or more brothers with their wives and children. The members are close relatives and bear a common totem-name, generally that of a plant, animal, or heavenly body. In central Australia, such a totem-district group lives under the rule of a chief. In south Australia this is lacking. Besides the chief, the medicine man exerts a considerable influence. The aborigines feel themselves closely bound to the habits and customs of their forefathers. Every transgression is severely punished. It is principally the old men who force the young ones to keep the tribal customs and ceremonies. Public opinion is an active means of preventing transgression; it is especially efficacious among people so closely related. Over wide territories similar customs are found among the various groups, and this also applies to marriage customs."

When considering the different marriage forms of the aborigines and their relation to one another, one must take into consideration the different degrees of development attained even by these low human tribes.[1] Among

[1] The author agrees with P. W. Schmidt's opinion that the oldest forms of culture are to be found in the far southeast, in the Kurnai and neighbouring tribes in Gippsland. To the north and west of these live tribes whose customs represent a transitional stage, such as the Dieri, who inhabit the country east of Lake Eyre. In the north the latter border on the territory occupied by the Aranta, who inhabit central Australia.

those of the three principal Australian races, the Kurnai, Dieri, and Aranta, the marriage customs are completely different and represent three types which will be dealt with here consecutively.

It is the custom in the Kurnai tribe,[2] which formerly inhabited Gippsland, for young men and women of marriageable age to become acquainted at the times when all the groups assemble together. The young people are permitted free selection, as the Kurnai do not divide their people into exogamic groups. On the other hand, they have to make their choice within widely separated groups, as those of the same river district are held to be too closely related, regardless of whether they are consanguineous or not. To every district group three or four other special groups are assigned with whom its members may intermarry. All over Australia the young women become members of their husbands' group, because the men can thus more readily protect and feed their families in their own districts. The children in South Australian tribes receive the name of their father's group and remain in the hunting-grounds allotted to it. Only the women who have come from outside the district group bear other group names. On the husband's death, one of his brothers marries the widow, thus establishing a form of levirate marriage, and consequently the Kurnai have a patriarchal system of relationship. They still consider that all the men and women of the same generation are sisters and brothers, and this still further limits the young people's choice in marriage. The old people, and especially the women, have a terrible memory for all the marriages ever contracted, so that the Kurnai once found themselves in such a position that hardly any marriage was possible on account of a too close "relationship." The only alterna-

[2] According to A. W. Howitt's *Native Tribes of Southeast Australia.*

tive was for the young couples to elope. The custom of seduction after an agreement has been reached must be, in the case of the Kurnai, very ancient. For some customs have developed which openly promote seduction against the will of the parents. Whether this custom can be taken as explaining the fact that the betrothal of quite young children or even of unborn girls is not prevalent among the Kurnai, in spite of its being the usual thing all over Australia, is still an open question.

As soon as the young people have become acquainted with one another, they determine on marriage in a characteristic way. They ask each other questions regarding mutual support in life, according to which the man promises to do his share toward the maintenance of life by hunting, and the woman by gathering bulbs, small animals, and insects. When at a corrobori the young women consider that the men do not pay sufficient attention to them, they take the initiative and form a closer acquaintance, according to their rude custom, by commencing an affray. For this purpose they kill some bird, the totem brother of the men, and by showing them this, awaken their lust for vengeance. The result is that the young beauties are attacked with sticks and have to defend themselves with their digging implements. A furious exchange of blows takes place, and blood flows freely. On one of the next days the young men kill a blue wren; the girls in turn have to avenge their "elder sister," and a new affray takes place. While the wounds are healing, many pairs have come to know each other and forthwith elope. Another proof of the antiquity of this custom of circumventing marriage restrictions by means of elopement is the fact that experienced medicine men often openly promote these elopements by their magical incantations. An exorcism or adjuration of this nature takes place when a youth has succeeded in persuading a medicine man by giving him presents, e. g., skins and weapons. During the rites, the medicine man, together with the youth and his friends, lie down in a place near the encampment, where all can see them, and sing magical songs addressed to the girl. If she does not hear them herself, her friends see to it that she is promptly informed. These incantations have such an irresistible effect on the young women that many follow the call at once, pack their chattels, and run away with the youth as soon as he appears. Of one medicine man the story goes that he had, by means of his incantations, bewitched the parents during sleep, and thus aided the flight of the lovers. As the parents married in the same fashion, one would expect them to show their children some leniency; but this is not the case. Even the old people of the Kurnai hold fast to their tribal customs, and this kind of transgression is strictly punished. The parents also call the medicine men to their assistance in order to discover the hiding-place of the fugitives. If a couple succeed in hiding themselves for a long time, e. g., until a child is born, then their return causes no special excitement. But if they are caught sooner, both man and woman have to defend themselves against the armed attack of an enraged crowd. Often they are seriously wounded. After this, however, the young couple are allowed to live together. Thus with this principal tribe of the most primitive southeastern Australians, monogamic marriage is based on the mutual affection of the young people, and the decision rests with the woman.

In the marriage customs described above, we see certain characteristic features that have been acquired on account of the isolation in which the Kurnai live. The Dieri, who inhabit central Australia and whom we will now consider, do not deviate so much in their customs from those of the other tribes. Occupying as nomads the territory east of Lake Eyre, and living in the midst of other tribes with similar customs, these aborigines were able to preserve their marriage customs in a pure state. The latter are distinguished by a two-class system, matriarchal relationship, early betrothal, and group-marriage. Of these customs, two may be taken as forming the basis of marriage common to all Australian aborigines with the exception of the Kurnai and allied tribes; namely, the formation of two intermarriageable classes, and the betrothal or engagement of the girls. The particular forms of matriarchy and group-marriage prevalent among the Dieri are not so widespread. From a human point of view, the most remarkable feature of these marriage customs is the amount of individual self-control expected. First, the desire not to contract marriages between people who are too closely related has caused the whole tribe, which is composed of small, independent, wandering groups, to split into two exogamic classes, Kararu and Matieri. The young men are allowed to marry only a woman from the other class than their own. The same divisions exist among related tribes, but these bear other names. In the case of marriage by exchange, which sometimes occurs, these classes are regarded as equivalents by the other tribes. Even when a man has won a woman by combat, he can marry her only if she belongs to a class considered marriageable in his case. Besides these restrictions, there are those of real blood relationship. Only the grandchildren of two pairs are allowed to marry where the men, according to the prevalent custom, have exchanged sisters in marriage. Each class embraces a large number of totem groups, but these do not exert any restrictive influence, as all members of the totem groups of the Kararu are permitted to marry with those of the Matieri. Paternal authority plays an important rôle with the Dieri, for the custom of betrothing a very young girl to a boy or older man, who as a practiced hunter or chief, or for some other reason, is a desirable son-in-law, is generally in force. These engagements are arranged by the mothers. It frequently occurs that a girl who has thus been betrothed falls in love, on reaching a marriageable age, with some one else and allows herself to be seduced. The tribal customs are kept so strictly that the pair run the risk of being caught and attacked with weapons, and thus many a young life is lost. The readiness on the part of the young men and women to sacrifice their own interest when it is a question of defending their marriage is, among the majority of the Australian tribes, most exemplary. If the engagement matures in the ordinary way and leads to marriage, the youth leads the twelve- or thirteen-year-old girl, with her mother's consent, to his encampment. He is usually accompanied by his own or class brothers. He waits outside for his bride and then leads home the young woman, who generally only pretends to offer violent resistance. After she has remained one or two nights with her escort, she is brought into the encampment of her husband's group. As his special wife, she takes her part in provisioning his group, and according to the ideas of the Dieri, she must be loyal to him. But this conception is very different from ours; it owes its particular character to what is known as group-marriage. The latter deserves special mention here, because formerly it was often described as a state in which all the men and women of a group mixed promiscuously and without restraint. This chaotic condition was even portrayed as the first stage of marriage. In reality the facts are as follows: A married woman can, with the consent or at the desire of her husband, become the second wife of another man belonging to an appropriate group. This happens most frequently where two brothers are married to two sisters, or if a widower is able, by giving him presents, to persuade his brother to allow him to contract a second marriage with his wife. A chief or other prominent person is allowed to contract this form of Pyrauru marriage with several women, if the husbands consent. But the tribe is informed of each new relationship by means of a festive assembly of all the groups in question. Side marriages, as may be expected, easily cause jealousy and discontent; so the elders of the tribe try to arrange that this kind of marriage is actually contracted with only the one woman in question. It is, however, a sign of distinction for a man to stand in this relationship to several women of his own or related groups. According to this custom a Pyrauru husband is not allowed to exercise his rights when the real husband is present or refuses his consent. Herr O. Siebert, a missionary who lived among the Dieri for years, writes as follows: "These Pyrauru marriages are characterized as regards morals and ceremony by a certain gravity and force. Thus group-marriage proves to be totally different from what it was formerly taken to be." The strictness with which these marriage customs are adhered to, largely on account of the peaceful life that is led, is a safe guide for estimating the aversion felt by the Australian aborigines to immorality. The latter is not completely unknown to them, *but before the arrival of Europeans it only occurred as an exception.* The children belong to the totem and marriage group of the mother, but the wife generally lives with her husband's group, so that the children learn the speech of their father's group.

The Aranda or Arunta, situated north of Lake Eyre, have a third system of marriage which is patriarchal. In the south the tribe is divided into four marriage classes, and in the north into eight. The members of these marry only within their class. Thus the choice of both the men and women is restricted to one quarter or one eighth of the opposite sex of their tribe. The children belong to the father's class. Among the Arunta also early betrothals are found, and these are arranged in accordance with the patriarchal system by the fathers. The result of these paternal conferences, which take place without any festivity, is told to the betrothed youth between his tenth and twelfth years, and he is also informed that he must wait to marry until his beard grows, or even until the first gray hairs appear in it. The betrothal is then also made known to the other members of the encampment. Now it becomes the youth's duty to make small presents to his future parents-in-law. He gives his father-in-law weapons or game, his mother-in-law edible plants. The bride, too, when she grows older, makes presents to her future parents-in-law. On the day of the marriage, the men assemble with the bridegroom, who is clad in festive apparel, in their midst, in the single men's encampment. In the meantime the women have also assembled in their encampment, where the bride sits weeping on her mother's knee. She is adorned with a wreath and black and red stripes. Then the bride's brother, accompanied by the bridegroom and some of the other men, go to the women's encampment. While the escort waits close by, the bridegroom goes straight up to his future mother-in-law, and seizing his bride by the arm, says to the mother: "Give me your daughter to wife!" The bride simulates resistance and clings to her mother; the latter rises and places her daughter's arm in her son-in-law's hand, which he then tightly clasps. This is the manner in which the marriage is contracted. The husband then goes out hunting with the other men, and the woman gathers seeds to eat. On their return they exchange their booty. The wife brings some of the game to her mother and remains the first night with her. The same thing takes place on the next day, but in the evening the wife returns to her husband. Under this patriarchal system of marriage, there is no question of dowry nor of an exchange of women, such as are practised by the Dieri under their matriarchal system.

In order to explain clearly the part played by seduction, which was formerly thought to be one of the most important means among the Australian aborigines for securing a wife, it should be remembered that the forcible seduction of women from strange groups only takes place as a great exception, during times of war. In such a case the woman, who is often the wife of a warrior who has been killed, is allotted to only one man, who must belong to the appropriate marriage class.

The marriage system of the Arunda is characterized by a very strict restriction of choice, which is still further limited by the fact that old and venerable men marry several women, one after the other, who remain in their respective groups. These wives have to work for their lord only when the latter visits their groups or at the corrobori. Thus it frequently happens that there are not sufficient women left for the young men, or that they have to marry late. Naturally enough, seduction often takes place with the woman's consent, but with the same risk of strict punishment as has previously been described. The personal and family property of the Aranda is very slight, and consequently such practical considerations as food supplies and maintenance play an important part in marriage, as well as mutual affection.

The desire to have children is also a factor, especially as these are expected to care for their parents later. *But there is the very curious fact that the central Australian aborigines fail to understand that pregnancy is the result of sexual intercourse.* This failure to recognize the relationship between coitus and pregnancy is vouched for by such excellent observers as Spencer, Gillen, and Strehlow, and is also met with in other districts. The aborigines imagine that a woman becomes pregnant by the soul of a dead member of a totem entering into her. In every migratory territory special rocks, caves, very old trees, or other striking objects, are supposed to be the dwelling-places of the departed spirits. These places are avoided by women who wish to escape pregnancy. This explains the striking fact that a child need not belong to the totem group of its parents but to that of the migratory territory where the woman first became aware of her pregnancy. This generally happens in the father's group where she lives, but during the great tribal assemblies it may also occur in the district belonging to another totem. Thus there is an actual case where the father belongs to the small falcon totem, his first wife to the rat, her daughter to some variety of caterpillar, his second barren wife to the kangaroo, his third wife to the lizard and her two daughters to the emu and water totems. Naturally the totem has no effect on marriage in this case—sexual intercourse before or outside marriage is only permitted during religious ceremonies; otherwise it is adjudged wrong and punished. Matrimony is usually an association of long duration, with strict compliance to the marriage laws.

LET us now turn our attention to marriage customs that exist at higher stages of culture, e. g., as found among settled agricultural tribes. The conditions here are entirely different. A difficulty that arises in this connection is that tribes which do not actually live in inaccessible deserts are often liable to acquire the customs prevalent among neighbouring higher forms of culture. We need only refer to the propagation of Hinduism, Christianity, and Mohammedanism and their influence on marriage institutions. Consequently the study of two Malay hill tribes in Sumatra—the Batak of north, and the Minangkabau of central, Sumatra—is particularly instructive. Both have been influenced in turn by India, directly, and indirectly *via* Java; they have acquired Hindu and Moslem culture. But their public institutions, especially those relating to marriage, have remained so untouched that the original Malay customs are easily discernible.

Although these tribes are on a much higher level of culture than the Australian aborigines, we find both patriarchal and matriarchal systems in existence, a proof to what an extent these correspond with the necessities and ideas of simple communal life. Here, however, wealth is a determining social factor. This is especially the case in the marriage customs of the Minangkabau Malays, as compared with the unpropertied, migratory Australian aborigines. Property also plays an important part with the Batak. In the case of both tribes the family is a large genealogical unit, where all live together and share a considerable family property in common. But the members are only permitted to participate, not to own for themselves. Their tribal and marriage laws are so framed that they not only do not permit a diminution of this property, but wherever possible foster an increase. The families are strictly exogamic, and any transgression in this respect is looked upon as criminal, causing the wrath of gods and spirits to descend on the whole tribe. Malay marriages taking place among the Minangka are distinguished by the fact that they are more in the interest of the family than of the individuals. This applies especially to the first marriage, which takes place between girls of twelve to thirteen years and boys of fourteen to sixteen years. The Malay families of central Sumatra consist of all persons who are descended on the female side from the same mother of the family; for example, two grandmothers and their brothers, three mothers and their brothers (all being children of the two grandmothers), and all their children. They all live either in the same house or in two separate houses situated on the same plot of ground, when the family has become too numerous to supply every woman with a separate room for her family. The grown-up and married men do not sleep in the family house, but in the sleeping-compound or with their wives. All members have a voice in family affairs. The oldest and most trustworthy man becomes the head. He looks after the property, is the bearer of all titles and distinctions, and represents the Bua parui (coming from one body) for the other families, some of which form a higher exogamic unit, the Suku. The Minangka tribe has about thirty of these Suku, each bearing a separate name, scattered all over the country.

The motive for marriage among these young Malays of the hills is mutual affection, which often lasts until death, the desire to have children, of which the Malays are especially fond, and lastly the advantages derived from an association with another family of high standing. It will be readily understood that the young pairs have less voice in the matter than the parents, whose main consideration is the family interest, and especially that of the woman's. This is natural, as the young wife remains in her own family. The husband also remains with his family, but the children are born in their mother's family and are maintained and reared by it. Consequently it is the girl's family council that takes the initiative and seeks for a suitable husband among the young or older men, if these possess special qualifications or riches. The girl's opinion is not asked. Besides the members of the same family and the Suku, persons belonging to families which have intermarried are also considered exogamic, in spite of there being no consanguinity.

If the proposal made by the family of the young man is accepted, the engagement follows soon after in the girl's house, but without her being present. The young man offers small gifts and receives similar ones for himself and his family as a sign of friendship between the parties. During the engagement, which can last two years, the pair are not allowed to see or speak with one another. Marriage is performed in accordance with Mohammedan rites; that is, between the Wali of the bride and the bridegroom; generally a Mohammedan priest officiates, and witnesses are present. The legal rights in connection with this type of marriage are based on the matriarchal principle. The woman is given a room in her maternal family house, also a part of the general household furniture, and whatever else she may require for the maintenance of herself and her children. A dowry is not given. Only by way of an exception does the husband live in his wife's house. In the beginning and also later on, even if as a personage of reputation he should have several wives, he only occasionally spends a night with his wife, helps her in agricultural pursuits, and also gives her some wearing-apparel. As his property and his own personal profit belong to the family, he can only do this with the consent of the head of the family (*mamá*). Later on, his relation to his children is similar to this. A distinguishing feature of the matriarchal system is the right of inheritance, according to which the children inherit from their mother, but not from their father. The latter's property is allotted to the children of his sister; this also applies to his hereditary offices and titles.

According to the position and wealth of the families in question, marriage takes place with either simple or costly festivities, in which many families take part and an extensive ceremony is employed. An important part of the latter comes when the young pair take food together. This is especially significant in the first marriage. These first unions, however, are very often annulled, as the young people scarcely had a voice in the matter.

If we now consider marriage under a patriarchal system of relationship, such as exists among the Batak of northern Sumatra, it will become evident that to look at it only from the standpoint of the legal rights would be to obtain too narrow a view. The laws underlying a patriarchal marriage of this sort strike us as pointing to the complete dependence of the woman, who is sold to her husband and his family. This does not, however, correspond with the Indonesian character; consequently a young girl even among the Batak has practically a voice in the choice of her partner. "The youth first attempts to make sure of the girl's affection; in fact as a general rule, the young people, who are permitted very free intercourse before marriage, are first formally engaged by exchanging love tokens before the bridegroom sends his relatives to the bride's father to bargain about the purchase money. Naturally cases often arise, especially if the man is old but rich, where the girl's relatives try to force her against her will and affection to marry for the sake of the large sum obtained as purchase money, but often the girl has still a way of escape by means of the Adat, that is, customary law. If she is in possession of a love token, she can run to the donor, who is then forced to accept her, and his relatives will have to see how they can come to an agreement with the owner of the girl regarding the purchase money."[3] The seductions that so frequently take place with the consent of the woman, a method which has become sanctioned by custom, show that the Batak women are purchased by their husbands for a price, but mostly not against their will. Something similar might be said of the woman's position in marriage, but before going into this, we shall give a short account of legal rights under a patriarchal system. Marriage among the Batak is largely influenced by their patriarchal conception of consanguinity. Their families are composed of the male descendants of the same father of the family in the male line, together with their wives and sisters, if the latter are still unmarried. For the women join the husband's family on marriage. The latter also possesses common property and lives in one house. It represents the interests of its members and both pays and receives bridal sums for the young women. The Batak family is strictly exogamic, and this is extended to a number of other families, which together form a Marga. An exogamic transgression is looked upon as incest, and the perpetrators were formerly killed and then eaten.

A large number of such Margas live spread over different districts. The chief always comes from the highest Marga and selects his wife from the second Marga, which directly follows his in rank; the men belonging to this Marga marry women of certain of the lower branches of the highest Marga. By preference they keep to the rule of marrying the daughter of their mother's brother, whereas to marry the daughter of their father's brother is to commit incest. When a young man marries he does not leave his parents' house, but receives a special room.

[3] A. Schreiber, *Die Battas in ihrem Verhältnis zu den Malaien. Ueber Sumatra im allgemeinen.*

The bridal sum (*djudjuran*) varies between fifty and five hundred florins (one florin = 50 cents U. S.). It must be paid before the completion of the marriage formalities. It is, however, considered good form and a sign of friendliness between the families if the payment is not made in a lump sum, but by instalments. When the sum has been paid up in full, the parents lose all influence over their daughter's lot. That the Batak actually look upon women as purchased goods is evident from their designation of them: goods, human being, means, a way of obtaining food, a food ladler. A woman eats only after the men have done so. "A woman has no private property among the Batak and is without legal rights. She is not looked upon as a person, not as an end in herself, but merely as a thing. She is always another's property, whether her father's or brother's before marriage, or her husband's when he has bought her, or of his heirs at death, whether these be brothers or sons" (Schreiber).

The right of inheritance corresponds with this in every way. Only the male agnates or descendants have the right to claim a share of the heritage of the dead man. The wife inherits nothing. And as she possesses nothing, she cannot bequeath anything. The first heirs are the sons or grandsons; if such are non-existent, then the brothers or their sons. The household furniture is not divided as long as there are any unmarried sons left. When distribution takes place the eldest and the youngest sons receive more than the rest. Unmarried sisters remain with their brothers, who support them, and who to cover this outlay receive the bridal sums of their other sisters. The widow, according to levirate custom, is given over to her husband's brother or some other blood relative. Her children belong exclusively to her husband's family.

Under this patriarchal system, divorce is impossible.

As a matter of fact, at later times, in very exceptional cases, it is met with; but neither protracted desertion nor abuse or faithlessness is ground for divorce. According to an old custom a man is allowed to return his wife to her parents only if she is barren; they are then obliged to give him another daughter. The same is true if the wife dies without issue.

Besides the bridal sum, the cost of the wedding festivities, especially those of distinguished families, is considerable. In order to avoid these outlays, the Batak practise seduction, much as takes place all over the archipelago, with the consent of the girl and her parents. The bridal sum is paid only after the flight. If the young man is not in a position to pay this, he must live with his parents-in-law after the wedding and work off his debt. Another way of discharging his debt is to give his parents-in-law one of his daughters later on. In the case of a family which possesses an only daughter to prevent its extinction, she may look for a man with whom she can contract an Ambilanak marriage without any purchase money being given. The husband is then taken into the woman's family, and the children belong to the latter and inherit their mother's property. Generally speaking, the Batak are monogamic, and polygamy is found in levirate marriages only.

From the above it will be plain that with the Batak, matrimonial rights are principally governed by material interests and the desire to have children. This sounds hard and mean and very loveless. But . . . when love is really present, the actual conditions do not tally at all with the description given here. In most cases, in spite of all theories, the woman is the mistress, and just as with us, where the law at times treats women as minors, the master of the house is by no means actually the master. Certainly more work falls to the lot of woman, but in general that is the case all over India and even applies to the matriarchal Minangkabau. If she has children, the wife occupies an important position in the family, and also as a widow, for then her sons can intercede for her.

Both conceptions of consanguinity which we have discussed can develop into the parental or cognate systems, the latter being prevalent with us. In parental marriage the father and mother have equal rights, and the children are related to both families and are the heirs of both parents. Where the Malays come into close contact with foreigners, and mixing with them gradually lose their original institutions, as for example on the east coast, the parental idea of consanguinity appears and is also applied to marriage. The Malays having also embraced the faith of Islam, their family rights and relations can not be considered as appropriate types of communal life and their marriage on a cognate basis. It is quite another matter, however, with the Dajak and Toradja Malays of central Borneo and Celebes. Their original form of culture, for a reason that has not yet been discovered, already embodies a cognate system of marriage. An idea of the marriage customs of the Dajaks may be obtained from the author's *Quer durch Borneo,* which was the result of observations made during a stay of five years in their midst. This long-standing intimacy with this primitive people enabled him to become acquainted with some aspects of their love- and marriage-life which do not so readily come to the fore elsewhere.

Puberty signifies for both the young Dajak men and women [he says] a complete revolution of their personality. They begin to pay more attention to their dress and their outward appearance in general. The young girls pull out the hair from all over their bodies excepting that growing on their heads; while the young men remove eyelashes and eyebrows and the scanty hairs from their beards. Together with the physical changes that take place in both men and women, there is a growing desire to please the other sex. The fashioning of gifts occupies a large portion of their free time. The girls make pearl necklaces, sword-belts, and adornments for sword scabbards. The men give in return finely carved bamboo vessels, flutes, oars, knife handles, etc. Thus both parties have an ample chance, in their desire for love, to find expression in art.

The young people have every opportunity of getting to know each other before marriage and to put themselves properly to the test. They do this all the more readily because marriage is looked upon as a serious matter demanding loyalty on both sides. Before marriage both sexes have full freedom to go as far as they choose. Parents try from time to time to influence their children, but usually with poor results. If the young people take a fancy to one another, custom permits them to indulge in an uninterrupted communion. The favourite pastime is to arrange fishing-parties. Before the fading away of the mild tropical night, when the light of the moon is just sufficient to rob the night of its dark strangeness, the youth puts on his best apparel: a broad blue loin-cloth and a variegated silk head-cloth. Black armlets and tufts of scented grass are special ornaments which he fixes to his arms and head. His finest sword is at his side, often adorned with gifts from his beloved. Thus, with fishing-net and oars, the youth hurries down to the river and with powerful strokes soon brings the boat to the place where she is waiting. The girl, who is dressed in the same manner, gets into the boat with her alms-bowl well filled and sits in the stern, steering with an oar. The young man stands ready to throw his net and propels the boat with powerful strokes to the place where he imagines fish are likely to be most plentiful. Thus the pair move down the river, and if the catch proves sufficient for a meal, they land. Usually an empty hut in the rice-fields or an intimate spot beneath the trees on the river bank is their final goal. The soft tones of the flute played with the nose add a special charm, for in the silence of the night these wailing but lovely notes awaken sensations to which the tender spirit of the Kajan is very susceptible. In times when the neighourhood is unsafe on account of wandering hostile bands, friends keep watch by night in the vicinity of the lovers.

Working together in the fields also gives the young people a good opportunity of becoming acquainted with one another, especially if the parents agree to this. Otherwise the fortitude of the lovers is often put to a severe test. I once observed how a beautiful young girl with great will-power brought home a lover who was anything but welcome to her parents because he could not do heavy work in the fields and was not yet able to build boats. Even after the marriage, which required a great deal of energy, the young husband had very great trouble in finding his place in the house of his parents-in-law. When marriage is being contemplated, the parents from both sides meet and discuss the dowry and purchase money that the young man must pay his parents-in-law. If the parents are no longer alive they are represented by relatives or by the chief. The amount that the young lover has to pay is usually not great; the parents-in-law are generally satisfied with one sword and a gong. On the other hand, rich chiefs have to pay as much as three hundred dollars. It is thought desirable that both parties should belong to the same class. Chiefs lose their prestige if they marry ordinary women, and their children have little chance of succeeding them. Among the Kajan-Dajaks of central Borneo, matches between not only close blood relatives but also between relatives by marriage are forbidden. Marriage between neighbouring but not related tribes is not prohibited, but it occurs so rarely that, for example, the Taman-Dajak and Kajan-Dajak have lived over a hundred years close to one another without mixing. They are eleuterogamic. There are so many restrictions regarding marriage, especially from the wedding up to the next New Year's feast, that the Kajan marry by preference shortly before the New Year, in order to avoid this unpleasant period. The ordinary Dajak wedding is very simple. The chiefs arrange big feasts when their children marry, which can last for two or three days, and in which all the notabilities of the village take part. The wedding takes place in the bride's house, whither the bridegroom is escorted by his friends. All the household furniture is taken out of the apartments, which are then decorated with green and coloured fabrics, and the walls are hung with all the gifts that the bride's parents present to their son-in-law's escort. The friends have also the right to take home with them all the good things that the chief's hospitality and the contributions of the villagers offer them. Pearls play a prominent part among the gifts which the bride and bridegroom give one another, and this also applies to the members of the family. First of all the bride receives from the bridegroom a "girdle for the wife" which consists of a string of four old pearls. At the common meal she finds two more pearls in her rice, besides which she receives one very fine pearl. The relatives and friends give her a string of pearls that has to be as long as she is tall, and the value of these is dependent on the wealth of the donors.

The household is managed by the stronger character. A breach of faith, which is looked upon as a misfortune to the entire family, is strictly punished, but it seems rarely to occur. The one at fault has to make atonement to the other's family. If he or she cannot meet his obligations, he is assisted by his relatives. In marriage the estates are kept separate. The mother and father together attend to the maintenance of their children. But once these are grown up, they remain in their parents' house, but plant their own rice fields with the help of male and female friends. Foreign articles of utility, such as salt, cotton, and tobacco, are often bought on a joint account. From this store each can acquire a portion corresponding with his needs, the father having the decisive voice in the matter. Man and wife do not inherit from one another. If the marriage is without issue, the property of the deceased returns to the family. If the partners agree to separate with good will, then on divorce each retains his personal property. The children are allowed to decide for themselves with which parent they will remain.

WITH this I will finish my sketch of the genesis of marriage. I need not go into further details, as the examples chosen are intended to serve only as symbols. What is then the result of our glance into the primeval age of man? *That the essential relations have from the very earliest times been the same as are found among highly cultured peoples of today.* Even in the most primitive ages, marriages in the highest significance of the word occur. Immoral conditions are most rarely found among primitive peoples. Consequently marriage can never be looked upon as a mere convention. In it eternal and universal validity finds its appropriate expression. Inasmuch as the modern world misunderstands this, let it go to the so-called primitive peoples to learn.

LEO FROBENIUS

Marriage and Matriarchy

ONE of the most curious legends that have come down to us from very ancient times describes the earliest sex relations of mankind and states that in the beginning men and women lived separately and knew nothing of each other. The legend continues to relate that at the first accidental meeting of members of these two sexes, the women defended themselves like men in battle, so that it came to a decisive combat; and only then did the difference in sex become apparent. These legends come from northwest Africa and in a variety of forms travel eastward right down to the Pacific, where on account of the existence of numerous islands a favourite version tells of a certain island where only women dwelt, but which one day was discovered by a man. These stories belong to the group of Amazonian legends. The legend finds its way into the Mediterranean, both by way of the African and Asian coasts, in the shape of stories of wandering Amazonian armies, of the wars they waged against other peoples, and of peculiar female types. J. J. Bachofen was the first to handle this material with regard to its sociological significance. The various forms of this legend, which described a rulership of women either in a past age or in a distant part of the world, led him to make his great discovery of matriarchy. Bachofen states that there were people living before classical antiquity under the rulership of women. This did not suffice for him.

He wished to prove from these legendary fragments and other data that the position of the two sexes had changed during the evolution of culture, and he made of the material accessible to him a ladder to reach his goal. According to him, the lowest stage was a form of hetairism in which all the women were held in common. The middle stage was matriarchy, the rulership of woman over man, the prerogative of woman. The third stage was patriarchy, the prerogative of man. The discovery of matriarchy was an important and decisive event; it gave rise to an extensive literature and became the saving grace and sole outlook of many who were not in a position to recognize the natural limitations of Bachofen's data and the error underlying his schematic system of a regular sequence of stages.

For his historical survey of matriarchy and marriage customs Bachofen had at his disposal only the most fragmentary material of antiquity, relating to the period before it, to work on. He had no conception of the immense insight into these matters that folklore, which was still dormant at the time, could offer by considering facts taken directly from life. Thus he made the mistake of not recognizing the patriarchal conditions under which Achaeans and Dorians lived. It was this patriarchy which influenced the higher Mediterranean cultures; this disproves the contention that matriarchy corresponds with lower and patriarchy with more highly developed peoples and cultural groups.

Nevertheless we must not forget that it was Bachofen who revealed this great monument in the history of sex relations and marriage. But to comprehend fully the relationship between marriage and matriarchy, we shall have to consider both patriarchal and matriarchal social and communal forms extant today.

FOLKLORE has shown that there was a time when in certain parts of the world patriarchal and matriarchal institutions existed separately and were in their own territory the decisive, determining, and motivating cultural factors. At one time, the two extensive regions comprising the interior of Asia (including eastern Europe) and the interior of Africa must have been patriarchal; that is to say, the vast steppe-lands were patriarchal. The Mediterranean countries and those of southern Asia lying in between these two expanses, that is to say, their coasts, were at the same time under matriarchal sway.

Patriarchy in its least modified condition is still prevalent among the Africans of the steppes. Here are found large groups of peoples and numerous tribes divided into clans. A clan of this kind lives in a farm surrounded by fields. In the farm the descendants bearing the same family name live together, divided into classes according to age: old men, men, youths, boys, and children. The eldest member still mentally efficient is the leader. Only in cases of complete senility can the next brother, or if he is not available, the oldest son who is in the old men's class, take his place. This social structure corresponds to natural growth. The age classes proceed according to the stream of life, one always taking the place of another imperceptibly. At the top the family dies out, while down below it grows anew.

The clan property is common to all. The oldest distributes the provisions from the warehouses, as well as the clothing and ornaments, and determines the time for sowing and harvesting, for hunting and for holding the manes festivals. According to whether the clan is considerably increased by its rising generation or is diminished by some misfortune, far- or near-lying lands are taken for cultivation. The actual amount of arable land belonging to the clan does not depend on some fixed constant, but on the vagaries of life.

I said: The family dies off at the top and grows anew from the bottom. An old man at his death is festively carried to his grave by all the members of the family amid expressions of cheerfulness; for the clan rejoices that now a young life can be born again. Children are just as much a spiritual necessity with these people as a physical one; they are the object of the ardent desire that fills the lives of these men. Consequently the youths seek playmates from clans living near or far. Great dances enable them to become acquainted with such playmates and a naïve happiness follows. If the clan agrees to the marriage, i. e., if it is confident that the young woman is the right one to bear it another worthy ancestor, a marriage is contracted.[1] This form of marriage is characterized by the fact that out of the man's yearning grows the idea of motherhood, the important phenomenon of the mother, such as is not found in a matriarchy. Woman becomes the holy vessel of matrimony; she is a member of the clan, a symbol of the plastic power to create, which must complement the man's desire.

MATRIARCHAL institutions are still in part very clearly evident, with sharply defined contours, among the Hamitic people of north Africa: from the Atlantic to-

[1] How organically the life of these patriarchates is bound up with the idea of constancy of soul (*Seelenkonstanz*) is clearly shown by the marriage customs. The bride has to be released from spiritual association with her clan. In order that no one should follow her from the clan, and through her fecundity reappear in the new clan, she is abducted; and thus the spiritual contact with the clan is severed. During the marriage ceremony the skull of a distinguished ancestor is placed before the bride by the head of the clan; then with an offering of holy grain, which formerly lay on the skull, the ancestor is invoked to permit himself to be born again through the newly married woman. For further particulars, see *Das unbekannte Afrika*.

ward the east the Berbers and Tuaregs, right up to the Bischarins on the Red Sea. The oldest form in question here shows woman supreme in all things. She is the property owner, the man being entirely without property. She bequeaths her property in the female line, and also her name and status. Descent from her determines the caste. The man may be a slave or a bondsman, but if she belongs to a noble caste, the children will also be high-born. Woman does all the work; she makes the skins into leather and prepares the leather clothing and tent. It is she who puts up and takes down the dwelling-place. She milks the cows, makes butter, mends, and weaves. The man only hunts, tends the cattle, and wages war. The woman, who is ruler over all, not infrequently loves her brother more than her husband, misuses the latter, and often treats him to cruel tempers and lets him feel her aversion.

The decisive factor in this curious communal order is the manner in which marriage takes place. The woman chooses the man. In fact she chooses him according to the same inward necessity that is naturally present in all women, hesitatingly and with the desire to obtain the very best. The men court the women, and then the play begins. Do this! Do that! The man is put strictly to the test. Rivals are made to compete with each other. Trophies are required as proofs of ability. And then finally, when the girl believes that she has found the best man, that is to say the one who suits her best, she accepts him.

But an allurement is necessary to keep the man keyed up during the period of probation, to keep him if possible at the highest pitch of expectation. Thus a natural instinct, which in these matriarchal communities is often manifested in a brutal way, causes the girl to flirt in such a manner as appeals most readily to men. She most scrupulously preserves her virginity (which affords the man the illusory pleasure of being the first), which is the means of her final conquest.

But under the matriarchal system the desire for selection does not cease with marriage. When in the course of time a man appears who is more courageous, daring, distinguished, and successful than the husband, she begins to woo him with the same insistence. Patriarchy, with its indifference to virginity and its strict conjugal fidelity, is a complete contrast to the carefully guarded virginity and conjugal infidelity existing under matriarchal conditions. I make a special point of this, because it is an indication by which attachment to a particular system may be ascertained. It is not, however, merely a question of variation. The two forms are contrasts in every way. This becomes especially clear when we consider the relation of matriarchal culture to the dead. In the matriarchal order, the expression of life is seen to be the continual splitting up of the body into new parts. The child splits off from the mother, and thus the life of the clan is assured. Adornment of the body, with all its members refined by breeding, becomes the significance and allegory of life. This cultivation of the body denies the existence of a disembodied spirit. The latter becomes a ghost. Consequently the dead and their bodies are not respected as they are by the Ethiopians, for whom everything is spiritual; but they are feared. The body is buried without ceremony; it is packed up and carried a long way off. Stones are dropped on to it, and it is shunned. Passers-by throw stones and dry wood on the grave to prevent the possibility of the spirit arising. A woman never touches a corpse, not even that of her own child. It is the man's duty to remove this strange burden. Thus physical existence becomes ever more isolated, perfection of the body is accomplished, and most important of all, by the selection and insistence of woman, man is driven to creative work.

Thus patriarchy produces motherhood in its deep spiritual significance, and matriarchy produces the creative activity of man in its joyous self-sacrifice.

From the above, it follows that matriarchy and patriarchy are not social phenomena that appear separately, for themselves alone. By taking into consideration all the customs bound up with these two conceptions and their corresponding outlooks, it will be found that there is no sphere of cultural, spiritual, or bodily activity in which the same contrasts and variations do not also occur: in domestic affairs and the division of labour, in housing and handicrafts, in all that manifests the depth of life. Matriarchal peoples are allegorical, and their attitude is a magical one, whereas partriarchates experience everything symbolically and are consequently mystics. In their own spheres, patriarchy and matriarchy are the same expression of culture, which manifests in all directions the same differentiation.[2]

It is my task here to point out the significance of the matriarchal and patriarchal structure of communal institutions and its bearing on the evolution of the different forms of sex relations into the highest types of marriage. To accomplish this we must understand the significance of this twofold division; namely, the manifestation of different cultures. This will enable us to obtain from the essential portion of the original symbols the means of comprehending the natural course of later phenomena.

The entelechy (i. e., development along a prede-

[2] Compare *Das sterbende Afrika,* Vol. II.

termined course) of culture seems identical with the essence of the general organic surroundings; that is to say, it culminates in both in the polarity existing between development and form, movement and rest, time and space. Just as the mobile pollen of the stamen falls on the stationary pistil of the plant, so in a similar manner as regards movement the semen of the male animal meets the stationary female egg-cell; and analogous to these reactions, we find essentially the same principle, though more complicated, in human sex. Man and male functions appear as solicitous, mobile, craving expansion, partial to novelty, urging and emanative, and taken all in all they are *centrifugal* attributes; whereas woman and female functions are in general characterized by hesitation, selection, permission to be wooed, taking possession of, absorbing into oneself, retention and economy; taken in their entirety, these are *centripetal* attributes. The close relation of these two principles becomes clearly evident when one notices that what is idly mobile and transient in the male, achieves in conjunction with the peaceful spaciousness of the female both purpose and form. In fact, this is what is known as polarity, which is an integral in itself. For polarity exists in every organic being; it is the tension between centrifugal and centripetal force—but by developing and stressing the differentiating quality of sex, one side is always in the ascendancy. This may readily give rise to a misconception of the real nature of the phenomenon. It is only possible, however, to comprehend the historical course of the evolution of culture and the development of primitive sex relations into marriage itself. With the spread of culture, large territories are recognizable today where the decomposition of polarity has taken place by either one of the poles becoming exclusively predominant. The great steppe-lands in the interior of Asia, Africa, and eastern Europe became the domiciles of centrifugal cultures and were consequently patriarchal. The countries lying on the coasts of the Mediterranean and (toward the east) of southern Asia represented centripetal cultures and were thus matriarchal. The movement and invasion of the mobile centrifugals into the territories of the centripetals resulted, in order of sequence, in the genesis of the high cultures of India, western Europe, the Aegean, Rome, France, and England. Naturally the mobile form of culture had more evolutionary powers, while the quiescent variety was more formative. These phenomena underlie the entire problem of what is known as world history, and it is my task to show how, in the course of these events, primitive matriarchy developed into the highest standards of *marriage.*

If we follow periods and episodes in the evolution of culture, the following will serve as a corroborative illustration of the various forms and extensions of matriarchy which harmonizes with facts.

I recognize three periods in the evolution of culture: that before polarity, polarity, and post-polarity. The first stage of culture is only found today on the edge of the Oekumene and in different outlying districts, and even here it is in a state of decay and senility owing to the influence of polar culture, with which it is in contact and by which it is being overrun. The internal structure exhibits the correlation to a narrow space; in this respect it corresponds to the conditionality among most of the higher animals. In general they feel themselves at one with their natural environment, and living in hordes, they make only the one distinction, that between males and females. There is neither matriarchy nor patriarchy. I term them pre-polar, because the cleavage due to the differentiation of types, which is necessary to sustain polarity, has not yet taken place. I cannot distinguish an episodic structure at this stage.

On the other hand, the general impression given by the second stage, culture dependent on polarity, is very clear. It forms a chain, both as regards time and space, with links that fit closely into one another. Four episodes are clearly distinguishable: the primitive manifestation of polarity in the west; the origins of the high culture on the Pacific coasts; the high culture of western Asia; the after-culture of southern and western Europe which ends with civilization. Let us now consider this in detail, and its significance and bearing on the history of matriarchy.

The first episode in the primitive manifestation of polarity is that in which the cleavage in culture has already taken place. Matriarchy develops as the expression of a new feeling of life, impelling a definite form. It comes on the scene with irruptive force and demands to be acknowledged as the principal significance of life. For this is the evolutionary and historical meaning of all materializations of culture, irrespective of whether the objects are spiritual, social, or material. The new order is expression and demands hegemony in all things. It possesses force of *expression* and causes all things around it to retreat. By its influence all is fashioned anew, until it has conquered and subjugated all and extended its modifying influence to every sphere of life. Thus it passes imperceptibly into the second form of differentiation; it becomes the part of a greater whole. The other aspects of culture which were at first pushed aside become animated as parts of a complex organism, ascribing to the new order its particular function. On becoming in its turn the old order, it reaches the stage of application (*Anwendung*).

The idea of matriarchy arises with irruptive force in its first and expressional stage. The power of expression is all the more extreme, as the development of some of the most powerful properties of the centripetal principle takes place here: the apprehension of facts (*Tatsachensinn*) and the immutability of rights. The conditions in this episode that marked the great revolution of women must have been strangely one-sided: Amazonism, legal hetairism, the pledging of men. This episode only served corporeal purposes, and the sense for facts created definite realities and evinced an uncouth aversion for disembodied spirits and ghosts. During this episode man was a servitor; his metaphysical aspirations and problems were completely eliminated. As a servant he had special duties to perform: to bury the dead, banish ghosts, and keep all supernatural things at a distance.

In order to understand the second episode, one must not forget the polar *bi-partition* which was bound to manifest itself both in patriarchal and matriarchal form, according to whichever principle was in force. In its patriarchal form it appeared, as has already been stated, in the vast territories in the interior of Africa and Asia. This patriarchy represents the high tension of centrifugal forces which emanate from the personal cosmos to the outer world, whereas the centripetal forces absorb things out of the outer world and both shape and give them definite boundaries inside the personal cosmos. Patriarchy is the expression of untamed, ardent desires, and matriarchy that of greedy fulfilment.

This is how it comes about that one side experiences

things spiritual, while the other declines them with what amounts almost to hatred. Similarly the one reveres the spiritual and supersensual, and those who are freed from the body by death; whereas the other reveres corporeal, sensuous, and living things. Consequently a change that was revolutionary had to take place when the representatives of centrifugal culture, following their natural bent for movement, brought their culture into the coastal countries of Asia, where the most extreme centripetal and matriarchal culture was prevalent. Fecundation took place, and a new episode followed, in which exaggerated empiricism and the veneration of all things corporeal reacted against cosmic spirituality.

This is the epoch that saw the birth of cosmogony and mythology; when man ceased to be the servitor of Nature and became the servant of the cosmic idea, in fact became a priest. Woman had won her place by means of irruptive force and revolutionary power, but in the course of gradual evolution man attained the development and use of his centrifugal forces. Thus it was impossible for him, as the representative of evolution, to substitute his patriarchy for the existing matriarchy on entering the formative sphere. He could only influence and modify it. Out of the old forms of matriarchy, where the children were the mother's heirs, a new form sprang up in which the "avunculus," the mother's brother, became the heir. But the ascendancy of the female line did not show itself in this manner alone.

The great conquest of cosmic space by means of mythology was the principal cause of the new order, which represented the application of the significance of the newly discovered universe, as ruled by the sun, to earthly conditions. The mundus, as symbolized by the temple, is the foundation of tribal organization. The four cardinal points (East, West, South, and North) and the point of intersection of the cross that joins them, become the symbol of the cosmic state. Four provinces with priests ruling over them, and in the centre the chief priest, symbol of the supreme divine ruler—this is the figure from which kingship evolves in an age of progressive reality.

And this god-king ("son of the sun") had to marry, as his first wife, his own sister or daughter. This and the rights of the avunculus are the typical symptoms of the stage of *construction* and *organization* (*Eingliederung*); that is to say, the second stage of matriarchy.

Still another phenomenon of this period (the significance of which is retained to this day) characterizes the irruptive force of matriarchal forms and conceptions: the myth of the *conceptio immaculata.* What was for the women of the matriarchal period a natural and powerful incitement by which to obtain man's service, the preservation and tendering of virginity as the most precious sacrifice, now becomes the point of departure for the birth of all the sun-gods. And in the temple only vestal virgins are allowed to tend the sacred flame. They are consecrated to the invisible god who can be known only by symbols.

In the first episode, the germinating period of polar culture, the latter extended only to the land. In the second episode it becomes littoral and passes through the fleeting sea and the magic world beyond the great waters which are subjugated by the newly discovered navigation. This was the time when the dragon-ship ruled the seas; in fact the age is entirely subservient to the male sense of width and distance. In the great swing of the pendulum, through southern and western Asia, the Aegean, Rome, France, and England, it passes from the coastal regions of southern Asia into the continent of western Asia. It passes into a land where conceptions were no longer lightly framed, retaining the shape of ideas, but had become definite phenomena; where the desire for representation, instead of being intensified by a symbolism ranging wide as the horizon, had become stiff and shackled by a logically restricted sphere. By the sea every rigid form melted in the play of the waves, in the alternating moods that accompanied sunrise and sunset. There was retained the image which could achieve its form and meaning only when taken as an artistic whole. It was the great age of a centrifugal world-outlook, based on things that are visible.[3]

But in western Asia every step leaves footprints; every tree-stump, rock, stone, and hill is a remembrance. Here symbolism turns to allegory, and the mobile and fleeting is changed to the constant and rigid. The sun that moved along the vaporous sea as lord of time and space becomes the glowing monster, the god of murder moving across the languishing earth. Here it is the cool of friendly night, the night sky, and the sea of stars that are reverenced. The illimitable rhythm, i. e., a temporal symbol of the universe, and the vital emotion of the former episode, give place to a symbol conditioned by space and dependent on the star-covered vault of heaven. No longer a feeling of vastness awakened by the vision of day and sea, but a feeling of the dismal pit, born of the night and the empty, monotonous land; no longer the playground of centrifugal forces, but the stage of centripetal intelligibility.

The result is the fecundation of western culture in western Asia. The new world arises: the world of reli-

[3] For further details see the new edition of Paideuma, *Erlebte Erdteile*, Vol. IV, 1925.

gions. The great difference from the former mythological vision of life is readily distinguished. In the latter, man is the object of cosmic occurrences, on the same footing with all earthly things such as plants and animals, fields and meadows. Now he becomes a privileged object. Different gods had arisen, but they were all equally reverenced. Tribes had different customs, but each was the equal of the other. In the cultural episode of western Asia a personal feeling arises: primitive nationalism and consequently centralization. The divine king of the cosmic order was centrifugal, while that of western Asia was centripetal. The significance of culture as a communal structure is no longer emanative, but absorptive. The personal conception, the unity of a people, no longer corresponds with the multiplicity of the world, but with a one-sided, narrow type of unity. The gods are supplanted by the national god.

All in all, centripetal force works in this episode of continent shaping, on the bridge-like territory between the Pacific, Caspian, and Mediterranean, much more powerfully than the centrifugal; but this is more evident externally in all other spheres than in sex relations. I said "externally" especially, for matriarchy gains ground inwardly at the expense of outward expression. Nationality is the first incitement to the problem of breeding. Centripetal nationalism since its very birth in this episode of culture has been, and still is, bound up with the racial problems of that age. Even if (in accordance with the ascendancy of patriarchy in the evolution of culture) the marriage customs of the high culture of western Asia bear outwardly more than ever patriarchal characters, and the women retire more and more from public affairs and seem willing to appear as servants, which was once the fate of man; yet inwardly they gain a considerable advantage, for the quiet work of woman continues mostly without man's noticing it or even comprehending its significance. This is the "quiescent matriarchy" which triumphs in the next episode.

In the history of matriarchy, this confident and secretive inward functioning also corresponds to external necessity; namely, the exhaustion of the exaggerated and fanatical old orgiastic forms which henceforth become ritual, consecrated to the gods. They pass through Thrace across the threshold of classical antiquity and reach Europe, where they become extinct.

By moving the centre of culture to the western Mediterranean—this corresponds with the fourth episode of polarity—naturally an intensification takes place which is in accordance with the two original principles: the centrifugal principle always develops more externally and thus gives the privileges of the male a more decisive form, while the centripetal principle gains in inward significance, stability, depth, and refinement. Thus external necessity strengthens its power to achieve unobtrusively its feminine character. And this all the more because, when the first high culture of the Occident arose in the Aegean Archipelago, it was accompanied by a freeing and expansion of the entelechy that was formerly bound by its continental situation.

As I have already pointed out, in the continental culture of western Asia, the significance of mythology had been degraded to allegory and magic. It can easily be shown that cultural evolution is invariably characterized by the appearance of external forms in the place of a decadent and rigid content; for example, the less political sense a nation possesses, the more laws it frames. Life in western Asia is overburdened with a mass of symbolism.

This penetrated the whole of its life and forced man in every custom and action, in every mode of experience, to adhere to the prescribed form and to make concessions to cultural requirements. This is true of everyday matters and applies still more to spiritual life. In fact, life becomes a self-inflicted slavery, the real slavery of those who feel themselves bound. A thin streak of this culture with all its attributes found its way from western Asia to the Aegean and held the archipelago as far as the Grecian mainland, veiled in a matriarchal wealth of form (Crete-Mycenae). Into this patriarchal culture the Achaeans and Dorians penetrated, as bearers of a primitive and virgin patriarchal culture.

This fecundation that took place on the shores of an inland sea proved a liberation. The new episode put an end to the superabundance of symbolism. The ancient forms of expression that sprang from the Oriental Paideuma had already acquired a place in the cultural edifice, and now find their free application. Tympanon, metope, and triglyphs become capitals; where formerly they were burdened with abstract interpretations, they lose their allegorical nature and become natural parts of architecture.

During the course of this liberation, one special feature is predominant, and this is decisive with regard to sex relations. In the episode of Pacific culture, mythology; in western Asia, religion; and in the Aegean, epics, were the natural modes of expression. Thus the course of evolution takes a new and most important direction. In the first episode of polar culture, mankind is divided into patriarchal and matriarchal families, which have intercourse with one another as such. During cosmogonal culture, families are established on a hierarchic basis. At this time all the members of the same family were essentially equal. All wore the same clothes and the same ornaments, experienced the same emotions and thoughts, and were subject to the same variations of fortune and fashion. This unity continued when the families grew into peoples. The third period, when religions were formed, gave the tribes their character as a nation. Nations stand to one another like isolated individuals. The outlook on life which sees man, together with the rest of creation, as a cosmic object, was supplanted by the conception of man and his nation as a *privileged object*. Oriental antiquity never advanced beyond this stage. If one reads such a wonderful compilation as the *Arabian Nights*, one finds not a single person, with one exception, who by personality or strength of character masters fate. Each is the toy of forces benevolent or malevolent, as the case may be. For every turn of destiny, common superstition finds an explanation in the occult world.

On entering the fourth episode of the polar period, a new thing came to life: the mythological matter that had its birth in the *expression* of mythology and religious emotions was now *applied* to construct the history of mankind. Gods become heroes. Supermen arise, who at first appear as exceptions among the herd. They are the natural efflux of the continually accumulating intensification stored up in patriarchy. The observance of personality was naturally at first a predominantly male characteristic. Thus individual man acquired independence, which found its consummate intensification in the epic period, and naturally also influenced the relationship of the sexes.

In Greece the civil position of women was characterized by two main groups. One group was composed of housewives, who lived a very retired life and apparently played no part in public affairs at all. In direct opposition to these were the hetairae, whose prototype was Aspasia.

They were very influential, and this was due not alone to their physical attractions. They were more or less clever and ingenious. These two types demonstrate the division in woman's character, woman as mistress and woman as wife: one, the representative of matriarchy working inwardly; the other, of its outward function. With the development of this phenomenon—the concentration of woman's personality on unnoticed but all the more efficient activity, by suggestive influence—matriarchy reaches its highest stage. This change, which was already taking effect in the previous period, then amounted to a definite guarantee of monogamy!

In the mighty struggle of polar forces, centripetal matriarchy has finally achieved the legal individual ownership of man.

Now that the high cultures have faded away, the third period of super-polar culture is in course of self-preparation. I will conclude by giving a brief sketch or indication of the relation between marriage and matriarchy in this age.

The period of polar culture extended from the *expression* of cosmic emotion in the mythological episode, through the *constructive* and *organizing* stage (*Eingliederung*) (religious, art, and philosophical episodes), up to the *application* of the knowledge thus acquired. For cultural forms as such, the age of high cultures, that is, of national unities of style, bound in their growth and life to a definite space, is for ever past. If one now reflects on the fundamental meaning of human progress taken as a whole and seeks to arrive at its predominant character, one is bound to notice a continual simplification, refinement, and dissolution of homogeneous wholes to the benefit of singular formations. In the beginning of polar cultures whole peoples were affected by an impulsive drive and agitation, gradually subsiding until they finally ended in border warfare. On the other hand, individuals became constantly more adventurous and energetic. They first opened up the world by sailing around it and wandering across continents, and then they travelled as merchants and pleasure-seekers to all countries. In the beginning of polar culture, whole tribes wore the same clothing; today every one tries to develop his own personal taste. In the beginning, poetry, through the influence of the myths, had a common character; whereas today it represents ethnological, psychological, and social observation of a personal nature. Formerly motivation and significance were embodied in the character of the tribe or people as a whole; now it increasingly depends on the strong personality of individuals whose characters can affect not only their own nation, but others as well. In the beginning, man's entire environment was a closed and self-ordered cosmos; today we are on the way to realizing a macrocosm in every microcosm, and consequently in every individual.

Thus out of the highest stage of the high cultures individual man is evolved, i. e., personality as the seed-corn in the rising period of unification of a world-wide culture. That signifies that the high tension of cultural polarity takes place in the individual, and thus individual personality bridges over the ever-fading contrasts and space-limitations of cultural forms.

Such a change must also bring a new expression for matriarchy. This is already evidenced in the way that women are leaving housework to take up professions. Other convincing symptoms are "the cry for the child," the new feminist movement, which springs up in patriarchal cultures, frequently near the borders of matriarchates (never actually in them); the easy annulment of marriage, etc. Ever more clearly and distinctly the two particular qualities deviate from one another, corresponding to the symptoms of the centripetal entelechy, mistress and wife. Again: in the matriarchal sphere of influence, which is continually widening, universal validity and particularity are separating. One thing is certain: that the action of centripetal force, which at one time was characterized by the grotesque form we have termed matriarchy, can never cease to exert its influence and will always, in accordance with the style and stage of culture attained, influence and modify the forms and essence of marriage.

The Indian Ideal of Marriage

A REQUEST has come to me from Europe to say something about the Indian idea of marriage. This puts me in mind of the difference between the European and the Indian idea—a difference which is not merely of outer method, but of inner purpose.

Like all distinctive features of civilized societies, the marriage system is an attempt at compromise between the biological purposes of Nature and the sociological purposes of Man; and both its outer form and inner aim depend upon the divergence between these two. For, in his individual as well as in his social life, man is governed by this diarchy.

Thus, where society is complex with a network of widely ramified relationships, the natural propensities have to be kept in check by social pressure from every side, while where wants are numerous and their supply difficult, and man is compelled to venture forth to distant places to make a living, there the social obligations needs must be light, and the nature and extent of the mutual claims of individuals over one another cannot be rigidly prescribed by society, but must be left to be adjusted by the individuals themselves.

It is a matter of comment by Europeans that we use no word like "thanks" in our own language for expressing gratitude; and they jump to the conclusion that our character must be free from that troublesome feeling. But the fact is that in our society the obligation of the giver of help is held to be stronger than that of the recipient. On him who has acquired learning is cast the duty of giving to others—that is not taken as a favour done by teacher to student. The offering of hospitality, even to the casual visitor, is incumbent on the householder for his own sake. Each of the domestic ceremonies, from the birth celebration to the funeral, is but an expression of the debt which each member owes to his community. From this it becomes evident that our society is not like a stream on which its members float in comparative freedom, but like the earth in whose depths their root-system is held secure.

The Aryans of India were at first forest dwellers. Then, as the dense screen of forest was lifted off the stage of their history, India's broad, river-served plains were converted from sylvan shelters of patriarchal communities into monarchical territories; and agriculture became the mainstay of her growing settlements. On the one hand, the close neighbourhood of peoples, racially different, giving rise to perpetual cultural conflict; and, on the other, the agricultural civilization claiming co-operation and the complex regulations of stable life,—these are the two forces that moulded Hindu society and still guide its course. Such a society can never exist and perform its functions unless peace is maintained among its members by a perfect system of mutual adjustment of rights.

In the beginning of India's history, of which we gain glimpses in the Rámáyana, three different parties are to be distinguished—the Aryans, the barbarians (variously called monkeys, bears, etc.), and the powerful, cultured Rákshasas. While all these were at daggers drawn, their constant dissensions precluded the establishment of any common social polity. Then, as the conquering

Kshatriyas extended their sway, and populous settlements grew up in their wake, the need for peace was felt and its merits were exalted. So, broadly speaking, the establishment of relationships between the Aryans, the barbarians, and the Rákshasas, forms the main theme of the Rámáyana.

Courage, in the ethics of Peace, means the courage of self-sacrifice; there, bravery has for its object the triumph of Renunciation. And, in societies where such sacrifice and renunciation are cultivated, not the individual but the household is the primary unit, and such household is broad, not narrow, in conception and content. That is why, as the Rámáyana evolves from a collection of ballads into an epic, its main function is transformed from a narration of struggles against the outrages offered to the cult of tillage *sîtá* into the exaltation of the Ethics of the Household. The unfaltering strength of self-renunciation which is needful for keeping true the varied relations between king and subject, father and son, brother and brother, husband and wife, master and servant, and among neighbours different in colour and character,—that is what it really glorifies.

Wherever many men have congregated, not for the purpose of attacking others, but for mutual benefit, there is evolved a mentality which eventually transcends all considerations of expediency and envisages Supreme Good as an absolute fulfilment. And so, in our country, there was a day when the household was glorified, not as a comfortable home, not as the enjoyment of proprietary right, but as the means of living the fullest communal life, and through it of attaining supreme liberation at the end.

The intimacy of relationship with wife and child is but natural, and so may hardly help to loosen the bonds of self—rather, it serves to strengthen them. But the household wherein even the most distant of kinsmen have a recognized right, where one's own earnings have to be shared by those who are almost strangers, where it is a matter of shame and censure if differences be made between near and distant relations,—there the claims of moral welfare override those of natural affection, and give rise to certain special qualities of heart. These gradually grow so powerful that both the individual as well as the social conscience refuse to tolerate any personal claims when these conflict with those of the household *dharma*.

Therefore, the home of the Indian has never been looked upon as his castle, the place where he is lord and master. No doubt the duty there cast on him, of considering the rights of others on any and every occasion, has involved him in expenditure of time and money, but his accounts have ever been cast up, not in terms of self-interest, but of social and spiritual welfare.

In societies where the household is founded on the comfort and convenience of the individual, his acceptance or non-acceptance of the householder's estate remains optional. If any such should say that he does not care for domestic joys, but prefers the freedom of irresponsibility, no room for objection is left. But in Hindu India, because the household is an essential element in its social structure, marriage is almost compulsory—like conscription in Europe on the threat of war.

According to our Lawgivers, any one making gifts to, or taking gifts from, a Brahmin who remains a householder, but does not marry, goes to hell. Says Atri: "No hospitality should be accepted from an unmarried householder." The household has been compared, in our *shástras*, to a great tree; for, just as the roots of the latter support its branches, twigs, and foliage, so does the life of the household maintain the different institutions of society; and the

Lawgiver lays it down that the King should do honour to the upholder of the householder's estate. But the mere fact of setting up a household, anyhow, does not constitute that estate according to our *shástras:*

> Grihasthopi kriyáyukto na grihena grihásramî,
> Na chaiva putradárena svakarma parivarjita.

Not by the house is made the household, but by the performance of the householder's duties—nor even by wife and children, if the householder be wanting in his own karma.

Karma here does not mean the looking after his family interests, but the performance of his specific duty—the fulfilment of his obligation to society.

> Tathá tathaiva káryáni na kálastu vidhîyate,
> Asminneva prayuñjáno hyasminneva tu lîyate.

With society are we connected, in it do we terminate this life; therefore should we do our duty as it arises, and not await our own convenience.

To perform the duties of a householder is in fact looked upon as a spiritual discipline. Says Vasistha:

> Grihastha eva yajate grihasthastapyate tapah,
> Chaturnámásramánántu grihasthastu vishishyate.

That is to say, because the life of a householder is a life of self-abnegation having its manifold obligations to gods and men, therefore of all the four *ásramas*, the *ásrama*, or estate, of the householder is specially distinguished.

In societies where the householder is but the means of ensuring the comfort and security of the individual, the notion of property also becomes intensely individualistic; for the right of property is at the base of the householder's estate. And when property is viewed as dedicated to individual enjoyment, it ceases as such to be a joy to the others who own it not, but becomes rather an object of their envy. Not only that, but in the process of its acquisition the question of social or moral welfare is lost sight of, and the spirit of rivalry and competition acknowledges no limit. And so, in ancient India, the class of merchants whose object in life was to acquire wealth in excess of the requirements of their livelihood, were held in contempt. Even today, water touched by such is deemed to be impure.

A school of thought has arisen in Europe which looks upon property as inherently vicious, and would advise its forcible extirpation. For, there, the irresponsible ownership of property is a potent factor in maintaining the antagonism between the claims of universal humanity and of individual man. And so far, western politics has devoted its forces to the protection of the rights of the proprietors. Hence the need for this counter-movement.

But many substances which are now good food were once unpalatable or even poisonous. Man, however, did not reject these at the outset, but made them wholesome and toothsome by a long process of culture. India, likewise, cultivated the viciousness out of property by converting the household into a field for spiritual discipline. And thus society in India stably maintained itself for centuries on the basis of the individual ownership of property; in fact India's wealth of food and clothing, education, morals, and religion were all so acquired—by virtue of that original precautionary measure.

When the welfare of society is left to depend on the voluntary generosity of its wealthy members, then is the vicious aspect of property brought out; for the indiscriminate acceptance of charity spoils the recipient. But, in

India, expenditure by the householder for social welfare was not a matter of generosity, but a primary duty in the interests of his own fulfilment. Such duty was cast not only on the rich, but also on the poor, according to their means. Manu says: "The *rishis,* the forefathers, the gods, the guests, and all living creatures expect to be maintained by the householder. Knowing this, he should act accordingly." By many such injunctions and in divers other ways are the Indian people kept reminded that the *dharma* of the householder consists in fulfilling the various claims of humanity. And further, in Manu's opinion, those who are of weak character and have no control over their passions—they are not worthy of the householder's high estate.

In order to understand the principle underlying Hindu marriage, it is necessary first to come to a true appreciation of this principle underlying the Hindu social system. It will then become clear that, in this type of society, having for its object the perfection of communal life, there is danger in allowing marriage to pursue the path of self-will. Such a society can withstand the encroachments of Nature only if its marriage system is walled round with a protective embankment. So the Hindu ideal of marriage has no regard for individual taste or inclination—it is, rather, afraid of them.

If any European would really understand the psychology behind this, let him bethink himself of the state of things that obtained during the last war. Ordinarily, in Europe, there is no bar to international marriages. But, when the one objective of the war overshadowed all other considerations, marriage with the subject of an enemy country became an impossibility; so much so, that European society felt no compunction in cruelly severing even long-standing marriage ties of this description. Not only was the marriage question so affected, but during war conditions food and all other amenities of life had to be cut down to a uniform standard. The personal liberty and elasticity of occupation, so characteristic of western civilization, tended wholly to disappear.

These war conditions afford a good parallel to the permanent conditions which govern Hindu society, where the encroachment of alien cultures has always been a constant danger to be guarded against. This vital objective of the twice-born leaders, who practically represented the whole people, therefore runs as a steady undercurrent through our society. The problem of keeping its civilization pure having been acknowledged as all-important, and its solution thus sought by India, her society has had to claim of its members the severe and permanent curbing of their individual liberty of choice and action.

Indian society, however, did not reach this stage all at once. It was gradually evolved through successive adaptations to changing circumstances. Meanwhile many relics of earlier stages survived into the later. Therefore Manu had to recognize, in his treatise, other different forms of marriage such as the *Gándharva* (by mutual choice), *Rákshasa* (by conquest), *Asur* (by purchase), *Paishácha* (by taking advantage of helplessness). In none of these is the social will manifest, but only the desire of the individual; for force, whether of arms, or money, or circumstances, is arrogant, and passion refuses to submit to extraneous considerations. But, while recording these forms, Manu censured them.

Though the *Gándharva* marriage, founded on mutual attraction, was also one of those which did not find favour with the Lawgiver, it nevertheless long persisted in Indian society, as our epics and other literature make clear. This only shows that, however conservatively stable a society may be, the principle of stability cannot be equally strong among all the classes which it comprises. In the Kshatriya character, especially, the cultivation of self-suppression was least likely to attain its fullest development. It is not possible to keep confined in a complex net of social obligations the warrior spirit which ever seeks fresh fields for expansion. It is for this reason that our *shâstras* prohibited the crossing of the sea. Any adventurous activity whatsoever, that may loosen our mind from its mooring and disturb the fixed habit of our thought and belief and behaviour, is bound to undermine the very foundation of our society.

Not only sea voyages, but also residence in foreign countries with antagonistic social ideals, was prohibited and penalized. In the West we find nowadays all kinds of forcible attempts being made to prevent the intrusion of Bolshevik ideas. This is comparable with our prohibition of foreign travel. No penalty is deemed too severe if it but keep in check the propaganda which, it is apprehended, may destroy the elements essential for the stability of the orthodox western social system. The liberty of the people to form their own opinions, to regulate their own conduct, is here no longer respected. The terrorist organization called Fascism, which seems to be daily gaining ground in Europe, is the exact counterpart of our rigorous social injunctions. There was a day in India when for the Sudra to aspire to the path of the Brahmin entailed the death penalty. The same psychological phenomenon is seen in the West in the cruel form of lynching, Fascism, Ku-Klux-Klanism, and the like.

It is no doubt conducive to a certain strength if all the members of a society are, in the main, moulded in accordance with some uniform standard. That may be a bar to the fullest development of its individuals, but it certainly does help to keep the society, as a whole, in a state of stable equilibrium. And if any society, on the cessation of its growth, should come to pride itself on being, not like a growing tree, but like a temple of which its securely established immovableness is its glory, it will inevitably feel the moving of a single one of its bricks to be a loss. Nevertheless it is not possible to keep all the members of any society uniformly bound in such unalterable fixity—that is against the nature of man and destructive of the principle of life itself. So that, as long as any people is vigorously alive, they or some of them cannot but keep breaking through the rules and prohibitions imposed by their society. Both in its biological and sociological phases, these opposing forces of conservation and experimentation are characteristic of life.

Anyhow, as long as the Kshatriyas were real Kshatriyas, it was not found possible to keep them rigorously bound down to the habitual performance of the prescribed rules for daily observance. That is why, in the history of ancient India, the Kshatriyas were at the bottom of all the social and religious revolutions. We must remember that Buddha was a Kshatriya, that Mahávîra was a Kshatriya; and that the clan to which Srîkrishna himself belonged was not famous for observing the precepts and prohibitions most esteemed by the Lawgivers. If we read through the Mahábhárata, we are reminded at every turn that, however determined may have been the endeavour to protect society behind a permanent embankment, there was not a single kingly clan of note which did not break through the walls. It was only in comparatively recent times, when the Kshatriyas had lost their virility and the Brahmins had gained almost unquestioned ascendancy, that it became possible to make the social bonds so rigorously inert.

Manu gives the name of *Gándharva* to marriage by mutual choice, and signifies his disapprobation by stigmatizing it as "born of desire." The way to marriage which is shown by the torchlight of passion has not for its goal the welfare of society, but the satisfaction of desire. Even in Europe, where the obligation of the individual to society is much lighter, it is well known how the mingling of the sexes under the impulse of passion often gives rise to anti-social difficulties; but there, society being mobile, the effects are not so deep as with us. In our *shástras*, therefore, the *Bráhma* marriage is considered to be the best. According to this, the bride should be given to a man who had not solicited her. If the institution of marriage has to be regulated strictly from the social standpoint, room cannot be found for the personal wishes of the people concerned; so the system which obtains in the case of the royal houses of Europe is the system which prevails throughout Hindu society.

Another way for the better understanding by the European of the mentality underlying our marriage system would be by reference to the discussions on eugenics which are a feature of modern Europe. The science of eugenics, like all other sciences, attaches but little weight to personal sentiment. According to it, selection by personal inclination must be rigorously regulated for the sake of the progeny. If the principle involved be once admitted, marriage needs must be rescued from the control of the heart, and brought under the province of the intellect; otherwise insoluble problems will keep on arising, for passion recks not of consequences, nor brooks interference by outside judges.

To return to our Kshatriyas: They were, as I have indicated, not in the habit of observing with any strictness the social rules relating to marriage. But it becomes clear from the poems of Kalidas that there was a struggle of protest in his mind against this laxity of their observance. The poet keenly felt the value of the eugenic restrictions which were directed toward maintaining the racial ideals pure, and yet his heart could not fail to be moved by the beauty of the play of the natural loves of man and woman against the background of the exuberance of the Universal Life. In most of the great works of Kalidas is treated the conflict of these opposites. The coming of the line of the Bháratas was a great event in the history of India. But though the prelude of unbridled desire, which ushered in the founder of the line, has been viewed by the poet in its aspect of beauty in the first part of the play, he has corrected it from the standpoint of the good toward the conclusion.

Amid the natural beauty of the forest hermitage, Sakuntalá's youth blossoms out in prodigal curves of body and mind, along with the ecstasy of form and movement in the flowering trees and creepers around her. Everywhere in this retreat does Nature beckon, but Society, as yet, has found no loophole through which to obtrude the warning of her uplifted finger. Sakuntalá's secret union with King Dushyanta, which takes place amid these surroundings, is not in harmony with the rest of society. So, according to the poet, the curse comes upon her. She overlooks, in her self-absorption, the duty of hospitality; for when Nature is busy securing any special purpose, she throws all other purposes into the background. Society thereupon exacts its penalty and, in the King's audience hall, the inevitable thunderbolt of insult and rejection falls upon Sakuntalá.

In the seventh act, the picture which the poet draws of the hermitage in which is consummated King Dushyanta's final union with Sakuntalá, now purified by discipline, is everywhere full of the rigour of renunciation, eclipsing the life-play of Nature. In the opening scene, the King is informed that the *Rishi* is busy expounding the *dharma* of the wifely estate. Sakuntalá, here, is seen as the emblem of devotion, the mother. It is clear that the poet's object was vividly to contrast these two pictures of the relations of woman to man, the one carrying the bondage of desire, the other the detachment of *dharma*.

Motherhood, in so far as it is concerned with the physical nurture of offspring, is not essentially different in man and the lower animals, being a function of biological, not of sociological, life, governed by instincts which are of Nature, not by man's own creative power. But where the mother undergoes voluntary penance for the elevation of the human race, keeping her natural instincts in rigorous subordination to the dictates of mind and soul, there indeed is her own creative power at work. Nowadays in the West, we often find women feeling a certain degradation in becoming subject to maternity; that is to say, they feel the insult of having to submit to this tyranny of Nature over their sex. But the way for woman to avoid such insult is not by abjuring motherhood, but by making it subserve her ideal, by bringing it under the control of her own intellect and conscience. How far India's conscious activity in the past—this striving of hers for the best possible progeny—was fully consonant with the conclusions of modern science, is not the question here. The point is, that just by such intellectual and spiritual vigilance can the human mother achieve her true dignity.

In his *Kumára-sambhava* it is the same thing that the poet tells us. There he has shown the divine aspect of the eternal love of man and woman. When the Titans have won paradise and banished the gods therefrom, the love of man and woman, transformed into ascetic striving, wins back heaven from the insult of defeat. The gods are eternally awaiting the birth of Kumára, the conqueror of evil. And, in order to achieve this birth, the passion of desire must be transmuted into pure, disciplined endeavour. The rigorous aspect of such achievement is the truth which is beauty. The beauty of illusion is gorgeous in its adornment, the beauty of freedom is naked.

In all three of his works, the *Raghu-vamsa*, the *Kumára-sambhava* and *Sakuntalá*, India's poet has looked upon marriage as a state of discipline, not intended for gaining individual happiness, but of which the method is the control of desire and the object to bring about the birth of the Slayer of Evil, the super-man who will make possible the achievement of heaven on earth. The agony of the poet which we glimpse in each of these springs from his consciousness of the degeneracy which was overtaking society through the flagrant disregard by the Kshatriya kings of the Aryan ideal of marriage. And the poet sends out his call to bring away the union of man and woman from the realm of Kandarpa (Eros) into the hermitage of Shiva, the Good. This Indian ideal of marriage can be much more vividly understood from the works of the poet than from any Dharma-shástra.

HERE the question arises: If desire be banished from the very threshold of marriage, how can love find any place in the wedded life? Those who have no true acquaintance with our country, and whose marriage system is entirely different, take it for granted that the Hindu marriage is loveless. But do we not know of our own knowledge how false is such a conclusion?

If we accept the institution of marriage, we must also admit that no system can be devised to insure that its original object shall remain true throughout the long period covered by the life of the wedded couple. That is why both law and public opinion have to keep such vigilant watch from the outside. But when external compulsion tries to bind together those whom only mutual love can truly unite, it makes their relations inherently impure—in fact, no greater insult can be offered to man. Yet, all over the civilized world, man submits even to this for the sake of the welfare of his children. So far, no society has been able to claim that it has arrived at a faultless solution of the difficulty. In entering the married state we all have to make our plunge into the doubtful and leave it to Providence whether we shall sink, or swim through.

The "desire," however, against which India's solution of the marriage problem declared war, is one of Nature's most powerful fighters; consequently, the question of how to overcome it was not an easy one. There is a particular age, said India, at which this attraction between the sexes reaches its height; so if marriage is to be regulated according to the social will, it must be finished with before such age. Hence the Indian custom of early marriage.

This brings to my mind the conversation I once had with an agriculturist. I was complaining to him of the lack of common grazing grounds in our villages, whereupon he told me that it was a mistake to suppose that a cow would thrive best if allowed to graze at will. Scientific feeding with specially cultivated fodder-crops only could yield the best results. These must have been the lines of argument, in regard to married love, pursued in our country. For the purpose of marriage, spontaneous love is unreliable; its proper cultivation should yield the best results—such was the conclusion—and this cultivation should begin before marriage. Therefore, from their earliest years, the husband as an idea is held up before our girls, in verse and story, through ceremonial and worship. When at length they get this husband, he is to them not a person but a principle, like loyalty, patriotism, or such other abstractions which owe their immense strength to the fact that the best part of them is our own creation and therefore part of our inner being.

There is also in our society the glorification of the *satî*, the ideal wife; and, accordingly, a real reverence for woman, as the embodiment of housewifely virtues, is not rare in our country. The idea was, in both cases, to replace the natural passion of sexual love by the cultivated emotion of wedded love. But it must be admitted that as woman is emotional by nature, it has not been as easy for man thus to idealize the married state as it has been for her. It must also be admitted that the restraints and restrictions prescribed in the case of the man have not been so rigorous as those for the woman.

Therefore, in coming to our judgment on the marriage system of India, we must not fail to recognize the fact that therein the man and the woman are not on a footing of equality. Such inequality would have utterly humiliated her but that, for the wife, the husband is an ideal. She has not surrendered herself to the brute force of another, but voluntarily consecrated herself to the service of her own ideal. And if the husband is a man of sensitive soul the flame of this ideal love is transmitted to his own life also. Such mutual illumination it has often been our lot to witness.

There is yet another vital element in India's culture which we must keep in mind. In spite of her exaltation of the household estate, India did not look upon this as man's ultimate stage. According to India's ideal, even the home must be given up in due course, in quest of the Infinite—the household, in fact, is only to be set up as an important stage in this quest. Even today, we see our householders, when their children are grown up, leaving their home to spend the rest of their life in some place of pilgrimage. Here is another pair of opposites which India attempted to reconcile. On the one hand, her civilization is essentially bound up in the home, albeit a home in which a wide circle of relationships find their place. On the other, its endeavour is, one by one, to snap all earthly ties in its pursuit of the liberation of the soul. In fact, it recognizes the social bonds because it is only through their acceptance that they can be transcended. In order to get rid of the natural desires of man, they must be used up; that is to say, guided by the spirit of renunciation to their own extinction. Here we find the difference between Hinduism and Buddhism. In its relations with Nature, Buddhism is uncompromisingly anarchist from the very outset.

The weakness of the Hindu system lies in the fact that its complex web is too closely knit and that the least loosening of its fibre in any of its parts tends to its disruption. It is afraid of the contact of the outside, because the bond which holds it together is that of external regulation, whose strength depends upon habitual conformity. But self-segregation for any society is no longer practicable in this age. For, while it may be possible to prevent the man on this side of the sea from crossing to the other, what about preventing those on the other side from coming over here?

So have alien ideas, alien systems, alien customs, breaking in through her embankments, dashed upon India in a multitudinous flood, making visible breaches in all the habits and beliefs which were the pillars of her social system. Further, apart from this disturbance of her inward life, there has been the more effective attack of an alien economic system; for without a sufficiency of food it is impossible for the various relationships of her complex society to be kept together. And just as foreign ideas come pouring in on our mental world, so do our foodstuffs, caught up in various currents of commerce, keep flowing away towards foreign lands, so that the people of our country, in their social dealings, are now compelled to keep careful count of their meagre resources. Lastly, there is the Nemesis of the unrealized ideal, which overtakes any civilization when, by reason of flagging vitality, it fails in the earnestness of its pursuit and lapses into the stagnation of mechanical habits. Every living organism is constantly confronted with the waste products of its own fatigue, for which its vital forces, while active, find natural means of elimination. The adoption of complex external devices is of no avail when vitality is on the wane, for they only tend to weaken the natural functions still further, if not to create new forms of weakness and disease. The civilizations which flourished for a time and have disappeared are those which committed suicide, clinging on to their own toxic products, by suppressing, under the urgency of their special purposes, the cleansing impulses provided by Nature.

Anyhow, the special qualities of head and heart which once found varied support in our broad social system are now dying out for lack of opportunity for their exercise; meanwhile it has not been possible to effect a corresponding change in the structure of our society, with the result that while all its restrictions keep on hampering us, their original object and justification have become impossible of acknowledgement. And so on every side are the members of this vast society overwhelmed with futility. In particular, the very basis of our marriage system having been undermined, there is no longer any harmony of adjustment between the underlying ideals and the actual facts of our modern marriages. One section of our people keeps crying out for a return of the *Satya-yuga*, but that golden age refuses to respond to their call. The time has, therefore, come for us to think out our problems afresh, to correlate our thoughts and conclusions with those of all humanity.

The gulf of separation which Nature has contrived between the sexes has preserved in its atmosphere the varied play of a powerful mutual attraction. This force which is creative—but destructive as well—continually sends its awakening message to our souls from behind the veil. If we screen off society from its forceful activity, that may conduce to its own safety but will surely reduce it to passivity. In our language we call the power of woman over man by the name of *shakti*. Deprived of *shakti* the creative process in society languishes, and man, losing his vitality, becomes mechanical in his habits. In such a case, though he may still retain many a passive quality, all energy of activity forsakes him. The manner in which the relations between the sexes have been regulated in our country has left no room for the action of this *shakti;* for as we have seen, our society, with immoveable stability as its objective, has been busy cultivating the passive qualities, ever in dread of individual forcefulness. Now that our country has awakened to outside influences, she finds herself powerless to resist alien aggression. She has even lost the faculty of recognizing that her weakness proceeds from within her own social system and is not the outcome of any outward accident.

In every society, its civilization is the territory conquered in its contest with Nature. And since in our country this contest was long and bitter, everywhere we find its fences more in evidence than its roads. But that there was once a good reason for this state of things does not help to save her when the reason has ceased to exist. Her barriers, which formerly protected her from the intrusion of outsiders, now imprison her.

It seems that in the age which has now come upon us, man is giving up the desperate hope of victoriously maintaining this constant struggle. He would now make his peace with Nature—and that duty has been entrusted to science. But the marriage system of every society belongs to an age when, in the parliament of life, man was sitting on the opposition benches against Nature's government. And Nature has ever retaliated against his obstructive tactics. Thus far they have nowhere come to any satisfactory agreement. That is why these ubiquitous attempts at the external regulation of man's most intimate relations have been insulting his best feelings and degrading the greatest of his institutions, all over the world.

LET me, as an individual Indian, offer in conclusion my own personal contribution to the discussion of the marriage question generally.

There are two parallel activities in the human world, the one which carries forward the stream of population; the other, the civilization of man. The first chiefly belongs to the realm of life, and the second to that of mind. In the creation of progeny man's part, though essential, is secondary. After he has once roused the passive seed in woman's keeping to vital activity, all the travail of child-bearing and parturition are hers alone. It is because of this comparative lightness of the male function in the propagation of the species that we find instances of the killing off of superfluous males in the insect world and of the keeping down of the number of male beasts by internecine struggles due to the savage jealousy which is their characteristic—showing the minor importance of this sex for the purpose of biological creation.

But when mind evolved itself into greatness, man found the opportunity to gain glory for his sex in the scheme of human development. For while woman remained entangled in the specific duties which life had assigned to her, man, with his greater freedom therefrom, was able to respond to the call of his intellect and engage in various works of creation in the world of mind—in fact he created the sphere of his own usefulness. In this, the first chapter of civilization, when mind was in the ascendant, woman in her turn dropped into the second place, not only as less useful, but even as an actual impediment; for the world which was her special creation constantly sought to throw its toils around the adventurous spirit of man as well. This comparative unimportance of woman in the birth-stage of civilization clings to her still. That is why the rebellious section of womankind would curtail her responsibilities in the region of life in order to enable her to claim equality with man in the work of his creation of society.

Opportunities, however, cannot be artificially created. The propensities of heart, strongly ingrained in woman's nature, cannot be dislodged by attacks from the outside. The tendency of these propensities of hers are toward holding fast, and not progressing onward. So it is only by adherence to the cult of preservation that woman can attain her true welfare. If she desperately engages in adventurous pursuits, she will at every step come into conflict with her own inner nature; and thus constantly distracted, she can never succeed in competing with man in his own special sphere. But just as man, after a long period of subordination during the ascendancy of life, was enabled to get rid of his disabilities in a subsequent stage, so woman too may look forward to a yet higher régime whereunder she will have the right to emerge from her present subjection. It is difficult to decide what to call this next stage, for the word "spiritual" is beset with controversy regarding its true meaning. However, let me for my present purpose give it that name.

The inner qualities of woman's heart result in an important by-product which may be called *charm*. This charm, like light, is a force. Intangible, imponderable though it be, the strivings of our intellect may not attain fruition if deprived of its life-giving touch. The nourishment which the tree draws though its roots may be classified and measured—not so the vitality which is the gift of the sunlight and without which its functioning becomes altogether impossible.

This ineffable emanation of woman's nature has, from the first, played its part in the creations of man, unobtrusively but inevitably. Had man's mind not been energized by the inner working of woman's vital charm, he would never have attained his successes. Of all the higher achievements of civilization—the devotion of the toiler, the valour of the brave, the creations of the artist—the secret spring is to be found in woman's influence. In the clash and battle of primitive civilization, the action of woman's *shakti* is not clearly manifest; but as civilization becomes spiritual in the course of its development, and the union of man with man is acknowledged to be more important than the differences between them, the charm of woman gets the opportunity to become the predominant factor. Such spiritual civilization can only be upheld if the emotion of woman and the intellect of man are contributed in usual shares for its purposes. Then their respective contributions may combine gloriously in ever-fresh creations, and their difference will no longer make for inequality.

Woman, let me repeat, has two aspects—in one she is the mother; in the other, the beloved. I have already spoken of the spiritual endeavour that characterizes the first; namely, the striving, not merely for giving birth to her child, but for creating the best possible child—not as an addition to the number of men, but as one of the heroic souls who may win victory in man's eternal fight against evil in his social life and natural surroundings. As the beloved, it is woman's part to infuse life into all the aspirations of man; and the spiritual power that enables her to do so I have called *charm*, and was known in India by the name of *shakti*.

There is a poem called *Ananda-laharî* (*The Stream of Delight*), attributed to Shankaráchárya. She who is glorified therein is the *shakti* in the heart of the Universe, the Giver of Joy, the Inspirer of Activity. On the one hand, we know and use the world; on the other, we are related to it by ties of disinterested joy. We can know the world because it is a manifestation of truth: we rejoice in it because it is an expression of joy. "Who would have striven for life," says the *Rishi*, "if this *ánanda* (joy) had not filled the sky?" It seems to me that the "Intellectual Beauty" whose praises Shelley has sung is identical with this *ánanda*. And it is this same *ánanda* which the poet of *Ananda-laharî* has visualized as the woman; that is to say, in his view, this universal *shakti* is manifest in human society in the nature of woman. In this manifestation is her charm. Let no one confuse this *shakti* with mere "sweetness," for in this charm there is a combination of several qualities—patience, self-abnegation, sensitive intelligence, grace in thought, word, and behaviour—the reticent expression of rhythmic life, the tenderness and terribleness of love; at its core, moreover, is that self-radiant spirit of delight which ever gives itself up.

This *shakti*, this joy-giving power of woman as the beloved, has up to now largely been dissipated by the greed of man, who has sought to use it for the purposes of his individual enjoyment, corrupting it, confining it, like his property, within jealously guarded limits. That has also obstructed for woman herself her inward realization of the full glory of her own *shakti*. Her personality has been insulted at every turn by being made to display its power of delectation within a circumscribed arena. It is because she has not found her true place in the great world that she sometimes tries to capture man's special estate as a desperate means of coming into her own. But it is not by coming out of her home that woman can gain her liberty. Her liberation can only be effected in a society where her true *shakti*, her *ánanda*, is given the widest and highest scope for its activity. Man has already achieved the means of self-expansion in public activity without giving up his individual concerns. When, likewise, any society shall be able to offer a larger field for the creative work of woman's special faculty, without detracting from her creative work in the home, then in such society will the true union of man and woman become possible.

The marriage system all over the world, from the earliest ages till now, is a barrier in the way of such true union. That is why woman's *shakti*, in all existing societies, is so shamefully wasted and corrupted. That is why in every country marriage is still more or less of a prison-house for the confinement of woman—with all its guards wearing the badge of the dominant male. That is why man, by dint of his efforts to bind woman, has made her the strongest of fetters for his own bondage. That is why woman is debarred from adding to the spiritual wealth of society by the perfection of her own nature, and all human societies are weighed down with the burden of the resulting poverty.

The civilization of man has not, up to now, loyally recognized the reign of the spirit. Therefore the married state is still one of the most fruitful sources of the unhappiness and downfall of man, of his disgrace and humiliation. But those who believe that society is a manifestation of the spirit will assuredly not rest in their endeavours till they have rescued human marriage relations from outrage by the brute forces of society—till they have thereby given free play to the force of love in all the concerns of humanity.

RICHARD WILHELM

The Chinese Conception of Marriage

In the earliest times, according to Chinese legends, people knew their mother, but not their father. The oldest clan names contain the determining sign "woman"; further, the word which today signifies "family name" contains the determining sign "woman" in remembrance of its origin. The "Hundred Clans" were composed of people fit for military service. All this points to original matriarchal conditions prevailing in China. It seems that it was not without struggle that the matriarchy was superseded by a patriarchy. In ancient history, traces of a matriarchate are still to be found. The patriarchate and patriarchal exogamic kinship was first established under the third Shu dynasty. This would be approximately 1000 B.C.

The Chinese conception of marriage can be understood only on the principle of consanguinity in which it became incorporated as a necessary component. The clan was under the leadership of the head of the family. Adjoining buildings were placed at the disposal of the sons and their families. The different generations remained living together as long as the venerable head of the clan was alive or a worthy successor could be found and the property proved sufficient for maintenance of the clan. The "partitioning of the home" was always an expedient of emergency, due to dissension among the brothers after the father's death or to economic difficulties. On principle, no limit is set to the expansion of the clan. In the holy edict of the Emperor Kanghsi, a family is mentioned where such harmony prevailed that nine generations dwelt happily together and even the dogs lived in such unison that they all assembled at common meal-times.

Most Chinese village communities have developed out of a clan which has later been joined by one or two others. This is indicated by the names of the villages, which are mostly compounded, as in German, with words like "home," "house," or "residence"—"Village of the Wang family," "Home of the Li family," etc. One of the best examples of the way in which these clans could expand is found in Kufu, the native place of Kungtse, where even today the majority of the inhabitants belong to the Kung family, which is the oldest noble family in the world. Its genealogy can be traced back authentically to the royal house that ceased to reign about 1100 B.C.

The clan is built up on the strictly moral relations that exist between father and son, elder and younger brothers, and husband and wife. These date back to very early times and were codified by Confucius. These relations depended on a sense of mutual duty. It is the father's duty to be benevolent; the son must venerate his father; the elder brother must be provident, the younger brother obedient, the husband considerate, and the wife submissive. On these relations, which are dependent on natural family instincts, is based the entire social order. For in reality the relations between ruler and servant and between friends are only a continuation and projection of family duties applied to society and the state. The most important of these ethical principles is the son's veneration of his father. This characterizes the clan as an essentially patriarchal institution.

Furthermore, the social foundation of the clan or

family rests in the religious principle of ancestor worship. The clan is not only a unit in space; it is one with the past generations. The ancestors are thought of as taking part in the family's weal and woe. Perhaps originally it was held that the ancestor was reincarnated in the grandchild. The old custom, according to which the grandchild has to act as the ancestor's incarnation at the sacrificial repast, points to this. As time went on, noble families tried to prolong the personal existence of their ancestors by establishing special cults. Three, five, seven, or even nine generations of ancestors were venerated, according to the status of the family. But the ancestors were always placed according to their generations, some toward the light (on the north side of the ancestors' temple) and others away from it (on the south side of the temple). Only the chief ancestor of the king's family is given the same rank as the god of heaven, i. e., originally they were thought to be identical; that is why the monarch was known as the Son of Heaven. The other ancestors, unless they had rendered some special service to the family, were superseded, once their time had come. From very early times, at least from the age of Confucius, ancestors have played a rather abstract part in the life of China; they have in a way been the religious representatives of the idea of the clan. They were absolutely dependent on the clan's continuing to live and on their being offered the appropriate sacrifice by the living head of the family. His wife stood by his side to perform certain offices, while the younger generations had appointed duties to fulfil at the sacrificial ceremony. This explains how it became the principal duty of the Chinese, whose religion was built up on the clan idea, to have male children in order to secure the continuation of the family and promote its welfare and activity in the future; they were also expected, by means of appropriate sacrifices, to let the ancestors participate in this future prosperity.

From this point of view we can best understand the Chinese idea of marriage. The marriage bond between man and woman, that is to say a lasting communion, is an integral part of the higher unit of the clan. Only in regard to these associations does marriage acquire its essential meaning. The natural basis of marriage in the erotic relation of the sexes is neither denied nor circumscribed. Eroticism has never been looked upon in China as debasing or sinful. Sex passion as such is appreciated without constraint as a natural instinct, just as the other instincts are. On the other hand, it is not given a mysterious and sacred meaning, nor is it looked upon as something to be worshipped, but simply as the human and animal operation of the two primeval cosmic forces, the creative and receptive, corresponding to heaven and earth, expansion in time and concentration in space. Passion in itself is neither good nor evil; only when it is uncontrolled and exaggerated does it become evil, just as every excess is evil. Moderation is the ethical requirement in regard to all impulses. It will be evident that in accordance with this view of eroticism, personal differentiation of feeling (and this refers mostly, if not entirely, to man) does not play a prominent part. Chinese lyrics do not sing of the one and only beloved, that lives once and will never be found a second time, but of seeking and finding, of happiness and separation, yearning and reunion, or of loneliness and renunciation. This also accounts for the fact that eroticism does not occupy such a predominant place in Chinese lyric poetry as it does in European. Other forms of emotion, such as the love between children and parents or between brothers and sisters, are shown to possess just as much pathos and to be capable of as fine a lyric handling as love between man and woman itself.

In order that the erotic relation may have an ethical significance it must be made a part of the family economy. Marriage is contracted in order that the family may be maintained. Naturally man thus finds that his comrade is also a consideration. But the main object is to raise up for the ancestors male issue, who shall offer them sacrifices and continue the work of the clan. This determines the sacredness of marriage; the moral obligation it entails is a part of piety.

The marriage form grows out of this idea. Monogamy is the rule, even the law, since male and female complement one another as do earth and heaven. But marriage does not lead to a separate family being set up. The woman becomes a member of her husband's family, and it is her duty to maintain, tend, and see to its continuance. She takes part in the filial duties of her husband. As son, he has in the first place to serve his father, while she as daughter-in-law has to serve her mother-in-law. She becomes a member of the clan's household, and her relation to her mother-in-law is much more important than that to her husband. If she bears sons, she has fulfilled her principal duty and attains a position of esteem. Barrenness is the main reason for divorce, i. e., for returning her to her family. In wealthy families, this expedient is seldom resorted to, if the relation is otherwise happy, for it is the woman's prerogative to give her husband one or more female servants, whose children then look up to her, his principal wife, as mother. Here is a motive for extending marriage, as is not infrequently the case in wealthy families.

From this peculiar position woman occupies, it will be clear that the choice of a wife, betrothal, and marriage are not altogether the private affair of the couple, but a family matter. A strict rule is that only members of families which possess different names are allowed to marry. Up to the present day strict exogamy is a custom in China. If a young man were to marry his cousin on his father's side it would be looked upon as incest. As regards a relation in the female line, more leniency is shown. The bride leaves her father's family and enters that of her future husband. As this almost invariably happens—for nearly everybody marries, as celibacy is not held in any esteem—so even at her birth the girl meets with a different reception; whereas the ancestors are informed with rejoicing when a son is born, this is omitted in the case of a daughter. In other respects also the son is treated preferentially. This does not, however, imply that the parents love their daughters less. The legend that the Chinese make it a regular practice to murder their female children has for some considerable time found discredit. One thing, however, is true, that the daughter is educated for another's family and not for her own.

This significance of marriage plays a decisive part in the choice of a wife. The proposal must come from the man's family. It is not done directly, but by the mediation of friends or relatives. Neither the wealth nor the nobility of the bride's family are decisive factors, for property cannot be transferred through a daughter but remains in her family, which she leaves on marriage. A man seeks a girl whose family conditions are about the same as his, so that there is a possibility of her readily settling down. In the case of friendly families, it often happens that the children are betrothed when they are quite small, in order to cement the friendship. The reason for employing a mediator is that by this means, if the suit is rejected, personal affront may be avoided, and that the virtues of the two wards can be spoken of by the mediator without self-praise. The significance of marriage demands that the engagement should receive the sanction of the cosmic forces. Horoscopes are cast and compared. If these prove satisfactory, the marriage may take place. There is an old saying that the old man in the moon in earliest childhood binds with invisible thread the feet of those who are intended for one another.

If the astral and other preliminary conditions are satisfactory, the engagement takes place with an interchange of records and bridal presents. The giving of presents has degenerated into something very similar to marriage by purchase. This was certainly not the original intention. The gifts were intended to loose the girl's bond with her ancestors, so that she might be free to enter her new family. All these formalities are both numerous and cumbersome. It is considered proper that the man's courtship should be met with hesitation. Finally the day of the wedding is determined. Then, in accordance with certain other customs that have to be observed, the bridegroom fetches his bride in a gaily decorated sedan-chair, and they proceed amid a festive escort from her parents' house to his. The wedding always takes place in the bridegroom's house, as a family occurrence which has its significance in the present and the future. The bride comes veiled in red. The marriage ceremony consists of drinking together out of two cups that are tied to each other with red string, the mutual veneration of the man's parents, the mutual veneration of the powers of heaven and earth, and the solemn presentation of the bride at the tablets of the ancestors. The bride enters her new home veiled. Only after the marriage ceremony has been completed are the veils removed, and she is now, at least according to theory, seen for the first time by the bridegroom.

In accordance with the fact that marriages are contracted more in the interests of the clan than of the participants, they often take place in early youth, and bridegroom and bride are about the same age. In country districts the bad practice arose, when there was a shortage of hands at harvest time, of getting one's son married in order to secure a daughter-in-law as a labourer. Usually a capable grown-up woman was chosen, even if the bridegroom was still quite a child. That this custom led to certain unhealthy consequences is not surprising, seeing that in the country the male and female members of the clan lived in a very close union; thus again and again we find this pernicious practice of child-marriage fought by new laws and ordinances.

As regards the relation of the married couple to one another, in Chinese marriage the housewife has more freedom than is generally the case in Japanese marriages. In Japan, the wife is a graceful, selfless, and devoted slave of the master of the house, and to be charming is the ideal that the girls are educated up to. In the Chinese family a difference is also made in the treatment of the future husbands and wives. An old song tells of the different lucky signs respecting the birth of children. When the master of the house dreams of bears, it signifies the birth of sons; if he dreams of snakes, it will be daughters. The song then continues:

Sons will be born unto you;
They will sleep on gaudy beds,
And be clothed in coloured garments;
Red garters they will wear,
And they will make your house famous by their rule.

Daughters will be born unto you;
They will sleep upon the earth;
They will be wrapped in swaddling clothes;

They will play with fragments of clay;
They will be neither good nor bad;
They will have to do only with eating and drinking,
And they will live without causing their parents grief.

But this difference in position does not mean that the women as such are inferior. In Chinese marriage the husband possesses paternal authority and represents the family externally—at least in such matters as do not affect the jurisdiction of the clan leader—but the wife has also her special domain in the interior of the house. Man is the image of the creative primal cause, and woman the image of the receptive. The man should be strong, active, and a leader; the woman, soft, receptive, and submissive. If this balance is maintained, each is useful in his appropriate place. There is never a question of woman's representing an inferior principle. Evil enters only when the order is vitiated. When the woman leaves her appointed sphere and wishes to rule where she should obey, when the "hen crows," then indeed things are in a bad way. And consequently it is woman who has the happiness of marriage and of the whole clan in her hands. It is written in the *Book of Transformations:* "The happiness of the clan depends on the integrity of woman."

What does this integrity of woman consist in? She must seriously fulfil her obligations to the man's family. She must not look back to her own family, but with all her powers must serve the welfare of her new family. Wherever in history a princess has neglected her duty to the house she belongs to by marriage, either because of her desire for power or her nepotism, chaos and the fall of the dynasty have resulted, as for example in the case of the famous Empress Tsehsi. But not only must all consideration for her own family be eliminated, she must also not be contentious in her dealings with her sisters-in-law. Here, certainly, are great difficulties. It is perhaps not merely due to chance that the Chinese hieroglyphic for "peace" is a woman under a roof.

For the proper understanding of marriage this qualification is important. The relation of the brothers to one another inside the clan stands foremost. The edict of the Emperor Kanghsi states that they should not allow their harmony to be dissolved by "the foolish words of the women," for "women's words sever flesh and bone." It should also be remembered that the marriage union does not imply an independent ownership of property in its full extent. The property, inasmuch as it is used for the maintenance of the clan, all belongs to the clan as a whole on a communistic basis. Its utilization and consumption is determined by the head of the clan, who is assisted in its distribution to the various households within it by all the grown-up members. Strictly speaking, private property within the clan only consists in articles of utility. It is evident that this common ownership of property is only possible in the country. Town life also had the effect in China of splitting up the clans into small families, which then become proletarianized, i. e., disintegrated. But in China this process was confined to the outer edges of the cultural system.

Another question arises regarding the relation of the marriage partners to one another. One might imagine that life in common of complete strangers of all sorts of different temperaments would lead to innumerable embroilments. In reality this is not the case. It cannot be asserted that even the most personal European marriage based entirely on mutual affection is any happier or more peaceful than Chinese marriage, which rests on parental authority. In fact, the reverse is usually the case. Divorce was much more rare in ancient China than in modern Europe. There are several reasons for this, the main one being the great similarity of personalities, which do not express themselves according to individual taste, but according to strict social rules. Consequently it does not make much difference to a man which woman he marries, for they are all more or less alike. More important by far than individual differences are those of education and milieu. A well-educated young man of good family is sure, if not of a passionately happy married life, at least of peaceful felicity, with a woman of his own education, if there is good will on both sides. This is made easier by the fact that both members of the newly married couple live in a family circle where each has his special task and work. Marriage is simpler because it is less problematic; it is not so much an epoch as an episode. This at least applies to the man. For the woman, naturally, an entirely new life commences with marriage. But in this the husband is not the only determining factor; other members of the clan play a part as well. The free outlook in China on sex questions does not leave it to demimondaines to attract and fascinate men. Girls of good family also learn both to adorn and make themselves pleasing. Powder and paint are freely used. The half shy, half roguish glance, the suppressed titter and modest blushes are weapons not unknown to Chinese women. The binding of their feet, which is now forbidden, was primarily intended as an erotic enticement. The "golden lotus flowers" and the gracefully wavering walk were considered alluring. This is the motive for regarding the woman's foot as an immodest subject for conversation—for in the presence of ladies in China one may not even mention the word "shoe."

However, one must admit that love in all its intensity of passion and pain scarcely ever makes its appearance in the tranquil conditions of Chinese marriage. But it can happen that the husband seeks to satisfy his aesthetic desires and impulses. If he has a wise wife, she will help him without evincing jealousy, and will help him to bring his beloved into the family. To meet such cases, the idea of the subsidiary wife was instituted. The less envious a woman is in this respect—and a good wife should never be jealous—the less will the new liaison influence the stable and practical love between husband and wife. Where the wife does not possess this wisdom, it frequently happens that the husband seeks his pleasure outside his house. Or if he makes use of his prerogative and brings his love into the house, a dangerous situation may easily arise, in which the wife fears her husband, the subsidiary wife fears the former, and the husband goes in awe of his subsidiary wife. In discussing Chinese marriage this part of the subject cannot well be left out. A certain amount of delicacy is required to understand it properly. These conditions are, however, by no means the general rule. By far the great majority of Chinese marriages are monogamic. Only in the higher and wealthier circles is the attempt made to resolve certain matrimonial difficulties in this open and considerate manner.

The sphere of experiences which the Chinese form of marriage can embrace is very wide. In unfavourable circumstances, marriage in China, as elsewhere, is an organized hell. A heartless woman not only destroys her husband's peace but harasses the whole clan to which she belongs, and can even cause its destruction. The worst tyrants of Chinese legend and history were as a rule spurred on to commit their abominations and follies by a beautiful but heartless woman. More than one dynasty came to grief in this fashion. But as a rule, under the patriarchal form of Chinese marriage, it is woman who suffers most. Man, in China, will always find some means of escape when, as the saying runs, "a little ogre sits at his bedside." Characters in plays, such as Bramarbas who says, "I fear neither heaven or earth, but only the mother of my son," may be taken as comic allusions. But in marriage it is the wife's task to come to an understanding not only with her husband, but with her sisters-in-law and more especially with her mother-in-law. Chinese legends tell of the spiritual conflicts of young husbands who are induced by their mothers to kill their wives; and more than one tale relates how the tormented young wife escapes this fate only by taking refuge in a Buddhist convent and renouncing the world. Especially when the husband is absent, which may be for several years at a time, as in China the wife is provided for by the family, does the anguish of separation gather force. Very often the last resource of the tormented spirit is suicide. On the other hand, this threat is often the only means of preventing the mother-in-law from tormenting her daughter-in-law too terribly, for it is always deemed a great disgrace for the family if a woman hangs herself.

But there is a happy side to outweigh these shadows. The average Chinese marriage is more peaceful and more a matter of course than marriage anywhere else. The very fact that the man receives his wife from his parents operates in this direction. He need never repent having made a false choice and is saved from attempting to better his fate by divorce and choosing another partner. Marriage is looked on as a fact, as something unavoidable, a sacrifice that has to be borne. This attitude facilitates contentment and the proper adjustment of the marriage partners to one another; besides, the family atmosphere is generally conducive to this. But there are also cases of great love and fidelity that approach heroism. The wife who remains immutably true to her absent husband and takes his place in the life of the family, in fact saves his family by laying down her own life, is not an infrequent case. It also happens occasionally that the wife becomes the man's comrade, sharing his troubles, helping forward his work, comforting him when he is tormented by self-doubt, steadying him when he would go too far; in a word, working and creating with him, and at the same time suffering for him and planning so that he should always have a tender and motherly care bestowed upon him on his return from the battles of the day. In this supreme relation, where marriage becomes a kind of friendship, in which two people complement one another and incite each other to progress, they build up together a world which in its turn changes the world. Even in the legendary times of old, women of this kind are found. They sit by their husbands in the saddle and are at his side to act as ministers. The Emperor Wen said: "I have ten trustworthy ministers, and one of them is my wife." But these conditions do not apply to ancient times only. The mothers of many of the famous men of China were examples of such wives, who not only made marriage beautiful by their goodness and wisdom, but at death honoured their husbands' memory by their manner of life.

A description of Chinese marriage would be incomplete without outlining the relation of the children to their parents. When the woman bears her first son, she is looked upon with love and respect as a full "matron." That is why wife and child are not only an indispensable part of the family, but even of marriage itself. Consequently the relation of the parents to the children is a part of the natural order. According to theory, the education of the child should commence prenatally. What the woman does, thinks, and feels during her pregnancy influences the child in her womb. It is related of many mothers of famous men that with the utmost care and devotion they helped with their purest thoughts to fashion the holy thing intrusted them. The children naturally belong both to the father and mother. They are loved and well cared for. There is a much more intimate relation between the mother and children than is usually the case in Europe. No school comes between the children and parents, but they grow up in the parents' house, and its influence works on them imperceptibly and involuntarily, without any special pedagogic measures. In earlier days parents were accustomed to exchange their sons when they were of the right age, for purposes of instruction, so that the necessary discipline should not be exercised by members of the same family and so vitiate the love between children and parents. For marriage and family life in China are built up on a great and beautiful harmony, which makes his native land so dear to every Chinaman.

Nowhere is the deepest significance of marriage and family life better expressed than in the words of Confucius in his commentary in the *Book of Transformations* on the sign of "the clan":

> The clan. The inward sphere is appropriate to woman, the external to man. That man and woman have their appointed places is Nature's greatest conception. There are strict masters among the members of the clan: these are the parents. When in verity the father is a father, and the son a son, and the elder brother an elder brother, and the younger brother a younger brother, the husband a husband, and the wife a wife, then indeed is the house in the right way. By building the house on a sound foundation, the world is made secure.

COUNT PAUL THUN-HOHENSTEIN

The Marriage of Convention in Europe

An Open Letter to Count Keyserling

Dear Count Keyserling:

YOU invite me to contribute to your *Book of Marriage* an essay on "conventional marriage" (*Standesehe*).[1] In order that I may accord with the key-note to which the entire work is attuned, and to which, in spite of its polyphonic modulations, it should always return, you furnish me with a definition of "conventional marriage" (*Standesehe*), as you understand it and would have it understood, and as your introductory essay proclaims it: "By 'conventional marriage' I mean, in accordance with its original and correct sense, marriage as the body of a specific ethos, the ethos of a definite cultural order, of a definite 'standing' in the cosmos. As a corollary, it also sets the blood limits within which the choice of partners is in each case permissible. Heredity is only incidentally a decisive factor, because marriage as opposed to monachism aims at the perpetuation and raising of stock to a standard determined by spiritual ideals." That is your definition. I have inwardly digested and thought the matter over carefully, and intend to expand this conception of conventional marriage to its very depths and heights. Further, I will attempt by means of introspection to apprehend and investigate this (as it seems to me)

[1] By "conventional marriage" (*Standesehe*) is meant the traditional marriage of convention, more especially in its cultural and ethical aspect.

immeasurable sphere. For here it is not a question of the narrower sphere of marriage according to rank, in its general social or specifically aristocratic and genealogical sense. This type of marriage is in fact the central point of our problem, but the problem itself is similar to such others as, for example, the idiosyncrasies of certain races, which only reveal their significance when they are apprehended broadly over their full extent, and are taken in connection with allied subjects. It is your phrase, "the ethos of a definite cultural order," that has struck a powerfully suggestive note in me, on whose waves I am borne out to the uttermost parts of the earth, and seem to mingle with similar waves that come from afar. The significance that underlies every marriage in India may seem strange and wonderful to us: to become the father of a family is man's highest aspiration; he marries in order to have a household, in order to establish a wide family circle, where alone he can develop and practise such qualities as make him in the eyes of his countrymen a perfect type of man. Strange and wonderful also must seem the ethos of Chinese culture, which comprehends man's entire welfare in the ancestral homestead, which has been handed down from one generation to another through countless ages; the conception of family is incidental to this. Care of the homestead makes regular cultivation and the certitude of future heirs a peremptory religious duty, and gives marriage today, as it did a thousand years ago, its primary significance. Here also the ethos of a definite culture is discernible, in accordance with which intercourse between man and woman is made to serve an ethical purpose. When I refer to our culture, the culture of the Occident, I use the term in its deepest sense, which is common to all cultures; namely, its necessary connection with the country and soil out of which it grows. Consequently, it can signify only something similar to what is understood as culture by the Indians or Chinese. Culture which is transplanted to a foreign soil deteriorates to civilization. Its ethos can only possess deep roots where it grew and ripened and found its natural habitation; where it is not an empty fabrication of the mind, but a living tree which spreads its arching branches as far as ever its roots stretch under the earth. The ethos of marriage has its roots lodged in the earth and is most intimately associated with Nature. It is built up on the innate nature of the darkest of all human passions, and in its operation it should never deny this natural quality. Thus marriage represents a definite status, for its origin is not due to any social order, no matter how primitive or vitally permanent, but it is a part of the cosmic order, the destiny of mankind. But in the social sense too I recognized only a status or class (*Stand*) in the real, the universal, meaning of the words, where their roots encircle man's sphere and are deeply and surely fixed in our earth, and consequently where to desert the maternal soil would be irrational. Peasants, nobles, and kings constitute real classes (*Stände*). The other groupings into so-called classes (and this is the tendency at present more than ever, due to the stress of competition) are only organized professions. To be a peasant, a noble, or a king is an organic vocation. The private merchant and industrialist, the private scholar—that is to say, professional men who treat life theoretically, playfully or as a hobby—are easily conceivable, because they actually exist; whereas the peasant without a homestead, the nobleman cut off from the countryside in which he grew up, the king without a kingdom or subjects, are in reality inconceivable. Yes, station or rank only denotes one's position in a definite natural and cultural order. When it fulfils this meaning, when it keeps its object always in sight, in the spirit as well as in the letter, then only does the blood and tissue of its race remain vital. The body which is inspired by a spiritual purpose cannot degenerate, degeneracy meaning the equivalent of ridicule in the bodily sphere. Here, in my opinion, is the secret of the preservation of races of hoary antiquity in the character of peasantry, nobility, and royalty. These have not avoided inbreeding, which tends to cause degeneration, but on the contrary often seemed to foster it; yet they continue to exist, because their life is significant, whereas all other male lines usually perish within three generations. Where the spirit of a conscious order or class is not bent on the life of the day but for its maintenance on a distant future, the natural qualities that are particular to a real class (*Stand*) receive a special significance that amounts almost to a mystical charm. Just as a deeply religious soul, through its absolute consciousness of the divinity of Christ, acquires a mystical ecstasy in reflecting on His purely human growth and development and His earthly parentage; or just as the human motherhood of the Virgin Mary always urges us to consider and express anew that most delicate of all secrets, because the extreme antithesis which it contains symbolizes the contradictions that occur in our own lives, and which are resolved by this symbolization: so in the high orders or classes which depend entirely on their ethos, the naturally human attributes have from the very beginning been surrounded by an intrinsic charm which converts the most natural manifestation into something unique and wonderful. How has this come about? Only through this has it first been able to fulfil its profound significance.

When at the commencement of her reign Maria Theresa, hard pressed by her enemies, made her appearance before the Hungarian nobles who demanded an armistice and speedy assistance, she bore her eldest son on her arm. This apparition of queen and mother immediately won the hearts of the waverers and gave rise not only to the famous cry, "*Moriamur prô rege nostrô,*" but also led to concerted action. The power of this plastic representation and the deep charm of its significance has become a symbol of the Hungarian nation. And Napoleon III. remarked bitterly after the battle of Solferino: "What is the use of victory, when the Emperor of Austria entering Vienna at the head of his defeated army will still be triumphantly welcomed?" Victory or defeat, in a higher sense it is inessential which it is, for all depends on the ethos; this alone reaches the heart of mankind in a thousand different ways.

The above may serve to all intents and purposes as a definition of what class (*Stand*) essentially signifies, what it has always signified in Europe. The same can be taken as a foundation for the historical European conception of conventional marriage (*Standesehe*). Here natural qualities become parts of a higher order. As, however, only marriage understood in this sense fulfils its ultimate purpose, it will be self-evident that only in this form can it receive the blessing of Nature. Only marriages which comply with the conscious conception of class (*Stand*) preserve the ethos of a whole race and consequently its vitality. And ethos alone can preserve Nature. In spite of the annihilating tendency of the Diaspora, the Jews all the world over have maintained their vitality, because their powerful ethos was never allowed to become quiescent or enfeebled, but kept alive an ardent aspiration which was transmitted from one generation to another by means of conscious marriage ideals. How widespread the inbreeding, and how slight the degeneracy! In a similar fashion their ethos guarded and led the old nobility through the centuries as a guiding principle for their lives and an unquenchable source of strength for posterity. One aim vitalized it, which, because it had its roots in the country and was directed toward the welfare of the people, made it secure against self-centredness and prevented it from becoming over-schematized. And as long as it performed this mission, the latter supported its existence. But only so long and no longer. This again proves the pre-eminence of the ethos. As long as the nobles remained feudal to their princes, their mission remained vital; loyalty was not a mere form of legality dealing with questions of rank, but a glowing call to free adherence. But when the kings themselves began to misunderstand their mission, when they made chains of the nobles' loyalty and kept them as wild animals, only to be let loose at the proper moment to work the king's pleasure; when they made courtiers of them, the thus tamed animal degenerated. Loyalty became toadyism; free adherence sank to slavish obedience. This decay became especially apparent in the France of the seventeenth and eighteenth centuries. Under Louis XIII. the disintegration of the free nobility began, while under Louis XIV., who no longer saw himself as the bearer of an eternal mission but as the centre of his own planetary system, the nobles were degraded to court satellites. The aristocracy became decadent, because their calling was converted into a playful service. And thus the fate of 1789 overcame it with an inevitability which lacked the quality of tragedy, because it was not destiny that overthrew it, but its destruction was due to its own guilt. But the sovereigns also who had in this sense become traitors did not escape the punishment for their disloyalty to their vocation. What did the introduction of fresh vital blood avail, as instanced by the early marriage of Louis XV. to a Polish noblewoman? What did the complete reform of royal morals lead to, as witnessed by the pedantic and foolish, yet moral, life of Louis XVI.? The spirit was dead, the vocation desecrated; kingship and nobility were devoid of significance and consequently predestined to fall. Of all this nothing has remained clear through history except the heroic conduct of the French noblewomen during the revolutionary Terror, as typified by the manner in which Marie Antoinette went to the scaffold; for she knew both how to live life beautifully and how to meet death proudly. She was born in Germany, whose first families had not yet lost their sense of duty and responsibility. But then Maria Theresa and Frederick the Great already slept in their graves, and Joseph II. had already given vent to the ominous saying that he felt himself to be the first servant of the state. And out of the dim but not too remote past rose the spectre of Wallenstein, who perhaps had met his murderous doom because he realized more clearly the mission of the German reigning house than its members did themselves. . . .

HAVE I gone out of my way to write this to you? I believe not, and feel convinced that you will understand.

I spoke of decay. It everywhere threatens the lofty, pinnacled creations of the spirit which an old culture fashions like slender spires mounting heavenward. The slightest damage done to the point of this sensitive cultural instrument makes it blunt and useless. Consequently the ideal can be kept pure and the instrument sharp and true only by the ceaseless labour of the many who remain unknown to history. But even this would not prevent its becoming schematic and decaying, if new vitality were not continually given to it from natural sources, by *marriage*, with the commingling of fresh blood and the springing up of new seed.

I will not intrude on the subject of the choice of partners, to which, you wrote to me, you were devoting a special essay. But it is necessary to say a few words here on the part woman plays in the evolution of mankind. Goethe once remarked that women are more concerned than men about the meaning of continuity in life ("*was um Leben zusammenhängt*"). True to their nature, they always succeed in establishing this continuity, which, in spite of a completely changed habit of life, preserves the connection with the past and yet leaves them free to see the vision of the future. This gives ample scope for the maintenance and development of an impelling train of thought, and it will be evident that the higher the ideals which a given status serves and evolves, the more must it depend for support on its women. Children may be the outcome of the most dissolute passion, but they can be properly reared only in a nursery where a healthy but strict pedagogic method and a hearty spirit are prevalent. This is only possible to achieve where marriage rests on a rational and invigorating base, and where befitting reserve has built up a world of proper reticence between the man who wooed and the woman who gave. A healthy mind establishes the ethos of marriage, but temperament is the ineffable product of the human soul. Both furnish the groping life of the child with its early purpose and comprehension; in a word, with *tradition*.

Taking into consideration the wonderful results of the conscious application of "conventional marriage," are the restrictions regarding choice of partners, the attaching of less importance to sensual love, in a word, the renunciation which is an integral part of it, anything but a joyous and splendid sacrifice? It is a renunciation that is veritably born of an ardent affirmation of life and its significance. There has been no great man since the world began who restricted himself for the term of his earthly life to matters of self-interest; who would not have laid down his life for his ideal, and who did not practise self-abnegation for the sake of something higher. Whoever is inspired by the ethos of his class to choose aright the partner with whom he is to mingle his life-blood and thus uphold the tradition which his children will inherit and grow up in and in turn pass on, is assured, by this triple principle, of joy and heroism.

It is indeed incomprehensible why the idea of breeding and pure stock should have led to so much general misunderstanding. It may be due to the fact that it is instinctive and innate, and thus not easily accessible to the intellect. Furthermore the upper classes soon began to speak of it and treat it more like a rigid principle than a vital, self-evident postulate. As early as the seventeenth century it was the custom in Germany to exaggerate the importance of genealogical trees—those ever-flowing fonts of tradition. The statutes of noble families were drawn up and accession to estate and property made a condition of their enactment, and in case of marriage, proof of ancestry was required. And when in the eighteenth century a scientific toying with genealogy took possession of the nobility, an arbitrary and rigorous interpretation of these statutes led to distortion. This great vocation of developing humanity was gradually degraded into an ornamental play, and the disregard of serious hereditary principles brought about degeneration. But how was it that, in general, ruling families escaped this fate? Because their mission was often stronger than they were themselves and thus retained its vitality; because they were borne up by the highest ideals, and the one-sided restrictions that prevented a free access of fresh blood were compensated by the amplitude of their vocation. In ruling houses where the ethos became merely a court procedure and the vital tradition dwindled into daily ceremonial, the restrictions mentioned above soon led to rapid enervation and extinction.

Thus it is due to human nature in its deepest sense that one finds just in the highest circles of life the most striking examples of premeditated "conventional marriage," of *real* marriage—the sharing of mutual destiny. Powerful above joy and sorrow, yes, overwhelming in its strength, is the ethos in woman. I have already pointed out that woman concerns herself more with the continuity of things than does man, and thus she is better suited than he to keep tradition alive. It is to this that posterity owes the glowing example of Queen Louise of Prussia. In those tumultuous days when despair was prevalent, it was she who upheld the idea of kingship and carried the popular ethos with her. And from this point of view also, one of the most remarkable women of the nineteenth century, the Empress Charlotte of Mexico, is best understood. She put all her energy and strength into this fresh ethical conception of empire, an empire that had yet to be established. Being herself childless, she insisted on adopting the last descendant of the old royal family of Iturbide, in order both to create and to transmit a tradition. She sacrificed her all to sustain the empire, and then finally, during her vain and abashing pilgrimage throughout Europe, overcome by disappointment and beset by doubt, she fell a prey to insanity. Those who according to their rank live on the heights, if they really comply with the conditions laid down by their station in life, and do not conform merely outwardly thereto, are living super-personally. Even the impoverished nobleman lives superpersonally, for pride of family and station give him a yearning beyond his own forgotten existence. And so does the peasant, for he assumes responsibility for the holy heritage of the homestead and in his turn hands it on. In all these forms of life, woman takes an intimate and essential part. Because here it is a question, as it were, of cosmic classification which is inherent in the economy of the universe, marriage essentially means to her participation in the life-ethos of man. *That is the significance of "conventional" in the only true sense of "cultural" marriage.* And in my opinion no other form of association deserves the title of marriage at all, for it cannot convey the wonderful meaning contained in the word "marriage." For other forms, a monstrous word coined by a modern sociologist is apt: *Hausrat-Gemeinschaft* (community of household goods).

But now it is high time for me to disclose the deeper significance of what I have written and to prove that I am not endeavouring to pile up a great tower of broken masonry; no, but to continue to work at what has already for ages been a mighty edifice in our German world of culture. This is the great mission of the present, the ideal of the future. I have spoken of a class ethos, by means of which all traditions become significant. Let me now further explain what the true manifestation of this ethos is in the German people and Teutonic culture as a whole.

Teutonism first appeared where it came in conflict with Rome. The aristocratic idealism of the young and vigorous Teutonic race opposed the orderly centripetal civic conception of the Roman Empire. And where it came to an actual struggle, the Roman legionary, one of many, the part of a mass conception, stood against the single independent warrior, quantity versus quality. On the one side, the world-wide conception of citizenship of the Roman Empire; on the other, the discipline and cultivation of massed strength and energy which forced the individual to make use of his whole personality. And later on, what were the Carlovingians but rebellious vassals, the rude usurpers of the legitimate Merovingian dynasty? Yet they do not stand in the history of the West as examples of disloyalty and treachery. Is this the case only because they were successful? Certainly not, but loyalty to themselves, requiring the introduction of the entire personality, was stronger in them than the hereditary relation to a reigning house in which the idea of rulership no longer existed, and which it was impossible for vigorous men to serve wholeheartedly. Again in the *Nibelungenlied* we see portrayed a princely house whose strength has been sapped. Hagen is grimly loyal to it; Volker, the musician, is his only friend; thus the heart holds to an ethos that all the others did but fear, for what can the heart achieve without ethos? It leads to the most empty thing in all the world: sentimentality. In the Danube, at Bechelaren, Hagen made the test: he knew now that none of the Nibelungs would ever see their native land again. He is the only one who possesses this knowledge, and yet he leads his royal house to a sure death, because loyalty is more to him than life, more even than the lives to which his loyalty is pledged. Kriemhild has transcended the honour of her body and life out of loyalty to Siegfried and has become Etzel's spouse in order to assemble new forces to avenge his death. Loyalty above death, above one's own life—indeed a treacherous trueness, which is perhaps incomprehensible to every non-Teuton—but it is all the deeper for that, taking on itself all the blame and acclaiming the ultimate tragedy of life.

Where the Teutonic spirit became paired with a foreign element, the unexpected and wonderful were sure to happen. The staunchness of its loyalty and courage had in conjunction with Gallic buoyancy established the idea of the Crusades, one of the most powerful conceptions in the history of the Occident. In the Maid of Orleans, the courage and faith to loyalty rose above adherence to reigning powers.

Two of my examples—which came to me unsought—are women. This is not chance; in such grave matters chance has no place. I am now coming to one of the most fundamental phenomena of the Teutonic character, the nature of woman. The Teuton sees a higher form in his loyalty to woman than to himself. She has always appeared to him physically weaker, and thus requiring protection, but also as more talented, nobler, and holier than he. He was the first in the Occident to honour woman, because for him marriage was not a mere object, as it was for the Greeks, nor a contract, as with the Romans, but an eternal part of the life of the soul. In the Teutonic world, married people are not of unequal status, as in the East or as they were even in Greece; nor is theirs the prosaic equality of Rome. They are one, for marriage is unity. But unity is only possible where unanimity exists. From the very outset therefore the same ethical nobility and courage and loyalty have manifested themselves in the Teutonic woman as in man. Thus, and only thus, could marriage naturally develop into conventional, in the sense of cultural, marriage; only owing to this were, in Romance times, religion and love the two ideas that governed the life of the knights. Thus Walther von der Vogelweide sang, "*Ohne Minne kann niemand Gottes*

Huld erwerben" ("Without love no one may win God's grace"). Woman possessed self-courage; so she had to be above sensual love, radiating lofty ideals and thus commanding devotion and reverence. And again it cannot be attributed merely to chance that the custom of priests' marrying lasted longest in Teutonic lands. Woman was reverenced, and consequently marriage also was held in high esteem. And more gradually and with much greater difficulty did the profound and consistent conception of priestly celibacy make its way. It was conceived as an intimate and indissoluble bond with God which could not tolerate any other indissoluble contract alongside it, for intimate association with the Divine cannot be transmitted by material heredity.

I have spoken of loyalty to oneself; that is to say, of ethical outlook and conduct. This loyalty must be the manifestation of an ethical idea if it is to uphold itself through the centuries, if it is to lead ever again to new and unexpected forms. The fundamental idea of Teutonism is *courage.* Courage is, with an otherwise unprecedented exclusiveness, the motive force of the Teuton's approach to all things and events. Courage even to defiance, even to the extent of refuting its aim, an irrationality of courage! But does not the courage to venture hold the deepest significance and beauty of life itself?

BE that as it may, the Teutonic world is founded exclusively on the ethos of courage. In this respect, more than in any other, its constitution is unique. This explains the special form of European "conventional marriage" which other races find so difficult to comprehend, and which even proves increasingly difficult for Europeans to understand the more the Teutonic component in their blood and tradition recedes. As bearers of this exclusive ethos of courage, the Teutons took possession of the European world. As the ruling race they were at first everywhere in the minority, but they secured the countries by establishing a hierarchic and warlike order. Thus Europe became a commonwealth of representative nobles. Only the lords of the manor counted. But these had in reality no private life. They *were*, so to speak, their feudal properties, and the king *was* his land. Even in Shakespeare's time, the King of England calls the French king simply "France." Thus all European life of any importance became the life of the representative classes. Thus the whole life of the nobility became founded on an ethical principle. And out of this, the specific form of European conventional marriage evolved, which represents, as in no other part of the world, a life-association based on super-personal grounds. The woman who married the lord of the manor knew full well that she had an office to fulfil that would mean setting aside all private and personal matters. Thus the particular part played by marriage in this system of life produced quite special and often very narrow restrictions. It was not permissible to marry any one who might endanger one's standing in the cosmic order or one's vocation. It was a heroic spirit of courage that created Teutonic conventional marriage. Thus the renunciation it entailed was similar to the hardships the warriors took on themselves without demur. It furthered and bred a corresponding mentality. In fact, this heroic disposition is from the very outset the principal distinction of the European woman of standing. In the Middle Ages, when she had occasionally to defend the castle for a decade alone, she was scarcely less hardy than the Crusader himself. The famous women of the Renaissance were just as courageous as the Condottieri, and superior in endurance and clever tenacity. In her great age, deliberation and superiority were the distinctive features of the European woman. And was she any weaker when she became a lady, when the life of the eighteenth century atrophied until it became a mere frivolity to which the guillotine finally put an end? It was just the lady of the eighteenth century—as I have already pointed out—who was filled with the highest ethos. The main point to regard is not her sometimes questionable morals; the main point is how much profligacy she could stand without losing caste or self-control. Private love-affairs did not destroy French marriage, they never even threatened the lofty ethos of conventional marriage. The frivolity and playfulness of the nobleman, as compared with the everlasting seriousness of the bourgeois, is the very sign of his stricter ethos. . . .

Looking carefully, one finds that there is much justification even for the prejudices of people of standing. Thus kings were justified, while they still felt sure of themselves, in proclaiming that they, as kings, were aware of certain things that the ordinary mortal could not comprehend. Lineage, early training, tradition, and ethos actually produce a unique outlook. Pride is not necessarily out of place. . . . Now let me take a look into the future. You told me that an essay on conventional marriage was indispensable to *The Book of Marriage*, because only conventional marriage fulfils the significance of marriage, and that improvement in the future was dependent on its rebirth. How right you were! Only marriage based on super-personal grounds has a proper objective. Our entire history has proved this without a doubt. As long as European life was healthy and strong, conventional marriage was its foundation. But in reality conventional marriage was something quite different from what it is today, a senseless restriction of the possible choice of partners to certain circles that are thought to be of equal standing. It is marriage as the embodiment of a high ethos that is needed. It follows that conventional marriage is not superseded, as many suppose, although it is not intended to live on in its present form. *It must be born anew if we are to witness a restoration of Europe.* And this especially applies to conventional marriage in its historical sense, as the ethos of courage. We are entering a new heroic age. Sentiment will die a natural death. Liberalism will become extinct on account of weakness of character. Only courage has a future. There is only one choice of alternatives: Is courage going to lead to construction or destruction? Up till now the latter has been the more powerful tendency. But its supremacy must not be final, or else Europe is ruined. The constructive element must win. But in these hard times, this presupposes that marriage, as the germ-cell of history, should rest anew on the austere but beautiful ethos which is the characteristic of historic conventional marriage. The rebirth of this conception would lead to the rebirth of the nobility. The latter fell on account of a lack of ethos, a want of tradition; lineage alone is not enough. On the other hand, it is indispensable. . . . But I must only write of marriage.

Ethos, tradition, and descent: I have come back to the lofty trinity of man's being. I have finished, for could I say more to prove that the deliberate practice of conventional marriage is more than ever necessary for man's present and future, *that there is no other marriage worthy of the name than the conventional, in the sense of cultural, marriage,* that it is only this form of matrimony which can lead mankind to the higher significance of things; in the ethos of courage to oneself, in the tradition of noble-mindedness, in the renunciatory but beneficial strength of blood-selection?

Farewell! I know in advance that you will agree with my exposition, for is it not largely the outcome of our correspondence and conversation?

Yours,

PAUL THUN.

P A U L   E R N S T

Marriage and Proletarianism

MARRIAGE is both a private and a social matter and can be comprehended biologically and sociologically. As it embraces the mutual destiny of man, woman, and child, it should not merely be investigated scientifically, but also considered from a religious and ethical point of view. Most people usually speak of marriage without realizing that they are considering it from a narrow point of view only. They think of the biological significance of marriage for the individual, of marriage in connection with the maintenance of the social order, of religious and ethical problems; how these affect the individual, and how the social form of religion (with us the church) is germane to the problem. The latter question cannot be answered with any degree of certainty today, because the state now attempts to deal with problems which were formerly under the jurisdiction of the church. This want of clarity in thinking reflects in the latter case the confusion of the actual conditions.

Proletarianization is a social event; it is externally an occurrence and inwardly a desire. Just as sex in the individual is connected with the whole of his being by means of very delicate and fine threads, so marriage in the case of both the individual and society is connected with all things and must alter if any factors change.

The social order today is becoming proletarianized. This has already gone so far that a large portion of humanity looks upon it as an ideal. The communistic state of the future embodies this ideal. Marriage too must change accordingly. Under such conditions a new aristocracy is bound to arise to govern proletarianized humanity. The latter does not notice this, just as the Russians do not realize that although their Lenin spoke in the Metal-Workers' Union, he was an autocrat. Now that his body is embalmed and lying in state for the faithful to gaze on, he has become something like a saint or a demi-god. A new form of "conventional marriage" (*Standesehe*) will rise up to oppose proletarian marriage. The first signs of this are already at hand. As it is brought into being only by contrast, it will naturally develop later, and as it only applies to the few, it is not so noticeable in a democratic age as the marriage order (or rather want of order) of the masses.

The marriage system is always dependent on economic conditions. The sexes are so differentiated that they cannot be treated as equals. The most happy economic relationship between them will be the one which establishes a division of labour based on this differentiation, thus enabling man and woman to form a higher economic unit. The education of the children is closely related with the professional occupation of the parents; in a labour-sharing partnership between man and woman, the children will receive different qualities from both parents, corresponding to each of these, who in this way continue the natural work begun with procreation. Modern European marriage, which is now in a state of dissolution, was of this nature. Its historical source can be traced back to the marriage of the coloni of the late Roman Empire. Externally it also resembled the marriage system of the invading Teutonic tribes, where these had to conform to surrounding conditions. At the same time, in their own territory, they were also partly affected by the social customs of the old cultures, through Christianity. The outward similarity was due to the fact that it served the same economic aim.

With the cessation of wars and the suppression of piracy, the slave markets became empty in the peace-abiding Roman Empire. One had to produce one's own slaves, but that necessitated a complete change in the economic structure. The condition of the slaves had to be improved, as they were being employed in industry and agriculture; at the same time that of the indigent freemen became worse, and the two together formed something approaching a new class. The patricians of the towns were exterminated. Towns lost in importance; the land and its claims became predominant. Consequently the social customs of the lower agricultural workers became the standard. It was at this time that the colonate was formed; big estates were broken up into small holdings which were rented to the former slaves or to the indigent freemen, in return for tribute or work. A man who had a small piece of land of this nature had to have a wife to assist him and to bear him children. This economic movement goes on through centuries of history. The marriage system of the coloni becomes eventually the marriage system of the artisans. Altogether the colonate becomes the social order for the small man. From the later times of the Roman Empire right up to the Frankish kings, the small landholders made their land over to the big estate owners and then had the use of it in exchange for tribute and work. The reason for this procedure within the Roman Empire was primarily to escape excessive taxation, and at later times it was the general insecurity.

One thing especially must be kept in mind. The common man cannot be expected to develop a sense of responsibility voluntarily, even if a strict marriage system is present to assist him in this direction. In the case of the marriage system of the coloni this was not necessary. The master, in his own interests, had to see that his people lived properly, and consequently he had to shoulder the responsibility for their marriages. The propertied classes of later Roman times were not descendants of patricians, but the sons of profiteers. But as they were forced by circumstances to act as lords of the country, necessity taught them their rôle to some extent—much as in the same way gentlemen will have to be evolved out of the mixture of rascals and idealists who make up the present Soviet régime; that is to say, if communism is to take root in Russia. The last survival of this authority was the permission to marry which the workers had to obtain from the landowners. This was abolished in Germany in 1848. Where the marriage system of the coloni became later a prototype for other classes, authority was invested in other bodies, such as guilds and the church; when these responsible bodies are disestablished, dissolution is bound to set in. It bore an external resemblance to the Teutonic marriage system. Our forefathers lived under simple economic conditions. Their land was uncultivated and barren. They had adopted agriculture, and we can well imagine that they did not get more out of their land than the coloni did in Gaul when they had paid tribute to their overlord. Just as with the coloni, the man ploughed the fields with oxen while the woman looked after the kitchen and stables; man reaped, and woman bound the sheaves. Besides which, the Teutons had another source of income, in serving as mercenary soldiers in the Roman army. These conditions made it possible for a particular kind of luxury to arise, consisting in costly weapons and gold ornaments.

The principal difference lay in the religion.

The Teutons in all probability still had their original patriarchal religion. Civilized Roman society was passing through all the different stages that accompanied the dissolution of this religion. The slaves had never even had a god. Under these conditions, Christianity made its appearance. Originally, long before the birth of Christ, it represented for the highest intellectual circles the myth of a crucified god, then a mystery cult, and finally the religion of the lower-class population of the towns. This religion evolved out of itself a new social order, embodied in the church, which undertook to fulfil the duties and obligations of the decadent state.

In the Christian religion and its social aspect—the church—the thoughts and feelings of the decaying social order are incorporated. On the one hand, the social catastrophe led the better elements to renounce the world and to come to the conclusion that woman was the principal cause of dissolution. That is how asceticism became part of Christianity. On the other hand, among the lower classes a new marriage system, which was both natural and moral, superseded the old decadent forms. This was also taken over by the church under the title of "Christian marriage" and was amalgamated with the ascetic ideal in a variety of ways.

When the Teutons embraced Christianity they took over these ideas and conceptions. They were not aware that their marriage system was similar to that of Christian marriage only outwardly. As is always the case, they looked on the differences as mistakes that had to be remedied.

As on the one hand marriage presupposes the existence of mutual love—not the infatuation that sometimes leads to marriage—so on the other it is dependent on a sense of responsibility, which cannot be regulated legally, but only effected inwardly by means of religion. This safeguard is found to exist in the earliest forms, just as individual sexual love is.

It is clearly evident that the safeguard marriage received from Christianity was not as firm as it would have been if the old patriarchal marriage system of our forefathers had developed independently of, but in conjunction with, a corresponding evolution of the existing religion. Christianity won its hold over the masses principally on account of the myth of recompense after death, regarding which the church had much to say. When the fear of hell disappears it can no longer operate as a popular religion, for then the church loses its power. The myth of God's Son dying on the Cross is only a symbol expressing insight into the tragic nature of life. This insight is only attainable on the highest spiritual plane. For the masses, the crucifixion had to be explained as if the Son of God laid down his life to cleanse tailors and shoemakers of their sins; the eternal value of the most insignificant soul had to become a dogma. By this means the masses were rated at a higher value than they could live up to, and this exaggeration was reflected in all the other spheres associated with religion. Thus the significance of common marriage was overestimated, and in this form it required more of the average man in thought and conduct than he was able to give. The Catholic Church introduced several wise extenuations, which, however, the Reformation again swept aside. Thus the following situation arose: Christian marriage is an ideal, the highest marriage ideal there has ever been, which only a few legendary characters of olden times can approach (Penelope, Damajanti, Dejanira), which only few can realize, while the great majority find themselves in doubt and tribulation. The less influence the church has on the life of the people, the more does this condition become aggravated. In the meantime the disruptive influence of democracy had set in, which was also inherent in Christianity, though in another sense. On account of its particular genesis, both democratic and aristocratic elements are found to exist beside one another in Christianity, and, according to the particular age, either one or other comes to the fore. In the Occident, the democratic factors became ever more prominent, once the struggle between Pope and Emperor commenced. This weakened the seigniorial bonds which took the place of self-responsibility for the lower classes. But not only the church, but religion itself thus fell into a state of dissolution, notwithstanding that by its democratic influence it won a new inwardness, the last results of which were the Reformation and Pietism. Thus Christian marriage developed into middle-class marriage.

Events follow the same course here as elsewhere; religious duties become middle-class moral prescriptions, which are then found to be without a proper basis, because they lack consecration. As soon as humanity becomes aware of this condition, complete disintegration is made possible.

Christian marriage, which later develops into middle-class marriage, is built up on the assumption that both husband and wife take a share in the work, just as naturally happens in the case of the small landholder. The latter's family life serves as model to the big landowners, noble families, and to the town artisans and patricians. With the advent of capitalist industry, there appears in history a power which has not even yet ceased to operate destructively. It also destroys the Christian middle-class marriage system. Thus the special work of woman becomes superfluous, because to an ever greater extent what she produces for the family can be made or bought outside. But on the other hand, her energies are thus set free, and she is able to take her part as a comrade in the man's work, outside of the family, for the general social welfare.

When woman becomes economically superfluous, artificial occupations arise (so-called education, reading, piano lessons, social intercourse, chattering, writing, painting, and studying—what is known as the development of personality, and so forth). These things make a person empty. The little bit of work that it is still possible for her to perform, such as preparing vegetables and dusting, is set aside, and woman becomes altogether incapable of educating her children. For only a complete personality can educate, and this completeness is achieved only by work, care, and struggle. When woman becomes active outside the household, there is no place where the children can grow up, for she cannot take them with her into the works or study.

This condition begins with the lower-class inhabitants of towns, who then begin to form the proletariat. In the country, too, conditions change, giving place to a rural proletariat, which is some stages behind that of the town. The movement gradually rises upward and affects the higher classes. Today almost the entire social order is proletarianized. The bourgeoisie, who are continually decreasing in numbers, cannot act as models. They also acquire their social form from the proletariat, and are essentially the same.

Altogether we have a very remarkable course of events

for observation here: the interaction of classes in their relation to life. What I have just said concerning woman's activity applies especially to that of the lower classes and the petty bourgeoisie. In the dissolution of the traditional marriage system, the lower classes played an exemplary part. In fact, they still continue to while destroying; the princess is just as much affected by the destruction of the existing marriage system as is the proletarian woman. In the present age, society is an integral whole; what reacts spiritually on one class does so also on another. Only the outward form is different. But I believe there were times when the upper and lower classes moved in different directions, and I presume that this condition is about to reappear.

We have examined the transitional stage from an economic point of view. But that is a mere abstraction. For the observer, men are governed by sociological laws; but in reality they choose their own path. And consequently the evolution of an emotional attitude toward life runs parallel to economic development.

The proletariat is a social class, but it is also an emotional attitude toward life. And no one can determine sociologically which was first. In individual cases, the cause of proletarianization will always be found to exist in the attitude toward life. Here we have reached the ultimate, impenetrable secret of life; impenetrable, because we can think only by abstracting particular forces and systems from the whole, whereas life is made up of the reciprocal action of all its component forces and adjustments.

What is the proletariat as an emotional attitude toward life? And emotion can be described in general terms only, and consequently such descriptions usually sound rather empty. Proletarianism is the lack of any high aims in life. A town forms a unit; so does a country or the whole of humanity. This unit is made up not only of the people but of the things pertaining thereto. A man is connected with his house and his fields, with the estate of his neighbour, with all the wealth of his nation, in fact with the whole world—everything is interconnected. The realization of the unity of all life must be consciously, or perhaps still more unconsciously, felt by every one in the shape of a sense of responsibility, love, devotion, or at any rate some sort of instinct. The person whose attitude toward life does not embrace such feelings of unity is a proletarian.

The proletarian is one of the basic types of humanity. He has always existed. Human history shows that different basic types play the principal part in turn. Today it is the turn of the proletarian, who does not feel the unity of life and who has no sense of responsibility.

The proletariat is a social class. Here it must be remembered that the conception of class does not tally with historical facts. The proletariat as a social class accords only in the sphere of abstract thought with the conception of the proletariat as an attitude toward life. In reality, judged according to the class system, there are many proletarians who are not so in their emotional attitude. Children are perhaps the best proof that our life is not a solitary atom, but a part within a vast whole. A mother in the midst of her children, a fading flower with ripe seed-pods, is a sign that our individual life has a higher significance, which the individual can never know, but at most only humbly believe in and feel. Consequently proletarianism as an attitude toward life must be hostile to marriage, not merely to any definite form of marriage which is historically doomed. Proletarianism as an attitude toward life is the denial of humanity and the world; it is the contention that individuals are solitary atoms; it means a process of self-destruction. In a healthy age individuals and larger groups sink into the condition of the proletariat and by their self-destruction rid the world of a useless burden. In times like the present, where the whole social order is proletarianized, it means the complete self-annihilation of society.

It was mentioned above that the bourgeoisie is essentially one with the proletariat—naturally the bourgeois idea is not the same as citizenship. The pre-bourgeois and pre-proletarian society of citizens is still a society and not a chaos. There is no difference between the American woman who possesses millions and is divorced for the twenty-fifth time and the factory girl who goes home after her work to dress herself showily for the dancing hall, from which she returns with a man who may marry her or may never see her again. There is no difference between the woman doctor who leaves her children to the servant, when she visits her patients, and thus thinks that she is fighting for the emancipation of her sex, and the working woman who sends her children on to the street when she goes to work and thinks that she has thereby taken the first step toward establishing a new order in which society has to care for the children. We know of savage people who die out when they come in contact with Europeans, not on account of diseases or alcohol, but because they do not wish to have any children. They simply cannot adapt themselves. We must look upon the self-destruction of civilization by means of proletarianism as a similar phenomenon, only that the subjective attitude is probably different. Industrial capitalism has brought mankind into a condition to which it cannot possibly adapt itself. It is itself the result of a higher cause that lies in the spiritual sphere.

Proletarianization is one of the forces working toward the destruction of marriage; it goes hand in hand with other forces that have the same origin, such as the greed for happiness, which is only felt by those who can never be happy; or what subaltern natures term individualism, in reality setting up their defects as absolute values. Another disruptive factor is the outlook that sees in life a pleasure and not a mission—in a word, that lack of general breeding and discipline which is bound to show itself when there is nothing to keep humanity in order and when its laws of life are dictated to it by machines.

What will follow the general débâcle in which we at present find ourselves cannot be foreseen: possibly a small master-class ruling tyrannically over a chaotic mass. These masters will then institute a new marriage system, which will no longer correspond to the middle-class idea, while the masses can live in their lust if they please.

Romantic Marriage

It was advice given regarding marriage that at one time injured Luther's reputation even among his followers, and which even to this day is used against him by his enemies, and over it his admirers sorrowfully shake their heads. The Landgrave Philip of Hesse had, in early life, as the custom was, married a princess for whom he could feel no affection, and with whom he soon broke faith. He fell passionately in love with one of the ladies-in-waiting, Margarethe von der Sale, whom he could not or perhaps did not want to get as a mistress, because of her social position; and consequently he desired to obtain a divorce. As in all classes among the Protestants, when difficult cases had arisen which one presumed or hoped would be settled differently than hitherto, the Landgrave applied to Luther as the responsible leader, and the latter found himself obliged to give him advice, which was as follows: If Philip could feel no affection for his real wife and could not free his heart of love for the other woman, he should, after obtaining permission from his wife, contract a second marriage with Margarethe, which should, however, remain secret; this was also to apply to this counsel given at confession. As far as the world was concerned, the second wife must be looked upon as a concubine.

This decision, strange as it may seem to us, was quite in keeping with Luther's outlook regarding marriage and human relations in general. When asked for an opinion, he was accustomed to seek inspiration from two sources: Nature and the Scriptures. He held that God had shown His will, both in life itself and in the Word which He had manifested unto men in the beginning. These two principles, he maintained, should be complementary. He found that marriage had always existed, and not that it was instituted by Christ, and that it was established by using definite, visible signs, as was the case with baptism and communion; consequently he did not regard it as a sacrament, but as a divine institution and the highest of all human callings. This follows from the fact that the commandment to honour one's father and mother immediately follows those relating to God Himself, and that God created man and woman and bade them live together and beget children. It was also his custom to quote the word of God: "It is not good for man to live alone." As there is scarcely any sphere of human activity where so much confusion, disagreement, and perplexity exists as in marriage, Luther was asked for advice and help almost daily by afflicted and despairing people. He did not keep strictly to the old canon in this matter, as he found himself at variance with it on account of his aversion to celibacy. The laxity which permitted illicit sexual relations of the clergy had greatly favoured a generally frivolous outlook, so that marriage was not held in much esteem. In order to better this condition, Luther took the matter seriously to heart and made use of every opportunity to point out how pleasing to God was the state that enabled men to conduct their lives in a chaste manner. He realized, however, that marriage was only good and beautiful when the partners loved or respected each other; but knowing the unstable nature of man's affections, he recognized that love was an unsure foundation. One might expect that Luther would have made divorce easier, because on the one hand he desired that marriage should be carried out with more warmth and affection, and on the other hand he was well aware of the frailties of the human heart; this, however, was not the case. If he had found some word in Holy Scripture, spoken by either the Saviour or St. Paul, which could have been interpreted as favouring divorce, he would certainly have made use of it. As this was not the case, he stood firmly by the saying, "What therefore God hath joined together, let not man put asunder," and by the idea of loyalty, which makes the promise once given irrevocable. He even strove against the customary dispensations, according to which princes and notabilities obtained divorce by payment. If he did not acknowledge the Pope's prerogative to annul marriages, neither did he claim that right for himself. Only in two cases did he recognize the right to divorce, and these were the customary ones, namely, adultery and impotence on the man's part. In regard to the latter point, his outlook was original. If the husband did not voluntarily renounce his rights, as was essentially his duty, the woman could elope with another man, and live with him, either secretly or in some other place. The children born of the second alliance were to be regarded as the first husband's rightful heirs, since he was in reality the culpable person. Here again it was St. Paul's injunction that man should not surrender to passion that influenced Luther, but he also felt its truth. Apart from the fact that he held it was a woman's right to have children, he considered that unsatisfied craving, which of necessity led to a passionate regard for other men, was detrimental. It is the internal, consuming desire which the conscientious man has to combat and which often only grows the stronger thereby, ravaging and poisoning the soul—the danger of repression, as modern psychology terms it—that this great knower of souls was endeavouring to spare men, but without freeing them from moral obligations. It is a question how far this is possible.

The expedient of a double marriage in the case of the Landgrave of Hesse was not satisfactory, because it had to be kept secret and the second wife appeared in the eyes of the world as a concubine, whereas the first wife would have actually been one if she had formed a relationship with another man. It seems that Luther, in spite of his friendly feeling for women, had no scruples in assigning the harder and less egotistical part in marriage to woman, just as if it was necessarily so, or as if Nature had thus planned it. Greater sensitiveness of body and soul, but above all motherhood, inclines woman to a constant form of marriage, whereas man, on account of his impulsive and vacillating desires, is the natural enemy of marriage. If man did not possess a deep-seated inclination for family life, marriage could never have been established as a form of life. Only the fact that a girl develops into a mother and a man into a father makes marriage possible as a divine institution. In spite of this, the different demands which man and woman make on marriage cause it to become a tragic relationship. The young man who is not yet a father has ample opportunity to satisfy his desires and fulfil his affections outside of marriage; so he only contemplates the latter either in order to improve his position, whether it be by marrying a rich woman or one of high social standing, or the daughter of an influential father; or to obtain a co-worker. The situation is entirely different in woman's case. Generally speaking, she first knows the sweets of love only in marriage, and is less able than man to keep bodily and spiritual love apart. Since marriage is for man a business and for woman a matter of love, discord arises in addition to the tragic element. At any rate, opposition to a strict relation based on loyalty will invariably be found to exist, on account of the weakness of human affection and character. Man's quarrelsomeness, his antipathy to restraint, his proneness to let himself go toward a woman whom he no longer needs to court, because he already possesses her, would entirely undermine marriage, if it were not that the mutual love of the children, the pleasure of watching them grow up, of reliving one's youth again in them, outweighs all these unpleasantnesses.

Above all, man is intended by Nature and his own reason to build up communities in which an orderly form of life exists. The idea of an integral whole, of a universality, which is innate in all men, and which always strives to find application to an ever-widening sphere of influence, enables the individual to relinquish his personal claims, in order to participate in a higher and richer social life. Man is accustomed to relinquish some of his individual rights for the good of the state, which personifies the conception of a whole people; and just as, in general, he demands that respect be shown the state, so he also requires that marriage, which represents the primary cell in the organism of the state, should be kept holy. Even if he permits himself considerable license outside it, he still looks on the order of marriage as inviolable. He coerces himself and others, because he knows that they are not noble enough to comply voluntarily. But since he does so on ideal grounds, he cannot fail, for the same reason, to champion in turn the rights of the heart when matched against force.

Luther was sufficiently broad-minded, when considering these facts of human life, to recognize their antitheses and paradoxes. He expressed it by saying that he distinguished between God and the world, and that God had contracted with the latter a morganatic marriage. One might be inclined to think that he would have liked to see the world perish, or that he held it of no account, seeing that he claimed the devil was its overlord. On the contrary, he recognized its reality, and only endeavoured to keep the law of the world separate from the law of God. It is natural that from this point of view there will always remain an indissoluble residue, for it is quite impossible to tear a man asunder according to his worldly and his divine natures, for man must become the citizen of both kingdoms. Luther held that the coercive factor in marriage was a necessity, since man's nature was burdened with original sin. At the same time, according to his opinion, marriage projected into the kingdom of God. He endeavoured by precept and example to fulfil its obligations with love and joy, and as far as possible to ease the lot of those who felt bound by it. The secret double marriages which he advised in certain cases were not intended to have any validity in the eyes of the world, which was relentless regarding the irrevocability of the first bond, but they were to have a significance before God and conscience, as forming a supreme court. Only a pure and courageous heart dared to entrust itself to a higher power than that which counted for the average man. But that was just the courage of the Protestants, who dared, by means of their conscience, to come into direct contact with God. The Protestant motto, "One should obey God before man," demands a conscientiousness which requires almost superhuman powers when the person's own happiness is at stake.

Luther himself suffered on account of his desire to appease this twofold nature of man, which shows itself in his craving for order and freedom, for happiness and duty. In accordance with his large-hearted character he did not adhere blindly to his own views, but recognized that other decisions were possible. The one thing he maintained was that if a man had advice to proffer, he must let brotherly love rule in his heart.

Although Luther essentially maintained the indissoluble nature of marriage as an inviolable form of loyalty, it can be asserted that he led the way to a much more tolerant treatment of the problem. He did this first by denying its sacramental character, next by endeavouring to found it on love, and lastly by establishing "conscience marriage" (*Gewissensehe*). In this consideration for the prerogatives of affection he went so far that during an age when it was still the custom for parents to determine the marriages of their children, he even at times took the children's part. A case in point is when he wrote most strictly to a certain Frau Ursula Schneidewin, who would not permit her son to marry the wife of his own choosing—requiring her to give way, as her obduracy was prejudicing her son's studies, and pointing out that she herself would not like a man to awaken love in her daughter and then desert her. "I have written that children should not marry without their parents' consent, but I have also written that parents should not hinder their children." Here also he recognizes an antithesis that can only be resolved with good will. If she continued to refuse, he would consecrate the marriage without her permission; and if later the young pair were in want, he would certainly come to their assistance. Luther's leniency is still more surprising in another case. The church permitted divorce in cases of adultery, but did not permit the adulterer to marry the woman with whom he had committed the adultery, and this is the law even among Protestants to this very day. Luther, however, held another opinion; even if a man planned the death of the husband in order to marry his widow, he should not be prevented from doing so. He referred to David, who had committed adultery with Bathsheba, caused her husband to be murdered, and then taken her to wife, and still remained a holy man. "In God's name," he cries, "why this harshness against one's fellow men, where God Himself did not require it!"

EVEN when taking into consideration differences of historical age and personality, Luther's outlook on marriage nevertheless bridges the way to the Romanticists. From the earliest times, a special dispensation in matters relating to love and marriage was granted to artists, on the one hand because they live more in the kingdom of God than on earth, and on the other, because they champion the rights of the individual against society. Even in an age when divorce still meant dishonour, the artist was permitted what was denied to other men, partly because he lived outside worldly conditions and escaped disapprobation in this particular by suffering general disrepute. A systematic demand for marriage reform was first advanced by the Romanticists. They held that marriage should be based on mutual love and that man and woman should possess equal rights. This outlook presupposes that woman is held in high esteem, and in a different sense from that of the Middle Ages or the eighteenth century. Women of character and spirit there have always been, but this did not prevent men from presuming that woman was content to live a selfless life, very different from that of man, which they thought it natural to assign her. The Romanticists' point of departure was the idea of a unity which was to balance the polarity of the phenomena. The main thing was that each person should be a complete human being. The man was to develop his feminine characteristics, and the woman her masculine ones. Woman should not merely think of dress in order to shine in society, nor should she be entirely merged in household cares and in her children; she was to develop her intellect, to take an interest in art and science, to have the courage of her own opinions and not allow others to treat her as a slave. They found Schiller's women, who swam in an ocean of femininity, and his men parading their masculinity, ridiculous and ugly. On the other hand, they admired Goethe's heroes, with their slight tinge of dreaminess and delicacy, his free and daring girls and women. They would also hear of no distinction between sensual and Platonic love. They recognized love as true and beautiful only where matter and spirit merged in a healthy union.

The Greeks divided their women into three classes, according to their usage: the matron, who in the capacity of wife bore her husband children, educated them, and ruled the household, and as recompense enjoyed the honour of this high office and lived in security; the hetaera, who was trained in the arts, satisfied man with her comradely allurements, and enjoyed his love in a variety of different relationships; and the slave, who was forced to serve as an instrument of passion. A man is rarely equally well developed in all directions, and it is seldom that he can satisfy all the requirements of life. A man usually also satisfies the requirements of a woman in only one direction. It is quite possible that an excellent paterfamilias plays a poor rôle as a passionate lover. If we bear in mind that the Greek classification, in one form or another, has been applied universally and in every age, because it corresponds with human nature or at least with man's inclinations, and because woman's wishes are not consulted, only then do we properly realize the magnitude of the change the Romanticists planned in their marriage reform.

A few young men undertook to refashion society in accordance with their subjective idealism. With the thoughtlessness of youth that exaggerates its own strength and does not properly gauge the limitations of human nature and the importance of tradition, they believed that the glowing eloquence and logical force of their conviction would also convince others. They looked with disgust on middle-class or conventional marriage, which hid, under a pretense of fervour, characteristics which soon caused it to deteriorate into an indifferent coexistence, or even gave rise to hostility. They were revolted by the soulless bodily intimacy and the mendacious manner in which a relationship based on avarice or convenience was represented as something holy and worthy of respect. It was termed love when the man simply felt the attraction of sex or the woman merely respected the man's social position. If only the outward form remained untouched, little notice was taken of the infidelity of men or women. The example set by the court of Friedrich Wilhelm II. had contaminated the hitherto strictly moral middle classes. It especially distressed the Romanticists that the woman's individuality was first obliterated by her husband and later merged in her children, and that even women found this natural. The spiritual coercion of woman they condemned even more strictly than the exploitation of her body. In the development of individuality they recognized the mission of humanity. It was principally Friedrich Schlegel and Schleiermacher who interested themselves in this question and championed it as writers. According to them, marriage should be the image of the Trinity, the union of the two halves of human life to produce a third; the latter did not in the first place represent children, but a dual harmony, a productive interpersonal relationship. Who has not heard that pleasant fable of Plato's, that every one is the half of a definite whole and must seek his complement on earth and can indeed find it? The Romanticists upheld this view by means of the plausible idea that for every fully developed individual there must be another person who suits him better than all the rest do, and is therefore actually intended for him. If this complementary relationship between the two individuals was to remain continually rejuvenative, they maintained that one individual must not merge himself in the other; but on the contrary, that they should help one another develop their own particular characters. The striving toward individual perfection was established as a religion. Not only should love and marriage be one, but also bodily and spiritual, heavenly and earthly, love. Just as human individuality flows in a mysterious way into the ultimate personality of God, or into the Universe (which were accounted identical), so the lover, if he entirely merged himself in his love, would find God. Sexual love is a ray from the divine sun of love which has penetrated to earthly regions and must finally return whence it came.

A love marriage in this romantic sense, which they termed real marriage to distinguish it from conventional or middle-class marriage, was to be indissoluble. This it already was by nature, for if the spirit and senses find simultaneous satisfaction and every longing regarding one's own imperfections finds fulfilment in the other person, then loyalty grows as the flower crowning love's stem.

If this strict outlook regarding the indissolubility of

marriage causes the romantic view to coincide with Luther's, then the very opposite is true of the distinction made between real and common marriage. The Romanticists held that this distinction was not only possible but necessary, because in reality common marriage was no marriage at all. Schleiermacher, who was a clergyman, published a catechism of reason for noble-minded women. Here he stated that it was their duty, if they became acquainted with real love and had the possibility of contracting real marriage, to set aside every obstacle that hindered them. But what should be the sign of real love? It is just the young girl who will be most liable to look upon the emotion aroused in her by the first words of love as real love and will give herself whole-heartedly to her first experience of love, for she has been told so much about its importance. Schleiermacher maintained that this glamour, which was the result of a false poetic impulse, was detrimental. First love and love at first sight was the bedazzlement of the senses, the attraction of sex and not of the whole personality. Real love, which embraces friendship, can only be founded on a close acquaintance with the whole personality and can only apply to fully developed individualities. This, however, could best be developed during an intercourse embodying love and friendship between man and woman. In this sense, not only did Schleiermacher warn people not to permit themselves to be misled regarding the alleged durable nature of first love, but he actually advised men and women and even girls to prepare themselves for real marriage by means of so-called preliminary experiments.

In *Lucinde*, Schlegel tried to give his ideas on love and marriage clear expression, but succeeded in the main only in reproducing himself, which meant a bombastic sexuality and an introspective intellectualism which denuded life of its pleasantness and left a shallow egotism. In order to come to his friend's assistance and at the same time enlighten the astonished and enraged public, Schleiermacher published the confidential letters which dealt with Schlegel's *Lucinde,* and in which he endeavoured to outline the moral foundation on which the romantic idea of love rested.

More important than the abstract statement of their theories was the practical application the Romanticists made of them in their own lives. Let us inquire whether their preliminary experiments led to real or ordinary marriage, and what example their own love affairs offered; in a word, whether they realized their principles.

Friedrich Schlegel, after a long and unpleasant preliminary period, first experienced real love when he met Karoline Michaelis, who was at the time already engaged to his brother. The renunciation which the circumstances demanded of him, and which he made manfully, out of love for his brother, showed him in a true light and did much towards his development. He withdrew, because he believed that the engagement rested on mutual love. He was not restrained by any consideration for legal marriage, as became apparent when he fell in love with Dorothea Veit, born a Mendelssohn, who was unhappily married. Dorothea left her husband, although she had two sons, and lived freely with her lover for some time before her divorce. Free love is not exactly a part of the romantic programme, but in spite of the evil rumours that were spread, their friends supported Friedrich and Dorothea, but disagreed with their conduct and urged them to marry, which Friedrich then decided to do. This marriage, it is true, lasted the rest of their lives without further mishap, but it developed into just such a commonplace middle-class marriage as the young rebels had at one time revolted against with disgust. Dorothea, who was ugly and much older than Friedrich, was scarcely liable to be beset by temptations, and it accorded with her own interests, quite apart from her duty, to remain with the man she had so dearly acquired. She chose a method of ingratiation best suited to his particular character, and subsequently submerged herself heart and soul in tending his bodily welfare.

If Schleiermacher did not attach much importance to first love and love at first sight, it was in keeping with his own personal experience. Only slightly sensual by nature, he was better suited for friendship than for love. He was able for years to maintain an intimate friendship with the beautiful Henriette Herz, who was also cold by nature, seeing her almost daily, without falling in love with her. Whenever he did fall in love it was always subsequent to a long friendship. The most important occurrence in his life was his acquaintance with Eleonore Grunow, who was unhappily married to a clergyman. Schleiermacher's friendly inspiration awoke a zest for life in the dejected woman, and they became indispensable to one another during an intimacy of several years' standing. When Schleiermacher had satisfied himself that even Eleonore's courageous self-abnegation was not able to change her unworthy husband, he advised her to get a divorce, and at this juncture mutual love sprang up between them. Eleonore, who, like Schleiermacher, had been brought up in a parsonage, had such a sensitive conscience that it was difficult for her to decide, in spite of the prospect of being happy with her beloved friend. Only with difficulty was he able to get her over to his way of thinking, that a loveless marriage was less moral than divorce. Finally he persuaded her to leave her husband's house, but she was not able to still her conscience, which told her that it was her duty to endure in marriage; and after much hesitation she returned to her cage. At that time Schleiermacher, who was deeply disappointed, looked upon Eleonore's decision as a deplorable mistake and a sign of weakness. He married a much younger woman, Henriette von Willich, the widow of one of his young friends, who looked upon him more as a father. The marriage developed into a very ordinary one, and Schleiermacher had to bear the brunt of his wife's melancholy disposition.

Ludwig Tieck's marriage was also quite unromantic, as he married, when quite young, a woman of only mediocre attainments, who did not share his literary interests and was content with being a good housewife. Later on, his middle-class marriage became more romantic when an intimate woman friend of his, much against his wife's and daughter's will, became an inmate of the family, and thus a kind of double marriage was established. Theoretically speaking, double marriage is not a romantic principle, but a relic of the *Sturm und Drang* period. It is a curious fact that Goethe, who in many other ways resembled Luther, returned in his *Stella* to the idea of double marriage, which Luther had suggested as a last resource. The latter had intended, however, that the partners of the first marriage should separate, whereas the young poets thought of it as a relation *à trois*. Jacobi describes this in his novel *Woldemar*, which in its time was much read and admired. He had a morbid conception of love, according to which the higher forms of spiritual love were impaired by the sensual love of marriage. He himself lived with two women after this manner, one satisfying herself with his soul, the other with his body. Such a cruel violation of woman's rights contradicts the intentions of the Romanticists. But only as regards intention or theory can one distinguish a special romantic outlook on love and marriage, different from that of artists in general. Creuzer, who has to be classed among the Romanticists, referred to Jacobi's example when he endeavoured to win Karoline von Günderode without having the courage to separate from his Sophie. The latter belonged to that large class of women whose stubborn perseverance wins the victory over the charm and passion of others more beloved. She always protested that she loved her husband, who was thirteen years younger, and by whom she had no children, disinterestedly, and that she wished to set him free; but nevertheless with patient tears she continued to feed him and care for him and spoil him; this disgusted him, but in the end broke down his resistance. One has the impression that he breathed more freely when Karoline's death put an end to the discord. The affectionate letters which the wife wrote to her husband's mistress—only Sophie's are in existence—divulge the tortures that such an unnatural relation occasions. Since sexual and spiritual love are as a rule aroused simultaneously in women, or one develops into the other, love is much more rarely a motive for double marriage with them, apart from the fact that they would find it much more difficult to find men adapted to the part. At that time people spoke of Therese Heyne and two men as "the trinity"; and in later times Turgenev lived as a member of the family in the house of his beloved singer, Pauline Viardot, who continued a normal marriage with her husband.

It was one of the ideals of the Romanticists that woman should retain her natural qualities and at the same time develop her higher spiritual attributes. This condition was fulfilled in Karoline Schlegel. Her first marriage with a Dr. Böhmer, who died young; her subsequent love affairs, and her second marriage with Wilhelm Schlegel, should all be looked upon as preliminary experiments from the romantic point of view. Wilhelm Schlegel, for his part, had always really loved her, and all his best qualities came to the fore in this affair. She had refused him when she was still happy, and for him to offer her marriage, now that she was deserted and expecting the birth of an illegitimate child, and to receive in return for his love her gratitude, was indeed chivalrous; and this remained his attitude toward her until the very end. It was he who always comforted and helped her in all her love entanglements with Schelling. Perhaps she would have been more loyal to him had he been less noble and shown more manly harshness and unjust jealousy. Schelling's vacillation between the charms of the mother, who was eleven years his senior, and those of her daughter came to an end with little Auguste's death, and his affections were then concentrated on Karoline. The marriage of Schelling and Karoline proved really happy for both. Just as Karoline's personality, full of grace and dignity, was the central figure of the Romantic movement, so her marriage was also exemplary of the "real marriage" that romantic idealism had always desired. Whether her death, which occurred six years after this marriage, enabled the highly poetic quality of this relationship to be maintained, cannot be determined. Schelling married a second time. His wife was Pauline Gotter, the daughter of one of Karoline's early friends; they lived happily together.

E. T. A. Hoffmann's conduct was typical of a disintegrated personality. He lived with a common woman, whose only desire was to be allowed to attend to his daily requirements. He loved a young girl to whom he gave music lessons and who contracted a marriage of discretion which proved unfortunate. Whether Julia resembled the ecstatic portrait he drew of her is inessential. He had never been happy with any woman, because he was not in harmony with himself; and for him it was the very best thing to be in love with a star, which he could not besmirch, since it was out of his reach.

In his excessive grief for a girl bride whom he lost by death, Novalis determined to die also. In the heavenly ether the insignificant girl took on a visionary importance and became the mediatrix of the Godhead. Love, religion, and death were all one in the young poet's heart. Later on, however, when he was worn out, he dropped down from the heights and became native to earth again. A new love awoke in him; he became engaged to a young girl, but died before the marriage could take place.

The least harmonious personality of all the Romanticists was Clemens Brentano. He had no luck in either love or marriage. When he was nineteen he made the acquaintance of Sophie Mereau, the wife of a Jena professor, and fell in love with her, she being eight years his senior. Sophie was very talented, pursued literary activities, and was pretty and vain. In reality she cared only about herself. She had married out of affection, but soon grew disappointed with her marriage; and the petty flirtations with which she amused herself did not satisfy her. Her liaison with Clemens Brentano came to an end, but she was divorced and met him again when she was free; he then fell passionately in love with her. Though still less capable of love than she, it was he who wrecked her self-esteem, especially when she became a mother. The glamour faded rapidly for him, leaving him despondent, empty, languid, and ill, whereas she became devoted and indulgent. He revenged himself on her by martyring her soul. When she died, in three years' time, she left him the best possible love-gift: the illusion that he had once been happy, and that only death had prevented the continuation of this felicity. Her three children were either stillborn or died shortly after birth; thus did Nature repudiate the alliance. A second marriage which Clemens contracted with a hysterical and stubborn girl soon necessitated separation, as existence together proved impossible for these two hypersensitive individuals.

How motherhood, inasmuch as it teaches resignation and sacrifice, makes it easier for woman to take part in the natural course of life, even if she has lost Nature's blissful unconsciousness, is seen in the case of Bettina Brentano, who, in spite of her resemblance to her brother Clemens, led an ordinary married life with Achim von Arnim until his death.

Rahel was the most independent, though not the most outstanding, character among the women of the romantic movement. She was invariably unfortunate in her love affairs, probably because of her natural predilection for handsome, weak, extremely sensual, and intellectually insignificant men. "Whoever has thought deepest, loves the most intensely": this was her idea. A brooding spirit, whether man or woman, attracts to itself the beautiful and the sensuous with magnetic force. Whether the woman's intellectual superiority proved irksome to the men, or whether their sexual needs required another complement, they reciprocated Rahel's love, but the intimacies never led to marriage; and here the fault was not hers. Weary with weeping and broken with disappointments, she eventually married Varnhagen, who offered her a sincere admiration, a respected name, rest, and security. Her marriage was based on friendship and gratitude, and proved happy, if one can term a respectful coexistence marriage at all.

If we take a summary view of the love affairs and marriages of the Romanticists, the despised family life of the petty bourgeoisie appears stronger and purer by contrast. Then the oppressive feeling of the unavoidable tragedy of life steals upon us. This, then, is love, the demoniac power, at whose mercy weak man lies! The Romanticists termed sexual love the hieroglyph of divine love. Is it not rather the invention of the devil? Is it not the nectar of the gods, made of the fruits of Paradise, into which the greatest antigod let fall a couple of drops of serpent venom, in order to change the life-flood into death throes? It does not always seize hold of and bind two hearts at one time, but it instills a blind craving for one who may be indifferent or turn away with aversion; and it leads to the cruel torment of unrequited love. And if two hearts are simultaneously smitten, love fades in one sooner than it does in the other; and in the place of delight come reproach, disappointment, bitterness, and repentance. Nor is this all. Love itself bears devilish lusts, the impulse to put the beloved one on trial, to excite and to tease, and to harry love to death with love. The lover often destroys the object of his affection, which no act can restore, much as a child does who breaks his toys to see how they were made. The magic enchantress casts a spell over an ordinary face so that it appears to the person who looks at it as the prototype of his love dreams. Thus it remains fixed in his memory, draws him irresistibly toward it, goads him on to madness, to risk all and to commit crimes, until one day the illusion glides away, leaving the commonplace. It was nothing resplendent that for days and years held the soul in its sway and expelled from it all that was good, progressive, and pure.

It was a brass coin that we mistook for fine gold. And if love joins together two good-natured persons, it forces on them the bitter-sweet experience that others are also worthy of affection, and that their hearts too are changeable. The vows of eternal love flow just as naturally from the lips of lovers as scent from the chalice of a flower, but the demon of love listens to them with a cold smile, as if it were the false pathos of a comedian. Love impels together such as can never learn to abide one another, and lets those pass by unheeded who would have made each other happy. How could people have sought to build the strong edifice of marriage on an element whose changeable, shimmering, and dangerous character resembles the sea?

The Romanticists looked upon marriage as essentially a private matter affecting two persons. It never struck them that society had an interest in such a relationship, and still less did they realize that it had the right to lay stress on this point. We are at the summit of an individualistic age. The development of the individual and his pleasure in evolving and observing his individuality appear to be the ultimate aims of life, and all the complexities of life should serve to mould the individuality of man and woman. The old world, said the romantic aesthete Solger, was a world of racial considerations, whereas in the modern world the individual is the first-born. Individuality is to be the destiny of mankind, and its expression love and friendship. "Man has now no other destiny save love." The exaggerated importance of love which we meet with in literature and life is the outcome of historical evolution. Since the fifteenth century the entire public life, the legislative, judicatory, and administrative activities, have been gradually taken out of the hands of the people and entrusted to functionaries of the princes. The self-governing, free Germans became mere objects of government. Thus a society came into being which existed alongside of the state and the governing class, which only busied itself with its own private affairs. Its folk spent their spare energy, ambition, and passion on furthering literature and art, but paid even more attention to love. At the same time a great economic change deprived women of their professional activity in the household, and the fine lady, having essentially no occupation, was evolved; she was almost compelled to spend her time in love intrigues. The man has at least the possibility of spending himself in his profession, but the artist (and especially the poet), who is without any profession, is a suitable partner for the lady of ease. The artist, on account of the feminine elements in his nature, is altogether dependent on private life and an extensive love-life. There are times, however, when this femininity of man, and the masculinity of woman which is a necessary corollary, become more general; and at such times the sex relations are more difficult to regulate, and greater prominence is given to the problem. The romantic movement overrated human nature and misunderstood the conditions in which individuality developed. They believed that man would choose the right course when left to himself, and consequently demanded freedom even for the child, which has an instinctive desire for strictness. They imagined that, by setting aside obstacles, they would further the development of the individual, while it is just in the struggle to overcome obstacles and to conform to moral customs that character is formed. It was assumed that highly developed individuals, who are the salt of social intercourse, must also be successes in marriage. They forgot that many of the most outstanding personalities are the products of unhappy marriages; while on the other hand, the marriages of relatives often prove to be love-marriages, but not infrequently the children are unhealthy. In fact, they never thought of the children at all, in spite of high-sounding words, which, for example, Friedrich Schlegel found occasion to use. Neither did they recognize the duties that would arise in connection with children. The mere word duty was for them a disharmony. Bettina Brentano once said that it was a good thing for duty that it had never come across her path, or she would have wrung its neck. Although too much importance must not be attached to the random words of a girl, this aversion was fundamental and general to the romantic movement. They did not realize that the good as well as the evil becomes barbaric and devoid of character without the application of duty. The Romanticists understood by duty merely something cold and mechanical, and did not feel the immensity and beauty inherent in the strict observance of a moral principle even when it contradicts Nature. As marriage cannot exist without a sense of duty, on principle they declined marriage altogether, and in their glorification of love-marriage they express their fear of marriage as it is in reality, and as it must necessarily be to a certain extent among a cultured people, if man does not desire merely to make woman into a slave. In Tieck's novel *Sternbald,* Woldemar on the evening prior to his marriage envies every man in the street: "How fortunate you are in still having to seek for your unknown happiness! I have found mine!"

This sighing over a happiness once attained caused a romantic philosopher named Kanne, on the day of his wedding, to escape the final ceremony by taking flight. Clemens Brentano, too, shortly before his second marriage had the desire to escape; and he must have soon repented that he had not done so. Incidentally he wrote in reference to his first marriage: "We shall live together as the snowflakes when it snows thickly; and as they melt at the coming of another spring, so shall we part from one another, if we are not intended to remain together"; we see that he had no proper idea of marriage in mind, but only contemplated a loose bond that could be terminated at will. Shortly after his marriage he had already begun to complain of misunderstandings. Instead of becoming more animated, more inspired to creative activity, he felt empty and was more despondent than ever. The same was true in the painter Runge's case, although he also married for love. For the weaker or delicately constituted artist, marriage proves a cage that prevents his soaring. Great geniuses have married without detriment to their creative powers: Bach, Luther, Dürer, Rembrandt, Veronese, and many others. And even if fewer works of art were produced on account of the influence of marriage, would not that be preferable to the demolition of a very ancient and sacred institution, under whose protection man has grown up and developed? Do the tears of two lovers outweigh those of deserted wives and children? The Romanticists evinced little interest in questions regarding the outside world, because they thought of the lovers only as strangely detached beings, cut off from the world. Man and woman appear alone in thin air, and stand opposite one another much as the hero and heroine do in a Wagnerian opera, and sing to each other without coming closer, as if they were under a spell. The unreality attached to romantic love was the cause of its not becoming popular with its contemporaries, who were more affected by the ideals of free love, which were only incidental to the romantic idea. The movement known as Young Germany was inspired by a group of young writers who wished to promote free love, and who in this respect allied themselves with the Romanticists, because they felt that the latter's revolutionary conceptions were aimed against the existing order. This furnishes an example of how extreme individualism develops into communism.

If one takes into consideration the "preliminary experiments" and the idea that marriage without love could not be counted as "real marriage" and was consequently readily dissoluble, then one is bound to admit that, whatever their theory was, the practical application of romantic tenets amounted to a kind of free love. Goethe in his *Wahlverwandtschaften* has suggested a middle course, whereas he usually advocated the inviolability of marriage. In the *Wahlverwandtschaften* he makes the Count propose that marriage should last for a term of five years; the possibility of ultimate separation would cause both parties to show their best qualities, and in most cases the union would be renewed, and thus in reality this form of marriage would be just as enduring as in the case of an indissoluble bond, but more liable to produce happiness. The authoress Auguste Fischer, who was not without repute and who had experienced all the horrors of marriage at the hands of her brutal and unscrupulous husband, reintroduced this idea of marriage for a term. Under the present complex social conditions this would certainly operate more to the advantage of the man than of the woman. Rahel Varnhagen realized this when she advocated the complete readjustment of woman's position, based on her rights as a mother. Nature, she maintained, had appointed the closest tie between mother and child, had planted in the mother-heart an enduring love and readiness for self-sacrifice, and thus in every respect had willed that the child should belong to the mother. Consequently it was only natural that the child should bear the mother's name, and the latter ought to rule in the family and possess its property. Nature must be obeyed, but one should strive to make her more moral. Nature was cruel in making it possible for man to coerce woman; this ought to be remedied by legal measures.

The Romanticists paid too little attention to the fact that man is ordained to establish communities, which have priority over the interests of any one individual. Family life causes man, woman, and child to influence one another in the most intimate manner, since it asks of each the most delicate consideration, because this has to be shown daily; it also educates them morally, by bringing together love and duty. But life is much too complex and contradictory to enable the family to uphold social interests against those of the individual, or to intrust to it, in every case, a higher authority. For in their turn, family interests become self-centred, and as a definite unit, the family tends to prevent a wider social life. Although family life demands sacrifices from its members, it can be very harsh toward outsiders. In fact, it is one of those bonds which must be firm but at the same time resilient. The very beauty and adventure of life lies in the fact that general rules cannot be applied to it, and frail man is entirely dependent on his courage and conscience. It would be unjust to the Romanticists to ban their attempts at marriage reform forthwith as erroneous, by merely affirming the sacred character of marriage. No earthly institution is perfect, but always stands in need of readjustment and renewal from the plenitude of unending life. Heart and fancy, with all their weakness and intemperance, oppose not only morality and duty, but platitude, narrow-mindedness, convenience, and calculated selfishness just as much. One thing is certain, that as much fine humanity is wrecked by family restrictions as by the very passion that seeks to break through these barriers. A high moral ideal towers above the world and its conventions and avarice. Out of the human heart issues the noblest love as well as the most dissolute, wild, and cramping lusts; heart and world are bound together by good and by evil. In the battle of life every person must, during his vacillations between the world and the kingdom of God, learn to give each its due. Love alone cannot guarantee a good and happy marriage, healthy children, and proper education for them; but neither can it be eliminated from a relationship of the sexes. All down the ages, passion has led to the destruction of marriage; and all down the ages, the authorities have made allowance for exceptions! But there has never been a decision that was just absolutely, or in all respects. In spite of Goethe's most charming description, in his *Wahlverwandschaften*, of the progress of forbidden love, and his obvious sympathy for the transgressor, he still maintains the sacramental character of marriage. On the other hand, he also pointed the way to freedom for several pairs who wished to separate.

The Teutonic conception of woman, which looks upon her as a divine manifestation and which found expression anew in Luther and Goethe, is the true foundation on which Occidental culture rests. This ideal is opposed in Germany by a thoughtless barbarism which causes the men to belittle, exploit, and even despise the women, because they are physically the weaker; the women in turn respect and pander to brute strength, and by their willing servitude increase the megalomania of the men. It is the chief merit of the romantic movement to have fought against this comfortable barbarism and to have championed equal rights for women; but even the Romanticists desired that their individuality should be taken into account. Goethe and Luther placed woman on the same footing as man—if anything, even higher; but they did not recognize her divinity merely in her artistic propensities and conversational abilities or in the charm of her personality; in fact, this lay chiefly in her motherhood, in her lavish love, in her readiness to assist others and to sacrifice her own interests. The wonderful description of woman's vocation and wealth of character which Goethe puts into the mouth of his heroine in *Hermann und Dorothea* emphasizes these unpretentious virtues, which nevertheless sustain society. "Twenty men together could not support this hardship, and it is not necessary that they should do so, but they should acknowledge it gracefully!" Goethe urges that men should be grateful for the services women render, and he speaks of the "deserved power" (*verdiente Gewalt*) which is woman's due in the home. The professional life of woman, which modern circumstances have forced her into, estranges her from her family and undermines marriage. Perhaps it was necessary for her to demonstrate her powers in different spheres of activity for which it was formerly thought that only men were fitted, in order that her practical accomplishments should be recognized and that she should also gain in self-confidence. It would be a great pity if the divine attributes of her nature were to suffer by this, for no matter in how many other spheres she may prove successful, she will always stand on the highest summit of human attainment in her capacity of mother. The general influence of an unmarried woman should also be motherly in this sense, and marriage should be considered from the standpoint of woman and children, and established accordingly.

Rahel once spoke of marriage as follows: "Can affection exist without an incentive? Is there any legal outward guarantee for either secret or open friendship? Is only the household to be accounted sacred? Does marriage consist only in rearing and educating children? Is not living together without charm or delight more indecent than the most immoderate ecstasy? Is sincerity possible where the unnatural can be demanded by force? Is not the condition of itself damned, where truth, grace, and innocence cannot find a place? Away with the barriers! Away with the ruinous heap! Let it be razed to the ground! Then all will flourish, vegetation-like, that has a right to live."

Should ever this wall, "the big, old, harmful wall of ancient prejudices," as Rahel termed marriage, be demolished completely, then the high tide of passion that had swept over it would soon commence to ebb and finally lose itself in the sands. To awaken passion, one would have to build up again the very thing that had been previously abolished in order to satisfy it. It is just the strength and beauty in human nature that depend on pressure, coercion, and opposition. One does not give a man wings by casting off his chains. For it is love itself which, in accordance with its innate longing for eternal love, requires an eternal bond. The double character of man, his weakness, commonplaceness, and wickedness, as well as his ready devotion, his noble endeavour, and his godlike fatherhood, require a strict constraint. And in turn, it is his weakness, commonplaceness, and wickedness, as well as his sense of freedom, his love of truth, and his godlike and titanic nature, that storm against constraint. In the past, the educative and evolutionary influence of marriage has been immeasurable. If this is to continue, marriage must not become narrow and fixed, must not make itself loathed by petty strictness. On the other hand, it must maintain its dignity and sacred character, which compel mankind to take it seriously, to reverence it, and to wrestle with it.

JAKOB WASSERMANN

Bourgeois Marriage

An Open Letter to Count Hermann Keyserling

DEAR COUNT KEYSERLING:

WHEN you invited me to write for *The Book of Marriage* I was busy just completing a novel dealing with marriage, which I had long planned and prepared for. This served me as another proof that each epoch is pregnant with particular ideas, changes, and preparations, and in this respect we can often only play the part of *accoucheur*. When such an outstanding intelligence as yours, which is so actively in touch with the spiritual and social requirements of the present age, decides to formulate a world problem of the day, to place it before an Areopagus of chosen persons for consideration and discussion, and to take part personally—then indeed the problem must be extremely urgent, and the evil of which it is the germ must threaten the very roots of existence.

I also became fully aware of this during the writing of my novel, *Laudin und die Seinen*. The crowd of the figures and life-patterns was hardly to be taken in at a glance, and it was difficult to bring it into shape and order. Experience and adventure mingled with and intensified each other. It was at the time more an intellectual fever than a matter of discipline and confirmation, and I felt while working at this book, as I had never felt with any other, that it was my mission to write it.

But let us leave the private aspect of the matter with its particularities and painfulness, and also the personal destiny underlying it. This would be more suitable for a private conversation than for public discussion. In a conversation of this nature, I could hint at the curious association applicable in this case also, between thought and suffering, experience and imagination, adventure and symbol, and could outline the temperamental forces, the change of attitude, and the internal focusing of the perspective that was required in order that this most delicate, adventitious, and dawning element should take on a higher form, conforming to law and order. At rare moments and in a tranquil state of mind, we feel and perceive all the wrong in the world. And in order to express even a small part of this, and by means of ideas or vision to offer humanity comfort or guidance, it is necessary that we should have had our eyes opened by some personal sorrow and should acquire almost the tranquillity of a god, who knows the purpose of the storm while it is still raging.

This is a hard task you have set me, and as I proceed to comply, I find the difficulties almost insurmountable. Apart from the necessary consideration of space, I am quite unaccustomed to express myself in thought and speech, and fear I shall appear a poor figure to a man of such system and order as yourself. The scope is so vast, the phenomena so numerous, that it paralyzes and confuses one; the thousandfold destinies, each positive in its own sphere, make one hesitate to form judgments. I see this and that man acting according to his nature, convictions, and character, in correspondence with external and internal circumstances in a particular way. Act thus he *must;* it is a question of necessity or destiny: and in the same manner I observe whole groups, social strata, and castes. Since they all possess particular features and characters, a uniqueness that cannot be repeated, I have not the courage, or possibly do not possess the ability, to find a suitable formula to account for their existence and effect, and to apply to individual conduct a general theory.

Foreseeing my difficulty, you advised me to attempt a simple description of middle-class conditions and to make use of as little criticism as possible. Such a description, even if it amounts merely to a rough sketch or conception, can virtually only mean quoting from the subject-matter of my novel. While your advice to avoid a critical attitude seems almost impossible to follow, because in each individual case and for every phase in general evolution one is bound to compare an imperfect individual or social state with an ideal or visionary standard (if this can be termed criticism), I have nevertheless determined to proceed in this way. In order to avoid repeating the data and the conditions laid down, together with the possibility of formulating them inadequately, I shall make use of a typical part of my book by quoting from it here. It deals with the life and activities of a famous barrister (Dr. Friedrich Laudin), whose specialty is divorce. The passage reads as follows:

Had he been a writer on social customs, he could have produced a most profound tractate on marriage and its developments during the twentieth century. He could have dwelt on the motives that lead to marriage and those that give rise to divorce. He could have noted down in his dry and professional manner, just as they had come under his observation, the innumerable marriages that rested on frivolity and indiscretion, on hasty passion and blind sensuality; then again such as were due to ambition, vanity, financial gain, good-natured weakness or a mutual and temporary infatuation; and last, what could he not have said of marriages contracted in complete indifference or disconsolate resignation? He could have sketched men who obtain a wife by craft, much as they would a position or a tip on the stock exchange, others who think of marriage as they would of going to a coffee-house and enjoying a game of cards, and those who have the choice of suicide or marriage and prefer the latter. Some men paid their mistresses with their wives' money; others made their wives into prostitutes and played the fine gentleman in a society that knows everything about them and shuts its eyes to it all, as long as scandal is avoided. He could have told of men who had been imposed on for years, who had pledged their souls for their wives' integrity; of moral sluggards who found it convenient to notice nothing, so as not to have to sacrifice their own comfort; of love-stricken men who became slaves for their wives, and men who wrecked their wives' health because they understood as much about a woman's body as a butcher does about silk spinning.

He could have told of women for whom a ball-dress meant more than the health of their children; of others who put themselves on a level with household animals, partly out of terror and partly to beguile their husbands. Other women deified their husbands, and in their idolatry would have preferred to tear their hearts out rather than allow themselves to be convinced that these men were puny mortals, a little given to roguery. There were women who used up their health in yearly pregnancies, while the master of the family, feeling that he had done his duty, spent his nights in inns and clubs or with mistresses. Some women wasted the money that their husbands earned with great difficulty, and others saved every *heller* while their menfolk threw away hundreds of thousands in senseless speculation. There were charity-furies, whose houses were as uninhabitable as railway stations. There were intellectual and spiritual minors, who had been forced into marriage to fade away there.

He could have explained how all these different people, pair after pair, dropped into marriage, frivolous and ignorant, often half strangers to each other, without sufficient sense of responsibility and stability of temperament. They both were disappointed and inflicted disappointment on others. They signed contracts which they had no intention of keeping, even as they set the pen aside and while the ink was still wet on the paper. There were couples who produced children to whom the lives of their parents were like a nightmare. How they came to him, both men and women, panting to get free of each other; how they bargained, how short their memories were, how they slandered and exposed one another! Hatred, contempt, satiety, and affront erased every dignity, every remembrance of the exchange of what had once been holy vows.

He could have described all this and have added to it the joy of the statistician, who shows irrefutable facts and pronounces the law of causation. But it appears that his mind was an abyss into which each case, with all its attendant associations, fell like a stone into a deep well. He kept them locked up in the depths; they could not be rescued or brought to the light of day.

Repetition often enervates a man's spirit. Nevertheless it must not be presumed that it was just this that pressed so heavily on Laudin as to make its effect remarked. It had nothing to do with his professional work. Perhaps circumstances were operative here that he could not account for, and these were stronger, more wearying and tormenting, than his deliberations, judicial examinations, and negotiations. Possibly a protocol with its dry enumerations and registrations was at times more eloquent for him than the loquacious statements by word of mouth and all the lamentation and discontent that men and women disclosed to him. There was so much hidden behind it all, so that what they actually said was not the principal matter, was not the terrible caricature, the tremendous disenchantment. But it was that which lay implied behind it all—it must be remembered that he knew it, had to know it: the many dim labyrinths of misery, collections of written and printed matter, receipts, and proofs of treachery and deceit contained in all manner of papers, which would have to be shown and then preserved until they turned yellow in the document cabinet. They were the keys with which he could open their dwellings, places of rancour and hatred; the bedrooms in which kisses turned to poison and embraces to spasms of rage. He knew their secrets, their hidden relationships; it was his task to do so. This arsenal of dissension teemed with proofs; both memory and imagination were filled with it, like a pedlar's pack stuffed with worm-eaten trumpery, with dirty, bizarre, petty, and abhorrent trifles, ranging from a soiled bed to an unpaid milliner's bill, from the arsenic residue in a coffee-cup to a garter found in a hotel, from a forged note to a forged cheque. Then the letters, mountains of them, mountains of lies, of suffering, insulting and full of hypocritical promises. Haggling, endearing, avowing, blaming, flattering, scoffing, execrating, and begging letters; some ungrammatical, others in a noble style. Then business letters: "I have the honour to inform you," followed by callous perfidy. There were poetic outpourings; threatening, spying, and express letters; affecting love-letters and letters of forgiveness, and again others full of hatred and devilish calumny.

Possibly you find this a very gloomy picture, perhaps too gloomy to be true. But you will doubtless take into account that in a poetic structure, the light and dark elements, as in life itself, shade into one another; and if one is taken out and looked at separately, the whole easily becomes deranged. I do not see that Laudin's experience differs materially from that of the persons who had to go through these things themselves, either in the capacity of negotiators, sufferers, or mere observers. The fact is simply this: Outward and inward law not only have nothing in common, but actually destroy one another.

Formerly mysticism, religion, church, and clerical influences and forces were at work deep down beneath the surface of middle-class life. These determined the life of society as well as that of the individual. Generation after generation were educated to conform to certain rules, inwardly and outwardly to conform to immutable conventions. In spite of the exceptions that private life afforded and the tragic confusion of some individual cases, however much destinies were intertwined the whole was governed by a fixed order, which though only apparent was indisputable. It rested on tradition, which in the course of time lost much of its strength and worthiness because of its decaying roots. Thus in place of obedience and conviction and all the many related virtues, a mere formal compliance arose, which ultimately degenerated into hypocrisy. At the same time the yoke and the necessary burden it implied were borne with growing discontent, which nevertheless, up to a short time ago, and in a few conservative circles right up to the present, operated on the one hand as a restrictive, moderating, and intimidating influence, while on the other hand it hastened the process of disintegration.

Not only have we experienced a vast political revolution and are still in its stress, but we have passed through an intellectual one of similar dimensions and importance. The main result is that the old ties have disappeared, and new ones have not yet been discovered to take their place. Thus, the individual man has in a strange, I might say frightened, manner claimed to be autonomous as regards his own destiny, and in every respect ventured to be responsible to himself alone (I say "ventured," because—and I am sure you will agree with me here—only the exceptional leader can be said to have achieved it), whereupon that kind of freedom evolved with which we see the whole world labouring today. This does not prove advantageous to social life and still less so to any guiding principle. But to me it appears as an intermediary stage, a transitional period, which can only be supported owing to the arduous efforts, which at times amount to complete self-sacrifice, of individual forerunners. The growing consciousness of responsibility to oneself and the sense of autonomy, a process which unquestionably cannot be resisted, since the whole social atmosphere is permeated with it and public life coloured by it, have made middle-class marriage appear more than ever a questionable institution. The restraint that state and church exerted in the traditional order, which regulated the motives of existence, is not only no longer willingly supported by citizens and populations, but even meets with resistance due to revolutionary and reformative aspirations. That the social system has long lost its sacred and inviolable character and has taken on in its stead a haphazard, superficial, opportunist, and even frivolous one, becoming a thing of the moment and the fashion, merely sensual and therefore shallow, merely economic and consequently spiritless, and has formed a mere outward alliance, can be no great surprise to you and me. We watched, each from his own tower for some tens of years, the growing symptoms of this disease, and dreaded what time has proved to be only too well founded. It may perhaps be objected that marriage was not always looked upon as a sacrament, and certainly not by all people; for example, during the romantic period in Germany, marriages were contracted, annulled, and contracted again, as if it were a matter of travelling to another holiday resort or exchanging furniture. First this was true only of an isolated group whose activities were looked upon with surprise, if not disgust, by the general public; in the second place, the custom was, in the main, the outcome of a rule of life that was carried to excess. It was nothing evolutionary or organic, but a voluntary matter, obtained by childish obstinacy or achieved by philosophic speculation.

I must naturally exclude here everything in the nature of adultery, and the alluring fashionable conventions from which it arose, with their mixed relationships, as well as the uniform tragic character or somewhat superficial irony and cheerfulness which brought a whole literature into being and was inspired by a specific cultural spirit (Goethe's *Wahlverwandtschaften* crowns this development with a majestic verdict). In reality adultery confirms marriage; the moral basis is accepted, defection from which entails punishment. Or, to put it better, it is accepted where the sin is recognized. Both conscience and society inflict punishment; woman loses her purity; the deceived becomes ridiculous; the law of might, modified by the marriage code, is introduced. All these things point to the indissolubility of the bond and the catastrophes attendant on its dissolution, at least in the case of woman.

Today this basis no longer exists. The tradition is outlived. New possibilities, new forms, are only in the process of evolution, and are only, so to speak, adapted to life by a chosen few, and forced upon society. It must naturally grapple with the trivial misunderstandings, caricatures, and *contrefaçon*, for there has never yet been an emancipation that was not compromised by the majority of its adherents. The dangerous, uncertain condition in which it is at present, can be noticed in every middle-class family. The realization of this impending shock may have urged you to sound the alarm that brought me to your side. Of what avail is substantiation, where the countless variety of the phenomena, each worthy to be considered and proved of God, mocks at the possibility of comprehensive treatment? I have attempted to give a rough sketch by employing a central figure. I see that this does not suffice. What is to be accounted right and what wrong? Which supports are to be pulled down, and which built up? Which is the most mortally wounded part of the social organism? The latter is like a veritable Job, leprous and unruly, rushing toward its fate. Each would need a doctor for itself—the wisest and most devoted physician he would have to be—and where suffering ceases and crime commences, a spiritual adviser and judge, with the attributes of saint and prophet, would be required. The serfdom of woman, which is a survival from barbaric times, prevents her from standing in a proper relation to her rôle in private and social life; on the other hand, there is her luxurious life to be taken into consideration, which degrades man into a beast of burden. Economic and material facts outweigh, under the increasingly difficult conditions of life, considerations of a higher category, such as moral and spiritual values. Birth control becomes a decisive factor in the peace and prosperity of the household. What toll has to be paid in nerves and spirit for the customary use of contraceptives! The damage caused by abortive surgical measures is not only bodily, but deeply wounds woman's psyche, though in some individual cases this is not always noticeable at once. Besides, it everlastingly burdens the popular conscience; but this is a chapter to itself. If any one, however, were able to calculate these ravages, he would arrive at a most astounding result. As long as the law continues in its bizarre stubbornness to proclaim the inferiority of woman, she will revenge herself by unconscious impulse and opposition; and by her embittered attitude toward the person and existence of man, she makes a veritable prisoner of him, because his desire for freedom still persists, in spite of life being beset by conflicts. In general the emancipation from a bondage that is considered unworthy rarely leads to a dignified condition. Confusion begets confusion, hatred increases hatred, and error grows of error, just as if the eye that was once dazzled, and the soul once spotted, could never again become completely pure. Naturally this is not the case. Only an ethical imperative is lacking; guidance by love or wisdom is necessary; authority is wanting. Above all, there is a need for right feeling and an instinct for the true, binding realities which come of the spirit. Where false and ephemeral things are held as realities, that is to say, where action and judgment are opportunist, all the suffering and misfortune naturally become contagious and epidemic in character, in the same way as low atmospheric pressure is favourable to the dissemination of virulent disease. You are right; it is of no use to criticize. What is the good of criticizing destiny? One can teach, warn, set an example, describe conditions; one can say: Have the right instinct, for yourself and for the choice of a mate; increase your watchfulness; depend more on mutual respect than on love or passion; don't waste yourselves, don't lose yourselves in words, don't squander your wealth. One can put one's faith in youth, by teaching one's sons and daughters to reverence the dignity of man and awakening them to the dynamic significance of even the least decision regarding life. All this can and should be done, for every change begins with activity, just as its final stage is form. The rest is merely incidental and auxiliary.

May I conclude with another quotation from my book? The passage describes something similar to the desired vision or dream, and reads as follows:

Laudin paused, stroked his forehead, and continued: I seem to see something like a reconstruction of the social ideal. It is a thought with which I have often struggled and which has always returned to me again in various forms. It was always a question of the ego and one's own personality, because we are all steeped in the idea of self, simply drowning in it. Sometimes it amounted to the extinction of self, or its disassociation; at other times, its transformation into other forms. If an individual is not content with his form or mode of existence, he seeks another which suits him better and which will give him more happiness. I cannot rid myself of the belief that the individual, as a separate personality, has lost his significance; this is due to the modern exaggeration of his importance and to the fact that Christianity no longer exerts a practical influence. Humus must first of all be prepared—human humus. I consider the individual as such as no longer of use to the community in respect to its moral and spiritual constitution. Only man and woman as a pair are of importance. I am confident that for every male and female individual there is only one complement possible. What human society would gain, by a continual increase of appropriately matched pairs, in peace, pleasure, buoyancy, and in purity and cleanliness, is hardly imaginable. Consequently all restrictions regarding the choice of a mate should be removed; neither men nor women should be hindered by moral odium, the burden of paternity or motherhood, or by considerations of virtue, from testing and experiencing all the different forms of phenomena and adventure which exist in their desires and imagination. If they possess instinct, they will make it all the keener; if they have a will to social life, it will lead them to their goal. Anything is preferable to what is at present termed marriage. Do not fear the suppression of morals or even their complete dissolution. What can be worse than that which stifles the spirit? No price is too high for even the attempt to bring about a change. In every person, even in such as appear most reckless, there is an inherent desire to attain balance. This must and will finally conquer every form of degeneration. A hysterical spasm has chained our world with laws and customs that were once significant and necessary, but which today are senseless and merely so many empty husks. Since capital punishment has been abolished, the number of murders committed has decreased. Prohibitions make criminals; punishments create crimes. There is something wonderful in man, an ardent desire that cannot be stilled, which was confided to the good in him, even if that good be merely as a tiny grain.

That is all that I have to say. And if you find my treatment of the subject inadequate, take into benevolent consideration the embarrassment in which the subject has placed me. I trust that I have not wearied you, nor taken up too much of your valuable space.

Respectfully yours,

JAKOB WASSERMANN.

MARTA KARLWEIS

Marriage and the Changing Woman

WITHIN the domain of Christian culture, both as regards time and space, the marriage order appears at a definite time to have been converted into a problem. Unhappy marriages there have always been, but they did not constitute a problem, any more than the appearance of ugly or defective children in a few odd families points to the general degeneration of the race. Marriage becomes a matter for extreme anxiety, care, and discussion only when woman, who is its feminine hemisphere, begins consciously to free herself from the feeling of dependence on the male hemisphere.

There is no other fetish that society holds to so firmly as the conception "woman," with all its usual associations of infantilism and dependence. Even today the middle-aged man is to be found who maintains in all seriousness that men seek the child in woman. The child requires protection, is a minor and consequently a serf, but above all it possesses no spiritual existence. Neither doctorates or other distinctions nor the right to vote have as yet been able to dispel this sweet idea of the childishness of woman, which man cherishes. Her sex alone, that ministers to his needs, is to incarnate her substance and dignity. Even worse: sexual serfdom for his benefit is thought to be the very foundation of her dignity, which again amounts to a glorification of man's self-indulgence. This constitutes a vicious circle of dependence. Woman won recognition only on account of her sex and is thus debarred from all intellectual and spiritual development. Only an intellectual existence can be called independent. Sex is the one thing that is constant and immutable. A fifteen-year-old girl is just as fit to serve sexually as a woman of forty. We see everywhere that there is nothing the average middle-class man objects to so much as to find that his forty-year-old wife lacks some characteristics of the girl of fifteen. This becomes the more evident if it is borne in mind how even the simplest young girl puts all her pride and honour into the determination that her husband should *become* something, that he should continually develop; that is, that he should not remain what he was, but change. Under no consideration does she want him to remain on the same level as that on which she learned to love him and chose him. But the stronger and consequently the more valuable the man's personality is to which she has attached her destiny, the more is she threatened by the precept which commands: Do not change; remain just as I chose you, for thus you are the stationary pole in my existence. There was nothing unreasonable in this as long as woman's evolution stopped at the moment she became fully developed sexually; this includes bodily maturity, maternity, and the innumerable variations of psychological change thus given rise to. But the life of the soul cannot be too carefully distinguished here from mental and spiritual life. What was a reasonable claim—the claim that woman should not change—became an endeavour to thwart the growth of life in the case of female individuals, whose minds as well as their souls were capable of development. For woman is subject to the same evolutionary laws as man. Now individuality commences only in the intellectual sphere, and here one might state a *jus individuationis* for woman, which man instinctively denies. Later on, we shall investigate one of the principal reasons for this denial, which is quite justified from the point of view of race preservation; but it is idle to argue about rights and the refusal to accede them, because a section, even if a small one, have already seized what was formerly an exclusive male prerogative. Here the problem implied in the beginning passes into the critical stage in which we see marriage at present. It might be objected that the inner achievement of a small group of women cannot bring about a general crisis. Nevertheless, what takes place at the extremes makes itself felt at the foundation also; the movement which has become conscious in the higher stages of development is nourished by the obscure revolutions of the unconscious.

The abolition of the bondage or serfdom of women took place from without and was recognized by external signs such as permission to study, appointments to public office, etc. Those in authority had finally, with the best grace they could summon, to allow this purely outward change. But right in the midst of the most lively struggle for women's rights, the conception of woman's activity as ranging between the sexual status of the mother and the prostitute received its indelible stamp, the mother representing the constant type, the prostitute the variable; both were infantile, as neither had a real existence. Doctorates, appointments to the judicial profession, the active and passive electoral franchise, were looked upon as toys, in varying degree dangerous, for those who were sexually unemployed. The abolition of serfdom did not practically alter the root conceptions. But those in power are very differently affected by the complete change in woman's intellectual and spiritual character. The woman who has seized the evolutionary principle and renounces the alluring characteristics of the fifteen-year-old in order to gain admittance to her new evolutionary phase possesses no lord or master, even if she gratefully recognizes her husband's thousand-times higher capacities. Beyond mother and prostitute, the student and worker type has appeared, struggling unceasingly toward the light. She also is permitted to struggle. No longer is the spiritual-sensuous side of religion her exclusive part. She has her pleasure in *creation* and *law,* and the more thoroughly she comprehends the principles, the freer does she become. Only at this stage can form become a vital question to the genius of woman. Consequently, the few great women who were creative geniuses must be looked upon as spiritual existences. For the woman who has changed in this manner, the world also becomes a pageant of wonderful, eternal changes. But here she is threatened by the precept of man as lover: Do not change yourself, for who can guarantee that you will remain loyal during the process?

When loyalty is made the battle-cry, then the reason for man's restrictive attitude becomes apparent. Since in reality only a person whose intellect is awake is subject to a law which he can understand, it follows that marriage and the idea of the family are no longer a matter entirely under the jurisdiction of men, but are equally dependent on the will of man and woman. Marriage seems originally to have been forced on man, his wife and children hanging around his neck, weighing him down; and human society looks upon these conditions as a necessary state of equilibrium. Woman functions in a passively centripetal manner against the active centrifugal force of man. But man as the representative of social life does not wish to lose at any price this passive limiting force, and he looks upon its transformation into an active force, that is to say, one consciously functioning, with grave mistrust. He knows what the demons of consciousness are in his own breast, and he shivers when he pictures to himself the soul of his mate. It is not merely despotism that urges him to offer resistance. A world that depends entirely on the male principle of evolution is rushing toward its own destruction.

Every movement of importance has its ridiculous side, and consequently it will not be out of place here to glance for a moment at the irritating caricature of the emancipated woman, at the intellectual pretentiousness full of swollen bombast, the want of foundation and reality, in all grades, from the simple bluestocking to the "high-brow" literary woman. The latter, by the way, is a figure that has been drawn often and clearly enough from Molière on down to Strindberg, so that in this case the caricature appeared before the reality, and the spurious proved the forerunner of the genuine.

Let us now return to the idea of sexual loyalty, which has been endangered. It must be admitted from the very outset that the mystic and sacred character of sex relations, and the taboo attaching to them, cannot exist, as such, for the intellectually conscious individual. Emancipated woman can never wholly and simply sanctify a function, an impulse, or a requirement, not even if it forms part of the institution of marriage. For her, only such love-relations are holy as guarantee the most ample scope for her spiritual and intellectual development. Of course, a sanction of this nature does not offer the same guarantee for the family that the mystical taboo relating to customs which are now becoming decadent did at one time. As a type, emancipated woman is well suited to motherhood, but not to the same extent to establishing a family from a social point of view—a phenomenon which law and morals will have to face. Woman conquers the world through the medium of man; it is no longer consistent to look upon her as a prostitute, because on her road to knowledge, to the conquest of the world, she has continually to give herself anew, in order to gain a new comprehension.

The masterful, progressive woman of powerful personality does not at first seem to belong to a discussion of the relation of the transformed woman to marriage. Nevertheless she does fit in here, inasmuch as the recognition of her existence should definitely influence the fundamental attitude of man toward the delicate and sacred subject of marriage. For, once the woman has made the male principle of movement her own, or rather, has been forced to do so by some inexplicable destiny, then it appears that the dislodged equilibrium can only be re-established by the man's acquiring a capacity which was formerly only possessed by woman and which is characteristic of persons in subjection. We mean here the virtue of *attention*, which developed out of a defensive attitude adopted by serfs and which is the most humane of all the virtues, if love goes hand in hand with it. Let us state it at the outset: Marriage in the case of the emancipated woman requires much more love, and creates much more love, than the average happy marriage of tranquil times did. By *attention* is meant the most delicate sympathy for one's nearest fellow-men; in this sense it has nothing to do with the polite attention of social circles. This delicate virtue is beyond chivalry and courtesy. It is never quiescent, always mobile, the gracious companion of every form of vital evolution. It is like a divinity, never tired; it is the humble little soul of that dual creature which a married couple essentially is. It never sleeps; it never trusts in the sense of letting things go; nor does it ever insist on rights, legal or erotic, as in the sense of property. It is this which, like a living genius, takes the place of the decadent taboo of sexual loyalty and the mystic inviolability of family honour. During the nineteenth century, marriage gradually changed from a social institution upheld by the state into a private relationship between two lovers. At any rate, from an ideal standpoint, marriage was looked upon as the endless extension of a love-relation. But we have already seen how man, as protector and avenger, has applied the idea of immutability to the loving and beloved woman. Emancipated woman has refused this requirement, together with the protector and avenger. She seeks a companion. She is forced to seek one. The corresponding demand in man, or to put it better, the conscious acquiescence of man, is still lacking. The signs of a change, *quand même*, are unmistakable; they appear, at a higher stage of cultural development, in the state of youth. In fact the man who today claims to be a protector is almost a curiosity, an obsolete form. At any rate the unwritten law of tomorrow will prove him so, and only such as can understand this law can do justice to the present.

This essay has had to force the most delicate and individual qualities of life into rough generalizations, in order to trace a connecting thread through all the complexities of experience. And at the end a vision that is both ironical and sublime rises before our eyes: that in all ages couples who were happy and complete in a pure way appear to be inclosed as in a thin shell that the ear cannot penetrate, but only the eye. The man or woman who has established his relation to the other half of the world soon grows mute and has nothing more to tell. We are aware of the solution, but we do not comprehend the secret measures that keep the harmony in delicate adjustment. The individual has found salvation, and the outside world remains full of the vexatious clamour of the problem.

BEATRICE M. HINKLE

Marriage in the New World

Among the many subjects agitating the minds of the people of the United States today none compares in its insistence and acuteness with the question of the future of the institution of marriage in America. A complete change in attitude, often in the form of a violent revolt against the former ideals and customs affecting the marriage relation, is in full swing, and the general uncertainty and instability in the relation is probably more marked than in any other country. People all over the land are aroused by the disturbed conditions and are arguing, writing, and preaching about it from all angles, in an effort to stem the tide of disaffection and disruption which is making such inroads on this ancient institution.

It is too late. The will of youth, together with the forces of social and economic change, are in full possession of the situation, and only a seer would attempt to predict what the outcome will be or when the final stage of disintegration will be reached. Nevertheless, there may be discerned definite tendencies which suggest possibilities of the future direction and render a study of the actual conditions of considerable importance in guiding, if not in stemming, the rapid movement.

The chaotic state of marriage is not confined to the United States; the same warnings are heard in England, where similar conditions are discussed and an anxiety is manifested which approximates our own. One questions whether the general disruption is peculiar to the Anglo-Saxon nations and, if so, whether it is due to the failure of the romantic ideal on which their marriages have been based.

There are differences in the American situation, however, which it is necessary to understand in order to account for the earlier beginnings of the laxity and the more exaggerated conditions manifested at present.

The most striking characteristic among the younger generation is the utter absence of any sense of responsibility or regard for anything except what affects their personal feelings. Obligations to society or custom, even duty to children, when they conflict with the individual's own wishes, scarcely exist. With none of the old restraining influences, marriage is entered into lightly and carelessly; even trial marriages and trial separations are frequent; divorce and remarriage follow each other in quick succession, and children are passed back and forth between the parents, whose only communication with each other is through their lawyers. The disrespect and careless attitude of children toward their parents is not a new phenomenon, but the disregard and neglect of parents, who pursue their own pleasures with little consideration of their duties to their children, is one of recent development. These conditions are found not only among the latest generation; the older group as well is swept along. Further, there is evident all over the United States a growing disinclination toward marriage, and this cannot be considered to bear any relation to differences in proportionate numbers of the sexes, such as exists in England; for here the numbers of men and women are about equal. Of much more influence is the frequency of divorce, the dislike of responsibility on the part of men, and the economic independence and greater demands in marriage on the part of women. In the thought of modern youth marriage is not the most important event in life.

In order to gain some insight into the forces operating to produce the extreme position occupied by the United States in this matter today it is necessary to review briefly the unusual conditions that have characterized our national and social life and to remember not only the youth of the nation but the effect of a primitive environment upon the spirit of a people. In the one hundred and fifty years of our national existence we have passed from a struggle with the wilderness and from the most primitive ways of life to a period of the most intense industrialism. Experiences and achievements which normally occupy many centuries have followed one another with startling rapidity. Intolerance of restraint, haste, impatience with delay, are all characteristics fostered by our environmental conditions, and they are now playing their part in the marriage situation.

American laws and social attitude and customs were modelled originally on the English code, and the same romantic ideal of love and happiness for the individual—so beautiful in theory and so difficult of attainment—ruled the marriage choice.

The severe legal restrictions surrounding women according to English marriage laws were rigidly adhered to by the early Puritan settlers. In addition, their conception of duty and responsibility was entirely opposed to the ideal of happiness for the individual after marriage. The people held to a stern moral and religious attitude and looked upon a divorced woman or one separated from her husband, regardless of the cause, as standing for ever in the shadow of disgrace. This was the beginning, and for a long time divorce was as difficult to obtain in America as it still is in England.

The most powerful force controlling conduct is public opinion crystallized into tradition, but in America these customs and this attitude were planted in virgin soil having no native substance of traditional life. Because they were taken over from without instead of growing up from within, there were no roots to nourish them; and for the coming generations they were bound to weaken and perish. Moreover, their disintegration was hastened by the very condition which at the time contributed to make Puritan marriages more enduring and in some ways more satisfactory than marriages of modern times. This condition was the sharpness of the struggle for existence in a primitive environment which made equal demands upon the women and the men.

The Puritan wife was noted for her devotion and unceasing labour beside her husband during the long pioneer period. Women were recognized as equally important with men in the general life. The small opportunity for social life, coupled with the mutually directed interests of husband and wife toward the same end—that of carving out a home and fortune for themselves in the new country—inevitably produced a closer bond in the marriage relation than exists when the major interests of one are separate from those of the other. Such a situation, unconsciously and regardless of laws, tends eventually to loosen the pressure of discriminating and restrictive measures surrounding marriage in its relation to women. A condition in which men are dependent upon women for their assistance and care tends always to produce in them a special attitude of respect and regard, which operates to lessen the frequently wide cultural distinction between the sexes and to bring about a more equal relation. This, in turn, affects the women, who become conscious of their own value and gain the capacity for that consciousness of self which has been the distinctive quality of masculine psychology and is necessary to command respect.

Thus, informally, great modifications were made in the old standards regulating marriage brought over from England. Moreover, because of the autonomous character of the states into which this country is divided, a curious situation of considerable psychological significance has arisen. Each state, as it entered the Union, brought its own laws, and these were either preserved or modified according to the predominant type and original nationality of its citizens. Thus it happens that there are scarcely two states that agree in their laws regulating marriage, and divorces and remarriages which are legal in one are null and void in another. There are only two issues on which all of the states have similar laws—bigamy and incestuous marriages. In other respects the restrictions range from no divorce at all to the greatest latitude.

Although such a situation arises primarily from the psychology of the people, it, in turn, influences the attitude of those living under it. Therefore, it is quite impossible to discuss the condition of marriage in the United States as a homogeneous affair, for there exist side by side all forms of and attitudes toward this ancient institution, forms quite as varied and heterogeneous as the laws of the different states.

This lack of uniformity in the external status has tended to produce an effect similar to that produced by too many laws: it has caused individuals to disregard law and the formal aspect and to take matters into their own hands, becoming a law unto themselves and conducting their relationships according to the dictates of their own immediate desires. As a consequence, we have groups for whom marriage possesses the same binding power as of old, existing next door to persons who are practically espousing a trial marriage.

All of these conditions are the special objective influences that have contributed to produce the particular state of chaos and disturbance which afflicts marriage in America today.

THE great change in the labour conditions of women inaugurated by the industrial revolution began when the country was still very young. The effect upon American women was not general or profound, however, for a long time, since our grandmothers in large numbers were still pioneers in some parts of this vast country. One by one, however, the factory took over the domestic occupations of women, while the men became more and more preoccupied with the pursuit of material values and the lure of the opportunities for exploitation offered by the new country. This left the women and children largely to themselves: the men, after their intensive labour, had little time or energy for the family or the love-life or for the development of those cultural and spiritual values which underlie a true companionship and are so necessary to women for any satisfactory married relationship. As a substitute for this—as soon as the men were able—they lavished money and material possessions upon their wives, looking to them to symbolize the success and prosperity which they themselves were too busy to enjoy.

As individual wealth increased, this condition spread and its influence permeated all classes. Practically all American husbands will say, when asked why they work so hard and intensively, that they do it for their families. This is the fiction which they repeat with monotonous uniformity, regardless of the fact that these same wives and families frequently implore their men to give them less of material things and more of themselves, that they may share interests together. The fact is the men are caught in a mechanism of their own creating, which now has become independent of the individual will and which drives them on, regardless of necessity or wish.

Nor is the problem less acute in the thousands of homes where wealth does not exist. The same industrial Moloch which with one machine has supplanted hundreds of brawny men is responsible for the curtailment of that other great labour of women—the bearing and rearing of many children, for which there is now no social demand. The few children and small routine household tasks left to women have permitted an enormous amount of unused human energy to accumulate without an adequate object for its employment. For ages women have been the steady labourers of the world, responsible for all that concerns the welfare of the family and the home. The reduction of this labour and responsibility by the machine and factory has fostered idleness and irresponsibility in many women.

Thus there is presented a social condition in which the most violent contrast exists between the sexes. The husband, even in wealthy circles, is so intensely occupied with his business interests that he has no energy left for more cultural fields or for the family, while the wife, because she has so much idle time on her hands, and no necessity to force her to independent constructive activity, becomes unhappy and neurotic—a waste product without meaning or purpose. This idle time lying heavily on the hands of such large numbers of women, who have been encouraged by their male relatives to seek out pleasure and personal gratification with which to fill the empty hours, has worked havoc not only on the marriage relation, but also on the moral character of many women, and contributed largely to the beginning of the present chaotic condition. American husbands have been notorious for their indulgence to their wives, but it has been similar to the indulgence of the fond father toward the child. Wives have been supplied freely with money; comparatively few demands or exactions have been made upon them; and they are able to travel, or to go on vacations, usually without the husbands, who are too busy to leave, or who prefer to take their pleasure unhampered by the responsibility of wife or children.

The men have been pathetic in their bewilderment at the turn of affairs. How many times I have heard husbands and fathers say, "What is the matter with my wife (or my daughter)? She has nothing to do but enjoy herself. I give her all the money she needs. Why can't she be happy? Why is she so restless?" It seems impossible for the masculine mind to realize that idleness and the pursuit of pleasure are as destructive to women as to men, and are accountable for much of the disorder and uncertainty so rampant among the present generation of young women.

However, this idle condition could not continue, since the energetic American woman possesses in her veins the blood of hardy pioneer life only recently behind her. There began a period of great restlessness and dissatisfaction. It is the dissatisfaction with, and unwillingness to accept, the rôle of parasitic woman, coupled with the complaisance of the American man and the lack of hard and fast tradition, that has resulted in the nearly free opportunity unequalled elsewhere in the world for women to engage in all forms of labour—professional, educational, and industrial—that are open to men. It is the refusal of the women to become a parasitic class, in spite of wealth and even facility to do so, that is the best insurance against the ultimate disintegration of marriage and the decay of American civilization. For the women in all healthy nations and culture periods have been the foundation and the upholders of the national life, and the final sickness and decay came when wealth and leisure produced a parasitic class of women, unable or unwilling to enter into the new and untried forms of labour which the masculine world offered.

The American woman is typically an active type, with a fund of available energy; therefore, in order to find a substitute for the old domestic labour, large numbers have pushed eagerly into occupations formerly monopolized by men.

The enormous expansion of industry, the constant development of new fields of labour, together with the pressure of the women for opportunities for remunerative work, created a steadily increasing demand for their services. It is safe to say that neither the men nor the women had any conception in advance of what effect the change in the status of women, brought about through working outside the home and the winning of economic independence, would produce in the marriage relation. For it is not possible to separate the changed attitude toward marriage from the changed status of women. One is dependent upon the other. It is women who have revolted and for whom the conflict over marriage has arisen.

The suppression of the woman's individuality and her personal needs and wishes for the sake of her husband, the submersion of herself in his life and interests, and in those of her children, has become no longer acceptable, since the whole social condition which demanded this has changed. And this applies not only to the present generation. Older women who have devotedly followed this ancient path have repeatedly told me that it had been a mistake, that it did not bring to either husband or wife the happiness and contentment which was expected from it, and that they would not submerge themselves in this way if they had the experience to live over again.

An interesting commentary on the submerging effect of marriage on women is afforded by the numerous instances in which wives separated by death or otherwise from their husbands have blossomed suddenly into happy, capable, useful individuals. Even among what have appeared to be successful marriages, there has come about, after the final adjustment had been made to the separation, the transformation of the wife from submergence, semi-invalidism, or a dependent, inconsequential existence to a healthy, socially valuable personality. This tells more eloquently than words of the damaging repression of the capacities of the women through marriage wherever social and industrial conditions place them in a situation limiting or inhibiting the full exercise of their active powers.

It is obvious why in the past marriage has been considered of far more importance to women than to men, for, owing to the limitation formerly placed upon women's occupation, it was only within marriage, as child-bearer and responsible creator and manager of the home, that she could find opportunities for the free exercise of her capacities.

It is the dislodgment of marriage from the supreme place in the interest and life of women that has produced the situation which a recent writer characterizes as the greatest revolution that has taken place in regard to marriage in all history.

To those who think in terms of the past and are unable to see any possible value arising out of the destruction of the old, the present chaotic condition of the marriage relation is a tragedy and means only the ultimate disintegration of our civilization. They forget that, if marriage as it has existed had been the satisfactory relationship which it was supposed to be, it is certain that women would not be in the revolt they are today; for even if it has ceased to be her sole occupation, every woman knows that marriage is still the most important function for her. But it is the disintegration of the outer shell that is producing the modern disturbance; the substance has long needed reorganization.

My own investigations have convinced me that there is little more unhappiness or mismating among modern marriages than there was in the days of our mothers and grandmothers. The great difference lies in the changed social attitude toward the married state itself. When practically the only occupation or position for women was marriage, and they were frowned upon or ostracized if they attempted anything different, both economic necessity (especially if there were little children to consider) and fear of condemnation kept them from expressing their dissatisfaction and deterred them from taking any steps toward a reconstruction of the relationship. Consequently, we heard little of their difficulties and unhappiness. Hard pioneering work still existed for the mass of women, and they were as inarticulate and submissive as of old to the demands made upon them. Only when the intense demand upon them was lessened, and the weight of necessity removed, did they begin to become conscious of their dissatisfaction.

The movement of women out from the home to the business and professional world has profoundly affected their psychology. They are fast awakening from their long sleep—a sleep in which they were unconscious of themselves as individuals and conscious only of the object—the man and the child for whom they lived. As Weiniger expresses it, the woman had no ego, no self, but patterned herself after the style or type desired by the man and the environment which he created. Woman's struggle today is the mighty birth throes of a new self.

The cult of the ego which dominates this age has produced its effect upon her, and she is becoming articulate and thinking. Her contact with the business and the professional worlds is creating a new consciousness within her, and she is demanding recognition for herself as an individual separate and distinct from man. Many of the forms which this unfamiliar attitude assumes are far from beautiful or attractive, and it is inevitable that this should be, for the pendulum has swung from one extreme to its opposite. It reminds one of the license and extravagance, indulgently known as the "sowing of wild oats," which occurs when a young man first escapes from the restrictions of stern parental authority. Women have escaped from the authority and restrictions imposed upon them as the result of the unalterable convictions of man that his wife was his property, and that she must live her life as he wished it. The twain are no longer one flesh—the man being "the one"—but instead they are two distinct personalities, forced to find a new basis of adaptation to each other and a new form of relationship.

IT can hardly be said as yet that the revolution of woman has gone beyond the stage of destructiveness. It is still closely connected with the divorce court and with extra-marital activities. In a recent series of interviews with hundreds of judges on the bench presiding over divorce trials in every part of the country, it was brought out that divorces had increased seventy-five per cent in ten years, and that eighty per cent of all divorce actions were brought by women. The attitude of the judges, who had listened to testimony given at thousands of trials, was unanimously sympathetic with the women; there was no condemnation, but instead a recognition that it is not divorce that needs legal restriction, but marriage that is diseased and in need of a complete reorganization. Meantime, women will not accept the marital conditions of the past, and the divorce court is the evidence of their discontent. The overwhelming part played by the economic factor in holding women to the marriage bond when marriage was their sole occupation has become tragically clear. Necessity held them for "better or worse," and "good" women remained married, regardless of the conditions, "when divorce barred them from heaven and human society." Now, when women, from those in the highest social positions to the mothers in factory and mill towns, can walk out with their children clinging to them and by their own labour provide for their care, there is no further necessity to accept the wretched relations. The entire attitude is summed up in the words of a young woman, "Why should I wait until I have six children? I will leave now while I have only three, for there is no future here for them or me."

Few men have any real comprehension of the situation. Only those who, like the judges, have had wide opportunity for unbiased observation of actual marriage conditions, are able to understand the psychology of the women. The others are aware that an unpleasant change has taken place, one which renders marriage conditions much more difficult for them, and they are in full retreat. The disinclination of men toward marriage is not a recent development, it is true; but their former attitude was more of an egotistic unwillingness to give up the pleasures of bachelor freedom or to assume the responsibility and obligations of a family. The present attitude is frankly one of fear and uncertainty regarding women.

The girls understand this change on the part of men little better than others understand their own attitude. One college-trained young woman gave the explanation that men are attracted only to morons; that the resourceful, serious, companionable girls are looked at askance; and only the irresponsible, incapable, physically attractive ones are sought in marriage. This may be a statement of fact, but it is not an explanation. The capable, intellectually developed girl demands much more development from the man than formerly and will not accept weaknesses and inferiorities that prevent her respect. This puts a strain on men and interferes with the operation of the pleasure principle. In addition, because of her mental qualities, this sort of girl is less appealing sexually than the purely emotional, sensuous type, and thus the relation is forced upon a new basis in which the intellectual aspect of the personality plays its part as well as the emotional. The girl enters the marriage state today with a full sense of herself as an equal partner in a relation which means a mutual give and take. She feels she has something to sacrifice for the new relation, as well as the man. There is little consideration of the claims of society or of its opinions. Marriage is regarded as a purely personal affair, and the major interest lies in the individual emotional problems and their solution. Even the children receive much less consideration than formerly.

One has only to talk with the young women just graduating from school—and this means not only college but also the finishing schools, which cater largely to the daughters of wealthy parents—to realize the attitude of modern girls. Marriage no longer holds the first and only position in their thought: they are busily concerned with the problem of what occupation they shall espouse and what training they shall take to fit themselves for it. It is this demand, so universal at present, that has influenced our colleges to establish courses in all sorts of practical subjects, for the whole tendency is to raise the status of woman's work, so that even in various household branches the college training puts the young woman in an equal class with the young man. I do not mean to imply that marriage is disregarded or out of the thought of these young women, for this is not so. On the contrary, owing to the timidity and fear on the part of men, they are more openly in pursuit of husbands than ever before, but with this difference—they want to make their own terms. Instead of conforming or fitting themselves to the ideal of the man, they are revealing themselves as they really feel. Marriage is no longer considered as the substitute for an occupation, nor does it take exclusive place in their thoughts. It is "my work" and marriage that they discuss.

Perhaps one of the factors influencing this attitude toward marriage is the freedom of thought and action on sexual matters that has replaced the former prudishness and coyness, so that the young women of today no longer look upon marriage as their mothers did. The ideal of virginity has largely lost its hold on the minds of young women, and the safety that modern knowledge has given them permits a freedom of action more nearly allied to that which men have always enjoyed. Their conduct has revealed more eloquently than argument how much fiction has been bound up with the traditional masculine ideas regarding their instinctive organization.

Instead of regarding marriage as the open door to all knowledge and life, their attitude is more like that of their brothers, and they think of it as something of a restriction and responsibility, even though a desirable and important state. The careless, superficial ones regard it as somewhat of a lark—a pleasant change in their lives, from which, if it becomes difficult, they can easily escape.

The conception of finality in relation to marriage has largely disappeared. The tendency in action is toward the trial marriage idea, although this is far from receiving social sanction, and the legal ceremonies still imply permanency and a contract for life.

Scores of young women are struggling with the problem of how to carry on the responsibilities entailed in marriage, the care of the children and home, and in addition, the occupation of their leisure time in some gainful and interesting way. For many it is necessary to add to the family income, for one of the results of the new economic freedom is a recently revived tendency toward earlier marriage. This is one of the contradictory phases of the present disordered condition. It is from the youthful impulses and willingness to take the chance and follow the fresh emotional urge toward mating that marriages are arising. Instead of waiting until the man has an income sufficient to maintain the wife and family in idleness, as has been the custom of the period just passing, the young couple, both of whom are working, decide to pool their interests. The wife's earnings often contribute materially to the income and, in a way, serve the same purpose as the *dot* in Europe—a custom which has never been known in America. The tremendous advance in the cost and the standards of modern living, however, has produced timidity and often inability on the part of the man to assume the heavy burden involved in the care of a family. The possession of an earning capacity by the wife contributes to a solution of this aspect of the problem.

On the other hand, many women in industrial life are earning more money than the men whom they could marry. Their positions are of the type that demand all of their time and cannot be continued in connection with other responsibilities. They desire to marry for the sake of the home and children, and their outside work is necessarily limited. They are thus confronted with the question of sacrificing for the sake of marriage the good position with an independent income often larger than that of the proposed husband, which must then suffice for two.

All these and numerous problems brought about by our industrial age are the external factors largely responsible for the chaotic condition of marriage today.

THERE is, however, another aspect and significance to all this disturbance which is less obvious, and before which the problem of the individual woman or of any one class of women fades away. This concerns its psychological significance and its effect upon the race.

For ages woman as an individual creature has been considered by the masculine mind to be inferior: only as mother did she possess a position and win recognition for herself. Therefore the mother-woman was the ideal toward which all women strove. But this was not woman as individual and differentiated; in this aspect she remained as far from attainment and recognition as ever. The present age is strongly individualistic, and it is impossible for women to remain untouched by this tendency. Consequently they cannot continue in their ancient path. Moreover, the need for a new direction and an awakening of their latent potentialities is very great, for if the women remain static and unchanged in their eternal maternal strength, as they are so often told they must, it is certain that the race will remain psychologically unchanged and bound fast to them. For a maternal woman is the weakness and the despair of man, the one to whom he at last inevitably succumbs. The race can move no higher than the women who bear it.

Today women are in a mighty struggle towards differentiation and an individual direction. They have cast aside the maternal ideal as their goal and are demanding recognition as individuals first, and as wives and mothers second. They are claiming the right to dispose of themselves according to their own needs and capacities and are often blindly reaching forth for that which proves to have no value. But this is an unavoidable part of all learning, and even foolishness has a value when learning is sought.

It is in this struggle that the women of America form the vanguard of a vast army. Through natural conditions and comparative freedom from the hoary bondage of tradition, they have had the opportunity to gain an independence of feeling and action which is unknown in the Old World. In the bloodless revolution that is in progress the institution of marriage, which for ages has symbolized for woman both her bondage and her power, is inevitably the greatest sufferer. Even motherhood is no longer held sacred and apart, as an end in itself, but is being subjected to the same disintegrating process. It is becoming clear that while all normal women can produce children, not all are mothers in the real sense of the term; and women are gaining the courage and honesty to declare this openly.

The sexual burden under which woman has struggled for so long is being rapidly cast away, and the safety from the consequences of her actions that modern science has provided is offering her an undreamed-of freedom, which is forcing upon her as an individual the responsibility for her actions. The relation between the sexes is perhaps in a more healthy and normal state than at any time of which we have historical knowledge. Sexual hypocrisy and pretence is largely a thing of the past. Men and women are meeting much more simply and directly as human beings and companions who have differences of opinion and attitudes needing understanding and adjustment, but who are unconcerned with keeping up a fiction which shall conform to an image each may hold of the other.

A complete reorganization of our ideas of the distinctions and relations between the sexes is being forced upon us, and if the man still fails to understand woman and see her as she really is—simply a human being full of faults and weaknesses, desires, and longings, not so different from his own—it will not be the fault of the women. It will simply be the man's inability to understand human psychology or else his unwillingness to surrender his subjective image of woman and his use of it as a symbol.

It is true that much that was beautiful and desirable in the past is being destroyed along with the ugly and outworn, and that the present condition of chaos is in no way satisfactory; but that is true of all revolutions. There is, also inevitably, much suffering and hardship, particularly accompanying the dissolution of individual marriages; but even here there is a complete change of attitude.

A particularly marked example of this change is found in a case which embodies both the old condition of marriage, with its insincerity and silences, and the modern shifting and instability, with its many inevitable unfortunate effects. The family, consisting of the parents and two children, is one of the best type, both husband and wife having a good family background, education, and cultivated tastes. Their marriage, entered into on a purely love basis when both were very young, had lasted for eighteen years, when quite suddenly the husband told his wife he did not love her any longer and wanted a divorce. The wife is the mother type, content with her home-making and her devoted care of the children, and quite unaware of what had been going on around her. Her husband's announcement was like the sudden dropping of a bomb into her Garden of Eden. With the blindness and unconsciousness typical of so many old-fashioned women, she had not the slightest notion that all was not well with those closest to her. "How could I know," she moaned, "that my husband did not love me any longer or was unhappy and dissatisfied, when he never complained or told me anything about it? He was a good husband and a loving father to the children, and did not complain about anything. I realized our relation was dull at times and there was little emotional stimulation, but I thought all married people became like that." On the husband's side, the subsidence of his love for his wife had been going on for years. Feeling that she was completely absorbed in her children, and that he was quite outside her circle, he had sought and found other companionship, and for several years, ostensibly to avoid having any more children, had had no marital relation with her. He had no other complaint except to tell her he felt he was merely wanted as breadwinner; and, with no effort to arrive at a new mutual understanding, he announced that he wanted to break with her and establish a new home.

The shock and pain of discovery brought to the wife the awakening she had needed. Instead of weakly succumbing, she inaugurated the discussions and efforts at understanding which should have taken place years before and which would have been successful had there been no other woman involved. There was a truer relation between these persons during the painful months of the wife's efforts to hold her husband and keep their home together than there had been for years previously; and although the husband did not recede from his position, the wife told me that she felt the experience had brought her an increased consciousness and a new understanding of life. After the first months of bewilderment and distraction the adjustment began, and she looked for and eventually found a new interest for herself outside of home and motherhood.

There was no ugliness between these people, for each desired simply to face the situation and, when finally the wife had accepted the idea that separation was inevitable, to make the change with the least possible injury to all concerned. It is to be observed that the children were not considered at all until the father's initial aim had been achieved. Then all possible effort was made to protect them from any unfortunate consequences that might arise from the separation of their parents. But the pursuit of personal happiness, which has so largely supplanted the conception of duty and responsibility to others as the dominant force in the marriage relation, is here revealed in its baldest form. Yet these are not careless, superficial people, but persons of high standards and ideals.

This case, which with slight variations is endlessly repeated, shows also the effect upon the man of the changed attitude toward marriage. He no longer wants the mother-woman but seeks a real companionship in which children are not the dominant factor. He has not yet reached the further attainment of being able to bring about the desired relation within the marriage circle.

It is these conflicting and varied aims and wishes that

are demanding a new consciousness and a differentiated type of human being in order to meet the new issues and needs involved in the marriage relation. The disintegration of the old conditions will force the differentiation required in the process of finding the new direction, just as it happened in the case of the wife and mother cited above. She will never again be the unawakened, ancestral type of woman which she was before her world crashed about her. The tragedy is that such disruption is needed to produce the effect.

It is safe to say that very few of the great numbers of disrupted marriages have any basis that could not be remedied if, with an awakened consciousness, husband and wife made a joint effort to develop a true relationship. What is needed is a deeper awareness of both self and the other person, coupled with a mutual desire to create a relationship, and a willingness on the part of each person to meet the difficulties directly and without evasion. The marriage must seem of importance and worth saving; then there will be a willing effort and sacrifice to make of it something of value to each.

The eager espousal by women of opportunities for labour in the various fields which have been occupied by men is bringing them into relation with collective life. It is giving them a clearer understanding of men and of their lives through their contact with an aspect of man's personality that is never seen under domestic and social conditions. The rending of the illusion and glamour surrounding man in the eyes of women, which the freedom of his life and the age-long tradition of superiority have lent him, is producing an objectivity of thought and feeling that will inevitably bring about that larger, more impersonal attitude in which women have been so lacking. It is also making for honesty in facing the facts of life and of themselves about which women have been quite blind.

The occupation outside the home which today carries for American women almost the same importance as marriage once carried has not robbed them of that altruistic spirit and impulse for service which has been the dominant spirit of women in the past, and which formerly found its only outlet in the interests of husband and children. This is shown by the eagerness with which all lines of work concerned with community life and social service are sought by women. The numerous welfare organizations, such as public health nursing, maternity care, and child welfare work, which are everywhere in evidence, are almost entirely in the hands of professionally trained women. At the same time there is the insistent desire for self-expression and for an occupation that shall enlarge the scope of the personality, so that a feeling of capacities fully utilized shall be gained.

It is this broader field beckoning women away from the narrow personal confines of family life which is giving them the opportunity for growth as individuals, and which is bringing a new attitude to the marriage relation. It is producing that new tendency toward a frank discussion of the difficulties and irritations arising, and an endeavour to clarify and alter the situation, instead of a quarrel with its accompaniment of bitter feelings, or an attempted concealment of the hurt and disappointment by resorting to silence, as was the former procedure.

It cannot be hidden from any one that there is a quickened consciousness in the world today, a sense of something inadequate and unsatisfactory in the ideals and conceptions we have held, and a groping after new values. Women are in the forefront of this awakening and this groping, even though the hasty actions, the avoidance of responsibility, the pleasure-seeking and noisy chatter frequently obscure the deeper-lying significance of what is occurring. These phenomena are but the bubbles on the surface of the swift-flowing waters—the most obvious and glaring accompaniments of this first stage of so-called freedom or equality for women. They are the inevitable products of collective psychology, and must needs be before any emergence of the new values can occur.

It is even probable that comparatively few women are aware of the new great social issues to which they are contributing any more than the common soldier is aware of what he is fighting for in war. They are consciously concerned only with their individual problems and welfare.

Nevertheless, a new ideal in relation to marriage is arising. The old ideal of duty and responsibility to society, to religion, and even to family, which kept marriage intact, is gone, never to return; but a new duty and responsibility, more solemn, more binding, and more imperative than the old, is here. Just as to all men of honour their unsupported word seriously given engages their feeling of integrity and responsibility, binding them far more securely than all the legal and business restrictions could do, so the new ideal of personal freedom in marriage places upon the individual a responsibility far heavier than that of the past.

Marriage is a duty of the individual to himself, for only within such a close relation voluntarily entered into can there be found those opportunities for the development of an individual integrity, of an adaptation to reality, and of those higher human attributes without which there is no such thing as a real happiness for the individual or for the world. A failure in making the strongest efforts to work out a satisfactory relation is a failure of the individual within himself. Therefore, instead of acting from impulse and personal gratification in regard to marriage, the necessity exists for an honesty toward oneself, for serious reflection and thoughtful action—intellect cooperating with feeling—in order to insure the basis for the development of a true relationship.

Furthermore, this ideal involves a far greater and more impersonal aspect than that of the individual or of the family; it reaches out to embrace the whole problem of general human relationships. For whether the individual considers it or not, the welfare of society depends upon marriage and the family more than on anything else. Therefore, a new ideal and a new reality attained by individuals in marriage is the first step toward the attainment of new world relations.

To carry this ideal through and to create thereby a new life of relationships is the great social task of women.

I am just in receipt of a letter from a gifted young woman who is in the midst of this struggle, first, to attain and preserve her individual separateness and express herself through her gifts, and secondly, to preserve and create something adequate out of a very difficult marriage situation. It illustrates the new condition very well, and I shall quote her words:

> I realize that I have been living a dream with Harvey. Now my eyes are opened and I see the situation as it really is. I have not faced it before, but have tried to pretend that it was all right and that things were as I wanted them to be. This has meant, of course, that I have been emotionally bound, and thus unable to come through to any real human relationship. Harvey has been so jealous of me in every way—he can't bear that I should be successful or have anything of my own, and he constantly criticizes everything about me and everything that I do. Our whole marriage relation is dependent upon his moods. But I've got to

work it through. I know I mustn't run away, although sometimes I think I can't bear it any longer. I think there must be some new relation between husbands and wives that can be attained. But to gain that there must be a real morality between them, for the new evolution of love and reality.

These words illustrate very clearly the deepened consciousness of the young woman, and the new attitude to the situation.

I have said very little about the deep-lying psychological problems involved in marriage, for they are the problems of the psychological development of the individual.

When the personalities are emotionally immature, caught in the auto-erotic phase of development, incapable of love for an object, but demanding that their emptiness shall be filled by the other person, there is little possibility of a satisfactory marriage unless a definite effort at recognition and overcoming of the personal inadequacy is made.

We have heard much of sex antagonism and the fundamental enmity between the sexes, but from a long experience I can say that there is no sex antagonism between persons who have freed themselves from their infantile desires and mechanisms and are emotionally mature. The struggle in the soul of man between love and power is the basis of sex antagonism and is at the same time the condition which operates to destroy the whole fabric of human relations.

The marriage ceremony marks the beginning of the great opportunity for the development of an emotional maturity in which the sense of justice, of consideration, of understanding, and of forbearance toward others shall be born. These attributes represent the greatest need of each individual today, not only to produce a satisfactory marriage, but also to bring about happier human relationships in general than those at present existing. The importance of an inward harmony of personalities in marriage is recognized as never before, and this vision and ideal toward which both men and women equally shall strive is the new demand of women in the marriage relation. These are the first fruits of woman's new-found individualism.

One of the happiest marriages I have ever known is conducted on a strictly modern basis externally, and internally the living of the new ideals has produced a reality not met in the finest marriages of the past. There are four children in the family, one of them adopted. There is a beautiful home, exceptionally well organized and managed; the domestic machinery runs without friction. But the peace is not that of a sheltered life. Besides fulfilling so capably her duties to her husband and children, the wife is actively interested in politics and in civic and educational reform. During political campaigns she makes most successful state-wide speaking tours. In all this she has her husband's sympathy, and often his counsel. Nor is she less interested in his activities. There are two distinct individualities here, with separate and mutual interests which they share in a rare companionship. A visitor feels the warm vitality of this home as soon as he enters it and, needless to say, there is no marriage problem. The wife's surplus energies are fully occupied in a socially valuable way. She is her husband's companion as well as his wife and home-maker, and their contentment is obvious to all. This is by no means an isolated case. Scores of such marriages already exist, and many women are making honest and intelligent efforts to increase the number. Homes like this are the islands that provide the soil from which the higher human society of the future shall develop.

Woman possesses, through her maternal impulses of love and service, the instinctive basis for the evolution of the new humanity in which the principles of understanding, of love, and of altruism shall supersede the principles of power and greed. She is the sex which gives birth to the new generation in the physical realm. The responsibility is upon her to bring forth the new humanity in the spiritual realm. But this is not an instinctive act, like the first one, but a task that requires the greatest self-consciousness, and a volitional effort of the highest order.

The great movement which is now sweeping over the land, affecting the women of all classes, carries with it something immeasurable, for it is the destroyer of the old mould which for ages has held women bound to instinct. The new humanity which is crying to be born needs a new womb and a new mother with unfettered capacities to bring it to birth, and to nourish it.

This is the underlying significance of the struggling woman, and of the new marriage which she is demanding.

THOMAS MANN

Marriage in Transition

An Open Letter to Count Hermann Keyserling

Dear Count Keyserling:

To entice people to skate on thin ice is a not very humane pastime which has characterized philosophers ever since the days of Socrates. I have often heard it said that you were one of these, and now I no longer doubt it, since you have intrusted us with subjects for literary treatment which are the most slippery and thinnest of ice—indeed, so slippery and treacherous that one has to evince much courage and a great desire to wish to dance on it at all, or to find it, as Nietzsche said, a "paradise." For this carnival on the precarious ice, which you have instigated, it would be advisable to have a number of Red Cross stretcher-bearers in readiness. One can certainly foresee that there will be accidents, and no one can predict that he will not be one of the victims himself. Nevertheless, it would never do to be merely a bystander. One's only excuse would be cowardice. One is married and has not the right to say: This thing, this extremely problematic thing, let the devil take it! The summons has something about it that makes it a duty to ourselves and our age to comply. *Hic Rhodos, hic salta.*

Marriage—a problem. This too has become a problem, as everything else has, with time. Our grandparents, bless them, would not have understood it. They are bad times in which the necessary, the original, order no longer seems spiritually possible, no longer suits the heart of man. The latter is a problematic enough creature as it is; bound to Nature, responsible to intellect, plagued by conscience, driven to ideals and to absurdities, with the propensity of invariably sawing off the branch on which he is sitting. Take, for instance, the case of domestic servants, who form one of the social pillars of the relationship, that is to say, of the original order, under discussion. Marriage is certainly not a middle-class institution; it is, using the word in its widest sense, the citizenship of life (*Lebensbürgerlichkeit*); but it has middle-class and social components which are at present deranged. The domestic-animal-like state of man- and maidservant, the status of retainer and menial, has hardly survived even in the country in its original primitive and epic sense, while in the towns it has completely disintegrated, having been dragged into the spheres of ethical criticism as applied to social conditions of emancipation and dissolution. Every one realizes that the domestic servant class, as a patriarchal survival, has, thanks to the generous stupidity of mankind, been already for a long time in an impossible condition, and no one can predict the end. For the epic conception of the household, as Kant still had it, composed of the man, wife, children, and retainers, is already disintegrated on this account. I maintain that marriage is not a middle-class institution. I wish to insure it against the most crushing deprecation of the time, and also against the mistake which so easily creeps in when the word is used in its revolutionary sense: the confusion between actual citizenship and that primordial form which is timeless and ageless, and is eternal with the human race. I do not know whether it is conservative of me to believe in it; at any rate I do believe in it. For example, I believe in the eternity, in the pre- and past-bourgeois validity, of the fundamental forms and spirits of art; I believe in the eternal epic spirit, which owing to the mistake already noticed is often stigmatized today as middle-class. It must be admitted that middle-class principles often appear fused with timeless, primordial, and immutable principles to a degree that makes differentiation difficult. For instance, the nineteenth century, which was essentially the century of the middle classes, cherished the primeval epic spirit, the "eternal Homeric"; Dickens, Balzac, and Tolstoy, and Wagner in the theatre, wrought with it their gigantic works. Whatever still exists of the great epic form, though disintegrated and intellectualized, belongs to the nineteenth, the century of the middle classes, and not to the twentieth. The ancient patriarchal relation of woman, as the "housewife," to man, was also civil. "And he shall be thy lord and master" is not merely biblical; it is Old Frankish as well. What we are experiencing, or rather, have already outlived, is the social undermining of this biblical and civil condition, by the emancipated woman who is free to ride bicycles, drive cars, and study. She has become intellectual and to a certain degree masculine. The emancipation of woman, which began in such a childish and ridiculous way, a bogey to all middle-class conservatism, which in its turn had mistaken middle-class tenets for eternal values, has yet produced many lasting effects that are irredeemable and irreparable and have become a part of progressive life.

Here it is all a question of a levelling up between the sexes, which gives rise to the most curious phenomena in the real inner history of mankind. Already Wedekind (I think it was in *Franziska*) remarked icily: "The difference between men's and women's clothing is vanishing all over the world." For his mincing taste (which at the same time sought the primordial in woman), dress that meant the liberation of woman's body, as sport and sports clothes did, was the most interesting feature. Naturally it did not escape his notice that all outward signs are the symbols of a corresponding internal state, and that interdependence exists between the two. Everywhere the feline character of woman has survived to a satisfactory degree and might with justice be termed eternal. It is the outcome of the will and the desire to allure man as something mysterious, with a sweet and strange contrast of sex. In general, however, the irresistible tendency is toward equalization and assimilation, and continues so in all spheres of life; in education, in professional thoroughness, in the freedom of movement in sports and politics. And this is no longer done from the standpoint of ambitious emancipation and in a competitive spirit, but much more as a self-evident and natural fact, which does not meet with any serious opposition from man, who is more inclined to meet her halfway; and this is by no means a merely formal attitude on his part.

I do not wish to imply that he becomes "effeminate"; so, too, to say that woman is becoming "masculine" is hardly correct. And the practical measure of hair-bobbing so as to avoid lengthy hairdressing, which can be made to look very womanly and charming, has nothing in common with the biassed way the former suffragettes used to do their hair. But certain aspects of manliness are lost: the gallant, cock-a-hoop, rough, arrogant, stupidly condescending, and venerating at the same time; the atmosphere of the middle-class ball-room, excited and puerile, erotic, stiff, formal, obscene, and stupid. In reality the change consists in both sexes becoming more fully "human," and this facilitates companionship. We only need to watch young people a little in order to ascertain that there is not much left of chivalry, courtesy, drawing-room behaviour; of *galanterie* and *minauderie.* The young man is no longer martial, stiff-backed, with heels clicked together, and heavily moustached. He shaves, making his handsome youth (inasmuch as all young life is beautiful) resemble more the beauty of a woman. His carriage has, in accordance with the fashion of the day, a somewhat soft and feminine air, and his movements are a little like dancing. He also wishes to appear "beautiful"—which is a human characteristic, but not a truly "manly" one; ambition is no longer set on being "manly" or "womanly." Or else he knows that he is beautiful. And this is in turn connected with another and more general emancipatory movement, which consists in *youth* demanding to be recognized, not as a preliminary human stage, subject to authority, but as possessing an independent significance; it even exaggerates its own importance until it conceitedly claims to be the actual and classic ideal of humanity; in any case it has discovered and represents its own specific beauty. Beauty was always, and today is more consciously and emphatically, the property of youth in general, and not merely a feminine aspiration and idea. Where this idea is at hand, the complete and rough conception of "manliness" is impossible: there is something feminine attached to the very essence of beauty—compare in this respect the artist, who has never yet been a complete and rough type of man. There is something androgynous, of which the Romanticists dreamed, in this human comradeship between the two sexes that I have spoken of. It is certainly not due to mere chance that this possibility of comradeship should just coincide with the psychoanalytical discovery of the original and natural bisexuality of the human race. And if our young people—and we wish them prosperity in this!—feel more clear and tranquil as regards sexual matters than former generations were able to do, it is because this subject is now practically free from all its former taboos. And doubtless it is on this account that homosexual phenomena are given a much more patient consideration by modern youth—in fact, since Blüher's time this is psychologically connected with at least one phase of the "youth movement," the *Wandervogel*.

Without doubt homosexuality, the love relation between man and man, sexual companionship, is at present considered impartially, and is no longer looked upon merely as a clinical monstrosity by educated people. It is not a mere coincidence that in France, the country of gallantry *par excellence*, one of the outstanding writers has lately published a dialectic and apparently passionate apology concerning this part of man's affective nature, after having for a considerable time withheld it from publication. In fact it is not seemly to decry and ridicule an affective sphere which has produced the Medici monuments and the statue of David, the Venetian sonnets and the *Pathétique*. The state, inasmuch as it blindly requires as many births as possible, an increase in the population *à tout prix*, may still adopt punitive measures, although antiquity teaches us that it might find several reasons for interesting itself in this condition quite apart from the fact that Hans Blüher, whom I have already referred to, has made it seem very plausible in his book that the genesis of the state itself may have actually arisen out of this affective sphere. Nor can homosexuality be deprecated from an abstract aesthetic point of view; still less is condemnation possible from a generously humane, emancipatory, anti-utilitarian, and consequently, by implication, anti-natural standpoint, while to decry it as unaesthetic is the least logical of all manifestations against it. The practical aspect of the matter is different, however. But does it not also finally depend on the idea of its being unnatural? At any rate, aesthetics is beyond morals and ethical considerations and has nothing to do with the law of life or with the conception of utility or fecundation. It will prove difficult to apply humanely aesthetic arguments against the emancipation of eroticism from the service of utility and propagation; that is, from the interests Nature has in the matter, the love-illusion which is only her seductive trick, a means of realizing her fertilizing schemes. Where the idea of beauty reigns, there the law of life forfeits its precedence. The principle of beauty and form does not spring from the sphere of life itself; its relation to life is that of a stern critic and corrector. It is indeed proudly melancholic, and it is closely and deeply allied with the idea of sterility and death. Platen says:

> Wer die Schönheit angeschaut mit Augen,
> Ist dem Tode schon anheimgegeben.[1]

And yet those two lines express the primordial foundation of all aestheticism, and consequently with good reason homosexuality has been termed erotic aestheticism.

But who will deny that from a *moral* point of view this is its very condemnation? It possesses no sanction excepting that of beauty, and that is virtually the sanction of death. It lacks the approval of Nature and life. This may be its pride, but it is a heavy-hearted pride, and at the same time it is also its culpability and infamy; and thus it is branded as hopeless and irrational. In questions of Nature and life, the lack of approval amounts

[1] "He who sees beauty with his eyes is already bespoken by death."

to a curse. A curse indeed lies on this free, all-too-free love, quite apart from the condemnation of society, which in this "humane" age, only too ready to amuse itself at any cost, is not over-strict and shows considerable patience. This kind of love is liable to end in coarseness and misery, even if it commences as a noble intuition. It is "free" love in the sense of barrenness and hopelessness, of inconsistency and irresponsibility. It leads to nothing and has no foundation to build on; it is *l'art pour l'art,* which is fine enough from an aesthetic point of view, but is certainly immoral. It harbours within itself a feeling of hopelessness, being without root or a sense of responsibility toward the future, and lacking connection. Its substance is libertinage, fickleness, gipsydom. It also lacks loyalty. If I am not mistaken there is no love so untrue, with so little sense of responsibility, and straying so much in all directions. That in antiquity it held the phalanx together and formed comradeships firm in life and death is only an apparent contradiction. "What kind of love is this," even one of the ancients asked, "that hangs by a hair and is past as soon as the beloved's beard begins to grow?" It skips about like a will-o'-the-wisp; it turns from one object to another, which is not so in the case of the love that obeys the call of life. I always found it humorous and naïve when Goethe, who was rather a "free" and egoistic lover before he married, admits: "It is a pleasant emotion when a new passion makes itself felt in us before the old has been completely extinguished. Just as it is nice to see, when watching the sunset, the moon rising on the opposite side, and to take pleasure in the double light of the two heavenly bodies." But it seems to me that this candid disloyalty is not to be compared with the freedom of homosexuality—which is a sign of its want of stability and instinct for enduring aftection: it is not creative; it does not build families and races.

Fidelity is the great superiority attaching to natural, creative love, which makes marriage possible. The laws of the Jews, who were from the earliest times well versed in these matters, threatened intercourse with boys with the death penalty. A contemporary philosopher who is a member of this moral race, Hermann Cohen, finds that fidelity is the synthesis of Eros and Ethos, of sexuality and morality. "For the sake of fidelity," he says, "marriage must exist"; real fidelity in love is only possible in marriage. Actually, marriage is only the working out and creation of the instinct of fidelity; it is at the same time its begetter, school, nourishment, and guardian. They are one, and it is quite impossible to say which came first, marriage or fidelity; and both seem equally absurd when imagined in connection with homosexuality. All that marriage represents—namely, durability, the foundation of life, propagation, responsibility—homosexuality does not; and as a sterile libertinage it is the very opposite of fidelity. Here it becomes more apparent than anywhere else to what an extent virtue and morality are essential to life—nothing less than its categorical imperative, the law of life itself—whereas all aestheticism is pessimistically orgiastic in nature; that is to say, it is a part of death. That the whole of art is inclined to lead to the bottomless pit is only too certain. But art, in spite of its connection with death and beauty, is still in a wonderful way associated with life, and finds in itself the antitoxin; friendliness and benevolence toward life make up the artist's fundamental instinct. He must possess to a certain degree the sense of citizenship in life and ethics, in spite of art and virtue having so little in common, if he is to be at all eligible for social intercourse. The artist, so it seems to me, is in reality the (ironical!) mediator between the realms of death and life. . . . Did you just call me to order? I obey, and become personal. In his early work, which was also intended to furnish his material life with a foundation, the youth had already dealt with the questions of marriage and fatherhood in a very pessimistic sense and spirit. The metaphysical experience on the strength of which Thomas Buddenbrook determined to face death had made marriage, inasmuch as it was "an attempt to continue one's life honourably and historically in that of one's descendants," seem a failure to him; and he denied that it could free him from "the dread of a final historic dissolution and decomposition." "I had hoped to continue living in my son? In a still more cowardly, weak, and vacillating personality? What a childish, misleading stupidity! What use is a son to me? I do not wish to have a son! Where shall I be when I am dead? I shall be in all people who ever pronounced the word *I*, and in those who are saying it, and will say it in the future, but especially in such as say it with vigour and cheerfulness. . . ." This alienation from the idea of the family and the perpetuation of the race, this flight into the metaphysical, is the expression of the same process of decay in the discipline of life, a return to the orgiastic freedom of individualism, which I described again in *Tod in Venedig*, giving it the shape of a homosexual love for a boy. The ideas of individualism and death were always closely connected (my book, *Betrachtungen eines Unpolitischen*, which dealt with the war, was written entirely in the spirit of romantic individualism, i. e., in the spirit of death; it was certainly a native sphere that I defended against social "virtue," which at that time seemed to me an affront and merely a literary fashion); it was a different matter with the idea of life and the duty of service, of social intercourse and dignity itself. Thomas Buddenbrook and Aschenbach are dying men, deserters from the discipline of life and morality, Dionysians of death: I very soon recognized this as a part of my own character. I will not call it the artistic impulse in me, for let me repeat again that an artist who has not a moral feeling for life is an impossibility; it is best expressed by the instinct to work; it is "thoroughness," it is sociableness, even when it produces a work which is furthest remote from life. I made clear at the very outset my conception of art, and the mediatory function I ascribed to it: We are the sorrow-bearing children of life, but nevertheless we are her children and were intended to participate in moral goodness. At twenty-four I could tell the story of my flight, as a broken man, into metaphysical individualism—I really had comprehended it at that age. But comprehension is something quite different from actual being; it is at best only a part of that. Goethe rather knew about Werther than was actually a part of him; otherwise he could not have continued to live and work. And the young author of Thomas Buddenbrook married a few years after he had led his hero to his death.

Hegel said that the most moral approach to marriage brought first the determination to get married, and then affection following in its train, so that finally both were present. I read this with pleasure, for it was exactly so with me, and is doubtless very often the case. *Auf Freiersfüssen gehen*[2]—which does not mean being in love or engaged, only desirous of and eligible for marriage—is the popular expression for it. In an idyllic poem I have described personally the motives for marriage and the es-

[2] There seems to be no English equivalent for this. Literally translated it signifies to walk on the feet of a suitor or would-be bridegroom.—*Translator's Note.*

sence of it, and I have left no doubt as to its psychological implications. The troop of children which the young father, who was but lately single, sees quickly gathering around him, surprise him and arouse his "childish pride," just as every reality does that comes true to the dreamer. In fact, for the latter, reality seems more fantastic than any dream, and flatters him all the more. The young master of the house "is not a little proud of his connection with the state and his part in middle-class security." But his fears and forebodings are also depicted, his secret aversion. The anxiety to retain his "freedom and solitude" made him rebellious against the life he had "honestly sought and morally desired." The unique experience of fatherhood is also described: to see the creatures of one's aspirations and destiny transformed into flesh and blood and appear as human beings, with a destiny of their own; to see oneself surrounded by a reality which appears to have sprung from the land of dreams, and not from real life—out of a dream that has on this occasion in some wonderful way become a "human enterprise," whereas usually his dreams only develop into literary works. And consequently one could speak of "adventure, of intricate adventure," when one glances at these little people, "the most cozy of all human beings," for they grow out of the dream and out of "a benevolent and upright attitude toward life."

This "benevolent and upright attitude toward life" and the will to adventure in the sphere of reality, to embark upon a "human enterprise, to convert emotions and dreams into real life," is the psychological formula for all morality and social life. It is the antidote to that metaphysical individualism which must be looked upon as the dissolution of the moral order of life, as an orgiastic liberation; and its erotic aspect is sterile homosexuality with boys.

The latter, as I have already pointed out, is intrinsically disloyal, whereas marriage, according to Cohen, "is the grounding of love in loyalty." Love that leads to marriage is creative love. The fact that makes marriage worthy of admiration and respect is that it converts a dream and an infatuation such as love, if it is founded on loyalty, into human enterprise and a marvellous producer of adventures in reality. Hegel has given us many beautiful definitions of married love. For instance, he terms it "morality in a natural form"; he could have termed it also "Nature in a moral form." Is not its significance much above that given it by the Catholic Church, which does not regard it as a sacrament, but merely as an indulgence; and is not marriage and its foundation of love a sacramental mystery? It is not without a purpose that the philosopher is desirous that it should maintain its religious character—piety, which should form an integral part of it. For it is not only a question of establishing morality in the flesh, but also the reverse, the establishment of spirit in the body; and the latter comes first, because flesh and blood are a part of all sacramental, sacred, and mystical beings, and not spirit alone is holy. If there are sacraments above the sacraments of the church, then there may also be institutions superior to society; and it is this reciprocal relationship between body and spirit in marriage that reminds one so astonishingly of the essence and relation of art; it is this that gives it its indelible sacramental character and its permanence as an original institution in the procession of the ages.

I return to my principal theme. It is the fashion of the day to turn everything into a problem; even eternal values, and things that are holy, indispensable, and axiomatic are treated in this manner—they are made to appear impossible, irretrievably disintegrated. That time should make the eternal values of the human race, the original institutions, problematical, can only be a *transitional* phenomenon, and does not imply cessation and dissolution. Like everything else, marriage is today in a process of transition; to think of its termination and end is absurd. Are there more unhappy marriages at present than in the days when the patriarchal and religious element was stronger, and a sense of holiness and consecration brought pressure to bear upon it and restrained the consciousness, functioning, and subjective effect of "unhappiness" and the idea of divorce? It is possible, even likely. Freedom, individualism, an exaggerated sense of personality (just where its justification proved most difficult), and the conception of "the right to happiness" accorded unhappiness and the desire to find a solution easier access to consciousness. Among other things, marriage is a problem of authority and subordination. One part—and this among other things explains its decay—must be subordinate to the other; and in the old, the "classical" form of marriage, in accordance with its patriarchal spirit, it was woman who was so. This has now become impossible, on account of her emancipation, individualization, liberation, and equality. "He shall be thy master" is an entirely obsolete attitude—and yet it was this very principle which, if it did not alone render marital community possible, at least incomparably simplified it. Not unlike this is the situation with the patriarchal-authoritative relationship of parents to children, which likewise, thanks to the emancipation of the young, can no longer be maintained. I say nothing of the servants, who, through decreased intimacy and socialistic legalization of the relationship, have become highly independent domestic employees. We see, then, marriage and the "household" menaced and rendered problematic by the husband through licentiousness, the right to happiness, and the right to change, if his felicity does not appear to him to be perfect; by the wife, by the children, and by the servants through emancipation, attained self-assurance, liberty, and personality. Cultural differentiation stands in connection with all this and comes under this head. It complicates and renders most difficult the binding together of two human beings for life—which in fact is possible only through patriarchal simplicity of feeling, of sense, and of the nerves of both parties—and makes indispensable an entirely different degree of consideration, indulgence, tact, diplomacy, delicacy, goodness, self-control, and art from that which pertained to a "happy" marriage in more primitive times. Naturally, irritability has inordinately increased. Comte Talleyrand's definition of marriage, *deux mauvaises humeurs pendant le jour et deux mauvaises odeurs pendant la nuit* ("two bad tempers during the day and two bad smells during the night"), must have struck many an intelligence. Consequently: separate bedrooms (while only a short time ago the patriarchal custom of sleeping together appeared an attribute of a good and righteous marriage), independence, different interests and occupations, reduction of possibilities of friction and irritation. And yet, the vibration of infinite impatience in the voices of married people, even in company—an expression which at every moment threatens shameful explosions of accumulated quantities of nervous torture and desperate irritation. Strindbergian remembrances arise even from a superficial observation of the majority of marriages—infernal recollections. Truly one may, even without malice, easily gather the impression that today ninety per cent of all marriages are unhappy—admitting the assumption that percentage calculations, or even conjectures and estimates, are permitted and possible in connection with such relative and fleeting concepts as happiness and unhappiness.

Why then, in view of all this, is not the possibility of the institution of divorce more often resorted to—since there is hardly anything socially scandalous still attached to it? Why, in spite of all this, do so many more marriages endure than are actually divorced, the great majority, almost all, one might say? Looking for the reasons, we find the most commonplace turning into the highest. Even in bad cases, practical difficulties combine with human indolence to resist the resolves of separation and even the thought of it, that slothfulness which, as Novalis says, "chains us to painful conditions." But in this natural inertia, something deeper enters, something more spiritual and more moral, something of that piety which Hegel mentions; the still trivial habit may furnish the transition; for it is nothing else than deep-rooted community of fortune, union in life, as well as through the children; it becomes piety, and even in faithless periods, it develops into a more or less conscious and discipline-creating sense of the sacramental character of marriage as "creative love." Even in bad cases, as we have said—and how much more in happier ones!—spiritualization and this awakening consciousness of the sexual bond, of which Hegel speaks, makes itself felt; it far surpasses the mere sexual bond, and at some moments—nay, always—leaves it far behind. Were marriage nothing more than what Immanuel Kant sombrely defined it in his abominable bachelor way, "the tying together of two persons of different sex to a lifelong reciprocal possession of their sexual qualities," it would never have shown this individual and institutional capability of resistance which it has so much opportunity to prove in our day. Such definitions recall the truism that the essentially brutal is the abstract.

Finer, richer in knowledge, and more human are those remarks of Hegel—dominated by all that insight which is appropriate before a theme so intimate, so manifold, and requiring so much piety. Hegel is delicate enough not to look upon marriage, so long as it endures, as a legal relationship. The law, he says, should be intruded into marriage for the first time when the family is about to be dissolved and its parties seek to become independent. He similarly declines to inquire after any principal aim in the relationship. He sees in it a peculiar unit, the purport of which is not impaired by the disappearance of any one or another of its possible ends. The marital relationship, he means, may "fulfil itself in mutual love and help." It is also clear that this is always the case with aged married people, and that, if the relationship rested alone upon the intercourse between the sexes, marriage as such would automatically be effaced with the coming of sexual frigidity—exactly the contrary of which is true. This does not prevent sexual intercourse from having a place in its sacramental concept. Marriage is "love"; that is, creative sexual union is transmuted into a sacramental foundation of an enduring partnership of life and fortune which outlives it. The sexual intercourse of marriage thereby differentiates itself from all others; "free," since with it there is associated the thought, the view, the goal of such creative love. According to Kant, marriage would exist for no other purpose than to facilitate sexual intercourse, and there do exist cases where it is so; where the passion for a woman, who is "not to be had" otherwise, determines the man, who for his own part would much prefer to remain single, to marry her. Such a marriage may still go not too badly, but that its moral basis is not of the best appears from Hegel's saying that in true marriage the resolve on matrimony is the primary element, the individual preference the secondary element. One does not marry a woman simply in order to "possess" her. The sexual community to which marriage leads and which lays its sacramental basis is something essentially different and more susceptible of spiritualization than that for the attainment of which one is not necessarily obliged to marry. It must be exactly this difference which exalts that "habit" which permits the persistence of the majority of marriages until death against all individual injuries and disturbances, even more than mere indolence, endurance, and resignation, and which confers upon marriage as an institution its stability through the ages, its character of the Eternal Human.

But the Eternal Human is capable of change. It must and will be; it cannot perish, but rather only proceed into new forms of life, like everything related to it. That it might in time become impossible is only an illusion; it bears within itself the powers which teach it how to consecrate itself anew after every desecration. Does any one seriously believe in the end of the basic phenomenon of *art*, which yet in the most persuasive manner appears theoretically to become impossible? The psychoanalytical recognition of its bearer, the artistic type, begun by Nietzsche; the intellectualistic analysis of art-forms; the nihilistic ridiculing of themselves which artists practise through their most gifted representatives, so that only the less gifted and most reactionary still appear to take art seriously: does not all this unmistakably bespeak the end? And yet art is also a sacrament; spiritual, but based in the carnal; so it was and so it will remain. So also will marriage be, and so will it know how to draw out of the depths of life a new consecration. But the worst thing and the most wrong everywhere is restoration. The time, which shudders before itself, is full of impulses to restoration, vacillation, retrogression, reinstatement of the old and worthy, restoration of destroyed holiness. In vain! There can be no going back. Every escape into historic forms which have become empty of life is obscurantism; all pious "suppression" of knowledge creates only lies and disease. It is a false piety, turned toward death and fundamentally faithless, since it disbelieves in life and in its inexhaustible powers of consecration. The way of the spirit must everywhere be travelled to the end, so that the spirit may exist again. It cannot be a question of suppression and restoration, but rather of the embodiment and the spiritualization of knowledge toward the growth of new dignity, form, and culture.

LEONIE UNGERN-STERNBERG

The Marriage of the Future

MARRIAGE is of a twofold character: first it is an institution, and secondly, it is a purely personal relationship between a man and a woman. The institutional character of marriage has prevailed through the centuries. Personal affection was not an important consideration in the conclusion of a marriage; marriage itself was a sacrament of the church, and as such was indissoluble. Under these circumstances the question of subjective happiness had not the significance which it has achieved in modern times. Marriage was at the same time security, destiny, and consecration; it was the background of the life of the man and the frame of the woman's existence.

This institutional character of marriage was closely connected with the economic conditions of the pre-industrial epoch. As long as the family was the unit of production, it was of necessity an inseparable entity, since only then was the continuity of domestic economy assured, and with it the material foundation of human existence. Marriage is the basis of the family; the family was the nucleus of economic life.

The state also had an interest in marriage as an institution. The purely human, non-specific artificial values which it represents were first created by men, since under primitive material conditions women were too much occupied by maternal and domestic obligations, too heavily burdened as procreative beings, to be able to outgrow these functions. Woman as such had consequently no part in the state; only through marriage was she made a member of it, and only through marriage did she win a social sanction for her existence. Only thanks to marriage could the life of the species be seized by the machinery, the law, and the administration of the state.

The extensive and revolutionary technical and economic changes of the most modern epoch have, however, effected a transformation in every respect. The family is no longer a unit of production; its connection with economic life, as far as that survives at all, is extremely loose; the household has lost its ancient character as the sole possible way of life. The present economic organization requires the working power of the individual, not that of the family. The effects of this economic breaking-up have been extended into all fields of human existence. Nor is a society organized according to groups or classes today any more the presumption or the object of the state, but rather the single individual. The most adequate expression of this fact is the democracy in which votes are counted and not weighed. Such a state had to confer civic rights on woman as an individual.

Through these changes, which struck deep into the social structure, marriage as an institution has lost its essential supports. For woman this was at first disadvantageous, since for a considerable time the change left her no longer so important a factor in the activities of life as she had once been. But the evolution of economic independence and its severance from family and home has had the effect of relieving woman. The domestic administration which in an earlier epoch filled her existence has become for the most part superfluous. Humanly, woman has won the possibility of a life of her own; she can now lead an independent, "manless" existence without perceiving it to be devoid of meaning. She takes an immediate and active part in the once scarcely accessible world of human values, which she might not have been able to create herself, but in the maintenance of which she shares today. That marriage in the last one hundred and fifty years has lost much of its value as an institution is evidenced not in the fact that marriages are now more rarely concluded, but rather in the fact that so many of them suffer divorce. Divorce contradicts the fundamental concept of marriage, which tends to exalt the purely instinctive coming together of man and woman into a lifelong partnership. The Catholic conception of marriage as a sacrament is indeed only a projection of the idea which inheres in marriage into the religious realm. Today the number of divorces mounts in absolute and pro-rata numbers even among the Catholics; in future it will probably increase still more. For newly arising forms of partnership will remain outside the life of reproduction, and consequently will not stabilize marriage.

Marriage will assuredly take a relatively insignificant place in the future structure of society; extra-marital relationships between man and woman will be more frequent, and the odium which hitherto attached to them will gradually disappear. Also, the state will assume the care of children in an increasing measure. Public institutions of every kind, with trained teachers and nurses, will more and more relieve parents. But the peculiar needs of human childhood will bring it about that marriage between conscientious human beings will endure, as an institution apart from all personal desires, on account of the children. For the process of spiritual adaptation, a harmonious relation with the individual child is obviously only possible in the family. All experiences with children, as well as the most recent psychological discoveries, point to this, that there can be no substitutes for parents. And the deeper the spiritual life of the parents, the less will they want to be supplanted; the more will their instinctive love manifest itself in an active companionship of feeling and experience with their children which will be full of understanding: the more will their self-seeking and their self-will efface themselves before the welfare of the children; yes, even before their own wishes. The longing for children is active in the majority of women, and man also desires a posterity beyond himself. But whosoever desires a child must desire marriage, marriage as a lifelong partnership, as an institution beyond all personal desires.

However, the institutional character of marriage will decidedly recede into the background as compared with its character of personal relationship. There is certainly nothing more difficult than to build up a lifelong partnership on a personal relationship. For relationships between man and woman have at all times an erotic colouring, and the essence of eroticism is mutability. The direct development, which is sufficiently well known to us from love-relationships, is invariably a rise and fall, a finding oneself and losing oneself. When a lifelong partnership of one man and one woman has nevertheless been achieved, it was caused by the fact that the relationship between man and woman may grow beyond the love-relationship, may grasp the totality of personality. In his depths, certainly, each one remains alone; there can be no complete merging, no absolute finding of oneself in another. Therefore the relationship to the "thou" (*du*) in marriage is of a different quality from the relationship to any other kind of "thou." The mental and spiritual development of the modern epoch has brought with it an enhanced differentiation of man, a finer consciousness of his spiritual multiplicity. Corresponding to this, the conscious content of life changes frequently: and friendships which continue throughout the whole life of human beings who do not live the same life become ever more difficult and more infrequent. To this the changing conditions of life today contribute something essential; no longer does any outward frame exist which would remain the same through decades and would embrace men as communities. Generally every one knows the other merely as an "episode"; only the fewest know each other as "continuity." This condition sooner or later becomes a torture to one who does not stand outside of life as a saint. One desires a human being who goes with him, who shares with him. Such a relationship is certainly not directly created through love between man and woman, since passion is essentially of short duration, nor can it change; either it is, or it is not. But in its shadow the "we" of marital unity can sooner come into existence than in marriages of reason, in which the partners face each other soberly from the beginning. And this "we" is the presumption of every marriage which desires to remain a personal relationship.

But if marriage as a personal relationship is to be an enduring creation, it must not be founded on the "typical," but rather on the consciousness and knowledge of self. Hitherto it has been connected chiefly with stipulations unuttered but taken for granted, which are essentially of a typical nature. One of these is the innocence of maidens before marriage. This requirement is quite natural; the sexual desires always tend to exclusiveness, wherever they can operate freely. Every man, every woman, wishes to possess his partner not only solely, but also as the first. But only man could enforce this wish, since in earlier times he had made woman a social creature, a human being within society; and therefore he could prescribe his conditions to her. Certainly virginal innocence possesses a peculiar charm. Besides, it is probable that the separation of love and voluptuousness is more damaging to the female than to the male personality; it remains entirely desirable that woman should not give herself lightly. But to exalt virginity as the prerequisite of marriage is in this day inappropriate, since it betokens emphasis on the sensual impulse of the race; and that is not conducive to success in the marital relationship, which should be essentially human and personal. The result is, indeed, too often that the maiden falls in love with the first acceptable man who offers her marriage, and that the man woos the virgin, but not the personality. These are bad foundations for a durable human relationship.

Another typical condition is that the husband must offer the wife a home of her own and must be in a position to maintain it. This requirement was necessary in the time when one could live only in a household. In the world of today, which offers so many possibilities of existence in which the woman can support herself, and in which even children are, or need to be, only in the rarest instances the gift of fate, this requirement no longer obtains. It hampers entrance into marriage from personal choice, since it forces marriage to take place according to wealth and income. To be sure, many a marriage concluded in this way on typical conditions turns out to be very happy. But the deterioration of married life today in the majority of instances arises from the fact that a relationship which has become an essentially personal connection is built up on a typical foundation.—This rejection of the typical does not signify that the existing social foundations for the conclusion of marriage will be completely altered. An essentially personal relationship arises most naturally between people of the same position in life, the same education, the same attitude. To the old class prejudice there now corresponds an active sense of the purely personal, the human—not casual opinions which experience many transformations through the years, but of an ultimate spiritual quality essentially constant. To become aware of them, to make them the guiding star when deciding matters of life importance, is the art of life.

MARRIAGE in the future can survive only if borne by a personal relationship from human being to human being. This new marriage will be more difficult in many respects than that of the past. For it will have valid claims not only on man's passive ability to endure, but also on the much rarer gift of living creative power. As long as marriage was a predetermined form, strife, whims, brutality, and self-seeking could exert but little power on it; in future, however, it will be a problem daily renewed, to be solved only by him who practises rigid self-discipline.

It lies in the nature of our epoch that objective norms sever themselves from life as such, and only shape the tools of life. All objects of use are more and more conformed to certain types such as were inconceivable in the time of craftsmanship. But purely human associations are ever more shedding their old traditional forms. Standardized kitchen-ranges, writing-desks, and automobiles may exist, but no more standardized marriages. External life runs its course more and more according to particular schemes. But whatsoever does not serve for the preservation of society as an economically established entity, whatsoever is merely personal, is deprived of its objective points of support and becomes founded on pure spontaneity, alert consciousness, and courage. In the domain of marriage, in the connection of human with human, we see going on a process similar to that once experienced in religion, in the relationship of man to God. Formerly religion was essentially magic and ritual; Christianity made it a purely spiritual affair. It corresponds to the growing humanization of our inner life—the counterpoint of external mechanization—that wherever we are valued as personalities and not as working force, we must consciously and firmly take hold of our life. This signifies that the inherent life of institutions is dying; they are no longer frames in which man may develop, but at the same time they are no longer a destiny which breaks him.

This may be an advantage for the individual existence; indeed, a step forward. The "misunderstood" woman is today already an outlived phenomenon, since her passive grief is contrary to the genius of modern life. The idea of the unhappy marriage is still current among us; in future it will probably be a curiosity. For two ways are open to the active personality; either one dissolves the marriage, or one accepts it with its suffering; and in this case one is not unhappy, but rather a human being who has mastered his destiny.

Certainly no consciousness, no will, no culture can deliver us from the problems and the suffering of marriage. These are eternal, for the relationship of the sexes can never be without problems and without pain. Marriage is a form of life; life signifies joy and suffering, and at root one desires suffering not less than joy. But marriage is a form of life and can be shaped as such, provided those who enter into it know themselves and have the desire for marriage and the courage to master it.

PART THREE

Marriage as an Eternal Problem

COUNT HERMANN KEYSERLING

The Proper Choice of Partners

THAT there are couples, however rare, which seem to be purposely created for one another, is an established fact. The reason for this cannot, however, be determined by intellectual processes. Is it, in accordance with Plato's teaching in the *Symposium*, a dualism arising out of what was originally a single entity? Does some god's eternal decree place in the world simultaneously two new souls intended for one another? Is the doctrine of reincarnation true? Or is what seems to signify a wise providence merely blind chance? No one can answer this question. Each believes what he must. The mystery is a problem beyond our intellectual powers. Consequently, the question of esoteric affinities, in its deepest sense, must remain outside the scope of this book.

But even a miracle can take place on our earth only within the compass of its laws. Just as Christ was able to express his sublime wisdom about God in parables that dealt with everyday occurrences, it can be shown that just the most profound and ultimate recognition has everywhere its corresponding part in the sphere of common sense. This means, as far as marriage is concerned, though the particular character of a given situation is not deducible in each case, that there are certain general laws of universal validity, within which this particular aspect manifests itself.

Two persons of different sex attract one another. Does it follow that they should marry? It is clear from the introductory chapter that this is not necessarily the case. Human beings are complex. And the marriage bond is only one of many; it is the most difficult to realize satisfactorily, and common experience goes to prove—unfortunately—that infatuation is the worst security for a prosperous marriage. This is not entirely due to physical attraction failing to satisfy man's soul completely, but principally because people usually fall in love—a careful distinction should be made between infatuation and real love—with a type different from that which would prove suitable for marriage. Every one is aware that the natural disposition of any person who is at all differentiated, if his heart is not fully possessed by one person, is to become attracted by the same type in ever new incarnations. Psychoanalysis teaches us that in the case of man there are usually two principal types: the mother type (the basis of this being either his own mother, or an imaginary adaptation, as he would desire her to be) and the "comrade," the natural prototype for the latter being a sister. His two types correspond to the general maternal and comradely qualities that enter into every woman's nature, and the latter aspect often finds its embodiment in the courtesan. Generally speaking, only the mother type is suitable for marriage. For it has its roots in the primordial nature of man; it typifies responsibility and is therefore serious in character. In the comrade type, man seeks adventure, stimulation, and sport. Exactly the same statements, *mutatis mutandis*, apply to the differentiated woman. By their very nature these two types are irreconcilable. Consequently it is a mistake even to try to bring them into agreement. Each must decide for himself in which way and to what extent he intends to realize the two complementary sides of his affective nature. One thing, however, seems positive: the comrade should never become the wife. It is a mistaken policy for a man or a woman to marry his comrade. And here we have the first definite answer to the question of the proper choice of partners. Marriage in the true sense of the word is only possible where the attraction lies (to use a musical term adapted from Wagner) outside the "comradely motive" (*Freundschaftsmotiv*). Friendship may prove to be the most intimate relation of all. It may even be that souls which seem created for each other are never intended to marry. The more personal a man is—here the artist creates the type—the less significance do superpersonal bonds possess for him. . . . Be that as it may, our fathers proved their wisdom when they claimed that marriage should be independent of personal disposition. Not because this was not desirable in itself; on the contrary, they only wished to imply that infatuation was not to be the decisive factor, because, for the majority of men, infatuation would directly apply to the "comrade." With most women the maternal instinct is so strongly developed that they readily fall in love with the right man. At any rate, they much less frequently come to grief in their friendships, as their feelings are more delicately graded. But as man is the suitor even when he is the captive, the idea of preventing personal affection from deciding, as a general precaution, is fundamentally correct. This is, moreover, confirmed by all modern experience. Only very rarely does marriage between friends prove successful. The attraction which in such cases leads to marriage—from the man's point of view, a woman's stimulating and inspiring quality; and purely personal sympathy on the woman's part—cannot be prevented from languishing. Consequently, most of these marriages are stormy in character and, as often as not, culminate in divorce. And as the marriage relation is essentially indissoluble, this inflicts serious injury and produces a debilitating effect, if the people in question are not at all superficial characters.

CONSEQUENTLY love matches, in the sense of marriages between friends, definitely preclude the conception of a proper choice of partners. If this statement appears disputable, it is due to the presumption that every one can find complete satisfaction in only one person of the opposite sex. This prejudice has now surely been outlived. At a high level of individual development, mankind finds again its absolute ideal in conventional marriage (*Standesehe*). Not in the historical and narrow sense of the expression, usually attached to the term convention; it has come to convey this meaning in Germany. But in the real sense: that marriage is essentially a special order, just as celibacy is in all things relating to monastic affairs, and consequently can be gauged only by its ethos. In this case, the ethos involves the maintenance of a special "order" both in the natural and cultural spheres. Neither does it oppose the will of the individual, where this is self-conscious, because to every man is allotted a definite position in the cosmic order, which he must fill properly if he is to realize his personal purpose in life. But to return to particulars. Generally speaking, whom should people marry? This question cannot be answered with scientific precision, because ultimately every vital phenomenon is unique in character, so much so that when a generalization is applied to any special case, it receives an interpretation reflecting the special character of the case. Knowledge of general principles will no more enable one to choose the right partner than mere knowledge of harmony and counterpoint makes a man into a composer. Moreover, on account of the very complex nature of the question, it is quite impossible to formulate any rules having general validity. From a theoretical standpoint the exception may still prove the rule, but in actual practice it is often just the exception that counts. For example, if it is generally true that an hysterical person is unfit for marriage, it does, however, occasionally happen that this disease is actually cured by it. Again, it is asserted with justice that marriage between near relatives is generally detrimental; but at times it leads to the very best results. This explains why at one time any preternatural qualities in a man were attributed to his incestuous origin. I can recommend a brochure entitled *Whom Should One Marry?* (*Wen soll man heiraten?* Frankfurt a. M.; H. Bechold); it contains in a convenient and handy form the most trustworthy information on this subject, the result of experience and research, mainly from a medical and scientific point of view. As I cannot go further into this particular question here, I refer the reader to the above-mentioned work, although he will not find much of practical value in it. In fact, generalities are only useful to the individual if they can be, as in the case of an algebraical formula or a paragraph of the law, a frame enabling him to fit in his personal factors, and thus to find for them a definite value. That is why, if the solution is to prove satisfactory, the problem of how to choose one's partner properly calls for a different formula from that one employed by all the specialists; it must be considered purely from the standpoint of its significance. Only in this way can the problem be formulated without contradictions arising. As soon as it treats of particulars, it breaks up into two separate problems, which can only partly be taken together: first, the choice of partners in respect of the partners themselves, and secondly, the same as regards posterity. It is evident that these two problems are distinct. As far as the child is concerned, the parents are only intermediaries, handing down to it the racial inheritance; from the individuals as such it receives nothing. Further, any one who has children renounces by this every claim to his own personal independence.[1] Moreover, if the child is the central problem, the question of personal happiness becomes secondary. For parental happiness is quite different from conjugal felicity; in the former case, different, impersonal impulses find their fulfilment. Lastly, the personal inharmony of the parents may evoke in the children that state of internal tension which is the necessary physiological agent for all productivity.[2] That is why the majority of great men are the offspring of unhappy marriages, or at least of inharmonious ones. Even gifted youths often do not turn out well if their early surroundings have been too happy. Freedom from difficulties to meet and overcome does not tend to awaken personal aspirations. But there is, as has already been pointed out, one standpoint from which the problem of the proper choice of partners can be treated as a whole: that which sees in marriage an independent unit, composed of two parts. In this respect it greatly resembles a child, which is also the product of a dual association.

According to Christian teaching, married people are no longer separate, but of one flesh. Psychic unity is experienced personally by all true lovers. I need not here discuss the reasons for marriage being an independent

[1] See my *Unsterblichkeit,* Third Edition, Darmstadt, 1920, especially the chapter *Mensch und Menschheit.*

[2] For details, see the chapter *Psychoanalyse und Selbstvervollkommnung* in my *Wiedergeburt.*

whole, after what has already been said in the introductory chapter. If we keep this in mind, we may now state that since unity is the fundamental characteristic of marriage, as well as of the child, then congruency in the case of the parents has apparently the very same significance as the agreement of various capacities and impulses has in an individual; then, surely, the problem of choosing the right partner must be treated from the same point of view as the harmonizing of differences and contradictions in one's own soul. How can this be accomplished? Certainly not by a levelling process, for all natural talents, as such, are immutable, just as are *genes* (the elements of heredity). On their own plane they can merely conflict with and exterminate one another. Harmony can only be obtained by establishing unity of a higher order, where the original problem is not solved, but dismissed.[3] From the servitude of instinct, only a higher force can free us: love. We can only be saved from the natural revolt against the superior forces of destiny by consciously identifying ourselves with the higher powers that promote destiny, in cultivating wisdom and religion. Consequently, the individual soul is accounted to that extent superior, the more irreconcilable elements it can unite together in a higher synthesis. From these summary considerations arises the first definite answer to the question under consideration. One should marry only that person who, on becoming his soul's partner, can assist him in becoming superior to those difficulties which he could not cope with alone, or which he realized were making him one-sided and incomplete. On the other hand, every one who is capable of understanding will find himself to some extent one-sided, because, as I have pointed out in the chapter entitled

[3] In this connection, see the chapter *Spannung und Rhythmus* in my *Wiedergeburt.*

Weltanschauung und Lebensgestaltung in *Wiedergeburt*, each individual is merely an abstraction of the cosmos of humanity, which is a real entity. Its actual existence is clearly established by the fact that a faulty social instinct leads to disease. This is why most good marriages rest on a complementary basis. At the lowest stage, the sexual complement is sufficient in itself, for where the individual is undeveloped the racial instinct plays the principal part. At all stages, the inherent complementary requirements of one's own generic type are the determining factors. This matter, however, is gone into more fully by Jung and Kretschmer. In cases of extreme individuality, the strictly personal aspect of one's complementary cravings is decisive. It finds its release, according to C. G. Jung's discovery, in the "soul-image" (*Seelenbild*) [4] which is stored in every man's consciousness and functions as a complement to his conscious ego. This image does not merely confine itself to general attributes, but even delineates sex. If one person arouses a feeling of love in another, the former becomes, wherever motives of the mind and soul come into play, the visible embodiment of what has been inwardly desired and consequently preconceived, much as another's words often express our meaning where we were incapable of expressing it ourselves. This is the origin of those intimations of recollection which make people feel as if they had always known each other, and which all true lovers experience. One sees in the person he loves, as in a mirror, the reflection of his own "soul-image" (*Seelenbild*). Consequently it is little wonder that one recognizes at first sight a person who essentially belongs to one; in fact it is surprising that the *coup de foudre* is not the normal commencement of love. In this we have

[4] Compare Jung's *Psychologischen Typen*, Zürich, Rascher and Company (English translation published by Harcourt, Brace and Company).

the explanation of absolutely all the precepts laid down for happy marriages, as well as of the contradictions involved in the well-attested rules. Thus, when it is held, on the one hand, that like associates with like, and on the other hand, that opposites attract one another, both statements are more or less true, according to the qualities required to complement one's nature. Natures whose development has been one-sided are generally attracted by their opposites, as only in this way can they overcome their limitations, whereas more balanced natures find their most suitable complements in those who are essentially like them, and show only a slight deviation from them in a few particulars. Details of special research in this matter will be found in the chapters that follow. But from what has already been stated, one thing is evident, which is at the same time the best answer to the question under consideration: that to ask oneself, "How can I, in a practical manner, recognize the person who best suits me for marriage?" *is to put the question the wrong way.* There is no help for the blind; that is to say, for those lacking instinct. But whoever is conscious of his own soul will readily recognize the person who is best suited to him, just as a man with eyes sees the landscape in front of him; for the contact between souls is just as direct as that experienced in the material world. One can only advise each person to open his eyes, to put aside prejudices and self-illusions, to be loyal to his experience and to judge it aright; then he cannot go wrong.

This directness of contact between souls also explains the significance of bodily impulses or motives, which should be taken into account much more seriously than is usually the case at present. The customary distinction between body and soul is erroneous. I have pointed out in *Schöpferische Erkenntnis* and *Wiedergeburt,* and shall not here go into further details on this point, that life is essentially "significant," and consequently an expression of the spirit, on all its planes. At the same time, every manifestation of life is a phenomenon, and thus material by nature. This is as true of the letters of the alphabet, which embody thoughts, as of institutions, laws, concepts, etc., which are the materializations of man's thought. Consequently, a distinction should not be made between body and soul, but between significance and expression. The customary distinction would be correct if the spiritual could be identified with the mental or conscious. But this is impossible. A picture or a sonata is not any less spiritual than a philosophical system, and yet they are certainly non-intellectual in character. On the other hand, a physical organ is just as significant in its functions as these and is only intelligible from its meaning and purpose. As regards consciousness, we know now that most mental processes are unconscious. Finally, we are aware that all expressions of life are essentially symbolic; and in this connection mental concepts and physical organs are on the same plane. Under these conditions, all material phenomena naturally possess intellectual and spiritual significance. Thus, beauty signifies the perfection of the race.[5] Even the smallest details have a spiritual significance. For this deep-seated reason the possibility or impossibility of receiving sexual gratification from a certain person, or the fact that being attracted or repelled often depends on small details, should be taken seriously into account. For these are always symptoms and symbols, whether we know how to appreciate them or not. This is why, in epochs when men were led by their instincts, marriages which were apparently based only on physical attraction often yielded the best moral and spiritual results, both as regards

[5] Compare the chapter on Aden in my *Travel Diary*.

the parents and the children. Soul and body are one. For the man who possesses insight, there is nothing really superficial or futile. He takes each detail as symbolizing the whole. Now a recognized harmony need not necessarily call for marriage. The latter, in accordance with its initial definition, presupposes the existence of harmony in regard to the totality of the differentiated being; and this totality, i. e., the possible unification of manifold qualities on a plane of higher unity, is not implied in the elements as such. However, in this case also there is a special point of departure that permits of a more exact definition. As a result of the researches of Alfred Adler, it has become evident that each individual's life develops in accordance with a mental "guiding image" (*Leitbild*).[6] This image anticipates the line of life and the possible course of destiny. It is a reality just like any other, but situated on a special plane. On this plane it is both self-evident and directly apprehensible to others, as in Nature all planes of existence react directly on one another; that is, spirit on spirit, soul on soul, "guiding principle" on "guiding principle" (*Leitbild*), just as one body reacts on another; in fact, much as directrixes describe the possible character of algebraic formulae. Only when two people have these in accord is a sensible marriage possible. Marriage is primarily, as the introductory chapter showed, a matter of mutual destiny. It is, however, necessary to avoid here a source of frequent error. To have the same line of destiny does not necessarily imply the same interests, inclinations, and world-outlook. In fact, nothing can be more foolish, both as regards the partners themselves and their progeny, than for an artist to marry a fellow-artist or the daughter of an artist, or for a scholar or lawyer to wed the

[6] In this connection see his books: *Theorie und Praxis der Individualpsychologie* and *Der Nervöse Charakter,* München, F. Bergmann.

offspring of another scholar or lawyer. The polarity of the sexes even implies that equality of experience does not mean equality of significance. If in history "conventional marriage" (*Standesehe*) seems to contradict this, it is due to the misconception of thinking of professional castes, instead of the reality of living types; for the born ruler is never a specialist, but a man of many-sided attainment. Consequently the same course of destiny essentially means polar correspondence. This is clearly seen in such frequent cases as when women dedicate their lives to "save" men, who from their own personal point of view are lost. The same applies when a famous man has the right instinct to choose a woman who by nature has nothing in common with his work. Woman desires to fulfil her own personal mission; in the former case as saviour, in the latter as helpmate. Destiny can only be played out if each possesses a separate rôle. As regards posterity, marriage is the natural archetype of this association. Father and mother do not operate in the same way. And even today, the instinctive woman, even if she only slightly resembles the mother type, sees in her husband also the father of her children. Even today every real man is aware, in the dark recesses of his consciousness, of a desire to fulfil his natural destiny as well as to conform to the spiritual laws of ethics and religion.

It is not of much use to refer to instinct for those people who do not possess it. Consequently it is necessary to formulate the conditions on more strictly logical grounds. At all times there have been strict regulations governing the contraction of marriage, ranging from the marriageable classes of the Australian aborigines right up to the order of rank of the nobility. These regulations have always proved indispensable, as it is only the exceptional man who takes the right course without compulsion. Here, just as with duty, it is a question of formulating what should in reality be self-evident to each man's conscience.[7] What is the ultimate common aim of all such regulations? The perpetuation of a special standing or rank in the natural and cultural order. And if the general conception is applied to the individual, we find that the maintenance of rank denotes fundamentally the maintenance of a *niveau* or standard; whether or not it is actually achieved in practice is another matter. And this brings us from the general conception of the directrix to a qualifying statement. Its relation to the standard is this: Each soul is an association of qualities and functions whose focus can be variously situated, as higher or lower, for example. According to its position the person's character is either superficial or deep, commanding or subaltern. The commanding character is not hampered by the conditions which dominate the subaltern. This focus is in reality the very centre of personality.[8] According to the position of the focus—that is, according to its plane—all qualities bear another significance. On the other hand, its conditionality is purely spiritual and cannot be deduced from Nature. In this respect the plane represents the empirical foundation to which all values are referred. It follows that to define the directrix of life is not sufficient to determine its significance; it is of primary importance to know on which plane it lies; for example, a young waiter who is predestined to become a head-waiter may have the horoscope of a Napoleon. It is the *niveau* which enables us to ascertain the ultimate significance of any data. The purpose and validity of the marriage laws now become evi-

[7] Compare the final section of the chapter on America in my *Travel Diary*.

[8] I have dealt exhaustively with this question in the chapter entitled *Weltüberlegenheit* in my *Schöpferische Erkenntnis*.

dent: Only people of the same standing can be complementary to one another in the true sense. If they belong to different planes they do not properly complement one another, as the very essence of harmony is lacking; secondly, in accordance with the laws of gravity, the lower tends to pull down the higher. If we recall the analogy between the unity of the single soul and that of the marriage relation, we shall realize that it is impossible to harmonize a member of a lower and one of a higher plane on the principle of equal rights; either the one or other will have the upper hand. *Consequently it is an essential condition for the proper choice of partners that both should be on the same plane of existence.* On the other hand to be on the same plane really amounts to equality of birth, in the proper sense of the term. Consequently, the claim for equality of birth is not only absolutely justified but imperative. Since each part of a man receives its significance from the plane of his complete being, it is irrational to marry a person, even though in some particulars one is in complete unison with him, if, taken as a whole, he is beneath one. This can never prove satisfactory either for the parents or their children. Soul reacts on soul, and gene on gene (hereditary factor), so that if marriage takes place between people who are not of the same status by birth, it leads with but few exceptions to personal deterioration and proves a cultural retrogression for the human race. And if we now pause to consider the majority of modern marriages, we shall immediately comprehend why most of them are so wretchedly bad. The decisive factor, the question of the plane, is scarcely ever taken into consideration. In this manner no tradition of cultural ascent can ever take root. This is due to the reaction against antiquated conceptions regarding equality of birth. Equality of birth simply means being on the same plane, and nothing more. With name and station it has only this in common, that a high standard is as a rule obtainable only by means of adequate education from the nursery up. But with the caste system and the consequent inbreeding, vitality is forfeited; and the type becomes so one-sided that eventually the difference between the outer and the inner plane amounts to contradiction. Then formal equality of birth is no longer a reality. That this is the actual state of affairs in the case of most of the old nobility can hardly be disputed. What still remains valuable is the merits of a genteel but one-sided character, and partiality contradicts the very conception of aristocracy. Compare in this respect the courtier with the independent nobleman—or the North German Junker, who is specially bred for occupying subaltern positions, with a Hungarian noble, who is the true type of the great gentleman. Everything depends on the plane actually lived up to. Nor can this be secured by any letters patent. In order to acquire this for the future, many of the noblest-born of our day have even been driven instinctively to marry women below their official station. They require a more vital psychic constitution and the infusion of fresh blood. But the ancient idea is right: For the man of good stock, complete equality of birth should be the one requisite when contemplating marriage. Here, however, a slight correction is necessary. A given plane does not embody ultimate values. Each person should aim at the highest, just as the Indian does by means of reincarnation, or the Englishman by concentrating on the common ideal of becoming gentlemanly. Thus the ultimate aim of marriage is not to maintain, but to elevate the plane. When this actually takes place, it is only thanks to the woman. If a man marries a woman below his station, he can rarely lift her up to his. But woman, as a born mother, is both able and specially fitted to raise the man; in this connection the dynamic and progressive principle lies with her. Whereas all highly-bred male lines become extinct, a careful fate has ordained that the female ones most frequently survive. This forces well-born women to marry below their station and thus allows a frequent admixture of young blood; thus at length, by intermarriage, the general standard is raised. Thus the eternal feminine again and again exalts sinking humanity. Here again we realize how wise our forefathers were in permitting their daughters to marry below their station, but not their sons. The male is unable to raise his mate. When all has been said, Nietzsche struck the keynote with his words: "You are not merely to propagate, but to exalt the species." Therefore equality of birth in its true sense is an imperative condition for prosperous marriage. The person who marries below his standard, inasmuch as he is worth anything at all, should be judged more harshly than if he had spent his whole life on lustful passion. And each person should attempt, if possible, to marry above his station, in one sense or another. In fact, every man's natural desire carries him in that direction. That is why every man looks up to the eternal feminine without possibility of disappointment; that is why woman desires to reverence her lover. This idealization signifies an ardently desired reality. As new things can only be created by the intercourse of opposite poles, the higher culture of soul as well as of blood depends on marriage making this its direct aim.

All depends on the standard and not on the feelings. Feelings alone can never prove that a thing is right, for they are only the result of satisfaction or dissatisfaction, quite irrespective of the contributing causes or motives.

In order to be justified, feeling must be the expression or reflection of correct judgment—this is often the case with women (consequently their feelings rarely urge them to make rash decisions), rarely with man. Here we are dealing again with the problem of lost instinct. Many people suppose that "conventional marriage" (*Standesehe*) was conventional from the outset. This is not at all the case. In times of harmony between vitality and culture, men fell in love only with women of the right status. This is how it should be, seeing that the plane of being determines the ultimate quality of man. Real agreement can never be reached between persons of unequal birth. Convention was only a precautionary measure against individual backsliding. It is quite impossible at the modern stage of consciousness to reattain primitive certainty of instinct. But education may, to use a good expression of Harnack's, re-establish candour. Actually, standard reacts directly on standard. This most essential of all realities can be accurately apprehended, just like any other. But such as cannot see for themselves must be taught to acquire vision. I have indicated the manner in which this can be accomplished, in so far as it can be done in a general way, in two chapters of *Wiedergeburt: Grenzen der Menschenkenntnis* and *Der natürliche Wirkungskreis.* The intuition of the teacher, who has seen the truth for himself, will find out the appropriate means of interpretation in each particular case. If only one generation would meditate on the insight of its ancestors, and thus fashion its soul anew, then the next generation would, thanks to the influence of nursery training on the unconscious mind, possess this insight as a matter of course, but on a higher plane than in times past. At any rate this would apply to the women of the next generation, and that would prove sufficient, as it is they who choose their partners in marriage. Then youths and young girls would no longer—what one must strictly advise them to do at present—need to school themselves in order not to marry the wrong person. Today most people marry inadvertently. When the majority of marriages no longer prove happy or efficacious, it indicates an incorrect choice of partners. Here we have the solution of the problem of proper choice of partners, from the point of view of the partners themselves. All details and particulars can be obtained from special medical, psychological, sociological, and statistical works.[9] The ultimate significance of all that the reader will find in these books has been anticipated by this essay. In fact, the special statements of science can be correctly interpreted only when taken in this light. So we must finally conclude that marriage is only complete when it is the synthesis of biological, eugenic, sociological, ethical, and religious ideals. On the other hand, this synthesis, which appears so difficult in theory, is quite easily attained in practice. An individual when analyzed is extremely complex, but he lives as a simple natural unit. The same applies both to the marriage relation and to the first step toward its realization—the proper choice of partners. *One need only be quite certain of what is actually right; the rest will then come of itself, as unconscious realization follows automatically on conscious perception.*[10] One even should not ponder these matters too much.

One thing more. As man is essentially a dynamic, aspiring, evolutionary being, marriage can bring fulfil-

[9] See Havelock Ellis's *Choice of Partners;* also the works of Forel and Magnus Hirschfeld and his colleagues, which deal with sex in its widest sense. Probably the most comprehensive work on the subject is Hirschfeld's *Geschlechtskunde,* Stuttgart, Julius Püttmanns Verlag. Very valuable is G. Schreiber's "Medical Examination Before Marriage," which appeared in *The World's Health,* August, 1925.

[10] See Baudouin's *Suggestion and Autosuggestion.*

ment only inasmuch as it intensifies life. Wherever it causes diminution it fails in its purpose. It is hardly necessary to state how fallacious are all counsels respecting the proper choice of partners which merely rest on indolence and convenience. Unfortunately this type of precept is often met with in books of a scientific nature and is frequently propounded by people who give advice on marriage questions. Marriage is primarily a matter of responsibility; and consequently, if it rests on a false basis, it can but lead to misfortune. It is not at all necessary that every Hans should get his Gretchen. To break down because of an unhappy love affair, where its continuance was not desirable, is indeed a disgrace, for it is in everybody's power to break off an engagement before it affects his actual destiny. Lack of insight? That is an unworthy excuse, for it invariably indicates a want of good will. At any rate, this applies whenever the unconscious is fully aware of the facts. And this is so without exception when a man and woman attract one another.

ALL that has been said concerning the proper choice of partners, in so far as it deals with fundamental principles, also applies to heredity; but in this case the statements can be made more precise. What produces a good or bad effect during an association of souls produces a corresponding effect in the hereditary factors (*genes*).[11] We

[11] The best book that I am acquainted with on heredity and racial hygiene is Baur, Fischer, and Lenz's *Grundriss der menschlichen Erblichkeitslehre und Rassenhygiene,* published by I. F. Lehmanns Verlag, München, in two volumes. When alluding in the following pages to these subjects, I have always referred to the works in question. For a special survey of eugenics, see G. Schreiber's *Eugénique et Mariage* and *Eugénique et Sélection,* Paris, 1922, and also the English journals, *The Eugenics Review* and *Biometrics.* As popular expositions, I can thoroughly recommend the works of Prof. Hermann Muckermann, Freiburg i. B., Herdersche Buchhandlung. They are written in an easy style. He is, by the way, a Jesuit priest.

know today that the natural elements of life are immutable, and that acquired characters are transmitted so uncertainly, if at all, that from a practical standpoint they cannot be taken into consideration. Further, since the discoveries of Mendel and his successors, we know that the hereditary factors possess specific characteristics which, on interbreeding, form a new mosaic-like pattern, but never mingle. On the other hand, we are also aware that the intellectual and spiritual character of a man, that is to say, the meaning that expresses itself by means of the alphabet of hereditary units, depends, inasmuch as it is not inborn, on the influences dominant during earliest childhood. Consequently, nursery training plays a more prominent part than has ever been suspected in times past. The seeds of what a man develops into, apart from his inborn character, are sown in him before his seventh year. Thus, with man, blood is not the ultimate propagative agent, as in the case of animals, but the synthesis of blood and tradition. If this were not the case, no civilization would ever have fallen, since biologically the ultimate material substance of man has scarcely changed, if at all, since the days of Adam. If this were not so, the fellahs would still be Pharaohs, the Arabians Saracens, and the Germans of today would be the same as in the glory of our Middle Ages. In this connection I need make no further mention of the significance of tradition. The state of affairs is only too evident. Family types are no less dependent on spiritual attributes than on hereditary peculiarities.[12] Every man has to build up his independent intellectual and spiritual life at first on the basis of what he has acquired and been taught, just as from a physiological standpoint he has to start out

[12] This idea is expanded in the Jeypur chapter of my *Travel Diary* and the chapter *Der Sinn des ökumenischen Zustands* in *Die neuentstehende Welt*.

from his physical inheritance. Consequently, it should be stated all the more strictly and clearly which precepts relating to marriage are known, according to modern science, to correspond with the laws of heredity.

What the children of certain parents will be like cannot be safely predicted, as the parents alone do not transmit the characters, which depend on the transmissible heritage of all the possible ancestors, so that certain characters appear while others are excluded. An ancestor who lived several centuries ago may suddenly appear to have come to life again. But on the other hand, it is certain that only what is actually extant continues to live on, and that the elements of the natural characters are never created anew; what appears to be the creation of a new type is due to a new combination of the old elements. Very often degeneracy may be predicted, and this usually can be determined with a high degree of probability, in spite of all complications, from a knowledge of the family tree. Usually one can foresee whether the children are likely to turn out satisfactorily or not. Knowledge entails responsibility. In the light of modern knowledge it should be deemed plainly criminal to bring into the world children who in all probability are bound to be degenerate. It would be irrational to forbid marriages which would prove happy for the partners merely on the probability of poor issue, for the present counts as much as the future. On the other hand, where there is a danger of degeneracy, birth control should be made obligatory. And in cases such that the necessity for birth control is not likely to be respected, the parents should be sterilized by the state.[13] One may find this cruel. But as long as war is still tolerated, this infringement of indi-

[13] This has already been frequently performed in America. See "The Legislative and Administrative Aspects of Sterilization," Eugenics Record Office Bulletin, Vol. X, 1914; also Günther's *Kleine Rassenkunde*, p. 193.

vidual rights for the good of the majority cannot be objected to. And today, as far as I can see, this form of social-surgical interference cannot be avoided, if the race is to be improved. As for some centuries everything has been done on humanitarian grounds to preserve inferior stock, so an anti-humanitarian period in this sense—such as is already at hand, a period of fearless thought and radical practice—is the only means of salvation. Consequently, the proof of ancestry should be generally introduced and as strictly kept as in noble families, but with a new significance. In the first place, for the sake of health, the breeding of bad stock must be prevented, until that extant today becomes extinct. Secondly, in order to maintain a high standard not alone for one special class, but to elevate the standard of all classes without exception, there should be only pure stock bred, regardless of the class in which it is found. This appears to be quite attainable, as wild animals are practically all of pure stock, and domesticated animals are being bred increasingly with this aim in view; there is in fact no single type which could not find its highest expression by its positive qualities completely outweighing its negative ones. And this brings us back to the claim for equality of birth as an imperative condition for every marriage.[14] Why are the children of so few great men equally capable? Because the latter have hardly ever married women of their own standing. If they had done this, as in Europe the old ruling families did (and as in the East the poets, artists, and philosophers did as well), then, although the exceptional endowment could not be preserved —it cannot be maintained for a long period, as it requires

[14] This idea is worked out more fully and from a slightly different point of view in *Zur Ueberwindung des Bösen durch Gutes,* Part V, in my *Weg zur Vollendung,* Darmstadt. Otto Reichl Verlag.

as its physiological base a state of tension which Nature cannot support as a permanent condition—the one thing essential to general culture would be retained, i. e., the standard of superiority. The chapter entitled *Der Sinn des ökumenischen Zustands* in my book *Die neuentstehende Welt* treats of this exhaustively, as far as it is a question of the organic conditions being analogues of the psychic ones. So today everything depends on the claim for equality of birth, in its true sense of the same level becoming universal. One often forgets that mankind ages every ten years, and what was of no consequence a hundred years ago now works catastrophically. In many European countries the educated classes have for some hundreds of years married only within their own professional circles, such as clergy, lawyers, and military officers. Consequently they have become, as types, so one-sided and lacking vitality to such an extent—for only where internal contrasts support tension can life truly flourish—that raising the standard requires, to start with, the breaking down and merging of all the fixations of the last few centuries. In this respect, the impoverishment of the upper classes and the consequent necessity for most of their members to take to new roads is most fortunate, for it will result in a new intermixture of stock. In spite of this, conditions are terribly serious. Without doubt, during the course of history mankind has certainly not improved but actually deteriorated, both from a psychological and physical point of view, although this does not apply to its ultimate elements. Everywhere the classes with the best spiritual and moral endowment have irresistibly died out, as they either faced greater dangers or spent themselves in other ways, from the suicide of the cultured classes in ancient Greece in the civil wars right up to the wasting of talented people in technical pursuits in our own times; or else they have become torpid. The caste system proved unfavourable to the racial instinct in the long run. In olden times it was primarily the nobility, which was as a whole extremely vital, and more especially the kings, who multiplied, so that often entire families were descended from a few heroes, whereas on account of the unfavourable conditions of life, the lower classes hardly increased at all.[15] Today the opposite is true. The tremendous increase of the population in Germany, for example, during the last hundred years has multiplied principally only inferior stock; so much so that the type of German of the great old times is rarer than red Indians in North America. Further it has been proved that democracy, which aims at raising the lower classes, in reality sterilizes and deprives them of endowments. In fact it can be shown that in England between the thirteenth and twentieth centuries proportionately less talented persons have constantly risen from the lower orders.[16] And when these have once risen, their hereditary qualities are lost to their stem. Nor was this in the long run favourable to the upper classes, because as a rule the progeny of talented upstarts could not adapt themselves to the new conditions of life. An extremely interesting discovery is due to Flügge, who showed that a race must be immunized to the effects of civilization just as to those of any disease, in order to survive it. Not the younger, but the older, a family is,

[15] Compare F. C. S. Schiller's "The Case for Eugenics," in *The Dalhousie Review.*

[16] Compare the extremely valuable works of Lothrop Stoddard, especially his *Revolt against Civilization,* New York, Charles Scribner's Sons, and *The Rising Tide of Color against White World Supremacy.* To what an extent the European races have deteriorated during the course of the centuries is graphically and terribly portrayed in Grant's *The Passing of the Great Race,* fourth edition, New York, 1923, and Günther's *Kleine Rassenkunde Europas,* München, I. F. Lehmann.

if it has conserved its vitality, the better can it adapt itself to changing conditions of life.[17] That is why ruling families, because they have lived longest under extremely favourable conditions, seem the least debilitated by their privileges, and this weakness apparently grows in proportion to the recentness of privileged standing. Under these terribly serious conditions, only the most rigorous selection can save mankind from an irredeemable deterioration. Today it should be recognized as a religious duty —everywhere growing public opinion points to this—to better the stock wherever possible. And then, in turn, better stock will again be rationally privileged. Today we are living a paradox; after several centuries of democracy—it commenced in advanced countries, according to De Tocqueville, already in the fourteenth century—a period of extremely aristocratic outlook is arising. Just as, in life insurance, the expectation of life rises with increase of age, so in the coming centuries the old stock, which is immune to the effects of civilization, will always gain ascendancy, naturally not quantitatively but qualitatively. Everything depends on the old families becoming vitalized by rejuvenation. Quite young families will prove themselves always more incapable of coping with the growing demands of modern life. The contrasts between types will thus rather increase than diminish. Here another point must be taken into consideration. Albert Reibmayr has shown that it is probable [18] that the civilizing of barbaric peoples in historic times was made possible only by intermarriage with civilized people. At any rate European history clearly demonstrates that the

[17] See Ludwig Flügge's *Die rassenbiologische Bedeutung des sozialen Aufsteigens und das Problem der immunisierten Familien,* Göttingen, 1920, Vandenhoeck und Ruprecht.

[18] See his *Entwicklungsgeschichte des Talentes und Genies,* München, I. F. Lehmann.

rise of civilization was proportionately rapid or slow according to whether intermarriage with families of cultural tradition was largely practised or not. That is why the cultural renaissance of Europe, following on the turbulent migration of peoples, appeared first in Italy and France and gradually penetrated into Germany, from south to north. Nations appear to produce talented people and geniuses in proportion to the amount of cultural heritage distributed among the population. The requisite "cultural ferment" is, in reality, everywhere at hand, because in the long run it is transmitted through the female and not the male lines. The latter are always comparatively short-lived. The higher the mental development attained, the more difficult it proves to maintain biological equilibrium, for this is, as has already been pointed out, hindered by a state of mental tension. On the other hand the feminine element is fundamentally indestructible. Thus the continuity of endowments as well as civilization itself depends on the one fact that throughout all the barbarian invasions, the women carriers of the cultural heritage were generally permitted to live and could thus transmit this heritage to their children. Also in the long run—Reibmayr has made this appear so probable that I myself believe in his hypothesis—cultural heritage proves more durable than savage. The stage of incubation may be long. But at some time or other the really valuable elements will break through anew. Now that the races of mankind, in comparison with former times, have (to a very great extent) deteriorated or become enervated, and more especially because of the satanically negative selection operative during the World War, everything depends entirely on full use being made of the existing heritage and its wise increase. That is why the hour of eugenics is at hand.

Eugenics made its way first in the New World, because the general development there started from a democratic and not an aristocratic basis, thus giving the conception of race ample scope, free from internal friction due to prejudice and the burden of outworn historic conventions. Statistics have shown only too clearly how bad qualities have been transmitted from generation to generation,[19] and that not only intellectual, but also moral, endowments are hereditary. After the intelligence tests which all Americans had to undergo on being called up for military service had proved how absolutely essential good stock is, and how alarmingly seldom it is to be found, immigration laws were framed with a right instinct for improving the stock. The intelligence tests demonstrated that nearly eighty per cent of the Americans in question had reached an intellectual standard which corresponded, at most, to that of children only twelve years of age, and that the small percentage of highly gifted persons, with always less exceptions, belonged to the higher races.[20] But the same state of affairs is prevalent everywhere; especially in poverty-stricken Europe, which has lost its best representatives through the war. Our best stock has irretrievably perished. Such great families as existed a hundred years ago are no longer found in Europe today. Neither is there any powerful, virgin people left with a great future, with the one exception of the Russians. Once again it is all a question of making the best possible use of the existing means. And this brings us once more to the question of instinct and standards. Intellectual man will never be able to recover

[19] Compare the accurately investigated case of Ada Jukes, which Günther describes in detail on page 191 of his *Kleine Rassenkunde*. A high percentage of the 2,000 descendants of this debilitated woman were hopelessly incompetent.

[20] Compare R. M. Yerkes, *Psychological Examining in the United States Army*, Washington, 1921. Lothrop Stoddard deals with these data best.

his original instinctive assurance. He should strive to put creative knowledge in its place. He must raise his intellect and spirit by conscious insight, to be enabled to establish the same immediate contact with reality as primitive man possesses on a lower level.[21] This is the principal problem of the near future as regards the proper choice of partners in its relation to posterity. This is the most important task, especially from the standpoint of spiritual and intellectual development. The spiritual and intellectual standard, and consequently the possibility of solving spiritual and intellectual problems, also depends largely on predisposition. Rudolf Kassner once said that aristocracy was an economy of experience. The age of the cultural heritage, if vitality has been preserved, is most certainly a point in its favour. Important problems can be directly solved only when subordinate and temporary ones have been settled; that is to say, when they are being solved automatically and thus leave the mind free to cope with more important matters. That this is the actual state of affairs, and that our forefathers were right in believing in the importance of ancestral lineage and inborn qualities, as opposed to modern conceptions, has been apodictically proved by the crucial experiment of the last century. A democratic age hoped to compensate for hereditary advantages by merely improving conditions and institutions. In this it failed, and such attempts will always fail. For we are creatures of flesh and blood, and only flesh begets flesh. The destiny of blood is also the destiny of the spirit, for only by means of a body can spirit manifest itself on earth. This accounts for the enormous responsibility of parenthood. Mothers are right in seeing in good children something

[21] How this can be achieved is explained in the chapter *Was uns Not tut* in my *Schöpferische Erkenntnis,* and also in *Die neuentstehende Welt.*

every bit as significant spiritually as the supremest work of art.

From this standpoint the proper choice of partners becomes a super-personal problem. The destiny of humanity depends entirely on the nature of the solution given it. If a spirit of collectivism seems to be gaining ground everywhere today, that is a sign that questions concerning the general welfare of all men have become historically prevalent. In this respect we are living under conditions that resemble war times; that is to say, personal considerations have to give place to general necessity. And here, finally, we return to a fact that has already been briefly mentioned; namely, that the problem of the choice of partners is different according as it is taken from the standpoint of the partners themselves or that of posterity. In actual practice also these two aspects have never corresponded. In former times it was simpler, because when people married, their first consideration was their children. Youth was instructed naturally to give precedence to matters of general welfare before thinking of personal interests, and strict conventions guarded against the possibility of defaulting. How shall we manage to cope now and in the near future with the monstrous intensification of personal and individual consciousness? In this connection it can only be stated that life has not become by the awakening of individualism less tragic, but more so. Cases will become ever more frequent in which responsibility to posterity and the interests of self-development will clash in an insuperable conflict. Every one will have to choose his alternative and decide what blame he thereby takes upon himself. It is most certainly the duty of the man of great talents to discharge his debt to humanity by first thinking of his own personal development. The value of every real marriage on a high plane, in the sense indicated in the introductory essay, is so high that it guarantees priority to individual interests over general considerations. Perhaps such highly developed couples, when they recognize that they are liable to endanger their children's welfare, will voluntarily renounce their claims to them. During the entire Middle Ages, though for other reasons, the majority of highly gifted men remained without issue; and this was not such a misfortune as many people suppose, because many of them were pathological from a racial point of view. In fact, this was more often the case in those days than now, because intellectual endowments had then to war against the extremely non-intellectual type of the age. But some form of renunciation is always necessary. This fact enables us not only to combat the sentimentalism which objects to rational grounds for marriage, but to divest this principle of its apparently inhuman character. Man is distinguished from the animals by the fact that his world is created by his spirit. He first proves his manhood by rising superior to his passions; these he should not mortify, but on the contrary, as the Talmud beautifully expresses it, "The greater a man is, the stronger are his passions—but the pure and consecrated man makes of his passions a chariot for God." Man is a human being only if he conquers Nature by spirit. That is why ethics demarcate the lowest stage of the really human. And consequently marriage belongs primarily to the sphere of ethics, or it is not worthy of the name. Marriage without ethos is a valueless concept. There is no need to marry in order merely to gratify one's passions. Whoever does so sins against himself as a human being. Under these circumstances, our investigation, which results in enjoining renunciation, cannot be said to make inhuman demands. To marry rationally is just as much in accordance with human nature, and consequently should be just as self-evident, as to trade honestly, to think logically, not to murder or steal. This is indeed the way to overcome the tragedy of life; it can be mastered only by man's raising himself inwardly above the plane on which the tragic conflict subsists. As an ethical being man is naturally superior to sentiment or passion. And he is truer to his nature when he rejects these at the proper time than when he weakly gives way to their demands. Proper conduct, even if it entails the conquest of self, will at all events bring a higher form of happiness than can be won by letting oneself go. Thus the strict rules regarding the choice of partners are no more cruel than any spiritual rules. Man can obtain freedom—seeing that he is essentially a spiritual being—only by sublimating sentiment and passion so that they become his spiritual expression. Thus we implicitly set aside the last possible objection to the main thesis of this essay; namely, that it represents a soulless ethic of duty. The latter is invariably negative, for wherever man is subject to it he no longer lives, as it were, from his vital centre, but is governed from an eccentric point.

Our assertions, properly understood, only require that *man should realize that he is a free being*. Man is essentially governed by spirit. Consequently he must give prominence to its claims, not, however, to the exclusion of others, but in a vital association with them. If we here take into consideration the facts proved by experience, that "conventional marriage" (*Standesehe*) proves by far the happiest form, and that only such marriages can continue to afford happiness as make allowance for impersonal and super-personal considerations—then we realize that, should the proper choice of partners cause a tragic conflict, it is fundamentally a sign of inadequate education. The vital form of marriage corresponds to man's nature. In marriage, if it properly fulfils its object, a part of which is the correct solution of the accurately formulated problem of the proper choice of partners, man achieves a truly comprehensive and many-sided fulfilment. Consequently, he need only comprehend the significance of his own innermost desires more clearly than most people are aware of them today, and then the renunciation which is essential to marriage proves to be the means, also in the case of the particular problem under discussion, toward achieving a higher and most joyous fulfilment.

ERNST KRETSCHMER

Physical and Spiritual Harmony in Marriage

Ueberall nämlich ist der Instinkt ein Wirken wie nach einem Zweckbegriff und doch ganz ohne denselben.

Instinct is an activity which always appears to be directed toward some idea, and yet is quite without any such.

SCHOPENHAUER,
Metaphysik der Geschlechtsliebe

AMONG all the reasonable and unreasonable causes which year in and year out bring about or prevent the conclusion of marriages, the judgment of the value of physical "beauty" or "ugliness" is apparently the most falsely founded but still the most effective. In the contest of motives it is frequently victorious, vanquishing considerations of money and career and judgments of intelligence and character. Again and again it conquers as one of the central focuses of erotic attraction and repulsion, with a silent, natural coercion, those other more rational arguments for the conclusion of marriage. Wherever we encounter such "irrational" elements in human actions, we are confronted by deep biological questions which extend beyond all personal interests and destinies into the cosmic.

This erotic valuation based on the physical appearance of a human being is, in individual cases, full of passionate subjectivity. It does not become more evidently sensible, real, or legitimate if we follow it from the personal into the sphere of ideals of beauty or ugliness held by entire groups of peoples or certain epochs. But we cannot save ourselves this little excursion, if we want to return with deepened perception to the connections between body and spirit in marriage. For much of this permits of understanding only superindividually; it is fundamentally impulsive—and as far as it is impulsive, it discloses its full sense only sexually; for the happiness of the individual, however, it is fate, destiny, and frequently paradox.

The ideals of beauty held by our European family of peoples, for example, seem to vacillate aimlessly. They vary over wide ranges in the various epochs of the history of art, in which the ultimate extreme on the one side was for a time reached in the Gothic, in an external sharpness, hardness, dryness, and boniness in the portrayal of the face and an almost brittle thinness and delicate slenderness of bodily form; this epoch's ideal of beauty, spiritually characterized by the inclination to ascetic mysticism, therefore evidently favours, within the multitude of variations of the European races, those physical formations which are denoted constitutionally and biologically as asthenic (without strength) or leptosomous (meagre-bodied). It soon swings, beyond the classical middle line of the Renaissance, quite over to the opposite wing of the multitude of racial variations, as we find it again in the paintings of the baroque, culminating in Rubens; it luxuriates in blooming countenances and even in a just tolerable degree of physical exuberance and fulness; well-made man, speaking from the point of view of biological constitution, stands at the apex of the idea of beauty of this time. From the heavy fulness of the baroque, the architectural forms swing in anthropomorphic parallels in accordance with the ideal of beauty in the human bodily form, to the almost childlike delicacy of rococo man, the narrow stylization of length in the Empire, thereafter becoming, with an increasingly more nervous variation, now fuller, now more ascetic. The ideal of beauty traverses the whole range of a race's physical possibilities of form, *in so far as regards the typical and frequently occurring formations of the healthy mass of the population.* Every healthy type of body finds, some day, its esthetic—and let it be said at once, at the same time its erotic—and procreative opportunity. It is stylized by the arts and by the fashions of the period, by which it is favoured with the greatest devotion, to the utmost limit of its possibilities of esthetic effect, and thereby at the same time is brought to the acme of its erotic attraction. The spiritual values belonging to the type of physical make in question swing parallel with this to the epoch's loftiest spiritual heights: the ascetic-metaphysical, the luscious-realistic, the childlike-playful. These great swings of the pendulum of the periods of art, like the short ticking of fashion, themselves pulsed through by the rhythm of wider, cosmic-biological connections, exert an influence on their side, advancing, fundamentally interfering in, and fatefully determining countless love-relationships and marriage compacts, which are thereby blessed or broken. Their "superpersonal" importance can only thus be explained: By a constant rhythmic flux, each of the physical and spiritual possibilities latent in a race is covered and is helped to its broadest possibilities of effectiveness and of sure procreation.

Just as this apparently capriciously vacillating valuation of "beautiful" and "ugly," precisely through these vacillations, accords all the potentially really vital forms within a population their rights, so it works with the same sureness of instinct for the elimination of varieties less fit to live. The valuation of "beautiful" does not by any means embrace all forms of the body coming into existence during an extensive epcch. The ideals of beauty in different periods fluctuate in the first place only with regard to the fulness of the body—slender or luxuriant—and in a slighter degree with regard to the size of body—stately or delicate; but with regard to the construction of the skeleton they all hold to the narrow limits of so-called "good proportion"; that is, within certain proportions of dimensions characteristic of a certain race, as especially the structure of the skeleton of the face, the relation of the lengths of the trunk and of the limbs, as well as the proportionate length and heaviness of the various parts of the limbs to each other. What falls outside this "good proportion" is likewise outside of every ideal of beauty of that group of people; it is apprehended sometimes simply negatively as "ugly," sometimes humorously, sometimes with fright: in short, with a great variety of feelings, but in every case not as "beautiful," and above all, not as erotically attractive for healthy desire. In this class are included the excessively large and excessively small creatures, the "giants" and the "dwarfs"; and above all, those who are badly disproportioned in face or body, who are stamped as "caricatures" or "freaks"—among the freaks, those forms which in biologically characteristic mixture with others affect the instincts as being of a strange species and therefore as erotically repulsive; for example, those of a bestial type or of a markedly foreign race. It is characteristic that in these "ugly" bodily forms certain definite variations of the spirit are thought to dwell; we speak of the "uncouth" giant, the "sly" dwarf, the "fiendish" monstrosity.

Here we come to a peculiarly accurate association of medical and biological with esthetic valuations, especially erotic esthetics, as far as they are naïvely, that is to say, impulsively, conditioned by instinct. The same physical creations, which are outside of esthetic "good proportion," are also usually physically and spiritually outside the realm of the greatest "healthiness." These creations, which are grouped together in constitutional-biological phraseology under the designation "dysplastic," are on the average like so many extreme biological varieties, less stable, of reduced vitality and strength, more subject to illness and destruction, less capable of procreation. Many glandular disturbances are frequently found among them; that is, forms which do not possess the internal chemical balance in the impulsive material of their physical and spiritual make-up; forms with excessively large hands and feet (acromegalous type), with excessively long limbs (type of the eunuch), heavy impediments of development in the middle face and chin (hypoplastic type of face), cretinous and other forms of dwarf growth, coarse variants of the sexual type (coarse-boned male women, men with infantile physiognomies), or those with the symptoms of general sickliness, high degrees of thinness or fat. In all these cases the esthetic valuation of "ugly" coincides with the medical-biological valuation of "abnormal."

Let us now return to our starting-point: to wit, the condition in life of young couples who conclude marriage. Pretty girls are married in preference to ugly ones. A girl announces to her parents with great determination that she will not marry a certain gentleman because she finds him unendurably ugly; and thereby the weightiest considerations of reason go for nothing. Personally, this is a whim of hers; superpersonally, it is an instinct. For her personally it is perhaps the greatest stupidity of her life; superpersonally, there resides within it, as within everything impulsive, a powerful secret reason. As behind the fashions of beauty, so also behind the perception of ugliness there is a universal rule of instinct for the preservation of the qualities of a race. The verdict of ugliness works steadily toward less frequent participation in procreation, and thereby ultimately toward the elimination of biologically inferior variants. This is not the place to determine whether this goal is usually attained under cultural conditions as they have developed today.

Is not the German word for ugly (*hässlich*) derived from the word for hate *(Hass)?* Is it sensible or reasonable to hate anything just because it is not beautiful? At the very point, however, where reason leaves off, the instincts begin, the powerful, dark forces of impulse from the depths. Hatred, the opposite of love, is erotic repulsion.

Has this valuation of the physically "beautiful" and "ugly" a bearing also on the spiritual harmony of married couples or a significance for the preservation of the spiritual qualities of the race? This has often been denied with great emphasis. A reasonable opinion says: Spiritual qualities alone must be conclusive for people of high value on entering into marriage; only superficial people would trouble themselves about defects of beauty. In individual cases this may be sometimes correct, since there is indeed frequent but not general congruence between physical and spiritual "good proportion." We find among the highly gifted and especially among persons of genius accumulations of symptoms of psychic and also, to some extent, physical degeneration, which forcibly lead us to the conclusion that cultural and biological standards of value do not everywhere coincide, but in many points diverge sharply from each other; also, the highly gifted are extreme variants of humankind, and as such are burdened with all the biological disadvantages of the extreme variant, with intensified bodily and spiritual susceptibility to sickness, very limited procreative power, and in part also with disadvantages in outer bodily form. We will here go no further into this very complex problem.

In what groups of mental disposition do we find statistically the greatest frequency and strongest impress of those deformations of physical development which we pointed out above as dysplastic and which are mostly met by the popular instinctive verdict of "ugly"? We find them in whole series in institutions for the feeble-minded, in houses of correction, especially in the sections for psychopathologically degenerate criminals, and finally in the parts of the insane asylums which house the cases of profound hereditary psychic disturbances leading to imbecility, particularly the severe brain-fevers and epilepsies. In short, where the most acute forms of psychic degeneration are gathered, we find at the same time the greatest frequency of hereditary bodily misformation.

This, as a fact of statistical classification of masses, says neither everything nor nothing for the individual case. Cautiously applied to our research, it means about this: Whoever marries a "pretty" example of humanity does not by any means necessarily marry a mentally well-developed person; and whoever, against his instinctive repulsion, chooses a pronouncedly "ugly" person (ugly through proportion, not through an outer deformity) has not because of that met a psychic degenerate. But the probability that an unbalanced mental structure will show itself in an unbalanced bodily form is greater than in a body of even proportions, and the reverse is likewise true. Or, to express it differently: In the selection of mates a beautiful body promises a slightly increased chance of happiness for the prospective spiritual harmony. This is what *mens sana in corpore sano* means—"a healthy mind in a healthy body."

A much more profound, more significant, sense lies, however, in the superpersonal; the physically instinctive judgment, "beautiful" and "ugly," works ultimately most favourably, through the mass of all marriages, not only for physical, but also for spiritual selection in propagation. At least in extreme instances, the chances of concluding a marriage will be thereby rendered forever unfavourable for many severe forms of degeneracy. And again for the preservation of the mental qualities of well-bred and cultured families, the erotic perception of beautiful or ugly bodily form is in the long run not altogether immaterial.

From all these universal rules in the choice of mates we come to the specific question, what definite individual temperaments attract each other erotically and are thus mutually inclined to marriage? The popular interpretation in this matter is not clear and tends to contradictory views. On one side there is the opinion that old married people often resemble each other in essentials of conduct and in outward appearance and become increasingly more similar; on the other hand, that opposites are most attractive to each other in marriage. There is nothing clear in this, nothing more than momentary impressions. I have consequently collected data on one hundred married couples, both parties of which I knew well enough in their true nature and in their outward appearance; the predominant majority belong to the educated class and mostly to the academic profession; obvious "marriages of reason," for the sake of money and of support, were excluded, but for the remainder there was no selection. I have reviewed and statistically evaluated the whole material from the modern points of view of temperament and constitutional biology. It is based, including all the varieties and mixed forms, on the six principal fundamental temperaments; that is: the hypomanic (vigorously alive), the syntonic (comfortably realistic), and the heavy-blooded, on the cyclothymic side; from the schizothymous series, the sensitive (finely-sensitive, delicate, idealistic), the schizothymous middle strata (coolly energetic, quietly aristocratic), and the autistically cold (cold, cold-nervous autistic eccentric).[1]

To obtain a comprehensive view, the married couples were judged by several of their acquaintances, to determine whether they were considered as predominantly mentally similar or dissimilar; the conclusions were then tabulated. The results showed that, of the one hundred married couples, thirteen were considered as predominantly similar, sixty-three as predominantly dissimilar, and twenty-four as about equally similar and dissimilar. Without putting too much emphasis on the results of this very cursory survey, it is at once apparent that those married couples who at first sight are designated by every one who knew them as dissimilar predominate strongly over the very few pairs who are regarded by their closer acquaintances as being essentially uniform. Many of the

[1] More details will be found in my book, *Körperbau und Charakter* (*Physical Form and Character*), fourth edition, Berlin, Springer, 1924. The cyclothymous types, who are yielding and incline to fluctuating periods of oscillation, vary in their feelings by several degrees between the vigorously active and the heavy-blooded handicapped. They incline to a realistic-humorous comprehension of life and physically to a thick-set bodily structure. In case of mental disease, they incline to manic-depressive (circular) insanity. The schizothymous types incline to autismus (that is, to spiritual isolation), to the development of a complicated inner life, to adolescent developments full of crises. Their spiritual life varies from delicate supersensitiveness (Hölderlin natures) to frigidity of disposition. They incline to humourless seriousness, to idealism, and physically to delicacy of structure (small-growing, delicate) or to an athletic physical build, or they display manifold dysplastic disproportions in bodily growth. In case of mental disease, they will generally be seized by schizophrenia (dementia praecox, youthful insanity).

"dissimilar" give the direct impression of contrast in their spiritual structure, especially in their temperaments, and appear as tangibly complementing each other in their personal life and in the transmission of their peculiarities to their children.

It almost goes without saying that people who have not a single point of contact on their entire spiritual horizon do not marry one another; in any case, none such are in our records. Even those who are strongly contrasted share in most cases minor partial complexes in their spiritual make-up, which serve as a bridge to mutual understanding; frequently also, in an inborn and almost complete dissimilarity, this common platform is created through the more spiritual principles gained by education, like similar family backgrounds and manners, similar convictions in views of the world and of religion, even when they are founded and felt inwardly and temperamentally in a wholly different manner by the two parties.

The results are still clearer and more tangible if we evaluate each single personality according to its dominant temperamental type. Thus, we find that among our two hundred persons, seventeen are plainly vigorously active hypomanics (in the entire temperament or in striking partial complexes); thirteen of them have the heavy-set physical construction. Of these seventeen hypomanics, the mate in not one instance has even a remote suggestion of the hypomanic temperament. Hypomanic temperaments, therefore—although marriages of two hypomanics may occasionally occur—have as a whole only a very slight erotic attraction of a lasting kind for each other. This is again a very peculiar fact, one only to be understood instinctively, for it is hard to comprehend why these exceptionally sociable, jolly, active natures, who are very easily approachable erotically, should not more often mate with their own kind. That they do not often do so is a great surprise psychologically.—We find as the mates of our hypomanics, without exception, temperaments in strong contrast with them, but frequently supplementing them favourably: quietly balanced mixed forms, 2; syntone of a quiet, friendly personality, 4; heavy-blooded (with strong nervous drive), 1; schizothymous middle positions (quietly cool, consequently energetic, aristocratic), 4; sensitive (fine-souled, delicate), 3; cold, nervous, 3. Or, to put it briefly, our seventeen cyclothymous hypomanics wed in the first place, that is, in ten instances, their utter opposites, schizothymous mates; in the second place, that is, in five instances, cyclothymous persons out of other temperamental groups, especially the quiet, reasonable syntone; and finally, in two cases, persons of similarly quietly balanced, mixed temperaments.

I have rarely found in my researches heavy-blooded natures touching on the melancholic of the soft cyclothymous type; specifically, only three women. The first has a highly intelligent, extremely over-energetic, schizothymous, cold husband—a very unhappy marriage. The second is married to a similarly energetic, optimistic hypomanic; the marriage is affectionate, but with very irregularly vacillating mutual discords. The third marriage, with a very reasonable, quiet syntonic husband, is happy. I have not found any marriages of two cyclothymous heavy-blooded people. All three marriages are exceptionally strongly contrasted.

As a counter-exhibit to the hypomanics we select now from the schizothymous groups of temperaments the more extremely developed, strongly schizoid personalities, touching on the abnormal; namely, all the strongly autistic types (living in and for themselves), the autistically delicate and the autistically intricate. Of such strong schizoids fourteen were found (of whom there were twelve with delicate leptosomous bodies). These often nervously delicate, agoraphobiac, and impractical natures showed a quite surprising predilection for energetic, life-loving marriage-partners. Twelve of them, the overwhelming percentage, were mated with such. Seven of their marriage-mates were decidedly cyclothymous (four hypomanic, three syntonic); the remaining five likewise energetic, realistic natures, mixed forms made up of cyclothymous components and cool, consistent, or sensuously refined elements of schizothymous stamp.

Only two out of fourteen schizoids chose for themselves similar predominantly schizothymous partners. In both cases it was a type of schizoid late marriage which seems to occur once in a while. Both husbands up to their fortieth year hesitated to get married, so that one might have thought them confirmed bachelors. One of them then found the realization of a latent ideal love of his youth; the other concluded a marriage of convenience with an impractical, esthetically gifted girl of a well-to-do family.

Here we pass on to those who remain unmarried by reason of natural disposition, the "born" bachelor and spinster, who are especially frequent among the strongly schizoid, with their unapproachable shyness and their complicated erotic predispositions—which sometimes lack impulsive drive—and with their tendency to solitude.

Reviewing the whole of our material of more extreme cases of one-sided temperaments, namely, hypomanics, heavy-blooded, and strongly schizoid—a total of thirty-four out of two hundred persons—we must state that inclination to marriages of similarity is quite scarce among them, while inclination to marriages of distinct contrast is so strongly predominant that it can almost be indicated as a rule.

Also in our complete material, marriages of similarity, as has been said, are considerably in the minority. We have examined individually, according to their temperaments, the thirteen married couples indicated as of this form. Apart from the two previously mentioned schizoid late marriages, they were all beings of the spiritual middle sphere, of more balanced temperaments. In four instances there are well-balanced mixed forms; one couple are self-assured society people. In not less than seven instances both mates were syntonic, and at the same time chiefly of the plump, short, pyknic body-type. These pyknic-syntonic married couples are also known to the casual observer and apparently form the foundation of the observations which maintain that older married couples become similar, as long as one does not mean by that the customary equalization of the emotional expression.

These pyknic-syntonic married couples attract attention through their bodily and spiritual likeness; they ultimately bring their manner of life into perfect accord with each other and harmonize in their movements as accurately as two well-regulated clocks: they are surrounded by a sunny, comfortable, quiet atmosphere as of warm coffee-cups.

The result of our researches can be summed up thus: Among a mixed material of sound human beings, marriages of contrast are decidedly more frequent, generally speaking, than those of similarity. The more extreme, the more one-sided, the temperaments are, the more strongly do they prefer marriages of contrast.

Homogeneous married mates are found chiefly in the equalized temperaments of the middle sphere, especially in the syntonic.

Here, as in the case of the effects of "beautiful" and "ugly," or that of the primitive horror of incest, we are facing wonderful regulations of instinct, great superpersonal principles which may not be completely explained by individual psychology, but to some extent operate directly contrary to our expectations. Also, the predominance of marriages of contrast, becoming stronger the closer we come to the extreme types of temperament, works decidedly against the multiplication of extreme biological variants through heredity; it prevents the accumulated ascendancy of those types which are less capable of resistance in health and in the struggle for life. The marriage of contrast is always carrying the imperilled extremes over into the next generation, where they must intermingle with the healthy, biologically adapted mean.

These are its general biological functions. In addition thereto it has still more important individual significance, especially in the creation of high intellectual gifts, notably the training of genius. A good number of great geniuses—I recall Goethe and Bismarck—were sons of exceptionally sharply contrasted marriages. The father of Goethe, with his dry, pedantic earnestness, and the *Frau Rat*, with her sunny, scintillating humour, are polar contrasts; and it is not difficult, with a knowledge of the more complicated connections of individual psychology, to follow the two parental lines throughout the poet's whole life: the distinguished classicism, the earnest, thorough industry of a scholar and a collector, and the somewhat stiff manner of the privy-councillor, on the one side; the effervescing, unconfined temperament, the warmth of soul and the capacity for love, on the other. Each half of his inheritance partly mingled with the other in his life and works, and partly stood side by side with it, in separate phases, acts, and attitudes. Similarly in Bismarck a sharp contrast is presented by the solid realism and instincts of a *Land-junker*, on the one side, and the lofty intellectual refinement of his mother's highly cultured middle-class family of scientists and her restless nervousness, irritability, and biting coldness, on the other. If one compares other such examples, one finds that, for the production of highly endowed men of genius, a sharp contrast in the parental heritages has a double sense. Through the union of two dissimilar dispositions, in such instances, an exceptional width of the intellectual field of vision and of appealing possibilities of emotion will be engendered. And through this sharp, unadjusted opposition, there then arises within the man that problematic inner complication, restlessness, and high intellectual tension which frequently create the prerequisite for novel and distinguished achievement. Yet the children of marriages of contrast are by no means always contrasted human beings. In many cases balanced intermediate forms are developed, while other children continue predominantly the paternal or the maternal portion of their inheritance.

Schopenhauer [2] comprehended with great acuteness and thoughtfully presented the predominance of the instinctive over the personal incentive in erotic attraction. He sees in the happiness of love in young couples a sort of "delusion," a fraud of Nature, which makes what is really only the "will of the race" appear to man as individual happiness. This "delusion" disappears directly after the union and paves the way in marriage for individually rather unsatisfactory conditions. It is not human beings who harmonize individually who attract each other erotically, but rather those whose qualities supplement each

[2] Schopenhauer, *Metaphysik der Geschlechtsliebe*, in *Die Welt als Wille und Vorstellung*, Vol. II ("Metaphysics of Sexual Love," in *The World as Will and Representation*, Vol. II).

other for the procreation of posterity useful to the species. The sovereign will of Nature, to serve the race with the greatest efficiency, therefore operates at the expense of the individual and his life's happiness.

Although in agreement with much that Schopenhauer has said, although our special researches clearly reveal the sovereignty of the superpersonal mechanism of instinct even in the case of the choice of a mate by a cultured modern human being, the one-sidedness of his presentation nevertheless cannot be ignored, a one-sidedness which is inseparably connected with the sharp, sarcastic pessimism of his whole sense of life. With Schopenhauer the discrepancy between the aims of the species and those of the individual in the marriage-choice becomes a tragic conflict which inexorably shatters the individual's happiness.

But such an absolute contrast between the two aims does not in fact exist. The individual choice of a mate is many times the result of a consciously or less consciously formulated compromise between different currents of emotion, which are in part mostly personal, in part mostly racial in origin. Rational and instinctive impulses are mingled therein, the instinctive usually prevailing. But the instinctive is not simply identical with the racial interest, nor the rational with the individual. Many instincts serve the species not against but rather directly through the prosperity of the individual, just through the furtherance of his personal vitality and his advantageous adaptation to life.

And thus accurate observation and psychological analysis of a large number of married couples teach us plainly that combinations most useful for procreation frequently lead at the same time to individually propitious life-partnerships; that, for example, the instinctive inclination to the marriage of contrast not only advantageously mixes the qualities of the offspring, but that this mutual supplementing of qualities often proves likewise of great advantage to both parties to the marriage themselves in the struggle for life. This harmonization produces a lasting feeling for personal life-partnership, while the psychological irritation and repulsion of dissimilar qualities discharge themselves in occasional stormy crises. This is perhaps the most frequent normal occurrence in marriages of contrast.

Aside from this, unhappy marriages are certainly frequent enough. But they arise only in part from the tragic conflict, of which Schopenhauer speaks, between the interests of the individual and those of the species. Much more frequently such marriages are concluded by two psychopathic or at least mentally ill-adjusted human beings, who not only do not understand themselves in the matter of their own life's happiness, but who also have had the instincts of the species within them somehow curbed, injured, or led astray. And when such marriages break up, it is not tragedy, deception, and mordant irony, but only another manifestation of the "will of the race."

We have thus far examined the question of the marriage of contrast, of the relative complementary attitude of two married people, under the aspect of the general theory of temperaments. Still another special problem, much debated biologically, arises here, concerning the harmony of two married people with regard to their sexual characters, their whole sexual nature. This problem refers to the great complex of the whole question of sexual determination, of the delimitation between "masculine" and "feminine" and the eventual forms of transition between the two, and consequently to a subject which has been discussed with growing thoroughness from Schopenhauer and

Weininger to Hirschfeld and Goldschmidt, partly under philosophical, partly under medical and zoological aspects, and which once more occupies the centre of the stage in contemporary biological research. We cannot here describe in detail this great realm of study, but can only formulate the train of thought which is of interest at this point, and which, supported by important facts, may be thus expressed: Man and woman are not absolute contrasts; it is rather possible that the factors of the "masculine" and the "feminine" are potentially embedded in each person, and that for instance in a masculine individual the factors of the "feminine" are more or less inhibited by dominating forces, and vice versa; and that this predominance of one sexual type over the other might possess different degrees in the same individual, so that, strictly speaking, one should distinguish not men and women, but more masculine and more feminine individuals. The degrees of masculinity and femininity might be so sharply graduated that one could obtain a continuous row of "sexual intermediate types" or "intersexes" between the two terminal poles, in the centre of which stand those rare forms of genuine androgyny of which one could not say whether they are of the male or the female sex. This theory, if it could be supported by additional material proof, would in fact supply a uniform frame for many of the facts of universal biology and medicine.

Aside from this special formulation, so much may be said with certainty, that in the sexual characteristics, within the physical as well as the mental realm, important variant formations are frequently to be observed, lesser or greater interstratifications, suggestions of the type of the opposite sex; masculine indications in the woman, feminine ones in the man.

In the spiritual realm we must to this end distinguish

two circles of sexual characteristics, a narrower circle of qualities which group themselves around the instinctive attitude toward mate and children proper to the particular sex, and to which are attached certain qualities corresponding to the will to accept one's own sexual rôle, in clothing, occupation, and other matters. Around this, then, is grouped a much wider circle of mental qualities, much more loosely connected with the sexual functions, and for the most part referring to the rôle of the sexes in the external struggle of life—qualities of character and intellect which permit of indication by expressions such as energy, courage, hardness, and clear, cool judgment. These certainly still have frequent connections with the sexual character, in so far as, in the true sense of the words, they are usually more strongly marked in men than in women. But it is singular that they are never parallel throughout with the narrower spiritual characteristics of sex. One might, for instance, observe in certain types of officers in war that many extremely over-energetic and over-courageous men were very frigid or reserved in their conduct toward women; an historic example of this type in the greatest style is Frederick the Great. One can occasionally make the paradoxical observation that men of this type, through their conspicuous "masculine character," exercise an intensively erotic attraction on women, but are handicapped in the enjoyment of their rewards by the frigidity of their mental sexual character, so that they feel this erotic adoration as an annoying burden.

The variants in the direction of instinct in a more restricted sense are generally found in the pathological realm. Yet their finer nuances, recognizable to the trained eye, are visible in marriages of healthy people. We do not speak here, of course, of the reasonably formulated perversities, with a complete reversal of instinct, which are occasionally met with, but rather of the partially masculine and partially feminine traits, much more interesting psychologically, which are incidental to the psychic structure of fundamentally normal married couples, and of the enigmatic warpings and deviations in the emotional life, the sympathies, and antipathies which are often a mystery to the persons themselves. The sureness of instinctive attraction, bringing together pairs who fit accurately together in mutually supplementing sexual type, is often astounding.

More serious cases of intersexual variants frequently lead to very unhappy marriages, because the conflicting psychic elements cannot be successfully harmonized.[3] Those who possess such dispositions are often torn and discordant in themselves and suffer under psychologically consistent but unrealizable impulsive aims in their desires with regard to their erotic and general psychic connections. This unevenness and this incapacity of fulfilment for contradictory aims of desire lead in marriage to the sharpest irritation; at the worst, when in an exceptional case two variants which are not complementary do meet each other, one mate assumes a normally directed sexual rôle and the other a metatropic.

The marriages of Strindberg are a pathological prototype of the psychic disorder in the relationship of an intersexual husband with his wife—a man who over-compensates his partially feminine traits by a rugged emphasis on the male part; for whom the conflict with the woman, and through her the woman-question in general, has become the perpetually renewed central problem of his life; who therefore has been driven into a prophetic rôle in the

[3] Compare the psychological study of Kronfeld, *Ueber einen bestimmten Typus metatropischer Frauen* ("A Certain Type of Metatropic Women"), in *Jahrbuch für sexuellen Zwischenstufen,* 1924.

modern struggle for power of the sexes, because the "masculine" and the "feminine" fight constantly within himself, since the desire for domination and the voluptuousness of subjection are mingled in the most irreconcilable contrasts of his own inherited predisposition. In this way his own marriages are always destructive tragedies, sizzling fireworks between ice and flame, hot amorousness and cold hatred, attracting and repelling, brutal, never satisfied, kept constantly feverish by the sensual desire to torture and to be tortured.

On the other hand, we so frequently find in married couples the reverse of the qualities which are significant for the sexual type in a broader sense that, disregarding extreme instances, we must look on these as normal variants, especially since in many cases these peculiarities do not offer disadvantages for the spiritual life together of marriage and for the struggle of existence, but rather more often represent very serviceable life-partnerships. We mean the cases in which the woman at certain points, or throughout the entire relationship, is superior to the man in the qualities of strength, energy, hardness, and finally also in a sharper power of discrimination. I count not less than eleven examples of this type among the one hundred married couples. We indicate this frequent type of marriage, with reversal of the masculine and feminine sexual rôles in regard to the qualities of the universal struggle of existence, as the F.-M. type. These F.-M. marriages represent a significant special case in the marriage of contrast and complement, as we have already observed in the case of the universal instinctive attraction of the temperaments. Of fourteen men among the cases in our record who may be indicated as weak and only slightly energetic, all but three have very energetic wives.

The combination of the hen-pecked husband and a

Xanthippe represents the most extreme case of the F.-M. marriage, a type which has been almost over-exploited by caricature in literature and drawing, but which is really quite rare. Out of our hundred couples I have only a single truly typical instance of this kind. This extreme type does not represent simply a normal complement of temperament; its occurrence can hardly be explained without suggestions from the sadistic-masochistic group. In contradistinction to popular notions, it is noticeable in our material that the F.-M. marriages are in large part exceptionally happy and harmonious, and in their beautiful completion of intellectual qualities, present to the outside world a worthy and sympathetic picture. Healthy, sensible, and well-bred women in such marriages for the most part avoid lapses from their feminine rôles; even wives who are dreaded by outsiders for their hardness and sharpness are inclined to idealize their weak, good-hearted husbands imaginatively rather than to minimize them. They instinctively seek to preserve toward them the "upward-looking" character of their normal sexual rôle; occasionally their feelings toward their husbands are transposed beautifully into the feelings of the painstaking mother. I remember instances in which a wife of this kind, in spite of the most authoritative energy in domestic matters, honoured her very clever, efficient, and good-hearted husband with devotion and conducted him every morning through the garden to the gate, even when she was an old woman.

Men who wed such "authoritative," energetic wives often have a significant type of constitution; the one group is of a very weak disposition, good-tempered cyclothymous, of pyknic bodily build; the other groups, intellectually very dissimilar from them otherwise, are sensitively delicate or impractical schizothymous people who are shy of life.—The "upward-looking" abandonment or half-maternal care of the wife for the husband is destroyed in such marriages only through fundamental discords, when, as in the rarer instances, the wife is too frigid of temperament and too tactless, or when the husband is so irreclaimably weak and ineffective in life that the wife's imaginative idealization of him fails; apart from this, features of real sexual inversion, metatropic peculiarities of desire, or sadistic-masochistic passion for torture may be present on both sides.

We contrast with the type of the weak husband of the energetic wife the reversed case of the "domestic tyrant" who emphasizes to an extreme degree his decisive position in the family. One finds him predominating in the older generation, with its more patriarchal notions, since he is somewhat out of fashion, and since even husbands who exhibit tendencies in this direction come under the influence of the spirit of the times, with its sense of the equality of the sexes. Nevertheless, we have eight such cases in our series. We are dealing with entirely different psychological structures in the case of these domestic tyrants. Several of our examples are men otherwise masterful in life, too; natures of strong feelings, powerful organizers in positions of leadership. Others are neurotic in Adler's sense of the term, egotistic people, weak, "neurasthenics" who over-compensate for their awareness of their own insufficiency by their emphatic claim to consideration, and who keep the family subjected to themselves by little hysterical devices. In another instance of an evil kind, where different wives succumbed under psychic maltreatment, sadistic motives appear to have had an influence—but we must leave this exceptional case to one side.

What sort of wives associate with despotic husbands? In half our cases we again have decidedly complementary, well-matched temperaments; that is, pyknic-syntonic wives, affectionately kind, but certainly not wavering personalities, who enwrap the harsh husband with goodness and who with comprehending foresight and humour direct affairs to some extent, but who anyhow hold their own at his side.

The three remaining marriages are decidedly marriages of contrast, but unhappy ones; the wife does not hold her own against her despotic husband and is spiritually crushed by him. One, the wife of an imposing, rugged schizothymous husband of the greatest intellectual force, could not keep up with his dizzy social rise; she failed under the burden of her great social tasks and was inwardly rejected by her husband; she herself, a pronouncedly pyknically built woman with a rather heavy-blooded, irresolutely soft temperament and of simple intellectual endowment, sank into a sub-depressive psychic condition. The two other women are quiet, unobtrusive schizoids of insignificant, pallid appearance, nervous, intimidated, with an expression of mute resentment in their faces; they have been completely pushed out of the way, and live in fear of people and like shadows in the background of the house.

HANS VON HATTINGBERG

Marriage as an Analytical Situation

As the closest sort of human contact with another human being, the one most different by reason of sex, marriage is a test of inner poise. We become so forcibly conscious of the problematic element in ourselves in this constantly problematic connection that many a structure of character is shattered. Marriage has a dissociating effect on those who are involved in it, for the union always remains a task. If, however, we here consider marriage as an "analytical situation," we do so primarily in a much narrower sense. Analysis or psychoanalysis indicates for us today a psychological method, a means of producing spiritual effects, and intelligence is therefore still required if we are to consider the great question through the instrument of the latest psychic research.

I. The Analytical Situation

The medical process of healing by psychoanalysis is directed toward the spiritual disturbance of nervousness, toward an inner division, the morbid exaggeration of the contrast between that of which we are conscious and that which causes our dreams which we do not understand. In the most extreme instances this connection is broken to such an extent that one arrives at a duplication of personality, at the creation of a second "I," when movements of the dream-world which is otherwise wrapped in sleep come to life, to a life of sinister independence, in the form of nocturnal somnambulism. But here a fissure always separates the realm of the unconscious from the conscious life of day to such an extent that its manifestations are experienced as something incomprehensible, something foreign to the ego. It may be morbid coercion or nervous fear whose meaninglessness one tries in vain to resist; it may be an apparently physical derangement behind which the actual impelling feeling is completely hidden.

This increased contrast between that which appears externally and the life of impulse in the unconscious arises through a handicapping of natural development. Nervous man is not capable of harmonizing the many-sidedness of his disposition with the demands of the surrounding world. For that reason he suppresses by force wishes and desires which are not consonant with what he would like to be, and this resistance, even in childhood, keeps the disturbing impulses from developing freely. For this reason, it is the task of analysis to relieve the strain of the suppression so that the stunted impulses may presently unfold themselves more naturally. The object is to smooth out a spiritual unevenness, and the influence of the method is directed toward stimulation of the repressed development. The nervous one must, so to say, recover what he has missed in his youth; he must live out his suppressed infantilisms, in order to win a better poise from the freer counterplay of forces. But this is accomplished in the realm of impulse, and therefore in the analytical situation the laws peculiar to it will govern, the significance of which for our psychic life has been revealed in its true light only through psychoanalytic research.

The essence of analysis lies in the fact that it emphasizes

the special right of the impulse-life in opposition to defence of the consciousness against everything that refuses to submit to the harmony of its logic with itself. It is directed toward the natural self-development of all the forces with which a human being is invested, and finds a hidden sense even where pure reason perceives only nonsense, in the labyrinth of dreams, in the large and small errors of our behaviour, yes, even in the nervous symptoms which indicate disturbance. But in its immediate sphere it shows those other sides of our spiritual life which we like to forget in our joy at the manifold play of thought, the peculiar blindness of instinct which only desires the gratification of the always limited interest of the individual. It demonstrates it in the analytical situation in the mechanism of the "transference" which dominates the relations of impulse between the analyst and the analyzed.

The process of this transference becomes most intelligible through observations of the more simple psychic organisms of the animal world. Here we see that any object is satisfactory to the instinctive impulse once the latter is aroused—in this way a cat, when deprived of its kittens, may become attached to young rats to gratify its instinct of maternal care—and we find further that the connection between impulse and object may often be nearly accidental.[1] It is known that something similar occurs also with human beings. The young maiden's awakening ardent need for love becomes directed by the same necessity toward any actor playing the part of a hero, and in other ways as well we are governed by a "law of position." To the man in the trench every one

[1] Newly born chickens attach themselves by instinct to every living being near at hand, after coming out of the shell; and they even follow the steps of their breeder, as they would follow a brood hen, if he simply busies himself with them at the right time.

who is opposite him becomes an enemy; and every adult, put back on the school-bench, directs—like a real pupil—compulsorily determined typical emotions toward the person in the teacher's chair.

The analytical situation shows, however, by weight of experiment, how unexceptionably rule is binding. When the nervous one makes up his neglected development here, the most widely different instinctive emotions are freed from their repression. These impulsive inclinations, which pertained to earlier periods of life, are now one after another transferred with almost mechanical necessity to the analyst, because he is near when they become active. In this way he is not only made a teacher, but even put into the position of a father; and thus all that need for tenderness which the child could not gratify, because his own father may have remained a stranger to him, attaches itself to him. In the same way as the friendly and erotic emotions, all the sentiments of repulsion which handicapped childhood are transferred to him.

No matter how many of these adaptations arise in the analytical situation, it always so happens that the emotion simultaneously confers on the analyst the qualities—hatred, the hateful ones; love, the lovable—which are needed to justify it. Irrespective of who he may actually be, he becomes precisely that one whom the other needs, through the clothing of the emotions which succeed each other according to rule and which take hold of him; and it is one of the most important tasks of analysis to make these changes conscious. Nothing shows more emphatically how we unconsciously dream out into the world, only to perceive the creations of our outward-directed imagination as the objects which our impulsive wishes desire.

The various impulsive emotions which the analytical situation arouses are transferred to the analyst not, however, because he is the most accessible person to whom they can cling, but rather from a deeper cause. The spiritual obliquity of nervousness arises in the struggle with the hostile surrounding world as the result of an unsuccessful attempt at adaptation. Its sense is defence against the inner world as well as against the outer. As the stutterer sets his defect between himself and mankind, of which he is afraid, as excessive weakness is often concealed behind severe harshness and wilfulness, so the nervous symptoms, like the exaggerations of the nervous character, generally aim to protect secret weakness. For the nervous person, his illness, his outward appearance, that to which he holds fast in the presence of others, is a fortress like a snail's shell, into which he retires in fear of contact with a surrounding world which he feels he cannot conquer. It is this fear, this aloofness, which has already hindered his development, which must be overcome by the one who wishes to help him, who really wishes to approach him. On that account every attempt to remove the repression, every step of the analytical unfolding, meets with resistance. When analysis disentangles the suppressed development retrogressively, the struggle out of which it arose is once more fought out in the relation to the analyst as the representative of the opposition.

Thus, what happens in the analytical situation is under all circumstances a battle. However intensely the nervous person longs for help, he is in the end like a wilful child who despairingly defends himself against what he most longs for. He suffers from this coercive instinctive opposition which separates him from the natural community of feeling with other human beings. The more he retires into the snail-shell of his isolation before the supposed menace, the more dangerously does terrified illusion change its object. He defends himself ultimately against the phantoms of his imagination. Therefore in all the different forms of resistance the same contrast exists. Like the stubborn weeping of the self-willed child, everything, exaggerated contradiction and submission, compulsory repression and exuberance of emotion, convulsion and paralysis, has a dual significance of attraction and repulsion at the same time. Fighting others, he fights himself.

The most important of the various forms of resistance also has the same double sense: the erotic misunderstanding of the analytical situation. The internal defence is likewise directed against the desires of the individual senses; fear of the questions of sexuality is therefore the most serious handicap to natural development. When analysis frees the sexual emotions from their suppression, they too are transferred to the analyst; thus his proximity turns into erotic attraction. But the more erotic tension becomes an aim in itself, the more surely it restrains analytical unfolding. The vacillations of a fantastic game of love hinder the progress of liberating knowledge. It now appears as though the human approach of the helper would require the closest bodily contact, as if a love-union with him could bring deliverance. But below the deceptive bridge of these desires which cannot be fulfilled, the psychic chasm gapes unchanged; the same undiminished fear separates love and sensuality. As though physical union would degrade the spiritual; as though sensual contact did not agree with the sentiments of devotion and adoration which are directed toward the helper; as if sensuality were necessarily impure. In this way, erotic misunderstanding conceals the most difficult problem: inward purification, the overcoming of the inner contrast between god and beast, between soul and body. It hides the uncomfortable truth that each human being can find his own salvation only in himself, in order to endure that last human intimacy which removes his loneliness.

II. Marriage as a Mutual Understanding

It is primarily due to the nature of the nervous disturbances on which it was perfected that psychoanalysis could develop from a medical process of healing to a psychological method of the most universal significance, so that it is reasonable to apply it to the important problems of marriage. Through it we have learned to know nervousness as a border zone of human nature, as a morbid exaggeration of the internal contradiction which differentiates it from the animal nature. The disproportion between what the conscious ego wishes to be and the life of impulse in the unconscious is never completely resolved, even in a healthy individual. We all put natural instinctive emotions aside, in order to adapt ourselves to the forcible requirements of our modern forms of life, under the pressure of which scarcely any one can develop himself unhindered. But even the freest development limits the original multiplicity of human temperament when we assume the sexual rôle, when we permit one of the two sides of our nature, the masculine or the feminine, to become dominant. Originally every one is man and woman at the same time: the most ancient myths and the most recent psychological discoveries are in agreement on this point; the psyche of the child unites the two poles. But as soon as we decide to become what we are destined to be by our sex, a revaluation of all fundamental values begins, which only in simple beings is accomplished without struggle and friction. The richer the temperament and the greater the contrasts it comprehends, the more inward labour is necessary to achieve a unified personality. That is never possible without renunciation, and thus the more human an individual is, the more profound remains his yearning for his other half, even where the impulsive forces are harmoniously arranged around the determining pole of sex. Intimate contact with the other sex brings therefore the strongest stimulus of life to a development which has not yet reached the best solution. In the other one, who *is* that to which unconscious wishes drive, the other side of human nature is experienced, which conceals for the adolescent, the young man as well as the young woman, the necessarily one-sided change to sexual maturity. It behooves one to discover himself truly in this experience. As the woman becomes a female only through the man, so also must the man prove himself as a male through the woman.

But it is different in those cases where a streak of psychic obliquity is concealed in masculine or feminine one-sidedness, where suppression hinders natural development, because fear stands between the two sides and morbidly enhances the inner contrast. Union within the narrow space of the married partnership, forcing an ever-increasing *rapprochement* of the one to the other, acts in such cases as an incentive to development which is frequently just as impressive as that which inheres in the analytical situation. For that reason the effect (as far as it is not produced by the deliberate direction of the analyst) is essentially the same, in the domain of impulsive actions. Here too, through the slackening of the artistic balance, suppressed impulses and neglected infantilisms awake in order to exercise themselves on the other, and the emerging instinctive emotions are by the same necessity blindly transferred to him, as the nearest person to whom they can be attached. In every stage of development the unconscious need invests him with the requisite clothing. Since the critical control of the analytical situation is lacking, the contradiction between the fantastically changed picture and the actuality is here often much more grotesque. Even the most good-natured and kindest man becomes thus a dread tyrant, an energetic, clever woman becomes a helpless child which must be led step by step, simply because it fits into the general character of just this phase of development: an unparalleled object-lesson on how the human mind is bound by impulse, how peculiarly blind instincts are.

As in the analytical situation, so also in marriage under all circumstances development is a struggle. One defends himself by the most various forms of resistance, conscious and infinitely more unconscious ones, against the proximity of the other, although like a capricious child one yearns for it at the same time. Fundamentally each one suffers from loneliness, and whatever resistance is shown amounts at the same time to a prayer for liberation from the constraint of one's own isolation. Above all, one defends his own weakness in resisting the other. So it is, when a basically all-too-weak man complains of the severity and coldness of his wife, which has only been produced by his unconscious (female) need for masculine firmness in the other, by his displaced passivity. Finally, in marriage, too, resistance grows with proximity. The greater the intimacy, the more conclusively the other becomes the representative of the rest of the world; and ultimately the whole life is lived solely in relation to the other, no matter whether the external form is one of attraction or repulsion, as the only standard, as the sole counter-pole of one's own existence. Yet only a very few know how far they are determined in their basic behaviour, as in the details of their outward appearance, by their marriage, by their instinctive movements of assimilation or their defence against a permanent understanding with the other.

Finally, the erotic misunderstanding which marriage so often inaugurates is common to both forms of human contact. This is at once recognizable where, for instance, the weak-willed man seeks an energetic partner for himself in order to become thereby more manly, or where a woman whose need for dominance cannot be satisfied by the part of the female gives herself in love to a weaker man, "out of pity," in order to help him. It is likewise active where a particularly strong erotic attraction comes into being between such contrary types, because it is strengthened by suppressed unconscious wishes,[2] whose sudden eruption is frequently the explanation of "passion" or "love at first sight." What drives human beings to each other in this case is in fact that their close approach may mean to them the most important stimulus of life in their handicapped development, when they live out their suppressed instinctive needs through the other person so as to overcome them. But the more erotic tension becomes an aim in itself, the more certainly does it hinder analytical unfolding, in opposition to the deeper sense of such a "development-love." Still another check presents itself next to this one when a marriage has been contracted through such an attraction. It is only too natural that the masculinity of the husband, growing in strength, should be turned against the now inconvenient energy of the wife, just as the awakening womanly sentiment of the wife no longer finds satisfaction in the weak masculinity of the other, so that the development in both cases is a menace to the marriage.

[2] In the case of the man "feminine" or passive, in that of the woman "masculine" or active, the most extreme developments of which become apparent in the phenomena of masochism and sadism.

What is here true in a special sense is likewise so in a much more general one. Out of the uncertainty of the period of transition which is ever further isolating us, we press with greater urgency toward the other, since we need more than ever the nearest human being, although we are disquieted by such proximity. At the same time, what is today in the process of formation is unquestionably a change in the relation of the sexes. Rearrangement can be fruitful only when we become conscious that each one must seek a solution within himself. But this problem is for the most part masked by the erotic misunderstanding which separates the sexes. Most frequently in the form of the quite common opinion: with men, that woman exists for nothing but sensuality; with women, that man seeks in them fundamentally only this one gratification; and therefore with both sexes, that comradeship and friendship between man and woman is impossible. Or in other words, as if "sensuality" were a remedy for sick souls, as if one could love oneself into health, as if sensuality could bridge over the inner contrast of two human beings whose souls are wrestling with each other.

In general we have likewise exaggerated the importance of the erotic for marriage. This certainly does not mean that, as in the analytical situation, the erotic tension should or could be eliminated in marriage. Just as love is duality in "yes" and "no," so simultaneous union and separation is the task of healthy sensuality. In marriage it preserves the natural distance between the sexes, since the most intimate union of bodies and souls is followed in natural rhythm by the movement to the proper pole; the man takes himself back to his work, the woman to her child.

This natural balancing is disturbed when we exaggerate the erotic toward the physical pole, in the direction of sensuality, and in the same way when we exaggerate in the opposite direction and combine the requirement of absolute understanding with the desire for love. The result of such pressing into one another all the way to complete spiritual amalgamation is constant lust of the soul, which of itself will grow further and further. The higher the emotion, however, the sooner every slackening can bring about the disillusion which demands a new ecstasy, since only for a moment can one merge oneself into another. But above all, through this requirement marriage becomes an "analytical" situation in the most dangerous sense. When the one accompanies every vibration of the other, deflections are reciprocally enhanced, and this give and take shakes the natural boundaries of the ego. Ultimately one loves only in self-defence, and the "hatred of the sexes" blazes up with redoubled vigour between husband and wife. So this most concealed erotic misunderstanding contains the germ of decay in marriage.

Marriage therefore works "analytically" primarily in the sense that it shakes every superficial equipoise, and what this may mean in the individual case depends on the direction of the development. Conditions are only seldom as favourable as in the analytical situation for bringing about this liberation, and not on that account alone, since the conscious guidance of the analyst must be missing. If both come into motion, the one very rarely will be able to serve the other as a fixed pole at which he is to arrive at an understanding with himself. When the two developments do not advance at the same tempo, their different phases must disturb one another; [3] and in this way, with two partners of different personal weightiness, the

[3] In the same degree as the too feminine man would develop his masculinity, his too masculine wife would become more womanly.

stronger becomes a handicapping pressure on the weaker, who must strive to keep pace with him, though without being able to follow him. Then, when the natural relation of the sexes shifts, a struggle for superiority unavoidably arises, which the analytical situation methodically eliminates, because there it is one-sided.

This conflict for superiority is accountable for the fact that development in marriage so often brings increased spiritual obliquity instead of liberation. Many avoid it in simulated childlikeness (which often goes so far that the married people talk to each other only in the manner of speech of little children) and thereby preserve a tolerable although artificial form of living together, although they thereby renounce spiritual elevation through each other. But only too often this does not succeed. If a nervous person is drawn into this conflict with one more robust and healthy, he will practically always (as manifold experience shows) be driven only the deeper into his neurotic isolation, through the increasing anguish to which the threatening proximity gives rise. Under such pressure a disturbance at first trifling can develop into a serious neurosis—marriage itself becomes a neurosis in the most unfavourable case, because each party doggedly continues his struggle with the other as an end in itself. A fight—fundamentally always about the same question, whatever the object of strife may otherwise be, as, for example, points of view toward the world or domestic problems. One suffers under this conflict; yet in spite of that one ever and again unconsciously seeks it with all the keenness of the suppressed instincts, with all the humiliations of despair, since one must neither win nor be vanquished, yet is powerless against his own compulsion. And all this, in order not to be compelled to see that one is fighting oneself in the other, that one is dodging the task of seeking a better solution of life by fleeing into this struggle and its isolation.

While this form of the neurotic conflict-marriage occurs only in the most unfavourable case, wherever the equipoise vacillates because analytical development does not follow a straight line, a wholly unconscious Hither and Yon is in action, which may be concealed by the most diverse external appearances—often beneath the surface of apparently harmonious living together. Thus, when the disappearance, to a certain extent, of the nervous depressed condition in the one and his now bright mood automatically produces in the other a downcast feeling which is beyond his understanding. As though it mattered who may be the more childlike, the weaker, and the sicker, each one unconsciously strives to enforce consideration for his own weakness, by exaggerating it, as he used to do as a child with his parents. No matter who from without plays the part of mediator, no matter which presses toward the other or which offers resistance in attack or defence, ultimately everything is an unconscious struggle for the goal of which each must understand the other; a conflict, therefore, again for supremacy, even to the other end unavoidable; as if the up of the one and the down of the other were tied by a "law of balance."

III. The Way of Analysis

One can maintain with good cause that all this Hither and Yon contradicts the sense of marriage. Not the "development-love," but only that other less passionate but deeper sentiment of lasting congeniality and esteem, with which a healthy sensuality is harmoniously united, must be its true basis. Therefore only the mature human being should be permitted to declare in public that which binds him to the other. But whatever our fundamental attitude as to this may be, marriage works today in an irresistibly increasing degree as an analytical situation,[4] and with increasing frequency in the sense of self-disintegration. Many people, who must experience this in themselves, feel it as a failure in the face of an ethical demand; and thus the analytical process is almost without exception burdened by severe struggles of conscience. Difficulties in marriage are still universally regarded as a distinct disgrace. Yet it is quite obvious that they occur not with fickle and irresponsible, but just with serious and conscientious natures.

What happens in this form to the individual is without doubt the outcome of a universal happening. We live in a time of transition, and this change attacks above all the more complex. It destroys the ties which gave a hold to the generation before ours, and it loosens every arrangement which covers unsolved questions. We are confronted by adjustments with the "other" as if with the "new"; and this development, which is just as responsible for the nervousness of the age as for many of the nervous disturbances of the individual, is experienced by husband and wife in the fluctuations of their relationship. All this occurs with the inward necessity of impulsive happenings, and on account of this the human *rapprochement* of the sexes is unavoidable, which works as an incentive to development. In this way marriage today becomes an analytical situation even for maturer

[4] This is not only proved by the increase of divorces. The unconscious fear of marriage, which often lies concealed under a directly opposed conscious demeanour, as well as the very frequent, mostly unconscious fear of the other sex (among others, one of the roots of homosexuality), is produced in its final analysis by a hazy premonition of the dangers of such an upsetting of spiritual equipoise. The bachelor and the spinster are therefore disdained by popular opinion, since they avoid the test.

human beings, and the question only remains: What is to be done in order to put the right significance into the development?

In this we can profit from the experiences of psychoanalysis. In any event it means liberation, if we understand that we seek upon the battlefield of marriage a decision which we can find only in ourselves; that we contend against our own weakness and the uncomfortable task of inner improvement in contending with the person nearest to us. In the same way we gain when we learn from psychoanalysis the many meanings of "resistance" and in what multiform external appearances the same occurrence can be veiled.[5] Often it is recognizable only to the eye of the physician, and often it appears in a form (as, say, "marital infidelity") the understanding of which must necessarily cause the partner exceptional difficulties. It is here important to hold to the methodological fundamental premises of the analytical situation, since the same double sense after all underlies all these detours. How-

[5] Thus nervous disturbances of the sexual life (as impotence in the husband or frigidity in the wife) often arise in this way. The theoretical interpretation of Freud has traced back the disturbances of human relationships in marriage, especially in the first stages, almost exclusively to such disturbances of sexuality. While this is often true, it is just as certain that it is an "erotic misconception of psychoanalysis" to overestimate the importance of sexuality, to such an extent, indeed, that the uninitiate have come to believe that it teaches that "everything depends on sexuality." This exaggeration was nevertheless necessary in the continuity of the great analytical process to which we are subject; and therein, that he had the courage to carry it through, lies not the least of the immortal service of Freud. "Sensuality" is still, however, quite universally looked upon as necessarily unclean. Although many people have overcome this inner contradiction of a morality which is today devoid of meaning, a handicap which we have mentally overcome is not for that reason alone removed in the realm of the instinctive. It was therefore necessary to demonstrate time and again in the broadest way how everything in our psychic life, the "highest" thoughts, are motivated by the impulsive force of the erotic; no matter that this force has thereby been understood as "sexuality." If everything is "sexuality," then the quotation-marks by which we emphasize "sensuality" fall of themselves.

ever simple the mental translation is made, it is difficult and often impossible to understand the mirror-writing of the unconscious in a vital way, to sense the longing for inner proximity in the exaggerated defensive attitude of another, when one is moving toward him.

For that reason, one never can become the analyst of his own partner in marriage, since one is not allowed that aloofness which is methodologically created by the analytical situation. Love as analysis, this inversion of the erotic misunderstanding, leads just as unavoidably to self-disintegration as too much stress on understanding. On the other hand, we learn from the mistakes which appear with particular clarity in the procedure of the analyst. Analysis differs from other means of spiritual influence chiefly through the fact that it does not start from a predetermined concept of the direction of synthesis. Agreement is the natural thing, and this can be achieved only through the breaking down of the resistance, by lifting the internal contradiction, in its profound senselessness, to consciousness. Analysis does not attempt to shape actively but takes effect through a patient evolution. When analytical breaking down arouses the fear which caused the suppression when one was solitary, the human nearness of the other helps to overcome it. Out of the living personality of the helper emanates the constructive power—not from explanation and instruction—which alone can serve as an incentive to further development. Thus the analytical situation sets a task for the helper which no one can fully execute, since it exercises his entire human nature, and nothing is more natural than that he too should fail. The expression of his defence, of his resistance, is theory. He becomes dogmatic and doctrinaire when he does not know how to extricate himself in a human way.

To the same extent, the arbitrary barrier between husband and wife hinders a natural unfolding, when one holds out to the other theoretical requirements as to what should be considered truly masculine or feminine as true love and marital duty. Here too one presumption only is fruitful: that agreement is the natural thing. But each alone, as his own analyst, can overcome the resistance within himself. When fear arises, one can find help in the certainty that the other is just as solitary as himself, in the same way that today all conscious human beings are solitary. Beyond this one can help the other through a human closeness offered with patient readiness, not as a violent demand.

This attitude of understanding certainly requires that one should first of all understand himself, and this to many an individual is impossible without instruction, which can only be offered by one who is sufficiently aloof—a true friend, therefore, but often a third person whom exceptional experience in life or exceptional gifts make capable of judgment.[6]

Even more important than all such assistance, which can represent no more than a means of help toward self-knowledge, is everywhere the analytical basic attitude that *every disturbance of the marital relation* must be regarded

[6] An almost terrified reticence prevents many from claiming such help, "since every man must cope with himself." Only when there is no other resort, when the internal contradiction has been developed to the point of nervous disturbance, does one go to the doctor as a "sick" man, in order to load the entire responsibility upon him. But just as general evolution pushes the tasks and opportunities of the physician ever further in the direction of educational and spiritual activity, so under the pressure of growing difficulties that reticence disappears which today is devoid of meaning, the residue of the individualistic exaggeration which had left the patient entirely to himself. It becomes a purely technical question, as the growing interest in the various branches of the scientific knowledge of mankind proves (physiognomy, graphology, and above all psychoanalysis), whether one permits oneself to be helped in order to overcome internal difficulties the more quickly.

primarily as *an expression of one's own resistance.* When each of the marriage partners is striving, in the inescapable conflict for superiority, to get ahead of the other in the knowledge of his own intricacies, then there arises in marriage that peculiar "objectivity of two" which the analytical situation methodically seeks to bring about and by which a correct direction can be accepted even from the marital opponent—a most beautiful realization of a new creed, that highest objectivity amounts to highest humanity.

Marriage as a Psychological Relationship

Viewed as a psychological relationship, marriage is the most complicated of structures. It is composed of a whole series of subjective and objective data, very heterogeneous in nature. As in my contribution to this book I wish to limit myself to the psychological problem of marriage, the greater part of the objective data of a legal and social character must be excluded, although these facts greatly influence the psychological relationship of the mates.

Wherever we speak of "psychological relationship," we presuppose *consciousness*. No psychological relationship can exist between two persons in a state of unconsciousness. From the psychological standpoint, they would be without any relationship at all. Some other relationship might exist between them, for instance, a physiological one; but this relation could not be termed psychological. Complete unconsciousness to the degree we have assumed does not exist, but partial unconsciousness of a not insignificant degree does exist. The psychological relationship is limited in the degree to which this unconsciousness exists.

In the child, consciousness rises out of the depths of unconscious mental life, beginning like separate islands which by degrees unite themselves to a continent, to connected consciousness. The gradual process of mental development means *expansion of consciousness*. With the birth of connected consciousness a psychological relationship becomes possible. Consciousness, as far as we understand it, invariably means ego-consciousness. To be conscious of myself, I must be able to make the distinction between myself and others. Only where this distinction exists is a relationship possible. This general distinction is always made, but normally it is incomplete, because there are very wide ranges of mental life that are unconscious. Unconscious substances cannot be distinguished; therefore no relationship can be established in their sphere: in their range the original unconscious state of a *primitive identity* of the ego with the other still prevails; that is to say, there is no relationship at all.

The young person at the marriageable age has an ego-consciousness (which is more true, generally speaking, of girls than of young men), but it has not long risen out of the midst of the primitive state of unconsciousness. Therefore, there are wide ranges yet shadowed by unconsciousness, and these, as far as they go, make it impossible to establish a psychological relationship. This practically means that a younger person has but an incomplete knowledge of the other, as well as himself, and therefore will not be sufficiently aware of his own motives and those of the other. As a rule, he acts chiefly upon unconscious motives. Of course, he subjectively imagines himself exceedingly conscious, for one always overrates the substance of the momentary state of one's consciousness, and it is always a great and surprising discovery to learn that what we imagined a summit achieved at last is, in reality, only the lowest step of a very long stair. The wider the range of unconsciousness, the less is marriage the result of free choice; subjectively this may be observed in the very noticeable compulsory *fatality* of love.

Where there is no infatuation, compulsion may yet exist, but in a less agreeable form.

The unconscious motives are of a personal and a general nature. In the first instance, they are motives originating from parental influence. There the young man's relation to his mother and the young girl's relation to her father is determinative. In the first place the relationship to the parents unconsciously influences, advancing or impeding, the choice of a mate. A conscious love of father or mother promotes the choice of a mate resembling that father or that mother, while an unconscious link (which need not consciously be manifested as love) makes such a choice difficult and leads to curious modifications. This cannot be understood before we know where the unconscious link with the parents originated and under what circumstances it will bring about, in an imperative way, modifications of conscious choice, or even prevent the choice. *As a rule, all that was artificially repressed in the parents is transmitted to the children in a perverted form;* that is, the children are unconsciously forced into a line of life that compensates what was left unfulfilled in the life of their parents. That is why over-moral parents have so-called immoral children; why an irresponsible and idle father has a morbidly ambitious son, etc. The worst consequences have their source in the *artificial unconsciousness* of the parents. For instance, a mother who closes her consciousness so as not to destroy the appearance of a happy marriage unconsciously attaches her son to herself as a compensation for her husband. This drives the son, if not directly into homosexuality, at least into modifications of his choice which really do not suit his character. For instance, he will marry a girl manifestly not equal to his mother, who consequently cannot compete with the latter, or will fall into the hands of a woman of a tyrannical and arrogant character, who could wrench him from his mother. Uncrippled instincts may keep the choice of the mate free from these influences, but sooner or later they will be felt as hindrances. From the point of view of race-preservation, a more or less purely instinctive choice would seem the best; yet psychologically it does not always lead to happiness, because the difference between the instinctive and the individual personality is often very great. In such a case, the race may be improved or revived by a purely instinctive choice, but at cost of the destruction of personal happiness. ("Instinct" is, of course, only a collective term for all sorts of organic and mental factors for the most part unknown to us.)

If we regard the individual purely as an instrument of race-preservation, an instinctive choice is by far the best. But as its foundations are unconscious, it cannot establish anything better than a certain impersonal relationship, such as is found among the primitives. In so far as one may speak here of a "state of relationship," it is a very vague and distant relationship of quite an impersonal nature, ruled by habits, customs, and prejudice—the very type of a conventional marriage.

Unless the marriage of the children has been arranged by the parents' reason or artifice or so-called thoughtful love, and if the primitive instincts of the children themselves are not crippled by the secret influences of suppressed and neglected parental complexes, the choice of the mate will be the result of unconscious instinctive motives. Unconsciousness produces non-distinctiveness; that is, unconscious identity. The result is that one takes for granted in the other a psychological structure similar to one's own. This feeling of unity and of identity is strengthened by normal sexuality as a mutual and apparently equally valued experience. This state of things is termed complete harmony and is justly, we may say, called a great happiness ("one heart and one soul"); for the return to that instinctive state of unconsciousness and unconscious unity is like a return to childhood (notice the childish behaviour of all lovers): one may even say it is like a return into the mother's womb, into the immensity of the promises of a yet unconscious creative wholeness. It is indeed a real and undeniable experience of godhead, whose overwhelming power effaces all that is individual. It is a true communion with life and impersonal fate. Self-will, bent on self, is broken: the woman becomes a mother, the man a father, and thus both lose their liberty and become mere instruments of progressive life.

Such a relationship keeps within the limits of the biologically instinctive purpose of generic propagation. As this purpose is of a collective nature, the psychological relations of the mates are in the main of a collective nature and cannot psychologically be termed an *individual relationship*. This can exist only where the nature of the unconscious motives is understood and the original identity is superseded. A marriage rarely or never develops into an individual relationship without a crisis. There is no coming into consciousness without pain. There are many ways to consciousness, but all these are subjected to certain general laws. As a rule, the change begins with the *second half of life*. The middle of life is a period of the highest psychological importance. The child begins its psychological life in the narrow sphere of the mother and the family. The horizon and the sphere of personal influence grow wider with the progress of its development. Hope and desire will aim at the expansion of the sphere of personal power and property; desire stretches out into the world. The will of the individual grows increasingly identical with the natural purposes of unconscious motives. Thus man breathes life into things, until they begin to live their own life and multiply; and imperceptibly they overtake him. Mothers are superseded by their children, men by their creations; and what was brought into existence by immense effort cannot be stopped in its course and growth. What was originally passion becomes an obligation, and finally an insupportable burden, a vampire sucking the life of its creator. The middle of life is the moment of greatest expansion, when man sets to his work with all his strength and will. But this very moment brings forth the eve; the second half of life sets in. Passion changes its face and becomes duty; choice grows into implacable necessity; and the windings of the road which formerly signified surprise and discovery become habitual. The wine has ceased fermenting and is beginning to clear. If all is well, man develops conservative inclinations. Instead of looking forward, he involuntarily looks back and begins to account to himself for the course of his life up to that date. He tries to find his true motives, and thus makes discoveries. Man learns to know his own individuality in a critical consideration of himself and his destiny. But his knowledge does not come to him easily. Only violent shocks lead to such realizations. By persisting too long in the youthful attitude, a division of will arises, because the aims of the second half of life are different from those of the first. Consciousness presses onward, following as it were its own inertia; but the unconscious hangs back, for strength and will can expand no more. This division within himself breeds discontent, and, not being conscious of his own state, he usually seeks for the causes in his mate. A critical atmosphere is the consequence; but this is a necessary condition, if consciousness is to ensue.

As a rule, this state does not appear simultaneously in both mates. The best of marriages cannot do away with individual differences to the point that the mates should be in the same state simultaneously. Generally, the one will more easily be reconciled to marriage than the other. A positive relationship to one's parents will make adaptation to the mate very easy, while a deep-rooted unconscious link with the parents will prove an impediment to adaptation. In this case, full adaptation will be arrived at later, and as it was attained with greater difficulty, it may prove more enduring. *Discrepancies in tempo*, on the one side, and the *range of the mental personality*, on the other, produce the typical difficulty, which exhibits its full force at the critical moment.

I do not wish to leave the impression that by a great "range of mental personality" I always mean particularly rich or big natures. This is not the case. I mean rather a certain intricacy of mental structure, a stone with many facets, as compared to a simple cube. They are many-sided natures, as a rule problematic, burdened with hereditary units which are hard to reconcile. Adaptation to such natures and their adaptation to simpler natures will always be difficult. Persons with such somewhat disassociated natures generally have the gift of splitting off incompatible habits of character for some length of time, and thus apparently becoming simple; or else their versatility, their changeful character, may prove their special charm. The other may easily lose himself in such somewhat mazy natures; that is to say, he finds so many possibilities of experience in them that his personal interest is fully employed. It may not always be in an agreeable way, for he will often be occupied in tracing the other through all manner of deviations. Nevertheless, so many experiences are possible that the simpler personality is surrounded by them, even captivated; it gets immersed in the larger personality; it cannot see beyond it. This is quite the rule: a woman, mentally, fully contained in her husband; a man, emotionally, fully contained in his wife. This might be termed *the problem of the contained and the container.*

The *contained* lives practically the whole of his life within marriage. He turns to the mate with undivided attention; no important obligations, no binding interest exists for him toward the outer world. The only disagreeable element in the "ideal" state is the disquieting dependence upon a personality somewhat beyond one's range, and therefore not quite credible or reliable. The great advantage is one's own undividedness—a factor not to be underrated in mental economy!

The *container* is, of course, surpassed by the simpler personality in the endeavour of uniting with the other in undivided love, although his somewhat disassociated nature renders the need of it greater. While seeking in the other all the subtle ties and intricacies that are to complete and oppose his own facets, he disturbs the other's simplicity. But in all ordinary circumstances, simplicity is the better condition as compared to intricacy: so the latter's efforts to call forth subtle and problematic reactions in the simple nature will soon be given up. The other, according to his simpler nature, will seek simple responses in him and soon occupy him sufficiently by "constellating" him (as the technical phraseology has it) in the expectation of simple answers. Willy-nilly, he will retreat before the convincing power of simplicity. Mental endeavour (the process of consciousness in general) requires of man such a strenuous effort that under any circumstances he prefers simplicity, although it may not even be real. But if it is not real, then he becomes its slave.

On the complicated nature, the simpler one has the effect of a small room, which gives him too little space. The complicated nature, on the contrary, offers the simple too many rooms with too much space, so that he never knows where he belongs. So the natural consequence is that the more complicated nature contains the simpler. It surrounds it, but cannot itself be absorbed and surrounded. Yet it may have an even greater need of being surrounded; it feels thus outside of marriage and at times plays the problematic part. The more the contained clings, the more the container feels himself forced out. By clinging, the former penetrates into him; yet the more he does so, the less can the other do the same. The container is therefore always to a greater or less degree looking out of the window, though he does so as first unconsciously. But when the middle of life is reached, a greater longing arises in him for that unity and undividedness so necessary to him according to his disassociated nature; and it is generally then that things happen to make him aware of the conflict. He becomes conscious of the fact that he is seeking a completion, that he has always failed to be contained and undivided. To the contained this event at first means the confirmation of the insecurity which he had always painfully felt; he finds other unwelcome guests living in the rooms that seemed to belong to him. The hope of security fades away, and this disappointment forces him back upon himself, unless by desperate and violent efforts he succeeds in forcing the other to the confession and conviction that his longing for unity is nothing but a childish or morbid fancy. Yet if this act of violence does not succeed, resignation brings him one great gift: that is, the knowledge that he must find in himself the security he was always looking for in the other. He thus learns to find himself and to discover in his own simple nature all those intricacies which the container vainly sought in him. If the container does not break down in recognizing what is generally called unfaithfulness in marriage, but keeps on believing in the inner justification of his longing for unity, he will begin by taking the severance on himself. A disassociation cannot be healed by splitting off, but only by severance. All the forces aiming at unity, all the healthy will-to-oneself, will resist severance; and he will grow conscious that the unification he was always seeking without is possible within him. He eventually finds the gift of undividedness in himself.

This is what very often happens at the height of life, and the curious nature of man thus enforces that transition from the first into the second half of life, the transformation from a state in which man is only instrumental to his instinctive nature into that other state where, no longer an instrument, he really becomes himself; a change from nature to culture, from instinct to intellect.

One should be careful not to interrupt this necessary development by moral violence, for any mental attitude resulting from the splitting off or repression of instincts is a falsification. There is nothing so disgusting as an intellect that is covertly sexualized; it is just as impure as an over-prized sensuality. But the transition is a long road, and may become mired on the way. If, as is the case with the primitives, it were possible to let all this mental development in marriage and by marriage remain unconscious, this transformation would be accomplished far more effectually and without so great a conflict. Among the so-called primitives, one meets with spiritual personalities which inspire one with reverence, as perfect and mature productions of an undisturbed destiny. I am speaking from personal experience. But where, among modern Europeans, are there such figures uncrippled by moral violence? We are still barbaric enough to believe in asceticism and its opposite. Yet the wheel of history cannot be turned back. We only can press forward toward the attitude which will permit us to live as the undisturbed destiny of primitive man really intends us to live. Then only will it be possible not to pervert intellect into sensuality and sensuality into intellect, for both must live, and the one derives its life from the other.

This transformation, sketched here in a few lines, is the essential part of the psychological relationship in marriage. Much more might be said of the illusions that foster the purposes of Nature and help to bring forth the transformation characteristic of the middle of life. The harmony of marriage prevalent in the first half of life (if such an adaptation was ever realized) is essentially founded on projections of certain typical images (as is proved later during the critical phase).

Every man bears in his heart the image of woman, not the image of *this* particular woman, but of *one* particular woman. This image is in reality an unconscious primeval inheritance, engraved on the living system, a "type" (archetype) of every ancestral experience of woman, the residue of all impressions left by women, a hereditary psychic system of adaptation. If there were no women, this unconscious image would make it possible to describe what a woman spiritually should be. The same applies to woman; she too has an inborn image of man. (Experience teaches us that we ought to say: an image of *men;* man, on the other hand, has rather the image of *woman.*) As this image is unconscious, it is always unconsciously projected onto the beloved figure and is one of the essential causes of passionate attraction or the contrary. I have called this image *anima.* I think the scholastic question: "*Habet mulier animam?*"—"Has woman a soul?"—very interesting, because I am of the opinion that the question is not irrational, inasmuch as the doubt seems justified. Woman has no *anima*, but an *animus*. The anima is of an erotically emotional, the animus of a reasoning nature. That is why most of what men have to say about feminine eroticism and the emotional life of women is based upon the projection of their own *animas*, and is consequently erroneous. The assumptions and fancies of women about men are the result of the activity of the *animus*, which is inexhaustible in the production of illogical judgments and false causalities.

An immense versatility is characteristic of the anima and the animus. In marriage, it is always the contained that projects his image on the container; the latter only partly succeeds in projecting his image on the mate. The projection is most unsuccessful where the contained is simplest and most transparent. In this case, this most fascinating image is projected into the air and waits for some real person to fill it out. There are types of women whom Nature seems to have fashioned purposely for the reception of the projection of the anima. One might even speak of one certain type. The so-called "sphinx" nature belongs to it most indispensably: a certain ambiguous and equivocal character, not a vagueness into which nothing can be put, but a vagueness full of promise, with the speaking silence of the Mona Lisa; a being both old and young, mother and daughter, of a questionable purity; childish, yet with a naïve wisdom, disarming to men.[1] It is not possible for every man of real intellect to be an animus, for he needs good words more than good ideas, words full of meaning that can become the mouth-

[1] An excellent description of this type is given by H. Rider Haggard in *She*, and by Benoît in *L'Atlantide*.

pieces of many unexpressed things. He must also be a little misunderstood; he must at any rate be in some sort of opposition to the surrounding world, so that the idea of sacrifice can enter. He must be an equivocal hero with many possibilities; and it is very probable that projections of the animus may often have found out a real hero much sooner than the slow insight of so-called intelligent commonplace people.[2] In so far as they are containers, the realization of this image marks a momentous event to the man and the woman, for here the possibility has come of finding one's own intricacies answered by corresponding multiformity. Here seem to open those wide expanses where one may feel surrounded and contained. I expressly say "seem," for it is an ambiguous possibility. A man may create a *femme inspiratrice* by the projection of the anima, just as a woman may really find out a distinguished man as yet unrecognized by the multitude, or more than that, may even help him to his real destiny by her moral assistance. But more often it will have proved an illusion of destructive consequences. It will prove unsuccessful because faith was not strong enough. I must tell pessimists that there are very real virtues in these psychic archetypes; yet optimists must be warned against dazzling fancies and the possibility of exceedingly absurd mistakes.

This projection must not, however, be understood as an individual or conscious relationship. It is nothing of the kind. It produces a compulsory dependence on the basis of unconscious motives that are not of a biological nature. In Rider Haggard's *She* is shown the curious world of ideas that originate these projections of the

[2] For fairly good descriptions of the animus, see Mary Hay's *The Evil Vineyard,* Elinor Wylie's *Jennifer Lorn,* and Selma Lagerlöf's *Gösta Berling.*

anima. Essentially they are mental images, often in erotic disguise, and clearly parts of a primitive mythological mentality which consists in archetypes; and in their totality represent the so-called *collective unconscious*. Accordingly, such a relationship is in reality collective, and not individual. (Benoît, who in his *L'Atlantide* created an imaginary figure corresponding to *She* even in details, denies any plagiarism of Rider Haggard.)

If such a projection occurs to one of the two mates, then a collective mental relationship faces the collective biological relationship and produces the above-mentioned severance of the container. If he succeeds in escaping submersion, he will find himself just through this conflict. In this case, the dangerous projection will have helped him to pass from a collective into an individual relationship. This is equivalent to a full consciousness of the marriage relationship. As the purpose of this essay is the discussion of the psychology of marriage, the psychology of the projection relationship does not come into consideration. It is sufficient to mention it as a fact.

It is hardly possible to speak of the psychological relationship in marriage without at least alluding to the nature of its critical transitional states, even at the risk of being misunderstood. It is well known that, psychologically, one understands nothing that one has not oneself experienced. This fact does not prevent any one from being persuaded that his own judgment is the only real and competent one. This strange fact is the result of the necessary overrating of the actual contents of one's consciousness. Without this concentration of attention, one could not be conscious at all. Thus it is that every epoch of life has its own psychological truth, its programmatic truth, as it were; and the same applies to every stage of development. There are many such stages, and even stages that only few arrive at—a question of race, family, education, gifts, and passion. Nature is aristocratic. The "normal" man is a fiction, although certain general laws do exist. Mental and spiritual life means a development which may be arrested at the lowest stage. As though every individuality had its specific gravity, it rises or sinks to the stage where it finds its limit. Its insight and convictions are fashioned accordingly. Little wonder, then, that the greater number of all marriages reach their psychological limit with the biological purpose, without damage to mental or moral health. It is only a few who become involved in any deeper dividedness within themselves. Where there is much external misery, the conflict is without dramatic tension for want of energy. But psychological insecurity increases with social security, unconsciously in the first instance, and causes neurosis; then consciously, and causes separations, arguments, divorces, and other failures in marriage. In still higher stages, new possibilities of psychological development open up; these touch the religious sphere, where critical judgment is at an end. In all these stages there may be a complete standstill without the least consciousness of what might happen in another stage of development. As a rule, the access to even the next stage is barred by the most violent prejudices and superstitious fears; and very appropriately so, for a person who feels induced to live on a plane too high for him becomes a dangerous fool.

Nature is not only aristocratic; it is esoteric. Yet no wise man will thereby be induced to be silent about what he knows, for he realizes only too well that the secret of mental development can never be revealed, simply because development is a question of individual capacity.

A L F R E D   A D L E R

Marriage as a Task

One does justice to a phenomenon of social life and personality only by leaving it in its setting and examining it there, without entirely leaving out of account its position in the advancing development within the stream of Eternity. Short-lived individual intelligence, in order to reap quick advantages, attempts to confine within an ever narrower and closer circle of interests what is subject only to eternal norms. We cannot bind ourselves in this essay to words or to traditionally sanctified concepts. That which dominates and compels us all is always, in the end, the immutable system of relations of man and the world, which perpetually burdens us with a problem whose iron adherence to its law appears inexorably in every human experience, now as reward, now as punishment. A man is murdered in short-sighted delusion—and the world is thrown out of joint. For thousands of years the excitement sends out its pulsations, when the longing of humanity for harmony with the universe takes form in a single occurrence and its effect. We others have only a premonition of the wonder; emotion and moods overwhelm us, until there comes one such as Shakespeare who is horrified by murder and who shows us that dishonoured sense of life does and must avenge itself.

One who plants trees considers the soil and the climate and does not permit himself to be led by caprice and vanity. For the rest, it is quite insignificant what he thinks, feels, or wants by his performance. Only the accord of his act with the exigencies of evolution can vindicate him. He creates for the community and for posterity, even if in so doing he considers only his own well-being, even if he is determined to act against the community and against the future.

Can any one recall an action, a deed, which could be termed beautiful, great, noble, for any other reason than because it was helpful to society, to the future progress of humanity? Does not every one bear the measure for such evaluation within himself? Is there a man in the complete possession of his senses who cannot discriminate between good and evil?

The point of view in an examination of all human relationships and institutions is consequently determined. Value and "correctness" are first and foremost conditioned and dependent on their suitability to the whole. If there is much about this which is controversial for thought—a contradiction of the logic of the facts will always make itself felt. It appears even though nobody comprehends its connection. The quickness with which we human beings raise accusations spares us most of the time the trouble of examining the connections. Likewise the fact that error and its consequences always lie far apart makes insight difficult and hardly permits of fruitful experiences for the individual and for posterity. The thousandfold experience of the many appears to yield itself with difficulty to the contemplation of the one. Thus life rolls on from generation to generation, without creating lasting traditions. And each individual still takes pride in using his own poor knowledge, often capriciously, in the upbuilding of associations of momentous importance for life—not caring that he is repeating thousandfold errors and seeking aims which destroy the happiness of his own life and another's.

The destiny of earth-man is knotted in three ways. His body and his soul cling to Mother Earth, to cosmic and mundane necessities; they are educated in these and seek, with ever-renewed strength, adjustment and adaptation, a living harmony with the laws of Nature. Culture and hygiene of the body and spirit originate in this compulsion. To it all beauty owes its powerful allure.

In the concept "Man," the "Fellow-Man" is inextricably included. All the prerequisites of his physical and mental development lie in the community and are created and wax great according to its necessities. Speech, reason, culture, ethics, religion, nationality, statehood, are social products and take effect in particular cases as precipitates of the community. In all these life-forms there lies a potent reflection of the presence of earth, strong and inexorable, as in the compulsion to unity. The destiny of man cannot unfold itself apart from these premises. The third premise is dual sexuality. But the quest of the sexes, perhaps eons ago mainly impulsive, aspires to a form which obviates conflict with these conditions. In the harmonious development of the erotic there is just as much impulse as communal sentiment. And in the bliss-giving ecstasy of lovers, a similarly bliss-giving power of creation unfolds at the same time, willingly paying homage to and affirming earthly life. If one views the love-life of man from this standpoint, one perceives that it is filled with laws of its own which do not just happen and which are not to be circumvented without the gravest objections. The logic of facts is cruel, much more cruel than we human beings. We should gladly be inclined to be lenient. And we do not appear as advocates of harsh revenge, if we demonstrate the inexorability of governing forces. Our task is only to warn, to mitigate hard consequences, to show to the present and to the future generation connected facts which otherwise might be entered in the books not as consequences, but as isolated fatal incidents.

Our present existence shows us the point of transition to a further development of humanity. This fact weighs so heavily on our life-process that, without our having to notice the fact, our love-relationships are formed with a view to eternity. The frequently excessive value which we place on beauty has for the future a significance of health and of increased adaptation. The loyalty and probity which we crave, the interpenetration of two souls toward which we strive, arise from our urgent longing for a stronger feeling of community; it is the same way with the desire for children, attachment to whom reflects the ideal of community and who at the same time represent for us an earnest of eternity. Loyalty and truthfulness, above all, reliability, the foundations of human community, certainly point toward the future of human morals and toward aims in the education of children.

That in the situation of love and marriage all these claims meet, are concentrated there and become binding laws, is only to be grasped mentally from the indissoluble connection of historic and organic development. Also, every wilful and erroneous departure vibrates afterward in the entire system of the relationships of life and impairs favourable tendencies in evolution. Damaging factors of inheritance take effect whether or not science has elucidated them. Incest falls under the interdict of communal sentiment, since it leads, like the marriages of blood relatives, to isolation, and not to that mingling of strains which furthers the community, and since the hereditary endowment can thereby more easily be influenced unfavourably than by a two-sided organic burden. Also, that courageous gaze, hopefully directed toward the future, which is indispensable to meet all the difficulties of founding a family, and that social bond which is a prerequisite to avoid a fruitless expenditure of energies, spiritless and isolated, within the narrow frame of a single family, seem to be lacking in the marriages of blood relatives. These and the other above-mentioned features gently and imperceptibly lead the partner and the children in the same direction, while their lack produces a feeling of distrust and constant insecurity, a family atmosphere in which only combative and hostile tendencies can thrive.

It is only another feature of the same spiritual force which we expect to discover when we measure by the rule of the true fellow-man. His perpetual, unchanging fundamental law on this poor raw crust of earth is: Give! All profane and sacred wisdom leads to the same conclusion. Thus it is likewise rightly ordained, in love and marriage, to think more of the other than of oneself, to live in such a way that one lightens and renders more beautiful the life of one's companion! To determine how many—or how few—succeed in so doing is not our object here. One thing is certain: that there are too many in our society who take and expect in proportion to the givers. Humanity seems too thoroughly dominated by the formula of love and marriage: "Because I love you, you must follow me!"

What mankind in our times still lacks toward fellow-feeling makes itself felt also in the strained relationship of the sexes. The struggle for personal domination, the outgrowth of a deep-seated, generally unrecognized inferiority complex, in most cases drives husband and wife to overstrain the semblance of their authority in a demonstrative way. Most married couples conduct themselves as if each party were afraid that one could see that it was the weaker. Spite, wilfulness, a negative attitude, and often erotic rejection, polygamous inclinations, and unfaithfulness, as well as nervous indispositions, come to the aid of self-love in defending the position of one's own arrogance of power. The man, through a long-outworn common tradition, possesses a slight advantage which he attempts to preserve, selfishly but to his own detriment. For him who shares our point of view, the master of the family is a thing of the past. He sees marriage as a duality in which both parties make a united effort to perform a common task, not on the line of their own will but according to all laws inherent in their problem. The organic and historic development of humanity toward a readiness for monogamous marriage, especially when one includes in this view the unique possibilities of the fulfilment of the most precious erotic expectations, is sufficient security that every one should be able to perform this task. Marriage is always understood as a creation of the communal sentiment, as the social form of love-life, as the safeguard and first school of children in their evolution toward the "fellow-man." Off this road lie marriages of convention, financial or speculative unions, the course of which always goes on slippery ground. For the union of the parents must serve as an example to the children as well, since otherwise, often in spite of their better knowledge and higher endeavour, they carry the bad tradition into their new home. Lust of domination or hardness in the father can terrify girls to such an extent that later on they distrustfully watch and misinterpret every step of their husbands; but it may also fill them with a sharpened need of warmth, which must remain forever beyond satisfaction on this earth. It may unfit them for matrimony or for the education of children, because they have lost their belief in themselves. Sons of hard mothers fly from women and are shy of society. This arises from a hitherto imperfectly understood function of the mother: to teach the child to understand boundless trustworthiness, and to make herself an example of noble womanhood. Again, mothers' darlings cannot give. Instead of desiring the friendly sense of community, they look for maternal kindness, which has its rightful place in life exclusively in the period of childhood. The choice of older, maternal wives has its foundation chiefly in this error.

Polygamous inclinations, perversions, and predilections for morally low people and prostitutes are always explainable through their tendency to eliminate and to debase the more suitable partner, and therefore through the fear of not being able to stand up before the other sex. In what great measure the sense and the task of love and marriage are thus missed, one can see from the growing prevalence of sexual diseases. Whatever their origin may have been, their spread is solely due to the misuse and aberration of eroticism. There exists one remedy only, one protection against these plagues: mutual love.

The connection of marriage with the most important necessities of society gives us to understand that it is not, as most people believe, a private concern. The whole nation, the whole of humanity, takes part in it. And each person who enters into marriage thereby fulfils, even if he is quite unaware of it, a mission of the whole. Among the most important requirements for the conclusion of a marriage are therefore a vocation and a livelihood in which both can participate and which insures the support of the family. The vocation, too, is a demand of society, cooperation in production. The contribution to the preservation of humanity is similarly not a private affair, and must be furthered through marriage. Likewise, the work of the housewife, at present mistakenly held to be inferior, can create real values, if through good management or artistic enhancement she can increase the man's capacity for labour. Invoking economic difficulties for the purpose of refusing marriage is often a subterfuge of the faint-hearted.

It is a widely circulated superstition that marriage can also cure evil, negligence, and sickness. Love and marriage are not remedies. In most such cases, one only creates new injuries without removing the old. The same error prevails in regard to the curative power of pregnancy. The marriage question, like all other problems of life, must be answered out of strength, not out of weakness.

Marriage is also menaced by disaster if people who wed look on themselves as martyrs. Unavoidably they will let the other feel this and cheat him incessantly out of his happy sentiments. Flaws in the marital relation, neglect, coldness, and infidelity, are the frequent results. The goal of marriage, that of each participating in the happiness of the other, is thus often destroyed at the beginning. For marriage is not a constructed edifice which one approaches, not a destiny which one goes forward to meet, but a problem of the present and the future, a creative performance in time which is rapidly flying, a task of building social values into the nothingness of the future. Always one will find in marriage only that which one has created in it.

We have so far enumerated essential main premises which must provide the basis of a firm and enduring marriage. We fear lest in the pressure of the everyday some of these necessities may too readily drop from memory. It seems to us desirable to look for a briefer formula which, in spite of its conciseness, will embrace all problems of marriage. Might not this formula be: "To be a true fellow-man"?

The decision to marry should certainly originate entirely in the striving toward fellowship. But this decision and marriage do not become identical with this striving alone. Only when they succeed in this sense are they able to solve their problems with regard to the commonweal. The fellow-man, as a sense of life, must therefore take precedence; and marriage then is tantamount to a further step toward perfection.

However one contemplates the fellow-man, one will encounter watchwords, maxims, and imperatives which at least say: To make oneself useful—to think more of the other than of oneself—to make the other's life easier and more beautiful. These are also the imperatives of marriage. Thus our question of "marriage as a task" reduces itself to the question: How does one become a fellow-man?

We can omit physical qualifications as a matter of course. The same is true of intellectual maturity. These are so seldom lacking that they can be left out of the reckoning. It is not so with maturity of soul. Despite all efforts, things are badly ordered for the soul in human society. The exploration of individual psychology has abundantly established the reason of this failure. Most men begin with a false start. An all-too-great inferiority complex compels them to use egotistical, demonstrative forms of expression, in which they think to find their will to mastery. Or else they give themselves up to pessimism without action, under the pressure of which they move as if under the effect of brakes. Arrogance from a feeling of weakness, or despondence through ambition, mark their way. At best they are properly prepared for a lonely life, but never for life with one companion or for life in society. Whoever falls in their way is their chosen object. They must be wrecked in marriage, since they lack the spiritual organs of social existence.

But marriage as a task aims at the right ordering of the claims of community, of vocation, and of eroticism.

HAVELOCK ELLIS

Love as an Art

THE primary end of marriage is to beget and bear offspring, and to rear them until they are able to take care of themselves. On that basis man is at one with all the mammals and most of the birds. If, indeed, we disregard the originally less essential part of this end—that is to say, the care and tending of the young—this end of marriage is not only the primary but usually the sole end of sexual intercourse in the whole mammal world. As a natural instinct, its achievement involves gratification and well-being, but this bait of gratification is merely a device of Nature's and not in itself an end having any useful function at the periods when conception is not possible. This is clearly indicated by the fact that among animals the female only experiences sexual desire at the season of impregnation, and that desire ceases as soon as impregnation takes place, though this is true of the male in only a few species, obviously because, if his sexual desire and aptitude were confined to so brief a period, the chances of the female meeting the right male at the right moment would be too seriously diminished, so that the attentive and inquisitive attitude of the male animal toward the female—which we may often think we see still traceable in the human species—is not the outcome of lustfulness for personal gratification, but is implanted by Nature for the benefit of the female and the attainment of the primary object of procreation.

This primary object we may term the animal end of marriage.

This object remains not only the primary, but even the sole end of marriage among the lower races of mankind generally. The erotic idea in its deeper sense, that is to say, the element of love, arose very slowly in mankind. It is found, it is true, among some lower races, and it appears that some tribes possess a word for the joy of love in a purely psychic sense. But even among European races the evolution was late. The Greek poets, except the latest, showed little recognition of love as an element of marriage. Theognis compared marriage with cattle-breeding. The Romans of the Republic took much the same view. Greeks and Romans alike regarded breeding as the one recognizable object of marriage; any other object was mere wantonness and had better, they thought, be pursued outside marriage. Religion, which preserves so many ancient and primitive conceptions of life, has consecrated this conception also; and Christianity at the outset only offered the choice between celibacy on the one hand, and on the other, marriage for the production of offspring.

Yet from an early period in human history, a secondary function of sexual intercourse had been slowly growing up to become one of the great objects of marriage. Among animals, it may be said, and even sometimes in man, the sexual impulse, when once aroused, makes but a short and swift circuit through the brain to reach its consummation. But as the brain and its faculties develop, powerfully aided indeed by the very difficulties of the sexual life, the impulse for sexual union has to traverse ever longer, slower, more painful paths before it reaches—and sometimes it never reaches—its ultimate object. This means that sex gradually becomes intertwined with all the highest and subtlest human emotions and activities, with the refinements of social intercourse, with high adventure in every sphere, with art, with religion. The primitive animal instinct, having the sole end of procreation, becomes, on its way to that end, the inspiring stimulus to all those psychic energies which in civilization we count most precious. This function is thus, we see, a by-product. But, as we know, even in our human factories the by-product is sometimes even more valuable than the product. That is so as regards the functional products of human evolution. The hand was evolved out of the animal fore-limb with the primary end of grasping the things we materially need, but as a by-product the hand has developed the function of making and playing the piano and the violin, and that secondary functional by-product of the hand we account, even as measured by the rough test of money, more precious, however less materially necessary, than its primary function. It is, however, only in rare and gifted natures that transformed sexual energy becomes of supreme value for its own sake without ever attaining the normal physical outlet. For the most part the by-product accompanies the product throughout, thus adding a secondary, yet peculiarly sacred and specially human, object of marriage to its primary animal object. This may be termed the spiritual object of marriage.

By the term spiritual we are not to understand any mysterious and supernatural qualities. It is simply a convenient name, in distinction from animal, to cover all those higher mental and emotional processes which in human evolution are gaining ever greater power. It is needless to enumerate the constituents of this spiritual end of sexual intercourse, for every one is entitled to enumerate them differently and in different order. They include not only all that makes love a gracious and beautiful erotic art, but the whole element of pleasure, in so far as pleasure is more than a mere animal gratification. Our ancient ascetic traditions often make us blind to the meaning of pleasure. We see only its possibilities of evil, and not its mightiness for good. We forget that, as Romain Rolland says, "Joy is as holy as pain." No one has insisted so much on the supreme importance of the element of pleasure in the spiritual end of sex as James Hinton. Rightly used, he declares, pleasure is "the child of God," to be recognized as a "mighty storehouse of force"; and he pointed out the significant fact that in the course of human progress its importance increases rather than diminishes. While it is perfectly true that sexual energy may be in large degree arrested, and transformed into intellectual and moral forces, yet it is also true that pleasure itself, and above all, sexual pleasure, wisely used and not abused, may prove the stimulus and liberator of our finest and most exalted activities. It is largely this remarkable function of sexual pleasure which is decisive in settling the argument of those who claim that continence is the only alternative to the animal end of marriage. That argument ignores the liberating and harmonizing influences, giving wholesome balance and sanity to the whole organism, imparted by a sexual union which is the outcome of the psychic as well as physical needs. There is, further, in the attainment of the spiritual end of marriage, much more than the benefit of each individual separately. There is, that is to say, the effect on the union itself. For through harmonious sex relationships a deeper spiritual unity is reached than can possibly be derived from continence in or out of marriage, and the marriage association becomes an apter instrument in the service of the world. Apart from any sexual craving, the complete spiritual contact of two persons who love each other can only be attained through some act of rare intimacy. No act can be quite so intimate as the sexual embrace. In its accomplishment, for all spiritually evolved persons, the communion of bodies becomes the communion of souls. The outward and visible sign has been the consummation of an inward and spiritual grace. "I would base all my sex teaching to children and young people on the beauty and sacredness of sex," writes a distinguished woman, Olive Schreiner, in a personal letter: "sex intercourse is the great sacrament of life: he that eateth and drinketh unworthily, eateth and drinketh his own damnation; but it may be the most beautiful sacrament between two souls who have no thought of children." To many the idea of a sacrament seems merely ecclesiastical, but that is a misunderstanding. The word "sacrament" is the ancient Roman name of a soldier's oath of military allegiance, and the idea, in the deeper sense, existed long before Christianity, and has ever been regarded as the physical sign of the closest possible union with some great spiritual reality. From our modern standpoint we may say, with James Hinton, that the sexual embrace, worthily understood, can only be compared with music and with prayer. "Every true lover," it has been well said by a woman, "knows this, and the worth of any and every relationship can be judged by its success in reaching, or failing to reach, this standpoint." [1]

LET us now look at another side of the same question. When we hear the sexual functions spoken of we commonly understand the performance of an act which normally tends to the propagation of the race. When we see the question of sexual abstinence discussed, when the

[1] Mrs. Havelock Ellis, *James Hinton*, p. 180.

desirability of sexual gratification is asserted or denied, when the idea arises of the erotic rights and needs of women, it is always the same act with its physical results that is chiefly in mind. Such a conception is quite adequate for practical working purposes in the social world. It enables us to deal with all our established human institutions in the sphere of sex, just as the arbitrary assumptions of Euclid enable us to traverse the field of geometry. But beyond these useful purposes it is inadequate and even inexact. The functions of sex on the psychic and erotic side are of far greater extension than any act of procreation; they may even exclude it altogether: and when we are concerned with the welfare of the individual human being we must enlarge our outlook and deepen our insight.

There are, we have seen, two main functions in the sexual relationship, or what in the biological sense we term marriage, among civilized human beings: the primary physiological function of begetting and bearing offspring and the secondary spiritual function of furthering the higher mental and emotional processes. These are the main functions of the sexual impulse, and in order to understand any further object of the sexual relationship—or even in order to understand all that is involved in the secondary object of marriage—we must go beyond conscious motives and consider the nature of the sexual impulse, physical and psychic, as rooted in the human organism.

The human organism, as we know, is a machine in which excitations from without, streaming through the nerves and brain, effect internal work, and, notably, stimulate the glandular system. In recent years the glandular system, and especially that of the ductless glands, has taken on an altogether new significance. These ductless glands secrete and liberate into the blood what are termed "hormones," or chemical messengers, which have a complex but precise action in exciting and developing all those physical and psychic activities which make up a full life alike on the general side and the reproductive side, so that their balanced functions are essential to wholesome and complete existence. In a rudimentary form these functions may be traced back to our earliest ancestors who possessed brains. In those times the predominant sense for arousing the internal mental and emotional faculties was that of smell, the other senses being gradually evolved subsequently; and it is significant that the pituitary, one of the chief ductless glands active in ourselves today, was developed out of the nervous centre for smell in conjunction with the membrane of the mouth. The energies of the whole organism were set in action through stimuli arising from the outside world by way of the sense of smell. In process of time the mechanism has become immensely elaborated; yet its healthy activity is ultimately dependent on a rich and varied action and reaction with the external world. It is becoming recognized that the tendency to pluri-glandular insufficiency, with its resulting lack of organic harmony and equilibrium, can be counteracted by the physical and psychic stimuli of intimate contacts with the external world. In this action and reaction, moreover, we cannot distinguish between sexual ends and general ends. The activities of the ductless glands and their hormones equally serve both ends in ways that cannot be distinguished. "The individual metabolism," as a distinguished authority in this field has expressed it, "is the reproductive metabolism." [2] Thus the establishment of our complete activities as human beings in the world is aided by, if not indeed ultimately dependent upon, a

[2] See W. Blair Bell, *The Sex-Complex*, 1920, p. 108.

perpetual and many-sided play with our environment.

It is thus that we arrive at the importance of the *play function*, and thus also we realize that while it extends beyond the sexual sphere, it yet definitely includes that sphere. There are at least three different ways of understanding the biological function of play. There is the conception of play, on which Gross has elaborately insisted, as education; the cat "plays" with the mouse and is thereby educating itself in the skill necessary to catch mice; all our human games are a training in qualities that are required in life, and that is why in England we continue to attribute to the Duke of Wellington the saying that "the battle of Waterloo was won on the playing-fields of Eton." Then there is the conception of play as the utilization in art of the superfluous energies left unemployed in the practical work of life; this enlarging and harmonizing function of play, while in the lower ranges it may be spent trivially, leads in the higher ranges to the production of the most magnificent human achievements. But there is yet a third conception of play, according to which it exerts a direct internal influence—health-giving, developmental, and balancing—on the whole organism of the player himself. This conception is related to the other two, and yet distinct, for it is not primarily a definite education in specific kinds of life-conserving skill, although it may involve the acquisition of such skill; and it is not concerned with the construction of objective works of art, although, by means of contact in human relationships, it attains the wholesome organic effects which may be indirectly achieved by artistic activities. It is in this sense that we are here concerned with what we may perhaps best call *the play function of sex.*[3]

[3] The term seems to have been devised by Professor Maurice Parmelee, *Personality and Conduct,* 1918, pp. 104, 107, and 113. But it is understood by Parmelee in a much vaguer and more extended sense than I have used.

As thus understood, the play function of sex is at once, in an inseparable way, both physical and psychic. It stimulates to wholesome activity all the complex and inter-related systems of the organism. At the same time it satisfies the most profound emotional impulses, controlling in harmonious poise the various mental instincts. Along these lines it necessarily tends in the end to go beyond its own sphere and to embrace and introduce into the sphere of sex the other two more objective fields of play, that of play as education, and that of play as artistic creation. It may not be true, as was said of old time, "most of our arts and sciences were invented for love's sake." But it is certainly true that, in proportion as we truly and wisely exercise the play function of sex, we are at the same time training our personality on the erotic side and acquiring a mastery of the art of love.

The longer I live the more I realize the immense importance for the individual of the development through the play function of erotic personality, and for human society of the acquirement of the art of love. At the same time I am ever more astonished at the rarity of erotic personality and the ignorance of the art of love even among those men and women, experienced in the exercise of procreative power, in whom we might most confidently expect to find such development and such art. At times one feels hopeless at the thought that civilization in this supremely intimate field of life has yet achieved so little. For until it is generally possible to acquire erotic personality and to master the art of loving, the development of the individual man or woman is marred, the acquirement of human happiness and harmony remains impossible.

In entering this field, indeed, we have not only to gain true knowledge but to cast off false knowledge, and above all, to purify our hearts of superstitions which have no connection with any kind of existing knowledge. We have to cease to regard as admirable the man who regards the accomplishment of the procreative act, with the pleasurable relief it affords to himself, as the whole code of love. We have to treat with contempt the woman who abjectly accepts that act, and her own passivity therein, as the whole duty of love. We have to understand that the art of love has nothing to do with vice, and the acquirement of erotic personality nothing to do with sensuality. But we have also to realize that the art of love is far from being the attainment of a refined and luxurious self-indulgence, and that the acquirement of erotic personality is of little worth unless it fortifies and enlarges the whole personality in all its aspects. Now all this is difficult, and for some people even painful; to root up is a more serious matter than to sow; it cannot all be done in a day.

It is not easy to form a clear picture of the erotic life of the average man in our society. To the best informed among us, knowledge in this field only comes slowly. Even when we have decided what may or may not be termed "average," the avenues of approach to this intimate sphere remain few and misleading; at the best the women a man loves remain far more illuminating sources of information than the man himself. The more one knows about him, however, the more one is convinced that, quite independently of the place we may feel inclined to afford to him in the scale of virtue, his conception of erotic personality, his ideas on the art of love, if they have any existence at all, are of a humble character. As to the notion of play in the sphere of sex, even if he makes blundering attempts to practise it, that is for him something quite low down, something to be ashamed of, and he would not dream of associating it with anything he has been taught to regard as belonging to the spiritual sphere. The conception of "divine play" is meaningless to him. His fundamental ideas, his cherished ideals, in the erotic sphere, seem to be reducible to two: (1) He wishes to prove that he is "a man," and he experiences what seems to him the pride of virility in the successful attainment of that proof. (2) He finds in the same act the most satisfactory method of removing sexual tension and in the ensuing relief one of the chief pleasures of life. It cannot be said that either of these ideals is absolutely unsound; each is part of the truth; it is only as a complete statement of the truth that they become pathetically inadequate. It is to be noted that both of them are based solely on the physical act of sexual conjugation, and that they are both exclusively self-regarding, so that they are, after all, although the nearest approach to the erotic sphere he may be able to find, yet still not really erotic. For love is not primarily self-regarding. It is the intimate, harmonious, combined play—the play in the wide as well as in the more narrow sense we are here concerned with—of two personalities. It would not be love if it were primarily self-regarding, and the act of intercourse, however essential to secure the propagation of the race, is only an incident, and not an essential, in love.

Let us turn to the average woman. Here the picture must usually be still more unsatisfactory. The man at least, crude as we may find his two fundamental notions to be, has at all events attained mental pride and physical satisfaction. The woman often attains neither, and since the man, by instinct or tradition, has maintained a self-regarding attitude, that is not surprising. The husband—by primitive instinct partly, certainly by ancient tradition—regards himself as the active partner in matters of love, and his own pleasure as legitimately the prime motive for activity. His wife consequently falls into the complementary position and regards herself as the passive partner and her pleasure as negligible, if not indeed as a thing to be rather ashamed of, should she by chance experience it, so that, while the husband is content with a mere simulacrum and pretence of the erotic life, the wife has often had none at all.

Few people realize—few, indeed, have the knowledge or the opportunity to realize—how much women thus lose, alike in the means to fulfil their own lives and in the power to help others. A woman has a husband, she has marital relationships, she has children, she has all the usual domestic troubles; it seems to the casual observer that she has everything that constitutes a fully developed matron, fit to play her proper part in the home and in the world. Yet with all these experiences, which undoubtedly are an important part of life, she may yet remain on the emotional side—and, as a matter of fact, frequently remains—quite virginal, as immature as a schoolgirl. She has not acquired an erotic personality, she has not mastered the art of love, with the result that her whole nature remains ill developed and unharmonized, and that she is incapable of bringing her personality—having indeed no achieved personality to bring—to bear effectively on the problems of society and the world around her.

That alone is a great misfortune, all the more tragic since under favourable conditions, which it should have been natural to attain, it might so easily be avoided. But there is this further result, full of the possibilities of domestic tragedy, that the wife so situated, however innocent, however virtuous, may at any time find her virginally sensitive emotional nature fertilized by the touch of some other man than her husband.

It happens so often. A girl who has been carefully guarded in the home, preserved from evil companions, preserved also from what her friends regarded as the contamination of sexual knowledge, a girl of high ideals, yet healthy and robust, is married to a man of whom she probably has little more than a conventional knowledge. Yet he may by good chance be the masculine counterpart of herself, well brought up, without sexual experience and ignorant of all but the elementary facts of sex, loyal and honourable, prepared to be, fitted to be, a devoted husband. The union seems to be of the happiest kind; no one detects that anything is lacking to this perfect marriage, and in course of time one or more children are born. But during all this time the husband has never really made love to his wife; he has not even understood what courtship in the intimate sense means; love as an art has no existence for him; he has loved his wife according to his imperfect knowledge, but he has never so much as realized that his knowledge was imperfect. She on her side loves her husband; she comes in time indeed to have a sort of tender maternal feeling for him. Possibly she feels a little pleasure in intercourse with him. But she has never once been profoundly aroused, and she has never once been utterly satisfied. The deep fountains of her nature have never been unsealed; she has never been fertilized throughout her whole nature by their liberating influence; her erotic personality has never been developed. Then something happens. Perhaps the husband is called away—it might have been to take part in the Great War. The wife, whatever her tender solicitude for her absent partner, feels her solitude and is drawn nearer to friends, perhaps her husband's friends. Some man among them becomes congenial to her. There need be no conscious or overt love-making on either side, and if there were, the wife's loyalty might be aroused and the friendship brought to an end. Love-making is not indeed necessary. The wife's latent erotic needs, while still remaining unconscious, have come nearer to the surface; now that she has grown mature and that they have been stimulated, yet unsatisfied, for so long, they have, unknown to herself, become insistent and sensitive to a sympathetic touch. The friends may indeed grow into lovers, and then some sort of solution, by divorce or intrigue—scarcely, however, a desirable kind of solution—becomes possible. But we are here taking the highest ground and assuming that honourable feeling, domestic affection, or a stern sense of moral duty renders such a solution unacceptable. In due course the husband returns, and then to her utter dismay, the wife discovers, if she has not discovered it before, that during his absence, and for the first time in her life, she has fallen in love. She loyally confesses the situation to her husband, for whom her affection and attachment remain the same as before; for what has happened to her is the coming of a totally new kind of love and not any change in her old love. The situation which arises is one of torturing anxiety for all concerned, and it is not less so when all concerned are animated by noble and self-sacrificing impulses. The husband in his devotion to his wife may even be willing that her new impulses should be gratified. She, on her side, will not think of yielding to desires which seem both unfair to her husband and opposed to all her moral traditions. We are not here concerned to consider the most likely, or the most desirable, exit from this unfortunate situation. The points to note are that it is a situation which today actually occurs; that it causes acute unhappiness to at least two people who may be of the finest physical and intellectual type and the noblest character; and that it might be avoided if there were at the outset a proper understanding of the married state and of the part which the art of love plays in married happiness and the development of personality.

A woman may have been married once, she may have been married twice, she may have had children by both husbands; and yet it may not be until she is past the age of thirty and is united to a third man that she attains the development of erotic personality and all that it involves in the full flowering of her whole nature. Up to then she has to all appearance had all the essential experiences of life. Yet she has remained spiritually virginal with conventionally prim ideas of life, narrow in her sympathies, with the finest and noblest functions of her soul helpless and bound, at heart unhappy even if not clearly realizing that she is unhappy. Now she has become another person. The new-liberated forces from within have not only enabled her to become sensitive to the rich complexities of intimate personal relationship; they have enlarged and harmonized her realization of all relationships. Her new erotic experience has not only stimulated all her energies, but her new knowledge has quickened all her sympathies. She feels, at the same time, more alert mentally, and she finds that she is more alive than before to the influences of Nature and of art. Moreover, as others observe, however they may explain it, a new beauty has come into her face, a new radiance into her expression, a new force into all her activities. Such is the exquisite flowering of love which some of us who may penetrate beneath the surface of life are now and then privileged to see. The sad part of it is that we see it so seldom, and then often so late.

It must not be supposed that there is any direct or speedy way of introducing into life a wider and deeper conception of the erotic play function and all that it means for the development of the individual, the enrichment of the marriage relationship, and the moral harmony of society. Such a supposition would merely vulgarize and stultify the divine and elusive mystery. It is only slowly and indirectly that we can bring about the revolution which in this direction would renew life. We may best prepare the way for it by undermining and destroying those degrading traditional conceptions which have persisted so long that they are instilled into us almost from birth, to work like a virus in the heart and to become almost a disease of the soul. To make way for the true and beautiful revelation, we can at least seek to cast out these ancient growths, which may once have been true and beautiful, but now are false and poisonous. By casting out from us the conception of love as vile and unclean we shall purify the chambers of our hearts for the reception of love as something unspeakably holy.

In this matter we may learn a lesson from the psychoanalysts of today, without any implication that psychoanalysis is necessarily a desirable or even possible way of attaining the revelation of love. The wiser psychoanalysts insist that the process of liberating the individual from outer and inner influences that repress or deform his energies and impulses is effected by removing the inhibitions on the free play of his nature. It is a process of education in the true sense, not of the suppression of natural impulses nor even of the instillation of sound rules and maxims for their control, not of the pressing in but of the leading out of the individual's special tendencies.[4] It removes inhibitions, even inhibitions that were placed upon the individual, or that he consciously or unconsciously placed upon himself, with the best moral intentions; and by so doing it allows a larger and freer and more natively spontaneous morality to come into play. It has this influence above all in the sphere of sex, where such inhibitions have been most powerfully laid on the native impulses, where the natural tendencies have been most surrounded by taboos and terrors, most tinged with artificial strains of impurity and degradation derived from alien and antiquated traditions. Thus the therapeutical experiences of the psychoanalysts reinforce the lessons we learn from physiology and psychology and the intimate experiences of life.

Sexual activity, we see, is not merely a bald propagative act; nor, when propagation is put aside, is it merely the relief of distended vessels. It is something more even than the foundation of great social institutions. It is the function by which all the finer activities of the organism, physical and psychic, may be developed and satisfied. Nothing, it has been said, is so serious as lust—to use the beautiful term which has been degraded into the expression of the lowest forms of sensual pleasure—and we have now to add that nothing is so full of play as love. Play is primarily the instinctive work of the brain, but it is brain activity united in the subtlest way to bodily activity. In the play function of sex two forms of activity, physical and psychic, are most exquisitely and variously and harmoniously blended. We here understand best how it is that the brain organs and the sexual organs are, from the physiological standpoint, of equal importance

[4] See for instance H. W. Frink, *Morbid Fears and Compulsions*, 1918, Chapter X.

and equal dignity. Thus the adrenal glands, among the most influential of all the ductless glands, are specially and intimately associated alike with the brain and the sex organs. As we rise in the animal series, brain and adrenal glands march side by side in developmental increase of size, and, at the same time, sexual activity and adrenal activity equally correspond.

Lovers in their play—when they have been liberated from the traditions which bound them to the trivial or the gross conception of play in love—are thus moving among the highest human activities, alike of the body and of the soul. They are passing to each other the sacramental chalice of that wine which imparts the deepest joy that men and women can know. They are subtly weaving the invisible cords that bind husband and wife together more truly and more firmly than the priest of any church. And if in the end—as may or may not be—they attain the climax of free and complete union, then their human play has become one with that divine play of creation in which old poets fable that, out of the dust of the ground and in his own image, some god of chaos once created Man.

MECHTILDE LICHNOWSKY

Marriage as a Work of Art

Il y a des mariages heureux, il n'y en a jamais eu de délicieux.

There are happy marriages, but there have never been delightful ones.

LA ROCHEFOUCAULD.

WITHOUT having died ourselves, we know what death is; without a personal remembrance of our birth, we know the whys and wherefores of human existence; hunger and nourishment, growth, illness, are, if by no means thoroughly understood phenomena, still ideas about which one can talk, and up to a certain point there is a possibility of acting appropriately. The same applies to science of a higher order, to technical matters, to the arts. For the investigation of these achievements, schools and books exist; there are times for exercise, helps, ways of avoiding error, the chance to reach better results through the selection of better expedients. In short, it appears that the world has progressed quite far in the mastery of manifold sciences and of sundry crafts, and that many of its citizens have learned to speak on these subjects, and some to deal with them competently. But in our existence there is a thing, a fact, a craft, an art, however one may choose to name it, a problem, a phenomenon of which we know less than we do of death, of health, of railway operation, or of landscape-gardening. This phenomenon is called in German *Ehe* [marriage], and that little word shows the coupling together of two vowels *e* through a sigh. These vowels are neutrally coloured in tone, not happily triumphant like *a* [English *ah*], not slyly ironic like *i* [long *e*], not agitated or disillusioned like *o*, nor indeed infernally awe-inspiring like *u* [*oo* as in "root"]. Marriage, which seems to have been modeled on Nature, but knows to some extent how to escape its sovereign laws, is first an idea and probably not much more than that, although it appears to have existed almost everywhere since time immemorial as a basis of life so fundamental that it is taken for granted. Created by thinkers, praised by the mass, accepted and employed with rage or in silence, is this concept, flickering temptingly like a fata morgana, or grey like a bourgeois statute, a social-political or a religious precept which many would very much like to raise to the status of a law of Nature. Marriage as an idea is, however, an old, a venerable, work of man; marriage as realization does not exist, though marriages there are, many thousands of marriages, as there are in the world millions of vehicles, from pushcarts to luxurious limousines.

As to marriage as a known quantity, as a thought which has been thoroughly considered and correspondingly worked out, as an explored territory, I could not name any quantity so unknown, any such *terra incognita*. Marriage is consummated; it is lived. Who or what is consummated or lived, of that nobody is as yet aware to the extent which might be natural in regard to other agreements which human beings enter on with one another.

What is a marriage that goes well? A thousand different answers are presented. Does the prosperous marriage depend on the love which brought the two partners together? And with what sort of love are we here concerned? Again the echo of a thousand answers rings out. But still from these two thousand answers no universally valid principle can be deduced, since probably the last judgment delivered would nullify the earlier ones, and it would be difficult to reach unanimity. Marriage appears really to exist only as an indefinite concept which cannot be considered in all its aspects, either on the basis of sociology or on that of religion, let alone transposing such general considerations into the realm of fact—although, for instance, the idea of scarlet fever has created a reasonable practical therapy which doctors and patients can follow. Of course, marriage is not a sickness; it is even said to be health. But this health is as far from being easily attained as a sickness may be from an easy cure, and assuredly it is more difficult to attain it than to accomplish a difficult cure and therapy.

In marriage there is one factor with which we must necessarily reckon, humanity as it actually exists, humanity divided into a million forms, which must claim for itself the strength and all the forces of Nature with its primaeval hostility to restrictions of civilization, culture, and art. Because it has need of this dominant hostility, this same humanity has produced from its core the thinker, the artist, who offers it that same quality with the enchanting word of "love." But he too, like Nature, cannot think with finality, can never produce deeds which could give it an easier rest, another sleep than death, the solution of all problems. There remains as the one rescue, as the one happy course—compromise. Marriage is a compromise which states and churches have conceived in order to give humanity a supporting mould of life and themselves a lever for control. Neither of the two admits the compromise openly; they invoke Nature, which remains silent, but which does not forego vengeance when provoked; or they invoke God, Who is always prudently invisible and Whom they have degraded to the rank of an inventor, while they themselves play the lords of the patent-office and meanwhile push forward their own discoveries, on which no God would ever grant a patent, the inventions of Morality and Ethics.

The characteristic feature of compromise is that no one likes to admit it, least of all the immediate parties—in this instance, the married couple. Compromises take form by necessity where inevitable and intangible factors have assumed control. Thus, in a higher sense, every poem, every work of art, is a sublime compromise with inevitable, intangible beauty, with inevitable, intangible suffering.

One speaks of wedding for love and of wedding for convenience, but not of love-marriages and of convenience-marriages. The act of wedding certainly does not constitute a marriage in itself. State and church want marriage—this abstract notion, from which only bridges which are difficult to cross can be constructed into reality—but they supervise only the wedding. After the wedding the chaos of humanity resumes its disorderly sway, and it seems as if it could, as a rule, hardly succeed in mastering it or in producing out of its midst a wise and godlike leader to whom it might subject itself in its deliverance. But restlessly and all confusedly it busies itself with the problem.

Let us first divide the matter into two great categories:

1. Wedding for love, with consequent marriage;

2. Wedding for convenience, with consequent marriage.

From the first there result:

a. Wedding for love, entered into in the age of unreason;

b. Wedding for love, entered into in later and in much later years. Here the problem is still more complicated, inasmuch as boundaries of age are difficult to determine, so that they would have to be drawn entirely differently for the two sexes; and here exceptions actually prove a rule which is hard to arrive at.

This very crude temporary classification of wedding shall constitute only the frame of the theme, and the subdivisions shall be concentrated in such a way that only the *wedding for love*, entered into in the age of unreason although in good faith and in presumed knowledge of love, and the *wedding for convenience*, entered into for reasons which have nothing to do with love, remain for further contemplation. Marriage is commonly an artful mixture of the two forms. Substantially different as they appear and may remain in their effect, in *one* point they resemble each other, probably in the majority of individual instances: of the two partners *one* is the persuader, the *other* the persuaded; one holds a definite goal before his eyes, the other has more of the nature of the dreamer; one is more active, more conscious, or more gifted, simpler or more passionate, than the other; and this is in no way determined by a law of Nature which might have allotted to the male partner the likelier priority in knowledge and leadership. In short, the famous equality which should bring two people together consists chiefly in their so-called mutual completion. Two wish the same thing, yet it cannot be the same identical thing. One could imagine that two engineers who come from the same school wish to build the same bridge; each begins the work from his own side, but it ends with a collapse in the middle and sinks into the river, since they have not worked equally, nor have they supplemented each other, or else their equality was so exact that they could not interlock at the point of meeting, and only a hard proximity resulted which could not stand pressure. It is significant for the mutual agreement which, beginning with the day of the wedding, is called marriage, that in the first place, in contrast to other agreements, it does not strive toward a set, controllable aim (for the management of the common household and the procreation of children is not a life's aim for human beings, but much rather an object of control for authorities), and that, in the second place, no monitor will guide the two who call themselves married people. Optimism, belief in miracles, confidence in authority, instinctive impulses, the natural bias of character, seem in the beginning to take the place of any guide. Many perhaps will say at this point: Religion! And yet again: Religion! But out of thousands, not even one-half understand what religion is; as to the usual concepts, I know very well that religion demands that one take up one's cross and follow the Lord; but this is only an admission that Christian marriage can be a real cross, and religion has never yet appointed for the participants, that is, the married couple, a guide who would do justice to reality in a comprehensive and honest way.

Marriage is a dual autonomy; the participants automatically transfer to it their native impulse of self-preservation, and thenceforward the impulse of self-preservation will be part of the substance of the marriage.

This will to combine the final, the enduring, nay, the eternal, with a phenomenon pertaining to Nature, which consequently is indefinite, changing, and of primaeval wildness, and which powerfully rules man, as in the case of spiritual and physical mating—this will to the eternal lays the cornerstone of this artful edifice and is part of the marriage which is a work of art. Here, in marriage, in contrast to other relations between the sexes, the motive of art enters; here the chords of Nature are played on; here the first tone of the metaphysical resounds.

An ideal dual autonomy is like a tree which forms a single straight trunk out of two principal roots. If, after the uniting of the roots, it splits itself into two parallel half-trunks, one may speak of its degeneration, and the wood loses in value and beauty—an instance of dual autonomy which is not ideal.

Bodily condition, spiritual disposition, character in its thousandfold varieties, dependence on impulse, knowledge and lack of knowledge of one's own forces, present in themselves tremendous cliffs or sheltering havens, which the ship of marriage must avoid or to which it must run; but in entering into marriage in youthful years, neither of the partners knows how to say to it much more than the important word "yes."

With regard to healthy and vigorous offspring, and because healthy youth in its carefree way bears burdens more lightly, feels difficulties less sharply, and conquers them more easily, and at times takes by intuition a path which is not too wrong, marriage at an early but suitable age for both sexes seems to me a necessity only to be avoided in exceptional cases, under one condition: *Marriage must be regarded as a work of art.* These nine words must be made clear to youth. Marriage as a social institution is a work of art—in contrast to the works of Nature, which rushes on in happy thoughtlessness and knows no consideration, no barrier, no time. Man, however, who lives within time, which for him has a beginning and an end, has to transfer this sense of the boundaries of his existence to the use of the epochs, to surround each action with a beginning and an end; man had to create speech in order to get a grasp on life as it passed, at least in the world of thought. Through the word he gave beginning and end to things; out of words he created laws; out of laws, walls between which life could flow as reasonably as might be. This entire edifice of speech, law, and attitude toward Nature, the hereditary enemy of every art, since only art can tame her, is in itself a tremendous work of art, at which humanity has laboured for thousands of years. Countless masters and apprentices with ceaseless and anonymous labour have created the artful work, which came into existence *with* Nature and *parallel to it* as well as *in spite of it*, that artful work which we call the civilized world, with its languages and its laws, and which, contemplated across the ages, appears as a work of art of tragic greatness. The path to beauty leads through suffering, and verily humanity has not been spared this.

What mankind in its entirety has accomplished, a work of art which, unlike the arts with which we are familiar, such as music, poetry, painting, and sculpture, which are at the command of only one master, was mastered by thousands, this is the task which two are supposed to perform. Two are in a fateful way more than a thousand and less than one. But enormous difficulty lies in the fact that, while every other work of art can be apprehended by the senses, that with which we are here concerned seems to reside in higher spheres, where the hand meets with no form, the eye sees no line, and the ear waits in vain for melodies; and even when the two artists have completed their work, but few will be aware of it, since it might well leave measureless abstract values to posterity, but no concrete traces. Here thought, sentiment, and an ever-renascent will to the good are bound to create beauty and the progress of mankind.

There exists yet another work of art in the metaphysical sense, which will be mentioned later.

Long before they call themselves independent, I would bring the greatness of this problem to the attention of young people and point out to them that more circumspection, foresight, self-restraint, and wisdom must be exercised in its solution than in any action which the individual has to perform; and again and again: If you have not this goal before your eyes, give up marrying, for you are not yet mature for the master-work of marriage! (How the young maiden, especially, should mature, without occupying herself at too close range with Nature's pattern for the work of art, is a matter which has only an indirect bearing on the theme and therefore will not be examined at this point.)

To the young I should like to say further:

However earnestly the world tries to present marriage as a matter at least half public in character, since it is sanctioned by it, it should not have the least part in it; married people should maintain an imperturbability, a terseness of communication, a discretion, which should be applied even to those who are closest to them. Two who love each other must protect themselves mutually against permitting the public to make their relation commonplace, because they are apt to infect themselves with this commonplaceness. Love cannot endure too great an exposure, and especially not when, through wedlock, a great step has been made toward publicity.—In love there are no insignificant things for which a different law would be required than for the so-called great moments, just as in art there can exist no comparative criterion for the value of the single parts. Art and life are integral and indivisible down to the smallest particles of their expression. Nothing is so needful of protection as love. Does not every lover know this? The fear of losing the other's love; the fear, nay, the certainty of being oneself of too slight value—is not this a certain sign of true love? Can this fear be turned into security through the mere formality of a marriage contract? No! This love must be protected otherwise. Precisely the relative lack of impediment which marriage offers to the lover is a menace to love; artificially constructed barriers will therefore not harm but serve it.

The imperturbability of the married couple should exhibit itself before witnesses, as much as possible as a neutral courtesy toward each other, from the first day on. But let the same courtesy prevail even when there are no witnesses. True courtesy in daily intercourse, that is, amiable formalities, the suppression of every personal ill humour, the abandoning of egotism, is the small coin which comes from the capital of the heart and is officially recognized by the world in intercourse between man and man. It has therefore, when this is its source, no more to do with unnaturalness and affectation, with a lack of genuineness or even with falsity, than the graceful, charming manner in which any work of art conceals from our senses in masterly fashion the greatness of the impulse which created it.

This courtesy is the purport of all restraint, and when it possesses the grace of true virtue, the grace of genuine art, it is perhaps the key to happiness. Beware!—if it be broken through, one finds the way back to it only with difficulty. The one who truly loves will understand me; it prevents nothing, it advances everything.

But it will be difficult for many, especially for youth not trained to it in *youthful years*—a sin of omission which I must regretfully put down to the account of the majority of parents. It must for once be said plainly—and I dare not shrink from so doing: Perhaps grace does not lie at the German's door; perhaps, in ignorance of its creative value and of its deepest root in the vanquishing of self, he considers it superfluous, since it is foreign to his nature; perhaps he is convinced that it has no part in his being, because he himself has never recognized that in his own education rudeness was regarded as genuineness, roughness as straightforwardness, and arrogant behaviour as frankness, and that the whole ensemble was taken for manliness. One thing is certain: that German youth is sometimes affected and insincere when it wishes to be polite; and as a result, this forced will to courtesy, to an absolutely misunderstood courtesy, does not endure. Even in the young women the performance of the duties of courtesy appears to me often purely external, having nothing to do with that gracefulness which arises toward one's fellowman out of the *vince te ipsum* (vanquish thyself); there is certainly nothing new in this requirement, but it appears to me that the ancient wisdom has fallen into complete forgetfulness in the high culture of the beloved ego. But marriage requires a mutual solicitude for the Thou; the ego can find in the marriage-partner a loyal trustee who will love it as he loves himself, and more. This "as thyself," which is taken from the familiar commandment of neighbourly love, happy in the highest sense, reveals a curious secret; it is certainly true that self-love *without any feeling of tenderness* is a silently accepted principle of Nature according to which man impulsively protects and furthers himself. It is also undoubtedly certain that nobody can love his unfamiliar neighbour with tenderness; the love of neighbours, when "felt," is at the best an automatic transfer of self-love; suffering that is known to oneself or the self-conscious joy of the individual will be perceived in another and ostensibly sympathized with; but this affective echo is only a crafty variety of egotism, which is not capable of separating suffering and joy from itself even in the mirrored picture. However, talent is involved here, and thus arises the chance of exercising an art; and here I speak of the second work of art from a metaphysical point of view, to which I referred above—of virtue. Only when exalted to a work of art can the love of one's neighbour be virtue: when it germinates "of itself," and therefore grows wild, it is neither the one nor the other. Love cannot be commanded, but its reflection can be, the "as if" which is contained in the commandment, and which in fact means: Behave toward thy neighbour *as if* thou lovedst him. Then, since one is not capable of loving oneself with affection and has only what he gives himself to offer to his neighbour, the wisdom of the commandment discloses itself as a magnificent call *to artistry.*

It is not love that is demanded, but behaviour as if one loved; not sentiment, but the act, as if one were carried away by a beauty which desires exactly this deed, in order to surrender itself. And it will let itself be captured, it will materialize as a work of art. This love is not emotion, it is religion. Some, like the artist, are born religious. Few are capable of creating works of beauty in the plastic arts, music, and poetry; but the way to the art-work of virtue stands open to every one.

And this art is tremendously fascinating and full of mystery. It consists in fact in this: that after one has studied his own cards sufficiently, one carefully conceals them from his fellow players, but peers industriously into the cards of the others and directs his game accordingly, not to gain a personal advantage, but to let the others win.

I am for absolute, authentic mutual honesty and frankness in marriage; but one need not always carry his heart in his hand—he may keep it in his head! The imperturbability of the marriage-partners, mentioned above, must be preserved not only in the face of the world, but also, and this is of great importance, from one toward the other, particularly because the unexplored and problematic element in the being of the man as well as in that of the woman exercises on the lover a beguiling charm, which ever and again prevents that dangerous feeling of security. The habit of permanent proximity can become just as dangerous. Imperturbability sets a healthy distance, that delicate tension which keeps hearts vigilant and lets love grow. The maintenance of poise and of distance between one being and another, however well wedded they may be, is necessary, since poise guarantees style, and distance, objectivity, two important factors in the exercise of any art. In marriage there is sufficient opportunity for woman to reveal herself as woman, man as man; therefore they must both—even the woman!—not be afraid of thinking how to give expression to that sentiment which the English attribute to the gentleman.—If marriage can be conducted as a work of art, every kind of art stands open to it; and I can but recall that saying of Voltaire: *Tous les genres sont bons, sauf le genre ennuyeux*—"All kinds are good, except the tiresome." To know the art of loving *beyond emotion*—that is, *although* a strong emotion is present, *or although no* strong emotion is perceptible—is a *sine qua non* for both partners in marriage. Love as an incident of Nature is always in peril of extinction, as on the contrary it is capable of flaming up again quite unforeseen. (I do not speak in this place of change in the object of love.) Every artificial element is foreign to it; it finds its element in the artistic.—Every lover is a poet, as we all are when we dream. Every one who is awake and every disinterested observer of the lover will learn here the connection of the "as if" with actuality. And this "as if" is the essence of art.—The artist stands before Nature, irresistibly attracted by its beauty and free of fear, as if he could seize and dominate it; and this "as if" becomes a fact. The poet speaks as if he were imprisoned behind a filigree of verses; and he *is* a captive, although he can free himself at any moment. The soul of the musician sings as if it carried all dissonances within itself and had only to arrange them, and thus it is, until the moment when he binds them into harmony; and he does nothing else through all his life. The actor stands on the stage as if he were the man whom he is representing, and it is so; he *is* the man. Married people stand—God knows!—in life! But it would do them no injury if they lived as if they stood on a stage, so that they would not so often step out of their parts and be unmasked as ordinary amateurs (lovers!). And indeed, the highest art of the stage is in a deeper sense a work of love, of which the deeply touched spectator must say: That was no longer theatricality; that was life!

Marriage may present a greater work of art than any other relation between the sexes, since harmony, the eternal longing of man, is thinkable in an artistic sense only within the confines of established principles. No art can do without the unfathomable principles of mathematics, which are as mysterious as they are endless; its principles can shift constantly and uninterruptedly in form, yet they will never escape life, never concede independence from themselves, and therefore never grant complete freedom. Liberty in bondage is the goal. Freedom in the unbound is really not freedom at all, but rather a state of immaturity.

A free bond of love is like the magnificent occurrences of Nature; the marriage bond is like a symphony. That which unites the artist with Nature is no longer a loose relationship; reverencing it, he carries on with it a marriage which cannot be sundered. His love is founded on deep respect, and he serves Nature with the utmost devotion, until it comes to life in his work and is capable of human speech. Even when he has become her master, Nature remains his mistress, and their converse lasts forever and is ever new.

Possession is a result which the denominator and the numerator project before them into eternity; so youth should speak thus to itself, when it contemplates approaching the great work of art which is marriage: He who knows not the pleasure of serving will never participate in the pleasure of commanding himself and an undertaking.

The small space at my disposal does not permit me to go into details, especially not into the details of technique or into the question of divorce, which is certainly in the sorest need of reform.—Divorce is thrice to be preferred to the awful drama of unhappy marriages lasting for years—marital vaudeville or marital burlesque—by people who are not artists! But usually the problem is not so simple!—I likewise cannot enter into the problem of the children, although they represent a leading motive of marriage. Perhaps the fundamental idea of this short essay can be indicated as a flash of light, a flash of light to which a path of thorns leads, which two honourable humans strew with the rose-leaves of their love. The human being is perhaps never able to create a work of art of absolute perfection, and everything, even perfection, is a fragment of the Nameless, the Eternal, the Divine.

Perhaps every star which we contemplate with longing from our lowlands is only a fragment, a flash of light.

PAUL DAHLKE

Marriage as a Fetter

MARRIAGE is a form of completion, of life-completion. Man is not an entity, as is clearly shown by the fact of "nutrition." This fact is, in the last analysis, nothing but the most universal and ever-renewed process of completion. All living beings not only depend upon nutrition but they are nutrition in themselves, a physico-spiritual nutritive process, comprising sensations, perceptions, thought, consciousness, as well as eating and drinking and breathing. This is what is implied in the axiom of the Buddhist canon: "All beings consist in nutrition" (*sabbe satta aharatitthika*). Marriage is the completion of the individual being, as illustrated by the phrase, "the other half," in speaking of married persons. It represents as completion a form of physico-spiritual nutrition, in which sometimes the physical, sometimes the spiritual, part is predominant. Marriage thus reminds man, as do eating and drinking, of his deficiencies, his lack of completeness. The passion for completion is the most universal, the basic, the all-pervasive feature of all kinds of natural life, and the desire to get rid of this compulsory desire and lack of completeness is the most universal, the basic and all-pervasive feature of all kinds of spiritual life. This desire or urge lies, in the final analysis, at the root of our idea of God: We, the created beings, mankind—we stand in need of completion. We feed; that is, we cannot help feeding: we woo; that is, we cannot help wooing—and we thereby forfeit our liberty. But we yearn for a being, for a state of existence, which will no longer stand in need of these base complements.

The loftiness of our idea of God is correlative to the urgency of this yearning. The gods of primitive races feed and drink and have their "other halves." The Homeric gods carouse and indulge in love. The Hindu gods require similar complements, though in a more spiritual form. And this is the reason why monotheism occupies a higher plane, as compared with these creeds: a fact which would otherwise remain unintelligible, monotheism being, as against the Hindu creeds, tainted with the flaw of deficient reality. The god of the monotheists is a lofty *abstractissimum*, paying for his disengagement from the necessities of eating and drinking and wooing (in a word, from nutrition) with his reality. He no longer stands in need of such complements, any more than a shadow requires a complement. This lofty abstraction has been weaned from every kind of nutriment. It neither eats nor drinks, nor does it wed. It does not need these completions, being the whole in itself. Still, being weaned of all this, it is a "whole in itself" without a living content. It exists, that is, only as an abstraction withdrawn from reality, and it depends upon the contingencies of individual experience, in what measure it is susceptible of individualization, and, thus, of efficiency in the individual.

From the viewpoint of marriage as a need for completion, one immediately understands why the attainment of the loftiest condition of existence has at all times and by all races been sought through celibacy. The world over, celibacy is the key to the more exalted regions of existence, to the higher spheres of life; and when Protestantism, with its Lutheran bluntness, proclaims it superfluous, it will have to bear the consequences of its thoughtlessness;

nay, it is even now bearing them. There are laws of reality that cannot be disregarded with impunity, the foremost of which is this: that all superior beings prove their superiority by their slighter need for completion.

Such as fail to see this will demand, with the specious and shallow assertiveness of men of the world, to be shown positive proofs of the superiority and necessity of celibacy. Celibacy, in their opinion, only serves to induce hypocrisy and immorality.

Celibacy unquestionably gives rise to such phenomena, and has, as a matter of fact, often enough caused their appearance. Yet this only serves to show that it is contrary to the essence of life, which is desire for completion, passion for completion. And everything hinges upon the question, whether life, as represented by this essential, should be regarded as venerable, and necessary, and worthy of approbation in itself, or whether this passion for completion should be considered as what it really is, a necessity, a deficiency, and in a word, an inferiority. It is here that Catholicism reveals its distinctly superior capacity for sensing the ultimate mysteries of life, as compared with Protestantism and Judaism and their all too exuberant affirmative attitude toward life, according to which the need for completion prevailing with life in general is held to be venerable and justified in itself, and thus to hallow itself and to render superfluous any kind of priestly celibacy. There are, no doubt, various kinds of life's self-completions, and they all appeal to man on the score of their "naturalness." Eating and drinking are natural. So are wooing and being wooed. Still, what ranks high above them all, as the higher form of life, is disengagement from such complements, lack of desire, the Great Poverty; and this proves itself to be the higher form of life by rising above and comprehending them each and all by virtue of its reaching an intrinsic conclusion, essentially unsurpassable, with its "no more." Who is the richest? He who has no more need. Who possesses everything? He who demands no more. Who is the most powerful? He who possesses himself.

A more crucial test of the quality of self-possession than celibacy hardly seems to exist. Nor is there to be found a standpoint from which, on the contrary, all these needs could be as forcibly shown to rise above the lack of needs; that is, a standpoint from which matrimony and its inherent worldliness could be shown to reach an intrinsic completion in the form of "no more celibacy." For need is never an actual completion nor an actual height, no matter what label be bestowed on it by dialectic. Thus freedom from needs clearly and *per se* proves itself to be on a higher plane, as compared with need.

Nevertheless, celibacy is a symptom. Symptoms admit of various interpretations, and that it is not symptoms alone that count is shown by the familiar distinctions between the monk and the bachelor. A man does not become a monk by remaining a bachelor; the reverence with which celibacy is everywhere regarded and treated stands in inverse ratio to the treatment meted out to the bachelor. His standing is unquestionably lower than that of the married man. What is the reason for this? Again we point out that symptoms admit of various interpretations. It is not symptoms that count, but motives. The meaning of life does not reside in facts, but in motives. This serves to reveal the fundamental difference between the monk and the bachelor: the monk is unwedded because of a morality surpassing the ordinary standard; the bachelor is unmarried because of a morality falling below the ordinary standard. This difference must be pondered, apprehended, understood; otherwise the monk might happen to become a bachelor, no more than a cowled bachelor; and *vice versa.* When this difference is apprehended, understood, and realized, the bachelor might chance to become a monk without the cowl, failing to exhibit himself outwardly as a monk for the reason that the actual circumstances are unfavourable, as, for example, in these present forsaken times, whose deficiency in cultural values and cultural sensibilities is pre-eminently shown in the deficiency of monachism and the lack of opportunity to lead a monastic life—of the cloister. Here again Catholicism, with its profound understanding of humanity, proves the only exception in the western hemisphere.

The question of the motive of celibacy confronts us in Buddhism, with all the differences that exist between it and the other religions, in this respect as in all others.

In religions based upon a creed, Catholicism first of all, celibacy is ultimately only an expression for an *imitatio Dei,* an imitation of God, the striving after that integrity which needs no complement and which is itself "God." Priestly celibacy has, to my mind, no other meaning: the priest on the one hand, the mediator between God and man, and the monk on the other, holding immediate communion with God, both show these relations to the Divine in disclaiming all manner of self-completion within the limits of what is possible to beings of flesh and blood. The ultimate and decisive complement, in this instance, is "God," the God in whom he believes. "Be ye therefore perfect, even as your Father which is in heaven is perfect." And to be perfect means to require no completion.

Thus, in religions based upon creeds, the fact of celibacy entirely depends on its metaphysical basis, without which it would be no more than an asceticism as devoid of purpose and significance as it is evidently thought to be by Protestantism and the worldly. And what, after all, could be the meaning of celibacy and its violations of human nature, unless it accomplishes a step toward that integrity which is "God"? Or in other terms: in religions based on creeds, celibacy is the expression of the striving after an ideal state, realizable only in the manner of a contrast-value with regard to the existing reality, and conceivable only as its transcendent opposite: the disengagement from all manner of complements in virtue of a wholeness in itself. To sum up: celibacy, in this instance, is a *postulate* subservient to an ideal object.

Celibacy in Buddhism, on the other hand, is not a postulate ministering to an ideal object, but *the result of a new way of thinking in harmony with actuality.*

There is but one actuality: that which I myself experience as such, or rather: that as which I experience myself. To realize this is the very axis and turning-point of thought, and by its side all other questions and problems, facts and convictions, descend to the level of mere symptoms, the meaning of which lies, not in themselves, but in their revelation of the nature of reality. It is to actuality that we solely appeal, finally and decisively, whether in the field of the conceptual, or in ethics or religion, etc. Nothing but actuality can really provide direction. Unless this be fully realized, all things, the symptomatically best not excepted, may turn out ill; that is, they may lead to a failure with regard to the object for whose sake one believes himself to be labouring. This is the meaning of the saying: "It becometh different from that, for whose sake they ponder it every time" (113th sermon, *Middle Collection*). Celibacy, when understood to be adopted for the sake of some ulterior object, no matter what might be its quality and nature, is bound to turn out badly, in one way or another, as, generally speaking, it is with all things that are not thought out down to their roots, that is, down to actuality, but that remain entangled in mere concepts. And it approximates an entanglement in concepts, when celibacy is adhered to for the sake of this wholeness that requires no complement, being in itself the Perfect. Wherever there is life and wherever life is accepted as such, the need for completion also exists. Life without completion is a concept as meaningless as a flame which does not burn.

Buddhism does not fall into the error of entanglement of concepts. Buddhism, in the final analysis, teaches the nature of actuality as it really is. One kind of actuality only is open to mankind: that which every individual experiences within himself. And the Buddhist doctrine of actuality tends, in the last resort, to demonstrate what the individual experiences himself: the restless, unstable, empty interplay of the five groups of attachment (*panc'upadanakkhandha*), that is, as a process which, in its nature, does not *possess* the attachments and completions as the functions of an ego, but which *is* these attachments and completions themselves and nothing whatever besides. An ego identical with itself and capable of completing itself to form a totality is, therefore, impossible. And this is the great sacrifice the unprejudiced thinker is called upon to make at the altar of truth: the sacrifice of the ego, the term being taken in the customary sense of identity with oneself. This is the great sacrifice to which Buddha referred when he said: "It is hard to find such as understand." For man understands best what lies in the direction of his wishes and his will. But Buddhism opposes that which man desires and intends: existence, well-being, and permanence. Therefore, Buddha calls his doctrine that which "opposes the current." And so it does indeed, since it eradicates the illusion of an ego and proclaims, in the place of an ego existing in itself, as a juxtaposition identical with itself, in which every one believes, the pure sequence of an ever-renewed remembrance, which must invariably spring anew from its preliminary conditions, if it is to exist at all. (Compare my essay on "Samsara and Nirvana," in the periodical *Der Leuchter*, 1925, Otto Reichl, Darmstadt.) The ego is thus not a metaphysical and purely spiritual entity no longer requiring any complements, nor is it a purely physical "becoming" receiving its complements from other beings, but a being complementing itself from within, a physico-spiritual entity requiring sustenance—corporeal and spiritual, base and refined—for its existence; nourishment, therefore, in either case, and thus need of completion, and thus deficiency.

Viewed from this new insight into the nature of reality, the problem of completion and its valuation undergoes a complete conversion. The aim that remains cannot be the completion toward an ideal "wholeness in itself," which would mean entanglement in concepts devoid of substance, forfeiting their actuality for the sake of absoluteness. The aim, in this case, is the *ending*, the *cessation* of these ever-renewed completions, which, it is true, are life itself, yet in which life experiences itself as potential *cessation*. Life is a potential cessation. Its totality consists in that it experiences itself throughout as a process of completions. "The whole, ye priests, shall be shown unto you. What is the whole, ye priests? The eye and the visible forms, the ear and the sounds, the nose and the smells, the tongue and the tastes, the body and the tangibilities, thought and states of existence. This, ye priests, is what is called the whole" (*Samy.-Nik.*, IV).

Whatever can cease, must cease! In the presence of potential cessation, cessation is the final object; that is, an object that does not belong to the sphere of transcendent concepts, but which experiences itself as a cessation of comprehension, both bodily and spiritually. "Perfection" is not, in this instance, the existence "in itself" of a whole perfected in itself and requiring no completions, but the complete cessation of all those completions that make up the whole of life and that must cease, since their cessation is potential. The object is, here, cessation (*nirodha*), extinction (*nibbana*), of the beginningless play of life which has unfolded itself, by virtue of its ignorance thereof, from unbeginningness. Therefore, this extinction is not the effect of resolve or of an act of will or of an ascetic compulsion, but the result of a new insight into actuality, according to which the root of all existence is ignorance (*avijja*) and thirst (*tanha*), with their passion for completion, which is the basis in itself and to which is opposed the cessation of this passion, the "*Enough now! Enough now, for ever!*" being the Noble in itself, to which thought presses forward as to the ultimate, the greatest, the irresistible comfort which consists in abandonment, relinquishment, and renouncement, and which encompasses and supersedes all the other kinds of comfort with their inevitable contrasts of pain and bliss. "There are two kinds of comfort, ye priests. Which are they? The comfort of the house and the comfort of pilgrimage. These are the two kinds of comfort. The higher of the two is the comfort of pilgrimage, ye priests. There are two kinds of comfort, ye priests. Which are the two? The comfort derived from sensual bliss and the comfort of renunciation. These are the two comforts, ye priests. The higher of these two kinds of comfort, ye priests, is the comfort of renunciation" (*Ang.-Nik.*, Book II). And: "Boundlessness is what I deem the greatest comfort" (*Majjh.-Nik.*, XIII). For where there is need, there is limitation. Where there is limitation, there is discomfort, insecurity, and uneasiness (*dukkhata*).

This serves to show how celibacy, with the Buddhist monk, is based on fundamentally different motives as compared with the celibacy of the Catholic monk. Marriage is a fetter to both; but celibacy, with the Catholic, is postulated for the sake of furthering the approach of the integrity requiring no completion, which is "God," whereas celibacy with the Buddhist is not a postulate, but the inevitable result of that new conception of the meaning of actuality which implies weariness of the interplay of completions that pretend to be mere functions of "life," while being life itself in its totality. The Buddhist monk does not vow himself to celibacy. He is disengaged from the desire to bind himself by marriage, since he realizes that marriage is merely one of the innumerable forms of completion, through which life lives and "sustains" itself and of which he no longer stands in need, having perceived his ultimate object to be the surcease of all completions, the definite cessation of the beginningless interplay—extinction. He is *bound* to strive toward this object when he realizes life to be a potential cessation; that is, something which must ultimately cease, or otherwise confront him with the reproach of an unrealized realizability. The ever-recurring catchword for the Perfect is this: *Katam karaniyam*, or, "What had to be done is done"; that is: what could be done and, in this way, had to be done, is done.

There exist numerous and explicit utterances of the Buddha on the danger of marriage for such as would attain to the highest state. "There is no stronger fetter than the mutual bond of the sexes." "O ye priests, I know of no form that fetters man's mind as much as the female form. The female form, O ye priests, fetters the mind of man. I know of no voice whatsoever, O ye priests, no perfume, no taste, no contact, that fetters the mind of man like the contact with woman. The . . . contact with woman fetters the mind of man. I know of no form, O ye priests, that fetters the mind of woman like the form of man. The form of man fetters the mind of woman. I know of no voice, no perfume, no taste, no contact that fetters the mind of woman like the contact with man. The contact with man, O ye priests, fetters the mind of woman."

Now marriage, as a form of completion, has been called a form of nutrition. If this completion is to cease, must not the monk, since he disclaims completion in marriage, disclaim completion by nutrition as well; that is, must he not, as a matter of course, choose voluntary death by starvation?

The answer is: No! for what matters is not the act of feeding, but that there should lurk no lust, no passion, no attachment to food behind the process of nutrition. The oil of the flame of life, the oil by which life sustains itself, and by which it has ever sustained itself, consists not in eating and drinking, but in thirst (*tanha*).

"It is thirst that creates man" (*tanha janeti purisam—Samy.-Nik.*, I).

The natural objection to this is: If the form of completion realized as eating and drinking is nothing but a symptom that depends for its significance and meaning on some other thing behind it, might not the completion realized by marriage be likewise a symptom depending for its significance and meaning upon some other thing behind it; that is, can there not be passionless marriage, as there is passionless eating: a marriage that would not be a fetter even for the Buddhist?

Our answer to this is that such a state would amount

to a play on the word "marriage." Marriage is essentially the adjustment of the sexual tensions prevailing between the sexes; that is, adjustment in an orderly and conventional form. This adjustment is accomplished, as a rule, by the sexual act, which, for the male at least, is the greatest confession of lust, that unique act of uprightness in which the word "upright" receives its real meaning, where concept and object, idea and deed, form a unity. There is, ultimately, only one upright member in man, the sexual organ of the male. It is impossible that the uprightness of this member (the erection), except in some cases of sickness, should be a mere symptom depending for its meaning and significance upon something still more remote. The act of uprightness is lust itself, a unique process in which form and essence, symptom and reality form a unit.

Therefore man is the upright, the open, being; woman, in whom this unique upright member is lacking, or rather in whom it exists, but in a rudimentary form incapable of generation, is the secretive, the hidden sex. It is for this reason that the *Anguttara-Nikaya* says: "Three things, O ye priests, live hidden, not openly. Which are these three? Woman, O ye priests, lives hidden, not openly; the wisdom of the Brahmins lives hidden, not openly; wrong opinion lives hidden, not openly. Three things, O ye priests, shine openly, not hidden. What are these three? The disk of the moon, O ye monks, shines openly and is not hidden. The disk of the sun shines openly and is not hidden. The doctrine proclaimed by the Buddha shines openly and is not hidden" (*Ang.-Nik.*, Book III).

Thus, eating and drinking may be accomplished without lust. The act of generation is lust itself.

But a marriage may be concluded with the explicit condition of the exclusion of sexual intercourse. There are cases on record of pure and chaste marriages, in which both "halves" live in absolute continence in respect of sexuality. Some cases of this description are even said to be historically proven.

This may be true. But the adjustment between the sexes, completion as between man and woman, need not be realized by the act of generation alone; it may also be accomplished in a great many other ways, as, for example, in the manner of a purely spiritual completion. Still, a marriage in which one of these completions fails to take place can no longer be called "marriage"; it has become a mere living-side-by-side, likely to be severed at the first shock it receives. On the other hand, completion as between man and woman may be equally well accomplished where there is no conjugal life. The spiritual friendships of men such as Dante, Petrarch, Francis of Assisi and Francis of Sales, are, from our point of view, fully equivalent to married life and its effects and consequences. Thus, Buddhism is seen to be, in the last resort, here as everywhere, a matter of honesty with oneself.

Gautama, the later Buddha, was married. That his marriage was not of the Platonic order is shown by the existence of a son engendered by him, at whose birth he is said to have spoken these words: "There has been born to me another fetter," meaning that there has been added to the old fetter, marriage, a new one in the son. These fetters were severed by the glow of the new way of thinking. During his later career as the Buddha, he was frequently in the company of nuns and female followers; but he never omitted the necessary precautions and, above all, never failed to impress their necessity in the strictest terms on the minds of his priests throughout his preachings. It is for her lack of uprightness that woman is, to him, the being in whom it is altogether impossible to be sure when and whether the passion of sexuality comes to an end. "In the pursuance of three things, O ye priests, there is no respite. Which are these three? In the pursuance of sleep, ye priests, there is no respite. In the pursuance of the partaking of intoxicating drinks there is no respite, O ye priests. In the pursuance of unchaste desires there is no respite, O ye priests. In the pursuance of these three things there is no respite, O ye priests."

He would most certainly not have been well disposed toward the endeavours of modern youth to blunt and overcome sexual attraction by means of early social intercourse. When questioned by Ananda in his old age: "How, Holy One, are we to conduct ourselves toward women?" he replied: "Refrain from gazing at women, Ananda." "Still, Holy One, how are we to act when we see women?" "Refrain from speaking with them, Ananda." "But, Holy One, how are we to behave, when conversation takes place?" "In that case, Ananda, keep advertence fully present." (*Digha-Nik.*, XVI.)

This is indeed taking a human view of man and a genuine view of reality. Avoid a possibility as soon as you perceive its avoidance as necessary, and necessities will spare you. Therefore, he bade his priests go forth upon their begging errands only at that time of day when womenfolk might not be expected to be about in the streets in negligent or scanty attire. A single glance, at a single unguarded moment, can suffice to kindle fresh conflagrations where the flame was presumed to be long since extinct. In the *Jatakas* there are to be found numerous accounts of how priests are occasionally seized with disgust with monastic life after having gazed upon an adorned or an unclothed woman. And the four-hundred-and-thirty-first *Jataka* relates that the Bhodisatta himself, as the penitent Harita, met with a fall from the loftiness he had attained into freshly kindled sensuality, through negligence in this respect.

Gautama, the Buddha, sought out lonely places until his death; and when asked his reason in so doing (*Majjh.-Nik.*, IV) he replied: "For mine own welfare and for the good of my followers." This again is indeed taking a human view of man and a genuine view of reality. And in this genuine reality married life is a fetter for him who has become aware of where the voyage leads: to surcease of all completions, relinquishment, cessation.

That this manner of conceiving married life, as derived from the Buddhist insight into the nature of reality, should ever lend itself to co-ordination with other conceptions as under some higher kind of unity, is out of the question, even as no standpoint exists from which doing and leaving undone could be co-ordinated as under a higher unity. Refraining from action, if honestly intended, if put into practice, that is, if realized, is always itself, and nothing besides. Any endeavours to place it under some higher concept, to present and to delimit it *as* this or *as* that, in a word to define it, is as unthinkable as it is impossible, since abandonment means also abandonment of all manner of comprehension. "And this priest, O ye priests, does not excogitate anything; he does not excogitate anywhere, nor does he excogitate for the sake of anything" (*Majjh.-Nik.*, CXIII.).

He abandons, having perceived that the nature of life is such as to allow of abandonment and that he who would be honest with himself must, as a matter of course, abandon it. To speculate on Buddhism, however ingeniously and pertinently, means misconceiving it.

In contributing this article on the subject of "Marriage as a Fetter" to this joint work on matrimony, I have not intended to suggest the possibility of working out the Buddhist conception of married life with other conceptions, nor have I meant to bring about its co-ordination with them under some higher standpoint. I have contributed my article simply because I wished to avail myself of another opportunity for pointing out that Buddhism, wherever and howsoever it may be approached, is wholly beyond the possibility of being reduced to a concept. Things like attaining to fullest maturity, abandonment, eternal cessation, are, in their nature, incapable of being co-ordinated with forms implying retainment or attachment, the categories of identity or contradictoriness being equally unavailable. There remains the incontrovertible fact that abandonment is what it is in itself, and nothing more. And any kind of endeavour to grasp abandonment by conceptual means and to co-ordinate it in the chorus of life as an individual part is destined to failure, provided that one does not toy with the subject as with a mere concept, in which case doubtless anything whatever can be managed conceptually, abandonment of conception not excepted. But whoever discountenances this process of transubstantiation, this substitution of mere concepts for actuality, will not be long in perceiving that the adequate formula is that *Buddhism is one thing, and everything else is different.* Let what I have said about married life be understood and remembered in the same spirit.

Verehrung dem Lehrer!—"Reverence to the Teacher!"

MATHILDE VON KEMNITZ

Marriage as Fulfilment

SINCE the chasm between man and man may be deeper than the "yawning gulf" of which our forbears spoke and more unbridgeable than the gulf between the soul of our most ancient ancestor, that liquid crystal, and our own, we are not surprised if by the word "marriage" the most different kinds of sexual relations are understood. In our examination of marriage as fulfilment we shall not apply the word to this diversity, but only to the highest possibility of the human race; that is, lasting, voluntary, spiritually compelled monogamy. All other forms are stages of development from remote pre-human times, or distorted phenomena of civilization which man chooses instead of his higher possibility. For the expert they may all have great significance, but they must never be taken as a criterion for spiritual valuations.

If we wish to understand why we may under certain premises term this lasting, voluntary, spiritually compelled monogamy a "fulfilment"; if we wish to get an idea why it has a far higher significance for the soul than all other lasting relationships of either consanguinity or friendship, we must above all clearly distinguish the nature of marriage from the emotions of human beings toward each other. This is the more necessary since the meanings of words are so very apt to be confused. Almost all languages describe the most dissimilar spiritual occurrences by the word "love"; what wonder, then, that the greatest confusion universally exists concerning their nature and their effects!

This nuisance I have attempted to check in my books,[1] primarily through express avoidance of the word "love" and by the application of the designation "eroticism" to all spiritually interwoven sexuality. But since the misuse of this word for primary sexuality is so general, I am frequently misunderstood. Only a fundamental view into the whole wonderland of the human soul [2] will preclude more confusion for the future. The community of the sexes, as I have stated at length, unlike all other relationships of human beings to one another, is not to be traced back to an "emotion," but to a will. I have called this the "will to selective amalgamation." The "emotion" of man is, however, a spiritual faculty of a different kind. It appears for the first time in the history of creation in the highest, the subconscious animals, and is therefore likewise found in the human soul only in the higher stages of consciousness. The subconscious animals and the unconsciousness of the human soul do not yet realize the presence of such a power. In the human consciousness emotion appears in a bipolar way as hatred and love, resembling an electrical power, and before the self-transformation of man it is completely at the service of the defective will to self-preservation. This will mistakenly conceives that the accumulation of pleasures and the avoidance of pain are the sense of life, and on that account throws the light of love on the one who gives pleasure and defends against pain, and the light of hatred on the one who gives pain and prevents pleasure. For the sake of this principle, the

[1] See *Erotische Wiedergeburt* ("Erotic Rebirth"), Verlag "Die Heimkehr," Pasing vor München.

[2] See *Der Seele Ursprung und Wesen,* Part II, *Des Menschen Seele* ("Origin and Reality of the Soul," Part II, "The Soul of Man"). Verlag "Die Heimkehr," Pasing vor München.

will to selective amalgamation unites itself with the emotions. It does this the more frequently and fervently because the pleasure and pain which it experiences are especially exuberant. Since this will, however, is a spiritual faculty different from emotion, it can associate itself alternately with both "poles," hatred and love. These couplings, peculiarly rich in variations, which we encounter in all defective beings, make plain even to the uninitiate the difference between the two spiritual faculties. If, however, the self-transformation of the human being in the sense of his divine function is brought to completion; if the will to self-preservation has placed above itself the self-creation of accomplishment as the sole purpose of life, then the emotions and the will to selective amalgamation are spiritually directed, and from that time on this will can never again associate itself with hatred. If the inspired hatred has reason to strike the chosen one, the will to selective amalgamation is extinguished.

The omnipotence of this will shows itself objectively above all in its sinister transforming influence on the soul. A magical activity, either destructive or brilliantly developing, can emanate from it. This, mankind has felt from the beginning, and for that reason has regarded the union of the sexes as a divine consecration or feared it as a demoniac enchantment which "can steal away a man's soul." Actually, not only the permanent union, but also the fugitive exchange of bliss, has a transforming influence on the soul—that influence so eagerly denied by all human beings who aspire to higher aims and who in primitive and unworthy unions attempt to fulfil their will to selective amalgamation. In the enduring union this reality is still more far-reaching. Here human beings who are conscious of God can pine away to contented or morose, garrulous corpses; but also, under the healing hands of eroticism, they can ripen into clarified, mature beings. Between these opposed, conclusive self-creations, which the union of the sexes furthers, we see all other human beings led part way in one or the opposite direction through the will to selective amalgamation. No one, not even the ascetic himself, escapes the transforming power of this will. The manner of fulfilment or of asceticism, the degree of spirituality—which determines union or ascetic resignation—decide the manner of transformation, the direction of the way along which the soul is led, without any regard for the stage of development and the capacity of the person thereby affected. An emotion can never effect a change of such a paramount and conclusive kind in the soul. But since mankind believes the will to selective amalgamation to be an emotion, so will mankind always fail to appreciate its transforming effect and prefer to interpret it as "immaturity"; if one grants the communal state of marriage such high significance in human life, one indeed calls it "fulfilment." It is therefore not without significance that I am able to illuminate in my works the reason of this singular and potent influence on the human soul.

The soul of man is the miraculous edifice of all stages of the creation of the cosmos, sheltering all cosmic revelations of will in accordance with their appearance in the universe.[3] Now, since the will to selective amalgamation made its appearance already in the stage preceding the first living cell, the colloid crystal, and has dwelt since those early creative phases in all higher individuals up to man, so it exists in the soul of man, in opposition to the emotions on all grades of consciousness and also in the unconscious soul. Yes, it glows through every single cell of the

[3] See *Der Seele Ursprung und Wesen,* Part I, *Schöpfungsgeschichte* ("Origin and Reality of the Soul," Part I, "History of Creation"). Verlag "Die Heimkehr," Pasing vor München.

body, and in the germ-cells it experiences an exceptionally clear objectification. In spite of this deep anchorage in the lowest spiritual stages, it rises into the human soul's highest forms of existence. In truth, in the supra-consciousness it is experienced as a powerful inspired desire, thanks to this fulfilled divine union. Thus it entirely penetrates the soul of man and together with the will to self-preservation represents the most extensive spiritual events. On the basis of this extent of experience we could already justify our conception of the highest possibility of mankind's selective amalgamation as "fulfilment." Certainly we must emphasize at the same time that the ascetic is not to be termed "unfulfilled" on account of his asceticism. In exactly the same way as we venture to praise only one kind of marriage as fulfilment of the will to selective amalgamation, there is only one kind of asceticism which leaves man entirely unfulfilled. The ascetic who, in his yearning for genius, renounces, of his own free will, an uncongenial partnership, choosing asceticism because he sees the inspired choice of his will to be unattainable, experiences just through this renunciation and through his suffering a powerful spiritual unfolding on to higher planes. But if a man lives ascetically because he is devoted to the insane idea that the will to selective amalgamation and its affirmation are things "unclean," he assuredly cannot escape atrophy of soul for the sake of this uninspired asceticism. He wanders away from God into the darkness quite as much as one who remains in an uncongenial union. I have elsewhere compared the "elective" asceticism of genius with the asceticism not in accord with genius.[4] The former is in harmony with

[4] See *Triumph des Unsterblichkeitswillens*, *Runen der Minne*, and *Moral der Erotik* ("Triumph of the Will to Immortality," "Runes of Love," and "Ethics of Eroticism"). Verlag "Die Heimkehr," Pasing vor München.

genius like the elective marriage partnership, and like it, by reason of the extensiveness of its experience and its effect, it can be called a fulfilment. Such an experience of the will to selective amalgamation subordinated to genius is, in the anguish of the resignation and in the joy of the amalgamation, an agent of invigoration to all the as yet unreleased genius in the human soul; and this so far entirely independently of the influence of the chosen one, simply through the experience in common of all the gradations of consciousness of the human soul.

But beyond this effect, we must now turn to those transformations which are produced in the soul not so much by the hope for selective amalgamation as by actual realization of transformations which the ascetic can reach only by different ways of self-creation.[5] The will to selective amalgamation indicates a deep-seated connection with the absolute idea of the universe, and thus with the will which first permitted the universe to appear; and in this way not only is its extensive anchorage in the human soul explained, but above all the intensity of its appearance in the soul and its effect on the "chosen" one. The world-creating goal of desire, for the sake of which the divine first made its appearance in this universe, was the will to create the consciousness of God in humanity. Since the will to selective amalgamation in its realization leads to the creation of a human being, and thus preserves the life of the species, this holy will assures the divine sense of the universe. For the offspring carries within himself the possibility of creating perfection in himself and bequeaths this to his posterity. He himself, or one of his posterity, may belong to those exceptional human beings who achieve

[5] See *Der Seele Ursprung und Wesen,* Part III, *Selbstschöpfung* ("Origin and Reality of the Soul," Part III, "Self-Creation"). Verlag "Die Heimkehr," Pasing vor München.

perfection through their own strength and through this are bearers of divine consciousness as long as they breathe. Through this inward intermingling of the procreation of the child with the absolute idea of the universe, the mighty effect which it and care for the development of the child have on the human spirit must not surprise us. The feeling of the close connection between the procreation of children and the divine sense of the universe has always permitted a consciousness of its holiness to dwell with the people most conscious of God. Thus the northern lore of the gods shows a positive knowledge of such consecration and teaches, under the cloak of symbolism, that the god Heimdold is present at the hour of procreation ("Creation of the Classes," *Edda*). Following the introduction of Oriental teaching of the ascetic ideal, this secure wisdom underwent a peculiar transformation. Marriage was barred as "sin" by the universal contempt for the union of the sexes, except when it was for the sake of procreation. The "morality" of the last century, deduced from the discoveries of the natural sciences, indorsed this conception to a great extent; and therefore insurmountable obstructions often stand in the way of "fulfilment" in marriage, as a result of such erroneous valuations. Against this, I have proved that marriage carries its consecration within itself, quite independently of procreation, even though the inspiring effect of parenthood on the soul of man can be so splendid that we would be justified in calling marriage "fulfilment" even if only on account of procreation, since in the experience of parental love lies the possibility of quickening genius. The ego, often for the first time, experiences in it an exaltation transcending the narrow limits of its particular individuality. The intensive common experience of the ego with the child or children is often the first step in the splendid ascent which the ego must accomplish in self-creation and which leads it to the sublime goal of overcoming hypercosmic distances in a single experience, as a bearer of divine consciousness. Parental love, above all, mother love, is moreover better suited than any other experience to stir the will to self-preservation from its monotonous devotion to the accumulation of pleasures. It demands sacrifice and yet again sacrifice, and does not hope therein for "return" and "payment." Therefore it is a possible bridge to the distant goal of divine experience which contains within itself the ultimate fulfilment of the human soul. Assuredly this event, too, like all those which befall man in his environmental and in his inner world, does not necessarily produce the same effect in every instance. The same experience of parenthood may just as well lead man to atrophy of the soul, if he turns it to such account out of his own choice. He then distorts parental love to a foolish monkey love, which may smother his own soul and that of his child. The act of generation carries thus the highest consecration, is "fulfilment" to man; but man can transform it into a soul-murdering poison. In view of the erroneous teachings which prevail today and destroy culture, in view of the underestimation of the peculiar value of marriage independently of procreation, it becomes a still more urgent duty to point out the consecration which inheres in it! I have had occasion to indicate in my works, from various points of view, on what clay feet the ascetic ideal stands, which chooses to stigmatize enjoyment of the senses as sin. In this brief discussion the knowledge to which wisdom and science lead can only lightly be touched on.

One who has penetrated into the entire structure of my philosophy will understand, what might seem in the first instance surprising, that the "potentially immortal" unicellular organism, the first living being of creation, resembles the human being, the highest step in creation, in many respects to a greater extent than all the intermediate stages. The human being is the only living organism to which, though subjected to the necessity of death, immortality is attainable, even if only in a spiritualized manner. That immortal ancestor teaches us thus the profound sense, the divine consecration of amalgamation, which it realizes independently of the task of propagation, in a marvellous way! But all mortal intermediate stages show, like distorted and stunted human beings, only an insignificant objectification of the will to selective amalgamation. The life of the "more highly differentiated" unicellular entities speaks clearly in regard to the exceptional value of the union of choice, for those beings propagate themselves through division and manifest the will to selective amalgamation at entirely different times. Then for a long period they attach themselves closely to the chosen being of like kind. Now the two united ones exchange, with a ceremonious transformation of nuclei, the hereditary substances which determine the being, so that each bears within himself the inheritance of both individuals. Then they return again to the solitary state (conjugation). Other species live a still more complete fulfilment. The cell-nuclei and the cell-bodies amalgamate in solemn transformation, and then form forever one single being (copulation), quite as do the germ-cells of mortal living beings. In comparison with this clear objectification of the will to selective amalgamation, its expression in the life of all unconscious mortal plants and animals and in a great number of human beings must be called very inadequate. Only the human being who lives up to his highest potentiality resembles the immortal unicellular organism. He too fulfils the task of propagation from a will peculiar to his species, and experiences independently of this the will to exchange spiritual qualities with the chosen one. He sees in this exchange the longed-for completion of his being, which is possible to him in consequence of the actual completing quality of the sexes.[6] Assuredly even those humans who, like unconscious animals, think only of sharing sexual happiness with the chosen one are exposed to actually consummated conjugation. Even the passing union of polygamy is accompanied by it. No reserve of personality, no strength of character, no endowment however conspicuous, protects against this mutual effect which accompanies the exchange of bliss. But it is incomparably greater and more enduring if those who are united in a union of choice are penetrated by this will to the merging of their beings. If they have both recognized the sense of life, the self-creation of completeness, then their marriage means the most splendid development of their personality. Qualities which they were not able to overcome in years of striving, in earnest struggling, fade away before the example of the chosen one as under a magic influence. Spiritual gifts which formerly dared only pallidly and infrequently determine action are strengthened, under the consecrating desires of the spouse, to a conquering force; and this the more wonderfully, the less a disenchanting educational attempt of the spouse impairs the mysterious process.

But how can this wonderful force, which overcomes in so disproportionate a manner all the influences of relatives and friends, be explained?

To this question too we must give ourselves an answer, if we wish to understand why marriage can be the fulfilment of man. Again the immortal unicellular organism

[6] See *Das Weib und seine Bestimmung, ein Beitrag zur Psychologie der Geschlechter* ("Woman and Her Purpose: An Essay on the Psychology of the Sexes"). Verlag "Die Heimkehr," Pasing vor München.

makes this wonder symbolically clear to us through its behaviour. Copulation is experienced in the domain of the immortal living beings only by the "more highly differentiated," which have developed single parts of the cell to cellular organs. It is a curious fact that such unicellular organisms (as, for example, *Trichomonas Intestinalis*) give up this ingenious apparatus before copulation and take on the original form of their ancestors, the form of amoebae, before they advance to the solemn transformation of amalgamation. The soul of man provides an analogue to this. It also, before the chosen one, in presentiment and remembrance of the hours of bliss, takes on again the original form of the child's soul. It, too, strips off all the involved differentiation which the struggle for existence has given it, and rests before the chosen one childlike, in more than one sense.

The bitter struggle for existence and harsh disillusionments have long since hardened the soul and cut it off from the influence of all other human beings, but it reveals itself again suddenly to the chosen one, with all the softness, the "plasticity," of childhood. It is this delicate docility which so wonderfully rejuvenates the expression of the "lover." The curious contrast of this receptive delicacy to the man's habitual reserve bordering on inflexibility, and his roughness bordering on hardness, has in it something peculiarly touching; in the woman it appears more as an increased originality. But in view of the mostly so imperfect mutual influences, this childlike plasticity must be taken very seriously. The wise man will not lightly regard the considerable peril which the new-kindled light of the human eye reveals, and yet he welcomes this transformation. Nothing is so inimical to the self-creation of perfection as the numbing of the soul in the state of imperfection. How can flight to the heights still be possible for man as long as he has exalted immature prejudices and sad misconstructions of reason to "life-principles," and remains true to them without ever putting them to renewed proof? What, in comparison with this death-sentence on his perfection, can the worst danger of childish plasticity amount to? Even when the choice has been unfortunate, even when the influences are most unfavourable, the soul still has a greater chance of experiencing through it the flight to the summits of perfection than in its mature numbness. That is the reason why many a soul experiences unimagined exaltation when it liberates itself from an unworthy union.

The return to the original form of the child soul represents for this reason also, in every case, an infinite gain, because every man led astray by reason, not to speak of educational influences, marches at least a considerable way downhill to distortion of the soul. A comparison of the adult with the child proves this at once. If he now assumes, in the union of choice, the original form, this must in every case be a step upward in the sense of genius. The soul-distorting, monotonous serving of a purpose is interrupted in a moment. As in childhood, time, space, and profit are forgotten. Once again, as before, the soul offers itself to reveries and does not ask whether reason rebukes them as "senseless." But meditating and longing for the chosen one, the dreamy forgetfulness of time is a wide, commodious bridge to the transcendental experience which stands above time, space, and purpose, and becomes for that reason from year to year less imaginable and less attainable to the struggler for existence. If the soul has thus rejuvenated itself to the child's estate, it is nevertheless far superior to it, since it forfeits nothing of the wealth of its knowledge and experiences; no more is it completely dominated by the mockery of appearances.

And thus it becomes a proper workshop for the creation of perfection.

Delicate plasticity toward the chosen one shows also a childlike susceptibility to sensation. "Like a heart without a skin," it feels the most delicate fluctuations. Sharp and profound are the pleasures and pains which the chosen one prepares. As in earliest childhood, the adult suddenly sees himself again, in an excess of joy, "exulting high as heaven"; and eyes which for years have not known the tears of sorrow overflow with suffering, as in the most distant period of infancy. This delicacy, and at the same time this keenness of the life of the sensations, is, however, of immeasurable significance on the road to perfection. Let this be emphasized with particular impressiveness, because unfortunate misconceptions have led to the teaching that the way to perfection lies through becoming superior to joy and suffering. This faculty of the soul, like every other experience of the consciousness, wears a double face and can lead men to spiritual death or to perfection. The perfected one experiences sorrow and pleasure with the supreme force of the divine, as far as they are in harmony with the divine. The warped soul, near to spiritual death, however, is merely capable of experiencing pleasure or its reverse. So the enfeeblement of sensitiveness is actually a perceptibly weighty handicap against the exaltation of the soul, and therefore childlike liveliness and delicacy of sensation, as selective amalgamation produces it, must be regarded as a way to perfection which is open to the choice of any one.

Fundamental as is this reduction to the child's estate through the magic power of eroticism, it is far surpassed in significance by the simultaneous strengthening of the godlike will to the beautiful which it creates in the soul. The divine will, revealed in every phenomenon of the universe, determines the form of all living organisms. Only the necessity of death compels sacrifices to it and moulds it to "useful" ends. But at no time does this will to beauty make its appearance so conspicuously as under the magic wand of the erotic will.[7] Whether the fish puts on his coloured marriage garment, although his eyes cannot perceive this splendour; or whether the little bird husband adorns the marriage nest for his chosen one with multi-coloured little stones, which she knows very well how to admire; whether the nightingale puts the longing of this will into melodious notes and lets them ring forth in song; or whether the human being expresses longing, hope, and love in words, tunes, or pictures, and even beautifies himself in love, it is in each case a splendid revelation of the divine will to beauty, which stands in a most profound interrelationship with the will to selective amalgamation, and therefore strengthens with it. But since this divine will, which illumines the capacity of the soul for permanency,[8] is just as important for the creation of perfection in the human soul as the rest of the divine rays which light up the faculties of the consciousness, the godlike consecration of selective amalgamation thus shows itself to be in the most profound accord with the holy sense of our existence.

If we finally view the paths to perfection, we become conscious of a wonderful sense which is often greatly misapprehended by human beings even in the highest and most gifted marriage which is imbued with it. It clearly proves its full superiority over asceticism. In solitude the

[7] See *Erotische Wiedergeburt,* Chapter II, *Entwicklung der Sexualität zur Erotik* ("Erotic Rebirth," Chapter II, "Development of Sensuality to Eroticism").

[8] See *Triumph des Unsterblichkeitswillens,* chapter entitled *Unsterblichkeitswillen und Genialität, Darwinismus und Entwicklungsgeschichte* ("Triumph of the Will to Immortality," chapter entitled "Will to Immortality and Genius, Darwinism and the History of Evolution").

man of genius grows to perfection. In dialogues rich in mystery with the God in his own bosom, there arises in him strength for steady, unyielding communion with God; that is, for an enduring life on the superconscious stage of the soul. The spiritual calm which only such solitude makes truly fruitful in man is granted him rarely, often only in old age, when his will to selective amalgamation has not found fulfilment. But if in a really gifted marriage this will has been appeased in the most precious way, then the longing for solitude can awaken with unfettered strength in the soul. The monk who flees to the desert unfulfilled, to live there alone with his God, knows nothing of the strong consciousness of the will to solitude as the hours of highest fulfilment in marriage awaken it in every human being conscious of God. So too in all creative human beings there awakens precisely the ever-renewed power of creation just in and through union, since true creation is assuredly always lonely communion with God. The will to create again permits, as far as it is fulfilled, the will to selective amalgamation to become strong and to seek communion. Precisely this mutual effect, which becomes most conspicuous in the creative human being, induces all those who believe that marriage is an unintermittent clinging of two people to each other to think erroneously that such creative ones are unsuited for marriage. In truth, they are those who, with all uncreative but gifted human beings, teach us that a marriage which desires to be a fulfilment must offer solitude and duality as well. The majority of mankind, who suppress the will to privacy for the sake of selective amalgamation, suffer in the opposite manner the same as the ascetic, who gave heed only to his will to solitude.

Looking backward at these rich blessings of marriage, and then contemplating the fate of even very highly exalted married people in the world about us, the disparity between the actual and the possible gives us an idea of the manifold dangers which menace a marriage and often allow it to become a blight instead of a fulfilment. These are of so multifarious a nature and are fraught with such terrible consequences that in this short essay we must content ourselves with a mere passing indication of the worst dangers. The evolving human being sees today in the world about him, in the so-called "civilized states," little more than sickness and depravity. Since the human reason can perceive the laws for the creation of pleasure, while the unperfected will to self-preservation regards the accumulation of pleasures as the aim of life, the human race has developed within itself an impulse from which all unconscious living organisms are free: the impulse to set ablaze artificially the quiescent erotic will through enticing glances and intoxicating poisons. The effect of this is the gradual acquisition of a malady which I have termed chronic hyperexcitement. The majority of men of all "civilized" peoples suffer from this illness, which, as its gravest symptom, desires change and enhancement of the stimulus. Since the fundamental principle of eroticism imperiously governs every human life, since the manner of the first erotic happiness determines in a far-reaching manner the laws of the individual's eroticism throughout his entire life,[9] the majority of men have become entirely incapable of concentrating their erotic will consistently on one human being; therefore they have become incapable of monogamy. The casualness of choice in adolescence has made them incapable of experiencing

[9] See in *Erotische Wiedergeburt: Die krankhaften Fixierungen der Sexualität, Aus der Stammesentwicklung der Sexualität,* and *Entwicklung der Erotik im Einzelleben* ("Erotic Rebirth": "The Diseased Fixations of Sexuality," "From the Race Development of Sexuality," and "Development of Eroticism in the Individual Life").

happiness as something holy, and thus they are generally unsuited to a gifted marriage; easily achieved sorts of sexual happiness, animal-like and fleeting partnerships, are the one thing for which they are suited, if indeed they do not sink far beneath the animal. Contemptuous insulting of the other sex and of marriage are the proven blinders which they put on to conceal from themselves what they themselves have flung away.

The female sex, influenced by the dominating ascetic ideal which ventures to call the pleasures of the senses "unclean," is just as little prepared for the consummation of a gifted marriage. Moreover, the sexual happiness of woman has been imperilled in a catastrophic manner by the development of the human race; and human institutions, above all the subjection of the female sex, have only increased the evil. Finally, the two fundamental laws of eroticism which from prehuman times determined the union of the sexes have been completely ignored. Therefore we stand confronted with the fact that in certain peoples sixty per cent, in others eighty per cent, of the women either never or only exceptionally experience happiness in intercourse, and for that reason live physically and mentally in an entirely abnormal condition in marriage. When frequent maternity does not occupy the organism, most of them degenerate more or less pronouncedly in an over-excitation of the nervous system, some becoming ill with hysteria. The hazy consciousness that the poise so necessary to life is denied them, that they experience only erotic excitement, causes them to desire communion ceaselessly. Never will the effect of that poise, quiet and the longing for solitude, enter into them. They never become mentally free for the strength of creation. They cherish every minute shared with their spouse; they misunderstand his healthy desire for solitude as "loss of affection"; and in this way the marriage is wrecked, in the majority of instances, without either of the married pair or the "physician" suspecting the real basis of their unhappiness. And if it should become suspected or known, it is falsely pointed out as abnormality; and thenceforth the evil weighs on the partnership with redoubled weight, most gravely felt in the gifted marriage. For here it is the strong wish of the husband, not only to receive happiness, but also to give it. The more profound the spiritual exchange, the stronger is the wish for solitude in the spouse. The suffering of those marriages in which the woman does not experience the equipoise of erotic happiness is so great that often the married couple, without suspecting the causes, in the evening of their lives praise as "wisdom" the monastic ideal of asceticism without choice.

But all these dangers, arising from the misconstructions of reason, permit of elimination through insight. Far more serious are those which have their foundations in the temperament and in the physiological laws of the sexes, and therefore are inescapable. The different endowment of the sexes, which in all the domains of the spiritual life must be acknowledged magnificently complementary,[10] while it contains the great consecration of mutual enrichment, is also the source of the frequent "misunderstandings" of the sexes which threaten the harmony of marriage. The development of the two characters is further imperilled by a sexual difference, which superficial observers frequently celebrate as a blessed completion; I mean the predominance of egotism in the man and of altruism in the woman (occasioned by the responsibilities of motherhood).[10] I cannot here go into the moral significance of both directions of will and their deflection toward im-

[10] See *Das Weib und seine Bestimmung* ("Woman and Her Destiny").

morality.[11] But I must hint at the fact that already within the individual soul the uninspired predominance of one of the two directions produces atrophy. Such a one-sided predominance as between the spouses has the same harmful influence. In those shallow permanent partnerships which have only the name in common with true marriage, the reign of egotism in the husband and of altruism in the wife seems to foster "marital peace" considerably. The wife more or less gives up her personality; in this way she fulfils the wish of the husband, who most of the time does not suspect what he is creating for himself through this arrangement of rank. Since such an arrangement runs entirely contrary to the laws of eroticism, the erotic enthusiasm of the husband for the completely enslaved wife disappears very quickly. Every "Gretchen" will be deserted without fail, even when Mephisto is not present, since man wishes to woo in order to possess! Moreover, mutual development of character is entirely missing, and both sexes pine away in such a marriage in a quite peculiar way. The husband does not free himself of the immaturities of his youth, but fosters and cherishes his weaknesses in collaboration with his uncritical wife. She herself degenerates into a caricature of her own being. She becomes a creature without the urge to independence, without the will to freedom, without self-responsibility, and exhibits an exceedingly distorted human pride. Even the highest marriages stand under the evil star of this peril. There lives almost no wife, however pronounced and sure of itself her personality may be, who has not in the first decade of her marriage bent herself with all too great a readiness to the will of her husband; who has not suppressed precious features of her person-

[11] See *Triumph des Unsterblichkeitswillen: Moral des Lebens* ("Triumph of the Will to Immortality": "Ethics of Life").

ality. When, therefore, after ten years the too stringently bent tree springs upward, it sometimes tears to pieces a valuable marriage in this sharp rebound. But even if this does not happen, worthy wives go the way of soul-atrophy. There exists on the other hand no man, however highly developed, who has not delivered himself too much to the egotistic course of his will in the first years of his marriage; who has not in the beginning expected and occasioned through love his chosen wife's sacrifice of her independence to a stupid degree, to the detriment of the higher unfolding of both!

Besides this peril of mental disposition there are still other precipices which threaten each sex, toward which, in ignorance, the ship is headed, in secure confidence that the strong mutual love has no dangers whatsoever to fear. But marriage, far more than life, is a high art. Nothing is more disastrous than blind trust in favourable premises; nothing is more necessary than a strong desire in both spouses to shape the marriage artistically. While the cliffs of sex menace all who are on a higher plane, they are in a far higher degree dangerous for creative man, and they turn many marriages into martyrdoms. The exchange of erotic bliss is rightfully celebrated as the invigorating agent of the power to create; yet it is no less possible to speak of a contrary reciprocal effect which makes itself noticeable quite specially in the permanent union, and for each sex in a different manner. Motherhood, with its strong demands on the whole soul, which in any case may considerably imperil the erotic happiness of the spouses, with all the rich fulfilment which it lavishes, has a serious consequence for the creatively gifted woman; it makes her uncreative for the time being—not in the very erroneous sense which man's will to domination has conceived, as if the desire to create were in woman a "perverse impulse to motherhood" and ought to be satisfied by motherhood. Every woman who knows how entirely different the two experiences are in quality will only smile at such a fancy. But the mental and physical claims of motherhood demand for at least a decade the sacrifice of creative work, which wounds many a woman's soul more painfully than the outside world ever suspects. Hence it is well that the woman who is alive to the divine and who is creative is capable of experiencing the happiness of motherhood in a much deeper degree than others. When powerful creation cannot follow the ten years of sacrifice, when indeed the husband does not see the justice, nay, the necessity, and with the best of intentions lays fetters on his wife—marriage may effect atrophy of the soul instead of fulfilment. In contrast to this hampering effect of motherhood on the creative strength of woman, she experiences on the other hand a harmony of the will to create with sexual happiness, such as is never permitted to the husband. Since with her this pleasure is not, as with the male sex, involved in the expenditure of millions of precious germ-cells, she experiences through it not debility of the powers of creation, but an enhanced alertness for creation, and she can experience a perfect harmony of the two wills for decades after the years of motherhood have passed. In this way marriage in itself never endangers her creative development, especially if the years of maternity lie before the time of creative maturity; it only demands in the beginning an exclusive surrender to motherhood, an offering which every woman who is not atrophied in her womanhood willingly brings to that great happiness.

Of an entirely different quality are the cliffs and the perils encountered by the man. He too experiences the highest unfolding of his creative powers, not through asceticism, but through sexual happiness. But the more profound the spiritual amalgamation of the spouses, the more active remains the desire to exchange bliss; and thus the danger threatens him of impairing his creative power through such happiness. This conflict between the will to create and the will to selective amalgamation may endure throughout his entire life, since the law of the enhancement of his creative force through the domination of the will to sexual happiness holds good for him within certain boundaries. Instead of an extreme sacrifice during the first decade and years of most complete harmony following upon it, he thus experiences a combat of both wills until he has reached old age; and only a few succeed in managing this situation wisely. This also explains how important is the insight of the wife and how essential is the fulfilment of the will to solitude, especially to the creatively endowed man. How often a marriage comes to grief from the fact that the husband, throughout the years, gives himself unsparingly to the will to selective amalgamation, suppressing the will to create until the latter bitterly revenges itself on him! The ideal of asceticism gradually comes to seem deep wisdom to such a man, and he rends his marriage asunder in order to be able to create again, only because he did not give their due to both the wills of his soul.

Looking on the great dangers which we have been able to mention only in small part, the frequent "asseverations of happiness" of married persons on a high plane seem almost beyond comprehension, for actually it must be only very rarely possible to elude all dangers. False choice, which, thanks to erotic ecstasy, which so often blinds one to another's failings, is very easily possible, and the conflicts of parental duties with eroticism, have not even been mentioned here. It is important, then, to emphasize that the affirmations of happiness of human beings, even when truthful, decide absolutely nothing in regard to the value of the marriage! "Fulfilment" we may call marriage only in regard to the inspired aim in life, never in regard to man's will to pleasure. There are married people who call themselves "happy" in marriages which in fact are no more than the mausoleum of their souls. And the nearer they are to spiritual death, the less they can know that the twilight of this vault is not sunlight and that its air permits no fresh, free breath. Therefore, nothing is more foolish than to measure the value of a marriage by affirmations of happiness; affirmations of unhappiness are more of an indication, although not a sure measure. What did the marriage evoke in the souls of the spouses? That is the one justified question, and the one also which always wins an unbiased answer! If one of the spouses was nearer to God in his unmarried years, and if in marriage he has descended from that lofty plane, then the sentence of death has already been pronounced on it; and even if the spouse himself should have been guiltless of causing the descent, he has nevertheless proved his impotence to ward off the fall, a fact which, in view of the strong possibility of influence in marriage, is sufficient ground to condemn such a union as worthless. But if a marriage is not good, then it is unquestionably bad, for this cruel law rules in every marriage: either up to the heights or down into the grave of the soul! Not one marriage exists in which the spouses can boast that they have remained the same after their union. But the more talented of the two is in the greater danger, since a still more terrible and inexorable law obtains, which provides that if a gifted, aspiring human being couples himself with a narrower spirit, with one that may be a harmless, yet "insignificant," little soul, he will not be able, in the long run, to lift this shallow being into the higher atmosphere of his spirit, since it is unable to fly. But on the other hand, the little soul every day, yes, every hour, with quiet, noiseless little tugs, draws the great soul down into its sphere; and very soon wounds and scars will show themselves. At first they are tiny abrasions of the skin; but gradually, from year to year, the injuries become deeper.

Thus, every human being who calls marriage in its highest possibility, the inspired union of choice, "fulfilment," assumes the serious responsibility of likewise praising elective asceticism. Never, not even "for the sake of the children," must a human being who is close to the divine exchange bliss with one who draws him down spiritually, for only this type of union, not the common home, has the power of transformation. He who has not the strength to renounce such bliss may extinguish in his soul the longing for the heights, for never will the path of his life lead him to them! Year after year he goes ineluctably downward, whether death lays hold of him when he has arrived in the valley, or whether, forever separated from God's sun, he dwells under the earth with the gnomes and busily digs shafts with them downward, ever deeper and deeper down!

ALPHONSE MAEDER

Marriage and Self-Development

In this contribution a special aspect of the problem of marriage will be treated, to which generally very little attention is paid; that is, marriage as a factor of self-development. What is the humanizing effect of marriage? In what does this self-development consist, so far as it is furthered and conditioned by marital life? Modern individualism, like a tidal wave, has swept away the conception of marriage which was handed down to us. Marriage itself is endangered. Here, once for all, it is necessary to provide the individualist with a new and deeper comprehension of marital life as a creative process through which he himself may arrive at a greater unfolding. We must begin with stating the limitations and the one-sidedness of the young man. If we observe the young man or the young woman from the standpoint of maturity, the unfinished, "temporary" element of their condition is the first thing which strikes us. The reciprocal attraction of the sexes is elementary for a good reason. Physically as well as mentally, there exists between them a mutually supplemental relationship which extends so far that one might speak of a bipolar division of universally human qualities between masculine and feminine beings. Thus, for example, conspicuous in the male are certain functions of an elementary or complex character, especially certain phenomena such as thought, moderation of will, the stress of the conscious, intellectual apprehension, the sense of reality, the feeling for individuality, tendency to the progressive and the constructive. These are in natural contrast to corresponding more feminine functions, activities, and phenomena, such as emotions, instincts in general, unconscious actions, adaptation and intuition, the power of imagination, the sense of community, the tendency to preservation (conservatism). This dual polarity is characteristic of antagonism. At each of the two poles an ambivalent power of attraction and repulsion operates, by means of which a tension is produced, as in a magnetic field. The differentiation and distribution of the individual functions and tendencies about these two poles is the expression of natural development. It leads to an adjustment between the two contrasted poles; differentiation has reached its acme; integration begins. It manifests itself first in the fact that the single different qualities gradually assume a new complementary relationship. What was in opposition and mutually exclusive appears now as part of a developing unit. Only the repeated experience of this dual polarity between man and woman, with the tensions and discharges which belong to it (the process of maturing), permits a new insight and attitude to arise; in this way the contrast becomes a complement. The married people have learned by suffering and torture that they need each other in order to fashion their common life fruitfully, as well as to arrive at their own realization. Here the notorious conflict of the sexes has ceased to rage. "Belonging to each other" has become part of life. The natural tendency of the man is to assume in the beginning a purely sensual attitude in love-life, while the woman is inclined rather to give primacy to the spiritual contact. This difference is the source of numerous conflicts; the stronger, the more intensive, of the two married people is victorious over the other, and this leads to voluntary subjection of the other. The actual solution, however, consists in the new realization that the impulsive nature of the man in love-life has to be tamed through the spiritual poise of the woman (tamed, not subdued), has to be filled with inspiration; and that the sensual nature of the woman must be aroused through the influence of the man. It is similar with everything instinctive (for example, the impulse to domination) in the husband, which has to undergo mitigation and socialization. Another example: Woman is inclined to regard and to do everything from the point of view of the personal, and in this lies the particular value and charm of her relation to husband and child, of her influence in the home; it characterizes her relation to all the objects of her environment and makes her the true centre of the house. It is only through the personal that the sentimental becomes active. But this personal element bears within itself a danger—the possibility of becoming petty, narrow-minded, unjust, and subjective. The man, on the contrary, is more impersonal, more matter-of-fact; his relation to men and things is rather sober (realistic) or abstract (general). The enriching, liberating possibility which emanates from him is the bridge to the superpersonal. The mutual supplementing of the two sexes is obvious. Let us take into consideration yet another point: Thought in our culture is characterized by emphasis on the causal and analytical, through its intellectual and abstract orientation. It is most decidedly masculine thought, which eminently adapts itself to the theoretical and practical conquest of Nature, especially of the inorganic, and which has furthered—nay, made possible—the development of the sciences. This particular and indeed sole recognized way of thinking is, however, not the only one possible. There exists another kind which might be termed, in contrast to the former, imaginative feminine thought, but which as yet is in the beginning of its development and which is arrogantly treated and set aside by the profession. This thinking is at root rather synthetically directed and is distinguished by its intuition and plasticity. The attitude requisite to it is contemplative, in contrast to the active and aggressive attitude of masculine mentality. Many problems hitherto raised in vain will find their solution only from this angle. When woman once stops thinking in the fashion of man, in which at best she can only become an imitative virtuoso; when she really dares to think in her own way (but to think, not merely to feel or to associate her spontaneous ideas), then this may lead to an amazing fertilization and revolution of spiritual life, in understanding as well as in action. This so-called feminine thought is naturally not a monopoly of the female sex, but a form of general *human* thinking.

THE self-development of man begins in the parental home. The child stands, so to speak, in a field of bipolar influences, the two centres of power being represented by the father and the mother. From these two centres emanate enlivening, checking, and guiding impulses of a special nature, in that they embody the two essential principles of life. In this way there is created in the soul of the child an organ of self-direction which in time takes over the function of educator. But the maturing being which emerges from this education is a unipolar, one-sided sexual being whose further development is conditioned by the sexual being orientated in the opposite direction. So, as both parents were for the child symbolic representations of vital powers, the wife represents to the husband (and vice versa, the husband to the wife) the bearer of that which is lacking in him. More is involved here than the desire for the attentive, pleasure-giving spouse; it is that elementary desire for experience of the being antithetical to oneself, which arises out of the profound suffering of one-sidedness and loneliness. An equivalence of the two married people is naturally a presumption of the arising mutual relationship, which, however, does not mean that husband and wife must from the start occupy the same level of maturity—for then hardly any marriage would be concluded. Naturally, the less mature partner is obliged to confide himself partly and temporarily to the guidance of the other. Not the sex, but facts, decide. Our laws, which still fundamentally sanction and demand that the wife should obey the husband, are barbaric and with time have become ridiculous, however much the arrangement was originally justified. Only reality determines and decides, not the dead letter. This guidance continues as long as the disparity of levels exists and is valid only in certain spheres. It frequently occurs that the man is superior in the intellectual; the woman, in the practical. As conditions may arise, they will interchange, the one or the other bearing the responsibility or taking a subordinate rôle. Generally, we may say that the period of subordination of one to the other is a disciplinary schooling of his own impulses, of his wilfulness and selfishness, and at the same time a preparation for independence. Guidance enhances strength and responsibility. This is realized successfully only where the dull spirit of force has been conquered and a clear insight into the value and significance of the individual has been achieved. The acknowledged equivalence and corresponding accountability of the married people brings with it the development of a special degree of independence of the one from the other. The one spouse can stand before the other the more independently, the nearer he is to him inwardly and the closer he dwells with him of his own accord in the community of marriage. Independence, and one's own dignity which is inherent in it, is, however, just as valid in the face of the environmental world. The co-operation is the more fruitful when two married people, in addition to their common relation and problems, retain and cherish their separate interests. It is certainly of value for the equipoise and harmony of married life if each one can retire to his island (in space or time) when he wishes to be individually free, for one must not forget that man has both an individual and a social tendency, and that both must be developed. The principle of "as well as" applies here, and not that of "either-or." Precisely this independence of the married people offers the best guaranty for the fruitful formation, for the continuance, of the creative process of marital life; it enhances the tension between the two poles. Thanks to this bipolarity, each suggestion can have its development and its correction; the one-sidedness which may easily lead to recklessness and ruin is thereby abolished. The marriage relationship is not hierarchic, but co-operative. Neither partner has to use (or to misuse) the other; each is dependent on the other. Mutuality is the rule of the relationship. The wife is the comrade for life, the equ .l in rank, the collaborator, of the husband. They carry their burdens in common, and thus they work at their task. They stand beside one another and yet are interwoven with each other. What a greatly promising and nobly elevating spectacle is this standing shoulder to shoulder of the two married people who develop into complete human beings through and with each other, in the consciousness of their situation and responsibility!

We have then arrived at the conception that the one-sided sexual being (man, woman) possesses another "latent" side which is only vivified and attains a gradual merging into the whole of the consort's personality through life with the chosen spouse. This formula confers a clear meaning on the idea of maturity. Husband and wife experience through their mutual influence a transformation from the masculine and from the feminine into the human being; this is the true goal of development. From that time on they are two human beings who confront each other; that is, two beings whose sexual polar one-sidedness has undergone correction and completion, so that they feel inwardly changed through their development. The mutual understanding of each other from within creates a new basis of fruitful collaboration in the common life.

No wonder that modern man experiences a newly-instituted gradual change in his behaviour, nay, even in his physical form, through the suppression of the barriers between the sexual beings, through this interpenetration of the masculine and feminine. One frequently speaks of woman becoming masculine and of man becoming feminine. But this does not touch the essential, but only conspicuous and exaggerated, phases of what is happening. It is in fact a *humanizing* of the man and the woman. The process has begun and until now has taken effect only to a limited extent. Nevertheless, the approach of the sexes, due to their perception of a super-sexual type, is already a fact. This has nothing to do with the ancient idea of the hermaphrodite—or, according to Freud, with that of a bisexual being—but with the homogeneous comprehension of the complete man.

In this research into humanization the physico-spiritual completion, not so much within the marital partnership as within the two married people themselves, has up to this point been of principal interest to us; but this does not embrace the process in its totality. We are in the midst of still another transformation of the relationship of husband and wife. The equivalence of the married people holds good not only in the sphere of the physical and spiritual (of Nature), but equally in the sphere of the intellectual; mutual stimulation, vivification, and completion is likewise possible, desirable, and requisite in this sphere.

The Christian epoch cherished and honoured woman chiefly as wife and mother. By it, woman was regarded and recognized exclusively as a sexual being. She stood at the service of propagation and education, at the service of the husband as the head of the family; her task was purely social. The destruction of the *ancien régime* through the French Revolution, the ground-swell of romanticism, and economic suffering have shaken and altered the structure of society. The outbreak of individualism has ruptured the collective orientation of the family. The demand for individualization has gradually taken hold of woman also; and not only in the form of her emancipation, but also in her positive attitude toward man. She can and will be, not only wife and mother, but also the beloved. She longs to face the man of her choice as a free individual, irrespective of child and family. People begin to distinguish types of women, to speak of the mother-wife and of the free woman-beloved (Blüher), both of which types have a right to exist. But these types can be regarded in still another way, that is, no longer as two structural categories, but rather as two possible Nature-given attitudes of woman in general. This means that, under certain circumstances, a woman can be interchangeably or at the same time the wife and the beloved of her husband. The woman has value and dignity not only as a member of the marriage partnership but also as an entity in herself; exactly like the man, she has her centre in herself. But in marriage the centre is neither in the husband nor in the wife, but rather above the two in a spiritual third quantity.[1]

Metaphorically speaking, the free woman has her island to which she can from time to time retire. The man must observe these new factors and try to adapt himself to them. With the distance thus established, the attraction between the lovers assumes a special tension, and the sexual conjunction itself a new significance. We are still suffering from a one-sided physiological, biological apperception of the sexual act. The love-instinct was simply transferred from the biology of the animal into that of the human being, and thus sexuality was indissolubly connected with propagation. As long as woman was regarded as wife and mother, this connection justly existed. It is different as regards the erotic relationship with the beloved, for here eroticism has no necessary connection with propagation. Sexual union becomes the outward expression of the inward spiritual-intellectual contact, the symbol of the tie of two fundamentally related human beings. Let us recall the "sacred marriage" (*hieros gamos*) of the ancient mysteries, the "mystic union" of the mystics of all ages—sexual union was to them a prototype of union in general. Man in his loneliness and isolation as an individual must ever again experience completion in the marital partnership and in himself in order to become focused and renewed. Sexual union attains only under such conditions its deeper significance, and therewith its full justification. Psychoanalysis has contributed much to

[1] See the important explanations of M. Buber in *Ich und Du* (*I and Thou*), Insel Verlag, 1923.

the understanding of these things, although its one-sided biological orientation has made a close approach to the heart of the problem impossible. The newly arising relationship of man and woman should in time produce a vivification and enrichment of marriage, although its importance is not exclusively confined to marriage.

A characteristic feature of eroticism is its tendency to idealize the beloved being; in the Middle Ages this was known as *Minne*, in the present as romantic love. This is not merely an exaggeration of emotion, as the realist maintains, but a presentiment of superhuman perfection which attaches to ecstasy. The lover gazes through the beloved on a spiritual ideal which would be foreign to him were he quite sober. The Dionysiac condition has a positive mission and a true function in the soul. The psychologist speaks of a projection on the beloved of an ideal picture of which one was hitherto unconscious. Life together gradually brings with it the correction of reality, which means that the projected ideal picture is withdrawn from the person of the beloved and transferred to the interior of the soul (intrajection). This picture is perceived from within as a spiritual reality; it retains its efficacy after detachment from the person who appears as the bearer and awakener of the ideal. It gradually achieves an elucidation and a differentiation which carries with it a sobering down in regard to the particular person, but not disappointment. Thus Gretchen, as one of the penitents, leads Doctor Marianus (the transformed soul of Faust) to the Mater Gloriosa, the embodiment of the Eternal Feminine. The significance of woman for the development of man can be very clearly seen in the Faust drama. After the experience with Gretchen, Faust finds in himself an entirely new relation to Nature (monologue of the woods and caverns). After the Arcadian idyll with

Helen, a profound transformation of character (soul) manifests itself in him. Faust renounces mere enjoyment; the man of action awakes. In a moment of inspiration he visualizes his task, to which he passionately devotes himself (the building up of the empire). The restlessly seeking, active man becomes quiet, contemplative, on beholding the Mater Gloriosa. He is entirely abandoned to the Eternal, the Divine.

Man and woman have not the same access to the spiritual world; man finds it through his thought and creation (work), but woman through love. Love makes her contemplative and receptive to the superhuman—in this way she can become the awakener, the "inspirer" of the beloved. Out of devotion streams belief in the eternal and the divine; thus she becomes the symbol of the amalgamation of the thing created with the creator, the mediator between God and mankind (Mariolatry, Beatrice leads Dante through the seven spheres of heaven). The woman believes also in the vocation and the destiny of her beloved; she refreshes, consoles, exhorts, and encourages him; she helps him to overcome the loneliness of high individualization. In the ethical sphere she readily attains a similar importance and becomes in this way the representative of his conscience (Dante feels the first look of Beatrice, when they meet in Paradise, as though she were judging him). Corresponding completions in masculine spirituality are to be found from the woman's viewpoint. In the spiritual sphere as well as in the physico-spiritual, man and woman thus supplement each other; they thus have in common many spiritual responsibilities for culture, which they have as yet hardly begun to discharge. One may, however, still expect many great things for the future from their mutual understanding and collaboration.

We may sum up what has so far been said in the statement that husband and wife become essentially human beings in the marital partnership. Their as yet undeveloped, latent complementary characteristics are vitalized and organized by what their partner experiences. A metabolism of the spiritual and mental structure is effected in this way. In the depths of the psyche, in the midst of the realm of the originally latent other side, a kind of centre of force arises which expresses itself in the man through a feminine image (the reverse in the woman). Let us call it, following Jung, "anima" (with the correlative "animus"), even though in a somewhat qualified sense. Before the anima appears a complementary ego which has arisen out of the longing and the maturing of the conscious masculine "I," just as man and woman stand before each other in marriage. Gradually a pair of images is arrived at through the approach and unification of the two images; the inner dissension is thereby bridged, and the one-sided individuality begins to become an undivided personality. The united pair of images symbolizes the higher self, the true centre, the kernel of existence of the human being.[2]

This briefly sketched formative process is characteristic only for the Occidental. It is profoundly motivated by his characteristics that his ideal of marriage permits his development as an individual at the side of the woman, for her and with her. His extraverted nature (turned to the outer world) requires of necessity the objective relation, in order to develop itself in it. The separation peculiar to him between subject and object needs to be overcome. Self-instruction starts this process. The Oriental appears to reach the goal by another path. His predis-

[2] Goethe's fairy tale, the tale of Novalis' Sophie, and Meyrick's *Golem* furnish interesting allegorical representations of this process.

position toward mystical introversion allows him to experience development, not in a dissociated object, but rather in his own still unified subject (*tat twam asi*, the principle of identity). The woman does not become for him, as in our sense, the symbol of the spiritual. Thus Buddha deserted his wife to go the way of spirituality and enlightenment. Marriage to him was a shackle.

So far we have studied the growth of the human being, his self-development, as conditioned by life in the marital partnership. This was done in the spirit of psychological method. Now we shall shift our point of view, in order to turn to an ethical method of observation.

As long as theology dominated the thought of man in the sphere of Christian culture, the dogma that man was monogamous by nature was held valid. The results of sociological and psychological research in the last fifty years have established beyond doubt that this assumption is contrary to the facts. Most especially the "psychology of the depths" has, by laying bare the processes of the unconscious, demonstrated the original polygamous disposition of man (therefore of man and woman). Nevertheless, the tendency toward a monogamous orientation of cultural man continues to exist in the Hebraic-Christian world (Occident). The contradiction is only apparent. Marriage as a social institution is determined, not only through the natural disposition of man, but also through the direction of spiritual life. The culture of the West has decided ever more pronouncedly for monogamy as an expression of a universally characteristic tendency, which also becomes manifest in individualism, democracy, and monotheism.

The marriage problem of the Occidental may be thus formulated according to this view: Man must transform himself from his primary natural polygamous position, through spiritual and mental development, to a voluntarily monogamous being. This is not a mere sublimation (refinement) in the Freudian sense, but a "transformation," a subjection of the instincts to an ideal, a subordination of Nature to the spirit—a creative process, the aim of which is the unfolding of the human being as a marriage-partner and as a personality. The transformation therefore possesses significance for marriage as well as for self-education in general.

The monogamous ideal of marriage demands the renunciation of manifold changing stimuli, individual choice, concentration. It emphasizes intensity at the expense of extensity. But thereby it makes possible an exaltation of tension, an enhancement of quality, a deepening, a spiritualization and an intellectualization of the relation between the married people. The characteristic attribute of monogamous marriage is its continuity, which holds within itself the potentiality of an uninterrupted creative development. The fact that the two spouses are interdependent throughout the entire married life creates the necessity of being and doing as much as possible for each other, in order to obviate the growth of frigidity or the Strindbergian hatred of those who feel themselves chained to each other. As one might expect, on the transformation of the polygamous disposition into the monogamous, arise difficulties which are the principal cause of numerous conflicts in marriage. Through the new comprehension of the individual and of the love-life the indifference or the tension between married people has strongly increased at present. Still more, in many and extensive circles, there is even doubt of the rightness of the monogamous ideal of marriage. Whereas at an earlier time infidelity was dogmatically condemned, people now incline to a cheap and frivolous condoning of it. This fact requires a deeper research, concerning whose general direction the following must be said.

The doctor avoids altogether condemnation or evaluation. It is his task to understand what is happening, to uncover the line of development, *to help him who is in error; to become a seeker.* Attraction to the fellow man, even when it has a pronouncedly erotic colouring, often represents a still unconscious search for certain complementary qualities, a longing for the establishment of unity and harmony within oneself. This seeking has a constructive character and must be distinguished from the longing for amusement and from mere flight from marital difficulties. A clarity early acquired in regard to this process makes it possible occasionally to understand attraction more clearly in its imaginative sense and to adopt a corresponding attitude. Preaching and moralizing have completely ceased to be effective; they have roused stubbornness, and with it frivolity and dogmatic amorality. One helps man better and more effectively by assisting him to perceive and materialize his problem. He must be directed forward. Experience teaches us that many men learn only through mistakes. Certainly many a *faux pas* has led to the renewal of muddled marriages. In time the concept of fidelity, which has hitherto been understood in a more personal manner, experiences a transformation to the sense of the superpersonal; that is, that fidelity has to be directed more and more to the common ideal of devotion, of unity, of harmony, while the life-comrade is felt rather as the visible symbol of this. Nowadays many situations are nontypical; no definite rules can be established. Every individual case must be examined anew and without prejudice. But this should be the attitude not only of the physician but also of the patients.

Much suffering and unhappiness would thereby be avoided, and a new and fertile life might grow out of the conflicts. Let not the ethically sentimental reader fear that through the doctor's refraining from condemnation the values themselves will be abolished. Medical art is helpful only until the situation is cleared and the new development is in process. Responsibility cannot be ingrafted, and it is therefore useless even to try it. Handicaps are eliminated through medical intervention, so that life can unfold itself freely according to its own laws—the valuation is generated and becomes effective in the convalescent. The position of modern man is exceptionally difficult, in that the process of individualization extends right up to the conscience, and the harmonious collaboration of the individual and collective components has not yet been reached; uncertainties and vacillations of a new kind thus occur.

We have followed the transformation of the primary polygamous-sexual to the monogamous-spiritual disposition. Much the same things may be said about the transformation of the impulse of aggression and of its integration into the entirety of the personality. The desire to dominate one's nearest, even in the higher, spiritual form of imposing one's views and feelings on him, will yield to the service of the common marital interests. Opportunity is offered to those who are married to each other, as it is perhaps to few others, to deliver themselves of the domination of an unhealthy egocentricity and egotism. Then only will the desire for mutual help (Kropotkin's *entr'aide*) be free, and the married life will become a school of love toward the nearest one and of social responsibility, out of which complete human beings may emerge. Friendship, comradeship, and other human relations, like that between master and employee or between state authorities and the citizen, unquestionably play an important part. Marriage owes its particular importance, in the process of man's maturing, to the close proximity in and the continuity of life together, and therefore to the ties of space and time. The problem which has to be solved is limitless. It remains a challenge of the ideal, whose influence can never be too strong for the attainment of the necessary tension, concentration, and seriousness. The difficulties to be overcome are manifold. Persistence and patience to conquer them advance the ethical value of man far more than the activities of his vocation, inasmuch as the marital life makes demands on the greatest part of his personality.

It remains to demonstrate more clearly the ethical standpoint for which this essay pleads, in order to prevent possible misunderstandings. We mean that the physician is not supposed to play the part of a judge, since it does not in any case behoove man to judge his fellow man. But this should not be taken as meaning that we look upon valuations as something subjective, almost imaginary (as an invention of the moralists), or as a mere "higher interest" of the species in the near or further future. By no means; we emphatically deny every psychologism. While we reject a dogmatic attitude as not in accord with the times and as inimical to life, we seek to orient ourselves directly to the manifestations of life itself. All departures and deviations from the right path, and self-correction and self-punishment as well, can be gathered from life itself.[3] *Life itself judges.* Man must

[3] See A. Maeder, *Heilung und Entwicklung im Seelenleben* (*Healing and Development in the Life of the Soul*), Rascher & Co., Zürich and Leipzig; and, by the same author, *Régulation psychique et Guérison* (*Psychical Regulation and Healing*), in *Schweizer Archiv für Psychiatrie und Neurologie*, 1925.

merely recognize his nature and his goal and learn to follow the path of his realization. *The inner guidance is the true ethical criterion.* The true help which one can bring to man consists therefore simply in helping him to find himself in this upward-directed sense. Therefore we do not reject "thou shalt" and "thou shalt not" in themselves but in their employment to enchain human beings who bear within themselves the possibility of liberal self-development. We rediscover commands in life, not as abstract words but as inner experiences, as personal forebodings, insight and action. Born out of the depths of the soul, they come forward in various forms, adapted to the momentary situation. The sacred words have kindled a new, fine life in man; they have made him fruitful.

LEO BAECK

Marriage as Mystery and Command

His own life's lot, the fundamental fact of his life, has been drawn and prepared for every human being. He has not created the primary and deciding fact in his life; rather, it has created him. He has received the lot of birth, and has been born without his choice. But another bond in his life which is of similarly fateful importance, of a similar capacity for determination and encompassment, is effected by man himself; it belongs to his own will and to his own doing. When two human beings are united in marriage, they represent to each other the inception of a destiny which is to become the arena of their life's fate. However much desire and illusion, the power of the attractive and the destiny of the fascinating, have seized on them and hold them, they still determine for each other their whole life's formation, their place in the world, their horizon. It is thus that two beings let their lives be born unto each other. Marriage becomes the second lot in life, the second fact of life.

It is decisive for what one is, what attitude he assumes toward the facts of his life—whether they simply exist for him, or whether his feelings and thought grasp them. All feeling and thinking is ultimately directed toward destiny. Destiny is the home in which the soul abides on earth. Here the line between the sacred and the profane is drawn. There is nothing more usual, nothing more commonplace than a destiny which remains unperceived;

nothing more full of reason, more distinguished than a fate which is felt and premeditated. The birth which man has received may make it either the one or the other to him. And so, too, may the marriage which he has entered into. It may mean to him the holiness of life, or it may become the triviality of existence, an insipidity in which all originality disappears. When a fact becomes realized in sensation and thought, it ceases to be valid in itself. It becomes the expression of something. And all expression in the human being is expression of mystery, or, what amounts to the same thing, of the unending and the eternal, since the unending and the eternal enter into our existence as a mystery. Inability to express is incapacity for mystery. What is settled and exhausted in the fleeting and finite world has no expression. True feeling and thought are fundamentally this feeling and thought of mystery. In it alone the sense of life unfolds itself; every ultimate word can be spoken only in it. In God every secret is ultimate clarity; in man the ultimate clarity is the secret. That which is hidden is that which comes to light; only the secret can reveal itself. Poetry and form, the knowledge which is belief, the thinking which is contemplation, issue out of the power which emanates from this. The human being around whose existence a light shines is the man of mystery. Thus Rembrandt, in his last and greatest years, has painted man, man as the expression of mystery. Thus are human beings shown in the Bible.

That also is the answer to the question of marriage: Marriage is an expression of mystery. Here the line between the commonplace and the holy is drawn. As long as marriage exists only as an arrangement between two human beings, concluded by them, as it is by so many, then it may indeed be honourable and useful; the two human beings can do a great deal for each other, and they can well fulfil that which is so often indicated as the moral task of marriage, namely, the elevating of the natural to the plane of the moral. There is a marriage which is consciously trivial, and it is perhaps from many points of view also the best; the so-called "good marriage" is most often this. What it lacks is ethical value, which is yet different from moral good behaviour, from abidance by the customs of the time and the law of the state. The ethics of marriage are the ethics of the revelation toward which marriage develops; it has its root in the divine mystery that two human beings experience in one another. This binds them together for life.

The ethics of marriage, one may almost say, can only be mystic. A merging with the mysterious, an eternal merging, is certainly sought by every mystic; for this reason religious mysticism likes to take its imagery from marriage. But how slight is that which a Kierkegaard indicates as the special quality of marriage, that it necessitates and requires permanent openness and full trust! Only the commonplace can possess such constant openness. The ultimate in man can certainly reveal itself, but it can never speak out. Two human beings, each with his own ego, with his most profound joy and sorrow—two destinies stand face to face and wish to become one. This tension overshoots all preached morality. To experience the mystery in it, to preserve it and to have faith in one another, is the true ethics of marriage.

Behind that which it demands, then, there is a living force, and not merely the precept of virtue's catechism, for the reason that there inheres in it an enduring longing. All longing, too, is longing for the mysterious. It is not a desire for something which one does not possess, to attain something which one has lacked. It does not derive from the senses and is never directed toward anything bodily, confined, earthly, but rather always toward the concealed, toward that which underlies everything that can be perceived as the profundity of life. It does not desire an increase, an addition, a completion, the filling of a void. Longing comes out of fulness. It is fed by the totality of man. It is a tension, a certainty which is yet a questioning, a possession which is yet a searching, a happiness which makes poetry; all happiness tends toward mystery.

Thus man experiences the longing for the secret of his ego, for the eternal and the infinite out of which he was created; the longing for that higher, wider life which is his true life. Thus he experiences the longing for the secret of the "thou," the longing to experience the mystery which he encounters in himself in his union with another human being. Many a man is capable of being led into such depths by that first longing that this other cannot bestir itself in him. It may be so ordained for the genius. To him alone the right and the might of celibacy may be conceded. But this other longing, that which reveals itself in marriage, is a longing just like that; and at its roots, too, lies genius, something of inspiration which marks even the human being who lacks creative genius. It preserves marriage as a living entity between two human beings; and in it the ethics of marriage expresses itself.

It has permanency because it draws them to the eternal; longing is longing for life. There is no longing for hours. This is the faith of marriage. All fidelity, too, is fundamentally toward the mysterious. We could not be true to the surface, that changing, breaking, aging thing. Only the continuity of what we are accustomed to, which is so often mistaken for fidelity, could hold us fast to the completing element. We can be true only to the mystery, which is always the same, always present, always youthful, always revealing itself. The unfaithful one is he who lacks mystery. The bases of his life reveal nothing to him, neither the one which he has received nor the other which he has prepared.

In trustfulness, man proves that there inheres in him an essence of his existence, an enduring element in the coming and going of his days. The essence of marriage is trust from mystery to mystery. For the sake of mystery and fidelity, marriage is in our life. Without trust it would be only something to fill the vanishing hours or merely the opportunity of the senses, an excitement which ends in despondency, something which dies at its birth—does not die in order to live, but rather lives in order to die. Through trust it is the belief of husband and wife in each other, in the mystery which surrounds both.

All mystery is one. As far as one God is from many gods, so far is mystery from the mysterious elements, and so different. Secrets are the secrets of hours and instants; mystery is the secret of life. Even death does not end it. It ends secrets, but not mystery—as it sets a term to the hours, but not the life. In secrets the sense for mystery is destroyed. They are that which lies just under the surface and remains beneath it, holding fast to it; they appear to be depths, but are really shallows. They uncover and display, but they do not reveal; they are always talking and never say anything. Secrets, with their twilight charms, are games; mystery is the sanctuary of the soul, the One which requires the entire heart. Marriage is the home of mystery, and for that reason it can be so only in the marriage of one man with one woman. Adultery is the betrayal of mystery to secrets. For that reason it served as a simile to the prophets of Israel for treachery against God. God, the One, is sold for the gods.

Secrets have their allurements; mystery has its command. Nothing can be revealed to mankind which does not also command. Therein, that it becomes a command and is never without a command, mystery proves itself; its truth, its genuineness carries within it its symbol. Secrecy without command is an illusion of the abyss. Its eternal basis signifies also the perpetual task, this steadfast direction to its goal, just as that which comes forth out of mystery is alone truly problem and goal.

Again the ethics of marriage present themselves, and they now attain their unconditional, categorical element. That gives them their unswerving and undiminished character, that they do not arise from human arranging, but grow out of this profundity. Human beings who have become to each other the mystery of marriage have thereby become to one another the command of marriage. They have become united, and to be bound for their lifetime has become to them thereby a divine command. They must realize and fashion their whole life through each other. Mystery has bound them to this command; without this command no marriage could exist. Otherwise it would be only a game with a phantom of mystery. The command is the absolute of marriage, and it is elevated thereby above all mere bonds and all destiny.

It also protects against a danger which obtrudes especially in marriage, the danger of the everyday. Marriage was entered into on the flowery path of poetry, but it is conducted in the realm of prose. That is the grey danger of marriage. The children who are growing up—those riddles which form themselves, draw near, and become distant—can bring new poetry into the years, but even to them the dreariness of the everyday will too soon cling. It is seldom that marriage breaks on the tragic; it is frequent that it perishes on prose. In the everyday which has conquered the whole of space there live next to each other two human beings who have become commonplace to each other—marriage as prose!

Only the command can resist this. The command of marriage governs the entire life, and therefore also draws the small and insignificant hours into its circle. It becomes the "law" of the everyday; everything must be its fulfilment. To guard the mystery, to preserve the command, everything within marriage must have its character of divine service, must be accorded its poetry. Nothing must be outside of the command. To the everyday of marriage must be given its freedom, which exalts it above craving and above depression—this freedom through law. This is the great venture which piety accomplishes, its *sapere aude,* in that it brings religion into the everyday, seizes its hours, the hours of prose: "when thou sittest in thy house and when thou goest upon thy way; when thou layest thyself down and when thou risest up." This venture piety accomplishes also in marriage.

The tragic, too, can confront marriage. In desire and intoxication or in the illusion of a glance, human beings may find each other and yearn for the mystery in each other—human beings who then become contradictory to each other and spoil each other's lives. Human beings may also gradually become antagonistic to each other, different from each other. It is the problem of the dissolution of the marriage, of the breaking of its command, of the tearing apart of its mystery, which here arises. This problem is not that of marriage alone; it is likewise that of birth. A man's own life as well, with its formation and its changes, can become to him a contradiction and a destruction; and the problem of separation from his own life confronts him. Not less important and not less serious than the question of laying hands on one's own life, that cleavage from existence on earth, is the question of laying hands on the bond of life which one has entered into, the dissolution of marriage. What the one means, this same grave question, the other also means.

Only with this full seriousness should it present itself to man. Can two human beings who have become mystery and command to one another part? And when the words of the tables are broken—the old saying has it: "The letters live on further." The command of life, for the whole of life, is always a path which will ultimately lead also to the tragic. There exists a "nay" to the tragic, the "nay" which that man pronounces who, not in insanity or fright, but out of a sense of tragedy, himself puts an end to his way on earth. And there exists a "yea" to the tragic, the "yea" which exalts and reconciles, in which speaks the command, which in the end still vanquishes and liberates.

Marriage is mystery and command, just like birth, just like the child. The birth of man, his marriage, and then the new life, the child which proceeds from him, these are the three facts in which life exists and realizes itself—to be born and to bear, and the tie of marriage which connects the two. One can disavow all three only together—never one without the others. Only he who condemns birth and the child can condemn marriage. And they can be affirmed only together. They are the great "yea" of life. In them speaks the "yea" of the answer in which man replies to his God. And thus marriage itself becomes a command. It is the command to give life and to develop life. This was the meaning of one of the old sages of Judea when he said: "Man the image of the Eternal; that is: man and woman—not the man without the woman, and not the woman without the man, and not the two, if God dwelleth not where their dwelling is." Revelation of the likeness of the eternal—that is marriage in its mystery and in its command.

JOSEPH BERNHART

Marriage as a Sacrament

To proclaim the sacredness of marriage in this age is to be a preacher in the wilderness. For many reasons it has lost its connection with the Eternal, as indeed the Eternal itself has lost the significance with which it once appeared, giving and demanding, in the religion of humanity. The secularization of marriage by the state was only the result and expression of the common worldliness or turning toward worldliness of that which was previously supramundane, conceived as the majestic autonomy of the divine. In the three thousand-year periods of history which may be taken in at a glance, rifts in the dams between "God" and "Man" have repeatedly appeared; today thought and the sense of life have almost come to renounce the belief that under the rushing waves any dam still remains, or may ever again appear. Not with right or wrong, but exclusively with the fact of this belief, or rather non-belief, are we concerned, at the point where the common life of the sexes forces the question: Do we really take hold of it as animals might—arranged indeed according to the aims of the individual, who seeks his own happiness, and of society, which for its welfare must maintain morals, rules, and regulations? Or do we grasp it in a fundamentally different manner—as a matter which is to be raised and transformed above Nature, even above the purposes of society, into some further realm of a higher but not less peculiar legitimacy? Then, of course, marriage, and marriage above all else, would have to be regarded as a sphere in which mortals may pass from Nature into a state above Nature, into a domain of quite different quality and inward order. This course may have its outlet and its end in an existing religion; it may be the result of a clear and profound comprehension of the essence of marriage; but it is no longer the course along which the thought and behaviour of all people move. The Roman Catholic Church alone honours and protects it, and accepts none other as right, even though it be therefore deserted like an Alpine pass which has lost its traffic to innumerable more convenient ways and means. The prophet in the wilderness, forsaken of mankind, will preach to the stones; for the voice of his mission is stronger than sorrow for the void that surrounds him. He also knows that the highest value and dignity once won by humanity on its road remain in its memory as the silent measure of things. He also has faith that the dull credulity of the five senses cannot remain the last word on the mystery of existence; and that man, while he remains a moot question to himself, ever and again takes the changeless elements of his species and its scene of action as allegory that the basis of the world is at one with itself, while the vacillation which is apparent is an attribute of man in motion.

If we are now to consider the question of the sanctity of marriage, it will be necessary to proceed from the simplest premise in regard to our conception of man and of the world, for the sake of purity as well as for the power of our insight. It shall be only this: that man is here to recognize order and to bring himself within it.—Then only the preliminary question remains to be answered, what we mean by sacrament. Nothing but what yields itself, for marriage, from the original sense of the word, which signifies the Roman soldier's oath to his colours: that it is holy, and that, once created through the reciprocal vows of the consummators, acting of their own free will, it remains indissoluble forever. In sharp contradiction to the modern usage which calls the dissoluble contract of the sexes for living together "marriage," the spirit of language itself arises against the falsification of this word. For marriage was once called *Ewa*, which signified both law and eternity, and in regard to husband and wife meant a perpetual bond, an inseparable belonging to each other—simply that same "sacrament."

The course of our research proceeds from the historical fact of sacramental marriage, examines its personal and suprapersonal bases as to the holiness of its essence, and seeks a correspondence between the inner piety of the holy marriage and the fundamental features of Occidental Christianity as it exists today.

1. The religious ceremony at the conclusion of a marriage is not in every sense an expression of a religious comprehension of its fundamental essence. As a primitive means of alliance with the powers of prosperity, in defence against the powers of destruction, it is found even where the union of the sexes has nothing to do with the world of ethical aims. Also, among the cultured people of the ancient East and West, the religious sanction is still far from establishing the bond of husband and wife as the moral and indissoluble welding of a pair into a unit. There remained entire or partial freedom for the husband's capricious pleasure, while the wife was far more strongly bound to the law and custom of chaste adherence to her spouse. Examples of the sacramental conclusion of marriage within the legal institution of monogamy appear among the Romans and Persians.

There, in patrician circles in the most ancient times, the religious sealing by the *confarreatio* was in vogue; essential thereto were the partaking, after the manner of the communion, of the sacrificial cake shared between the bride and bridegroom, and the accompanying pronouncement of a formula which was binding in the sight of the gods and which invoked their protection. A priestly marriage-prayer of the Zoroastrian religion, reminiscent of the Catholic ritual of today in spirit and in sound, consecrates the indissoluble contract between the betrothed, three times questioned concerning the sincerity of their will to marry, with exhortations to the recognition and moral imitation of Ormuzd, the creator and lord of all good, and to the extermination of Ahriman, the evil one. If elsewhere, as with the Egyptians, Romans, and Spartans, adultery, though usually only on the part of the wife, was subject to severe penalties, the crime appears to have lain considerably less in the injury to the religious character of marriage than in the violation of righteous statutes and of the husband's claims to overlordship.

The later Christian foundation of marriage as a sacrament is rooted, with its most peculiar idea—of which we shall speak later—in a fundamental feature, springing from the pre-Christian religious marriage-practice of polygamous as well as monogamous peoples. A still deeper and truly religious desire *to be* a symbol corresponds to man's profound need to create symbols. Whether we here do or do not come to a kind of self-confronting, as in a mirror, the fact remains worth remembering that the union and bond of the sexes puts itself into the condition of portraying greater, and preferably ideal, relationships. God created the human being; He created him man and woman; on the basis of these beliefs, Israel exalts marriage to the highest consecration, taking it as a representation of its union with Jehovah, from which Emmanuel, the man conceived in God, should arise. Confucius considered marriage as an image of the connection between the bright spirits of heaven and those of earth. The myth of the heavenly marriage of the sun with one of the astral sons of God (morning star, evening star, or moon), a tradition of the Aryan peoples, transformed its natural-religious character in the progress of the ages, as wedding-ceremonies of humans combined with it as the magic background of worship, into the sense of a metaphysical support of an archetypal ideal happening. The marriage of the Hindu goddess of light, Sûryâ, the Hera of the Greeks and the Juno of the Romans, becomes a prototype of human wedlock and bestows a sustaining consecration on that marriage which is concluded with reference in worship to the heavenly precedent. Those divine wives demand of all those who wed the same fidelity and chastity as that with which they are devoted to their husbands. The ideal patroness seems to embody herself anew in every woman who consummates marriage. The prototype of the heavenly couple reappears with the Romans and elsewhere in the establishment of that priestly couple, the Flamen Dialis and the Flaminica. Bound together in the old ceremonious form of the *confarreatio*, they represent Jupiter and Juno in their ritually ordained life together, made noble by most delicate morals, and officiate at the marriages which are concluded according to the rite of the *confarreatio*,[1] administering the blessing of the divine married couple.

This feature of the portrayal, which has its counterpart on another plane in the setting up of exemplary marital alliances (like those between Nala and Damayanti, in the

[1] Leopold von Schroeder, *Arische Religion* ("Aryan Religion"), 1916. Vol. II., pp. 392 ff.

Mahabharata, and Odysseus and Penelope), has significance for our purpose primarily only as a fact in the history of religion; even outside of Christianity, the bond of the sexes strives to raise itself from its mere natural basis upward into a metaphysical realm of inward shaping and sanction.

2. To demonstrate the progress and the deepening of the above-mentioned idea in Christendom, where it has become the innermost nerve of the sacramental understanding of marriage, the Mosaic basis of Christ, as well as His own position and its religious and moral motivation, must be discussed.

The practical result of the precepts of Jesus on marriage in the Evangelists finds its most conclusive statement in St. Paul (I Cor. 7:10-11): "And unto the married I command, yet not I, but the Lord, Let not the wife depart from her husband: But and if she depart, let her remain unmarried, or be reconciled to her husband: and let not the husband put away his wife." This command, which affects Roman as much as Jewish jurisprudence, is based on a revolutionary line of thought. The post-exile period of Judaism had overcome the polygamous character of ancient Israel, which was not prohibited by any command, and had approached the monogamous custom of the Graeco-Roman world; but the polygamy of successive unions, which was in vogue at the time of Jesus, in consequence of the laxity of the Rabbinical schools (especially that of Hillel), insisted on the permission of the Mosaic law for the husband to send his wife back to her old family clan with a bill of divorcement; that is, a certificate in writing that he had separated himself from her and that she was once more free to dispose of her person. Jesus opposes this marriage-law with the whole force of His "Verily I say unto you." Not that He wrecked the entire "law": He builds up the half-finished work of Moses, which for Him rests on God's good bases, to the dizzy height of its logical end. He goes back beyond the law of Sinai to the order of Paradise. Man was created as husband and wife, and once "yoked together" the two are as *one* flesh, nevermore to be separated by human power. Divorce is adultery if the divorcing or the divorced party enters on a new marriage. Such was the law from the beginning; the freedom of the bill of divorcement was, however, a concession by Moses to the Jews, who in their obduracy resisted the original sense and seriousness of marriage. It is indissoluble, and so for the one as well as for the other part; for the husband and wife are equal to each other in birth, since they both share in the one image of God. "Have ye not read, that he who created man also created woman?"[2] Of so sensitive a delicacy, however, is the holy bond that a covetous glance at a third person destroys it.

Jesus' comprehension of marriage is as free from juristic as from ascetic elements. God's creation is good, including the sensual intercourse of the sexes. The "one flesh," once united "by God," sundering with its might all the other ties of Nature, is the basis and demand for a unity and community of a higher nature. Not only in view of the new order of all things following the catastrophe of all that was earthly, which was believed to be near, not only the heroic ethics of the man of the Kingdom of God, in which he shall stand for approval before the eyes of the One, the Perfect; but more and deeper still, the law of the winning of life through its renunciation, the law of the higher form of human existence arising from the connection with the higher forms, requires in

[2] So, according to the old Syriac translation, read the revolutionary words in Matt. 19:4 concerning the equal rights of the sexes before God.

the eyes of Jesus the exaltation of the sexual life over the roaming impulse of Nature, and its mediatorship and employment in the service of an order which is not the order of impulse, but rather its opposite: His saying about the adulterous eye is followed by the counsel to pluck it out.

Consecrating the marriage bond, Jesus nevertheless understands the higher lustre of its renunciation "for the sake of the Kingdom of Heaven." Herein lies the motivating cause of the indecision of the Christian epoch concerning the fact of marriage. But what is the significance of this for the question of its sacramental character? That the exaction of marital chastity and fidelity shall be sustained and strengthened by the heroic ideal of the complete chastity of those who can comprehend it. The law of *noblesse oblige,* valid also in the domain of values, exerts a secret force of obligation from the condition of religious celibacy on the status of religious marriage. In all its long history it has been a blessing for the sacramental marriage that it could look on the bond of trust of the *Solus cum solo,* of the solitary one united with the One God; for here was the strength which marriage needed in cases of its inward danger—holy, sincere reality. The uncertainty of attitude toward the questions of virginity and marriage in early Christian times and later, finally the religious preference for celibacy, has prevented the shaking of the sacramental character of marriage itself. From the great contrast of the "No" to the world, which is in a bad state, and of the "Yes" to the other, God's own world, a most profound struggle arose in the valuation of Nature, of the matters of human life, and of society. How shall the Kingdom of God come, in what manner shall it appear, if not in the material of what exists on earth? So the cry is soon for the transformation of the temporary and evil through the medium of the Eternally-Good and Perfect. The Jewish heritage of the contrasts of two worlds and world-periods becomes associated with forms and contents of ancient thought, to fashion the message which has come down from Jesus into dogmatic teaching. But what Jesus applied to the "Father in Heaven," Paul applies to the Christ which Jesus became for him. He makes Him into an axis of the world of yesterday, today, and forever. In Him as the centre and the source of life, he applies and founds the still half-visionary bond of those who adhere to Christ, and writes a constitution for it. In spite of the unworldly aspect of the trend of his communal ethics and of all offensives against the "body of sin," he employs asceticism as a means to his will for construction. In the struggle against the "old" for the creation of the "new" man, he is led upon the way of the spirit, which repudiates sensuality, and whose goal and might and figure are the Christ, in Whom we must live. Toward Him the course of marriage is likewise directed, and if it indeed must exist—it would be better if man refrained from it—then let it endure according to the command of Jesus, as a holy and indissoluble bond; yet, in a still deeper sense as a mystery, through Him and upon Him. The flesh twain and one—this great secret is the same in the exchange of love between Christ and His community as in the unity of marriage. The ancient idea of the imitative founding of marriage in a supramundane relationship of devotion returns and mixes the moral essence of indissolubility with a mystic element. The Christ of the Faith finally took the rôle of the ancient Logos; and by this means philosophical thought also declared itself for the religious character of sacred marriage. It is explicitly named as a sacrament in the old, broad sense of the ancient *mysterion*, of the symbolic materialization of a hidden metaphysical reality; and the concept brings itself ever more clearly to the indication of indissolubility. It is, however, such a sacrament—this Augustine says—by reason of its nature and idea, not on the strength of its Christian consecration. While, since the days of Paul, marriage had to fight for its existence and its divine right against its denial in Gnosticism and Manichaeism, nay, against the *hybris* of virginity, a philosophical and mystical cultivation of marriage had already developed. The idea of sacredness here proves a breakwater to the perils on either side. The deep suspicion against the panther-beast in man demands the shackling of the impulse which had wrought destruction in the Roman Empire of the West; it is now considered as the most powerful cause of ethical disorder; but this habitual evil of the libido becomes of value in the service of a marriage which on the sexual foundation erects the temple of permanent moral union. If the sexual union sublimates itself to *caritas*, of which it is the symbol; if the holy God-spirit, on which rest husband and wife with their common eternal quality, is maintained above the tension of the sexual nature as a third and higher element, then such a bond of trust of the spouses between themselves and toward God is not less charism than virginity. Holy in its essence, marriage is also holy as a task of participating loyally and steadfastly in the birth pangs of the Church for the spiritual, godlike human being.

The mediaeval Christian period, and likewise the Catholic Church of our times, has not added any new thought to this. The fundamental preference for virginity, for the sake of a higher fruitfulness, was always matched by the praise of holy wedlock (*sanctum conjugium*), the "order of marriage," which was to surpass the religious through the direct divinity of its establishment and the still more profound persistence of its rule. Its essential sacredness found beautiful expression in the Roman precept (the Greek church thought otherwise) that the people entering into marriage, while they verbally guarantee their will to marry, should themselves administer the sacrament to one another. Against all attacks of the sophistry of impulse and the pantheistic dissolution of dogmatic foundations, the idea of marriage has maintained itself in the consciousness of Christendom as a bond sacrosanct in itself by its natural character. Like the whole order of human beings, it was supported by the great structure of the religious cosmos, in which the world of space and time was observed from the other world of the disposing God, and in which man and the human were not aim and goal in themselves, but rather the material and subject of God, for the supramundane and absolute end.

When Luther, in the surge of his chaotic nature, willingly or not, destroyed a thousand-year-old order, he demolished the old sacred marriage as well. Through his overstressing of a religious motive, he brought about the tragic revolution of the secularization of morality, and likewise of marriage. The God in the heart is always molten to nothingness by the heat of the human, and has done His human work under the empty name which remained to Him. "Thou dost not owe God anything, save to believe and confess. In all other things He makes thee loose and free, so that thou mayest do as thou wilt without danger of conscience; nay, He does not even inquire for His sake even if thou wouldst cast away thy wife and run away from thy master and failest to keep thy bond. For what is it to Him, whether thou keepest such a thing or leavest it?" "God is not concerned by the fact that the husband forsakes his wife, for the body is not bound to God, but is given by Him free to all external things, only inwardly belonging to God through faith. But before man the tie must be preserved. . . . Against God one cannot sin in this, but rather against his neighbour." The course of nature, asserted with radical pessimism—"We are all whoremongers"—is for him deserted of all good spirits. A fateful apotheosis of inwardness as the exclusive moral tribunal, a religiously exaggerated conception of sex-life in marriage as a permanent sin, despair with regard to the power of marriage to dam and regulate impulse, added to the prevailing sexual valuation of woman—all this led him—although he occasionally sounded the most beautiful praises of marriage—to discard the "human discovery" of the sacrament. He turned the "outward bodily thing like other functions" over to the arbitrary action of posterity and to profane handling by state and society. The puritanic purging and deepening of marriage into a bond in which God was the third and strongest participant did not occur without a reactionary movement toward the ascetic ideal of monasticism and against the original spirit of the Reformation. Meanwhile, for the majority of Europeans the old metaphysical support has been broken; and sacred marriage requires a new foundation.

To prove the indissolubility of marriage by its own essence is logically an attempt replete in perils. At the left and right of the road we are warned by the sacrifices of the vicious circle, which after the manner of fakirs has easily taken away the ring of indissolubility from the fundamental "concept of true marriage," possibly because they have regarded it from the beginning as of such value. But the seriousness of our problem requires its most difficult presentation. There is, then, primarily the knowledge that marriage, as a private and as a public matter, is involved with the most mobile elements of historic happenings: faith, attitudes to the world, and customs. That "essence" does not reveal itself in every epoch, and within a given epoch not to every stratum of civilization, in all its aspects, and still less in its ultimate depths. And if it were to be definitely assigned, for a time, a place in historic life, the comparative valuation, and much more, the determining of norms, would depend just the same on these mobile elements. Thus the natural law could well be reconciled with the rejection of polyandry, but not with that of polygamy, while in the discussion of indissolubility, it could not get beyond acknowledging that this was a very highly desirable form. For only when the guiding laws of moral consciousness have affirmed themselves through the experiences of society, through the differentiation and integration of personal life and possibly also through a kind of agreement of the best; when, in a word, a moral ideal governs the peoples of one cultural structure, at least in secret validity —then, resting on such grounds, a moral relation of the historically changeable regulation of marriage can be subjected to the question of its essence. While we apply, for the time being, in order to arrive at a firm ground of discussion, the name of marriage to the dissoluble tie as well, through whose recognition the civil law of today permits successive polygamy, we shall lay our ban on the partisans of polygamy and of the fundamentally esthetic and pleasure-seeking concept of life. With them we have no common ground of discussion.

Now, for the intellectual examination, the reality of marriage is designated as nature (physis), desire (eros), and morality (ethos). Of these three elements, which in the Logos of the entire phenomenon are certainly as interwoven with one another as in the drama of life, let us endeavour to understand the indwelling requisite of sanctity.

1. The sense of every community reposes in a third thing suspended above it. Friendships, alliances, peoples, nations, are more than the sums of their members. That of which a community has been formed or established is expressed in a flag and fashions itself to the genius which is the mainstay of the whole. Sexual union, as the most elementary, engenders also the most elementary symbol of its bond: the child. Arisen from the selfish, it turns itself against selfishness and seals the sexual tie as a moral bond. With it arises, as has so often been stated, the most powerful advocate of holy matrimony. But the fact of this power stands and falls with the power of the fact. The polygamous marriage also, which was less of a hindrance to stable relationships in its patriarchal form than the soluble monogamy of today, knows how to deal with the child; and where it is missing, should the sacramental tie between the spouses be missing with it? From them, and not from the child, antiquity has already pronounced (we here disregard the Bible) the postulate of duration and fidelity. When Penelope had already for a long time gone unimitated, when the marriage practices ran counter to Euripides' words—"to love *one* wedded wife and not *two*, in the manner of barbarians, was the Greek custom"—Aristotle led the way back to the good primitive state, pronouncing that the union of the spouses took place not merely that they might live with it, but that they might live one through the other in perfection; marriage was self-perfecting union in sexual contrast, therefore permanent and exclusive, and every union outside of it was wrong. The humanism of the middle stoa

has deepened this thought—"*unus homo nullus homo*"—and has deduced from the pure idea of man and society the concept of marriage which entered into Roman law and continues, in its essence, to live also in the more recent idealistic philosophy. With it the purely natural view is vanquished; the husband and wife, of equal right, are summoned to their share in the alliance aspiring toward moral unity from the polar pairing of nature; the sublimity of this knowledge may in the future be given up by the practices of life and by social theories, but never by the innermost conscience of cultivated man. This is, however, not sufficient to establish the sacramental character of marriage, the imperishable sanctity of its bond. For this Logos of alliance to physical and moral union ceased to be binding where the material was lacking for its realization. In the face of the internal ruin of the community it could explain of its own right: It has dissolved itself, its parts are not pledged to each other any longer, and each one is free to enter into a new union. It is incontestable; just the refining of personality, the complete internal equalization of the position of the sexes (with the consequence today of the economic self-reliance of the wife), but chiefly the reference to emotional inwardness, to the demands of conscience in the point of agreement of beliefs and actions—all this has wonderfully deepened successful marriage, but in so doing has made success more difficult. Its problematic character grows as marriage is removed from the basis of Nature and transported to the height of the spiritual and the moral. Yes, the moral indeed threatens the "sacrament." Does this need explanation? One knows the fate of the "inwardly untrue relationship" from "moral motives"; one also knows how soon, how often the Cana marriage-pitcher stands waterless—and that there is an esteemed court of jurisdiction whose judgment is: destruction. It is conscience. What conscience? Your personal conscience, of course. And are you quite certain of its holiness? Really? And *God* speaks from this altar, not *your* God, not *you?* And if you yourself had committed that "inward untruth"? Be it as it may—conscience is useful for all things, even for conscienceless-ness. In a case of emergency it does not refuse its blessing even to him who is a slave to impulse; he acts out of inner conviction, out of his fidelity to himself.—And his fidelity to the other? Indeed, his fidelity to the underlying laws of the bond? With the apotheosis of personal conscience, of pure inwardness, the fateful jurisdiction has been created in which the moral stands upon the brink, always in peril of transformation into its counterpart. Against the monstrous error of the Protestant Germanic world, where morality (and religion as well) is entirely entrusted to the disposition and conscience of the individual, we must call to arms the opposite Catholic world, in which subjective conscience receives measure, form, and advice from the objective conscience, from the law, and from other things necessary and established.—Morality, in the absurd sense of the autonomous conscience, excludes sacramental marriage as the highest conception of the immoral. Yet it is a question whether the common life of a pair does not contain in itself the source of its moral order, whether the sense of the unity aspired to in natural pairing be not identical with the sense of the sacrament.

2. Were man no more than a natural being, only a passively driven life, he would stand beyond all moral responsibility. But when as a person he enters into a higher order beyond the natural state, he must pledge himself to it in his totality, also as a physical and sexual

being. In the span between the sub-moral impulse and the gravity of the moral world, being a person, he again and again feels the conflict arising from this double order. No matter in what one may recognize the personalizing principle, it always appears as superior to the blind world of impulse, and its last result is personality, which before all (I do not speak here of God) exists as an aim for itself in itself. But just this independence which is its dignity is also the basis of a liberty limited by that dignity; nay, a liberty which loses in freedom of what is permitted as the height of the dignity increases. Personality is ordained as the highest law of its nobility, not to be subjected by nature or by any peril to its dignity of independence. Such peril is given in its destiny to exist for another. The tendency to devotion—whether it is in its affirmation of existence a Christ-like self-commitment with the aim of completion and expansion, or, from its negation of existence, the expectation of being extinguished in Buddhistic self-surrender (Buddhism covertly according infinitely more importance, if not indeed to the world, at least to the ego as the world, as the sole reality, than does Christianity, to which it is only the symbol and shadow of the divine universal reality)—the tendency to devotion is bound to the command of nobility in the free personality: that it shall not become an object. If it once with the whole of its existence has entered into a union with the totality of another, with indeed the will to enduring, full union—and this is the case of the monogamous marriage—retreat leaves the partners no longer as whole human beings, but used properties. Neither metaphysics nor religion is required to prove this dignity of the person as a non-object, of a being which is not merely animal. But if it is once recognized as holy in the sense of its own self-directed sovereignty, then the most complete existing amalgamation of persons is holy and indestructible; and it is a matter of the same importance whether the being who gives up the bond of his own free will (there is no such thing and never will be as a rending asunder) treats the other partner or himself as an object. The domestic servant, the labourer, the official, every partner to an agreement in the pursuit of non-personal aims, is dischargeable or exchangeable; but where the personal itself comes into play as basis of a union, there grows with the depth and breadth of contact the command of duration and exclusiveness. Who would want to appeal to his freedom at this point? He could only mean the freedom of the beast, which allies itself changeably with whom it will, not the freedom to preserve his ultimate dignity in power against the impulse and intrigue of Nature. Nature, the perpetual builder, the perpetual destroyer, blindly friend and foe of the order of spirit and of soul, nourishing and wasting it, creates good and evil also in the bond of the sexes. Here is at play the chaotic magic of impulse, the kindling of fires, relationships of choice, all that in the earthly realm of the moral produces joy and sorrow. But in this same Nature, for all its fickle luxuriance, an admonition to fidelity is perceptible. In the language of the religious man: It sighs for the revelation promised to the children of God. The bond of love entreats a boundless length of intoxication, an eternity of possession and of being possessed. Still more, the exchange of the bodily leads the spiritual as well, in a singularly binding way, to a sharing of joy and sorrow. "I breathed out my soul in the first kiss. Why is it that I torment myself, as to whether it found a house?" (Arnim.) "And the kiss remains within" (Goethe) means: By conjugal love, the moral being in man is aroused and called to take over the experience into its jurisdiction and there to perfect it in its own fashion. A secret feeling for the logic of this perfection is part of each love, but if the fatalism of a passion of the Tristan and Isolda or Paolo and Francesca kind does not chain the couple together forever and to all eternity, there gather about it a hundred causes of decay; and decay cannot be arrested unless, from beyond "Nature," free, exalted powers of knowledge, of will, or of faith elaborate the happening of Nature, lead it forth into the sphere of a new order and lawfulness. This, however, will be perceived by morally developed human beings even in the morning of love. Then the condition of forfeiture governs forever. Thus it has been said by mediaeval scholasticism in a dry sentence of the schools: The eternal duration of the bond lies in consent; otherwise, it does not establish marriage (Thomas Aquinas). The Catholic Church says that marriage is holy and religious Nature; not by virtue of an added human convention in Christendom and elsewhere, as an agreement of free wills, it is in itself essentially a sacrament. As such it proves itself more deeply still in the inner law and sense of the marital Eros, in its inborn destiny to be seized by the right of superhuman powers, by reason of which Goethe too understood marriage as a mystery in the sense of the Christian sacrament.

3. In the course of the bridal Eros to the married state, the way from flower to fruit, a consistent order is consummated; and it rests with man to decide what sort of fate he will allow it to become for himself. In the sexual sphere the conflicts of man and woman and of flesh and spirit are crossed, and in the vortex of their point of intersection the destiny of "human being" is decided for the man and for the woman, as the destiny "marriage" for the two, or rather of the one which they desire to be

and must be. If unanimity rules how they for their part wish to decide the conflict between the flesh and the spirit, and thereby as well the deepest antinomy of existence, then the conflict between man and woman is adjusted into the harmony of a duality, either by the common decision which declares for the flesh; that is to say, the mere use of life for the satiating of sensual appetite—or for the spirit; that is to say, a suprapersonal basis and sense of their human existence. The marriage of strong personalities irresistibly raises the occasion for this decision and in fact compels it. In this case it lies in the nature of the matter that the harmony which has come into being on the side of the flesh is more threatened by ruin than that on the side of the spirit. But no marriage escapes the law of the tragic, which is connected with these primal conflicts especially in their crossing; the unsuccessful marriage corroborates this by its very breaking upon it; the successful one succeeds only as it submits to the tragic law of sexuality, which escapes the character of the tragic only from an exalted and superhuman aspect.

The eternal myth of voluptuousness is written in the myth of the fall of the angels; the totality and the fulness of life, which one can grasp only from the distance of renouncing veneration, in the moment of contact thrusts the assailants back, far below the abodes of their original dignity. And as the pair in Paradise sought covering before the eyes of the Lord, so every consummation of love in flesh stands before the silent tribunal of a strange power. The egress from the garden of delight leads past a flaming sword. All the self-accounting of reason, that only the natural has happened, does not silence the voice of an accuser out of the dark. He desires satisfaction. And this, in the true understanding of the word as the fulfilment of an obligation, lies in the merging of all the possessions of the joined natures. Their agreement in the mere state of Nature justifies itself before the higher court of personality only as a symbol of moral intertwining. Through it alone is the sexually created bond satisfied. In this knowledge lies the demand for indissolubility (as for Kant and Fichte).

It results further from the natural law of transformation of the eroticism of a single pair. Whoever submits to it and does not, in order to perpetuate the sensual pleasure, leave his work of beginning as an unfinished torso, finds himself on the road to the eternal significance of sensual desire. He perceives the way if his Eros, liberated from the bondage of Nature, becomes open-eyed. This is the course of the voyage to the promised shore, which does not yet reveal itself truly in the first dawn of the promise. It lies in the twilight of knowledge that fulfilment of passion has likewise been deliverance from it.

Does it mean also deliverance from the partner?

The time comes when our inner potentialities contest the throne; disunion with oneself, and with it the menace of disunion of the tie. The crisis is nothing less than a crisis between Nature and culture. Here passion and love, sacrilege and sacrament become separated. Eroticism turns back to Nature to renew itself and repeats in its oath before a third presence the words of the broken one; or it submits to the law of transformation in some other form. Not separated from Nature but free from its compulsion, it then steps over from love (*amor*) to affection (*caritas*), from "I love you" to "I hold you dear." The third presence which now appears is not the countenance of an adulterer, but rather that of the angel who binds them. He has extinguished the flaming sword of the expulsion, since the creation of the bond beneath the Tree of Knowledge is expiated and blessed by the fidelity which has preserved it. The angel, transfigured Eros himself, protects marriage as a school of humanization. It stands, like all righteousness, under the sign of renunciation, which is the irremissible path to personal perfection. The ingenuous quest for happiness, though it might be the right of the childlike man, is exchanged by the clever man for the struggle for inner form. The superiority of *being* over *having* presents itself in an ever clearer and more pressing way, and marriage is the unceasing opportunity to perceive and to complete the structural law of existence. It lets itself be understood as the symbolic case of the ego-world tension, like the polar duality of the entire universe. But, like a drama, the acute conflict between the individuals as representatives cannot be wilfully suspended at any point; for its meaning can only be understood from its natural end: the transition from Eros as motive-power of life around the centre of the ego to Eros as the force which moves the ego around the timeless universe of valuation, in which it is mysteriously founded. But this knowledge, which thus is the fruit of love, in its turn marvellously increases love in height and depth. At the point when marriage produces boredom between frivolous souls, so that only habit makes them still fare together across insipid wastes, for others a transfiguration of passion takes place. "Marriage: thus I call the will of two persons to create that which is more than they who have created it. Reverence toward each other I call marriage, as toward those desiring such a will" (Nietzsche). To those who have possessed between and above themselves a higher third as an immovable mover, the way of trust and patience gives reward in the fulfilment of the "eternally" which the passion of the beginning has vowed. But what now comes to pass is eternity of a different kind. "Thou" becomes a symbol to the "Thou"; "Amen" to that trust in existence, testimony of good will, which binds all beings, guaranty for the One and All in one most exalted value. The sacrament stands unveiled and unveiling between those who have come together in its name. On it rests, on it feasts, the glance of the eyes which, after the "in one another" of bridal love and the "for one another" of wedded love, together rest on the likeness to which their union, receiving here its significance, has developed.

When viewed and lived in such a way, the sacrament of marriage is the most worthy reply to that covetousness of Nature which is called love. That also was Goethe's opinion: "Indissoluble it must be. There is no sufficient reason for separation."

None? The law-books say otherwise, and the great European tradition of holy marriage has already been destroyed through the right to divorce. The Catholic Church alone holds fast to it, even at the cost of the defection of the insubordinate. Its marriage-law grows out of the idea of the institution of God's will and grace and is, like everything Catholic, decided by the sovereignty of the matter itself over the persons. The logic of sanctity ignores the individual's fate and is deaf to the protests of the exceptional case, to yield to which means the violation of the principle and the recognition of the contradictory logic of chaotic Nature. Where the foundations of marriage are destroyed, dissolution of living together is permitted; but never, either for the guilty or for the guiltless party, is remarriage with a third conceded. In this gravity of the tragic appears no more than the gravity of sacredness, and the plaint of the happiness so sacrificed is not more weighty than the moral value which it pretends to possess. In every case this is slighter than the value of the sacrifice made to the ideal of an unconditional value. Man can do thus, or he can do otherwise; but his decision is governed by the law that there is no liberty in the most sublime. Liberty, however, to resign this most sublime remains with him. The temptation to do so is most intense in marriage whenever its necessary catastrophes, verbally understood as "turnings," divest a new profundity (or height) of its significance. Then appears the lure of a flight to a new and better ease; Eros reverts to the childlike ways of its inception, impulse to the crudeness of its exuberant nature; or fidelity goes the way of marriage up to the last word. Then the danger of the break, which is spared to few marriages, and which has been overcome, justifies itself, and even the state of inward defection, as an evolution from the order of the ingenuous and the natural into a higher one. The union which has been wrecked by hidden or open guilt, even if it be the most profound and noblest, proceeds organically to reunion; and this new bond is deeper and more secure than the first, since it is knotted by higher forces. Herein the law of sin and salvation consummates itself; the preference which is accorded the redeemed sinner over the righteous one who does not need mercy is seen as the prime law of the inner mysticism of humanity; the highest values of existence draw their life from their antithesis, and they are enhanced, in their struggle for redemption from their fall, to a deeper preciousness before themselves and their sphere. This law of fall and atonement, which is not to be understood in a trivial sense but rather as a way through negation to affirmation of the marriage-bond, is the natural grace of the sacramental marriage, inimitable as deed and as fate. Nothing but such marriage can offer it, since it alone dares venture the tragic sacredness of the firmly knotted bond, while the one which can be broken, which has its centre of gravity anywhere save in the thought of the partnership which is perfecting itself, the bond with a reservation, as if only in play, uses a mere slip-knot for the tie. "If the case of the man be so with his wife, it is not good to marry" (Matt. 19: 10). The word religion is upon my lips and the reader's, and it is time to pronounce it.

The objection will be raised that we have rather disclosed the character of the sacramental marriage than advanced proof that marriage is sacramental in essence. The answer lies as close to hand: The concept of the holy which is involved points to an ultimate immutable dictation of the moral, the reasons for which cannot be shown without trespassing on the realm of the metaphysical and of faith. To put it otherwise: The moral reaches out beyond itself, and this other world can be grasped only in assertions, in dogmatic explanation of world and of existence. The fact that marriage has come to be acknowledged as a holy relationship permits the elucidation of this sanctity, but it does not extend to the fathoming or establishing of the value "holy" itself. Here the prime phenomenon of the religious arises before us, and thanks to the connection between it and the entirety of man, who is held and determined by it unto his innermost essence, the last word on marriage as a holy bond falls not to knowledge, but rather to faith. On faith alone every personal decision in matters of marriage is based, and faith remains also the ultimate and most powerful factor where knowledge has said its "yea" to the holy character of marriage.

This state of affairs then decides our course as a progress from seeing to contemplating, from the objective to the personal; and whoever opposes it, since he does not wish to be led into the uncharted darkness of a personal world of belief, may dispute with the nature of things itself about the failure of all logic in the question concerning humanity in its analysis.—That connection between religion and marriage still requires, therefore, another examination. But while the perspectives of this matter run in every direction into the infinite, this only shall be considered: What is the mutual effect between the perfect marriage, that is, not the "happy" marriage but that which materializes according to its essence, and the common religious element of the religions of faith (not, then, of Buddhism, which is a religion of negation consistent to the point of absurdity, and therefore also of unbelief)?

First the fact must be considered that the highest religious forms of the ancient and of the Christian world pronounce the unqualified or qualified negation of marriage. It may be for the reason that it appeared to endanger the highest personal values in their earthly development, or the moral preparation of the personality for the perfect existence in the life to come; it encounters a profound scepticism both outside of and within Christendom. In Christendom, in so far as it has preserved the innermost spirit of its beginnings without having descended to the worldly ideal of a materialization of God in cultural activity, marriage clearly takes its place, not after mere celibacy, but after virginity. This prevails, as far as it is understood and lived as a sacrifice of love for the sake of God, of the highest, unconditional worth, as the heroic act of religious devotion through the life *Solus cum solo*—of the solitary with the solitary. In the fight between the flesh and the spirit the side of the spirit is stronger from the beginning and defends itself against the claims of the flesh, but in marriage the way leads from lust and deception by the flesh over the vanquishing of all its consequences to the sublimity of the justified spirit. The eternal goal of personality is the same here as there; the way to it, its sanctification through the ethos of the Cross, passes through marriage as through virginity, but the higher rank of nobility falls to him who achieves the required surrender of his ego without this tribute to the flesh and its danger of becoming self-indulgent. So marriage, although an *officium societatis humanae*, is surpassed by a higher value; and for that reason, according to Catholic teaching, divorce can be effected when the marriage-partners enter monastic life under the vow of chastity. Thus negation of marriage, like its affirmation, is bound to a most exalted significance and purpose. This purpose desires in every instance that man should be made free for it—*vacare Deo*, "to be open to God," it is termed in monastic phraseology—at the same time, regarding its effect, the perception of the basis of the world: *vacate et videte*, "be open and see." This conflict, with a large span, between the infinite need of man, his "hunger and thirst after righteousness," and the inadequacy of all worldly attempts to satiate it, provides that marriage too should be recognized and mastered only as a step at this juncture. Where Buddhism with curious logic denies the questioned being of man because it asks and thirsts, while his thirst is met by submersion in thought and contemplation, the connection between sacramental marriage and religion appears as a reciprocity of cause and effect. Goethe's saying that man, in the highest reasoning of which he is capable, touches divinity, "which reveals itself in prime phenomena, physical as well as moral, behind which it remains and which proceed from it," acknowledges this connection.

The holy marriage, which is true to its essence, possesses religion in itself. The ethos which we have outlined is the starting-point, indeed, the very likeness of all the fundamental features of religious reality—theologically speaking, a *testimonium spiritus sancti,* a witnessing of the Holy Spirit. All great human values, personal as well as objective, point beyond themselves to a giving and fulfilling realm of the unconditional, and this most of all in their antinomial, conflicting state. Although the desire of the sexes is explained and experienced as basis and likeness of the devotion to God (Max Müller), and although love, springing from soul to soul, ennobles, strengthens, and purifies itself in the divine love which has been kindled by the human prototype (as the begetters to the begotten), yet the matter always appears as if ordered from somewhere beyond and demanding another world. Thus in marital fidelity there lies a feature of belief in the loyalty of the world's foundation to itself, and in the experience of the delight of subjugating the raw material of Nature to the spiritual, a growing trust in the spirit, especially as essence and power. The command of asceticism, which irresistibly presents itself in right marriages, leads those who carry it out to the knowledge of this great antidote to passion—inborn, no less than passion, in the nature of man—and leads him along the essential line of true religion, unfalsified by cultural formality. Yet more: Indissoluble marriage is the enduring opportunity and direction for approaching and classifying the values of existence. The most prominent among them is the person of the partner. Then it is generally true that with the passage of the years its religious vocation for the other part, if this other's religious sense is not entirely missing or reduced to insignificance, becomes constantly of increasing importance. The happy—to speak naïvely—like the unhappy marriage is a loss of power to the first Eros. But this occurrence, in all instances when the marriage does not shatter on it, possesses the significance of a disturbing knowledge. Either it stops at resignation, which is so often invoked, or it comes to conversion into a transcendental Eros. The gradual comprehension of the "Thou" as a representative, as a "sign" in the sense discussed, is consummated in the harmonious union, as if human beings, hand in hand, understanding themselves and existence, were laid hold of by something beyond their love. Then their combined tears reply to the tragic law of love that it must always remain only an effort toward an impossible end. "Can a human being belong to another on the earth entirely, as he would wish?—I thought it over the long night through, and was compelled to say: No!" Even the greatest love remains only an attempt; human and human fundamentally cannot even with the utmost exertion reach each other and be united with each other, as their love urges and desires. Passionate love rages only because it feels its insufficiency. Eros must despair of himself; he is always *Eros thanatos*—mortal love. He does not die, but he is governed by the law of death; he is himself the law of death in the sense that he cannot become possessor of life even in its exuberance—then, indeed, least of all. In the quiet of unification, as in the tempests of the union, he realizes that it is denied to him to possess life in its reality, or indeed to be, as it is decreed to him, an urge into the infinite. The universal destiny of this experience forces the human beings whom it drives before it along different paths. The indifferent average, whether virtuously or not, acquiesce in being driven; but the strong and passionate personality, who sees himself scoffed at by his eternal Eros, takes up, while remaining in the domain of Nature, the tragic struggle (under another aspect it is also comic) for the perfecting of his Eros in new relationships, or—and this is the decision of the religious—he breaks for himself, by virtue of his knowledge of *Eros thanatos*, an entrance into another world. Whether we call it "supernatural" or something else, it is another Nature of a new, wonderfully liberating and delivering kind, most delightful through the light of the knowledge that in it Nature is not disposed of and destroyed, but rather fulfilled, exalted, and to its last degree beautified, as the material and substance of a higher, controlling order. What has occurred in this breaking through above Nature? I draw, for answer, the picture of a religious marriage.

In an hour of clear, quiet self-contemplation the spouses know and feel the structure of their bond and its affiliation with the structure of the entire world, which arises from the external and the internal. If chastity did not prevent the exchange of a word concerning the profoundest matter, the husband might break the silence with a confession somewhat like this:

"I hold thy hand in mine, and yet I yearn for thee. Our intimacy, profound as it is, is contested by a still deeper feeling of the distance that stands between us. The more our marriage has become knowledge of Mine and Thine, the more despairing the effort at union has become, which is the essence of our love. Our ultimate happiness, which fires us ever anew, is the impossibility of such union. No common delight, not even the deeper force of common suffering, has bound us so closely together as our mutual experience, growing with time, of the unmarriageableness of our being. Thou a human being, I a human being, like trees intertwined at their roots; but not ever one and the same being—each a mystery to the other, an ineffable individuality. It is a Third outside of us in which we are One—the soil in which each of us takes root, the space in which each of us grows, nourished, revived, and preserved by both. Not I and Thou are significant to one another, but to each of us that Third, and this in the vicarious appearance of a human Thou. Nameless, it has bound us from the beginning, though still covered by a dazzling light when we met each other, unconscious that the Third is more powerful than are both of us. But now we know it. It has disclosed itself to us between your and my isolation, and our love has become a testimony to our impotence to love, our bond an indication of something over us. Now we know it, we poles eternally separated, eternally drawn to each other, imposed upon each other; we have and hold one another, not for our sake, but that in this event of I and Thou that Third may take form, and with it we two as well. As long as we were to ourselves and to each other nothing but natures—*moi seul,* I alone, in the pitiful attempt to sublimate our nullity through Eros—one abyss then only called to the other, and our happiness was soon in its weight hardly different from the pressure of suffering. Then, gradually and imperceptibly, came education through the mortal essence of Eros. He has, to our eternal gratitude, chained together the human elements in us; he has, to our still profounder gratitude, thrown us back upon ourselves and led each one by himself to the truth that the last solitude of any human being is not to be filled by any other human being, even the most beloved. He has blessed us with the knowledge that marriage also, in the idiom of religion, is created 'toward God.' I do not care whether grace, wonder, or whatsoever sort of compulsion brings the name of God upon my tongue—it is enough that we know and adore the might of the Third as a will above us. He, the Third and One in whom we are united, is henceforth our law and our liberty; in Him and through Him is our bond holy, our solitude relieved, Nature freed from its dumb existence in itself, the dualism and the opposition of our souls bound up in the more exalted and relieved from the tragedy of their separation. Now for the first time can I love thee. Now thou art more than thou alone, and my love no longer founders on thee, since it reaches out beyond thee to all that is worth loving, which thou art to me. I love thee; now it means this: I love, I am a lover, because thou existest. Now forever we embrace infinitely more than merely one another; in embracing each other, we give testimony of that by which we are embraced. So thou hast become to me the best that one human being can become to another: the sign and pledge of the lovableness of the ultimate ground whence all things arise. If it is of such that it is said: 'What therefore God hath joined together let not man put asunder'; then it does not lie in our power to become divorced—for our bond is knotted and preserved by a third hand. Therein lies at the same time the significance of our divided self—also the sense of our 'one for the other.' While we, Thou and I, belong above all to it, our community is also in right order. We are no longer terrified at the truth that God alone is sufficient, but not any human to any other human. In Him we honour the common law of fidelity, the domination of the spirit over the roving animal in us; and when we are tormented by the reproach of sin, there still remains to us—since we are not appointed judges over each other—the path to freedom, in confession and pardon at a third place. Thus bound in God, we possess a true liberty. Thou, like me, an independent person pledged to duty to Him—we have not the right to fashion the form for one another according to our own inner law. But, so that we may each help the other to shape each other, that we should achieve through each other our true being—and that in the settlement of our differences, in the friction of our natures full of self-will and defect—this is the temporal significance of our marriage before God, and also the heaviest obligation that is imposed on us. I should have been forced, dear wife, to despair of success without the thought of eternity. But now I believe, as thou dost, in our eternal destiny and duration. See! Our life, destiny, hazard, occupation, and also marriage, is only one single opportunity to take shape under the hand of God the Artificer. It matters little whether we experience happiness or unhappiness; little, what we do, whether we make platters or pots; little, what human beings cross our path; but everything depends on this, to be and to remain in the right. All labour has significance only in relation to existence. Let us term that in which all things find their just proportion and their ultimate dispensation the eye of God; thus only comes to our eye true sight, with the belief in that eye: and let us call the mysterious sense of the world-occurrence the glory of God; thus our faith in this sense is our incentive to assume, without much protest and without arrogance, the tragedy of existence. So let us not tremble, if it falls on us, perhaps arising out of us ourselves; through it the world must be convinced that it is not God, but is of God. This belief, the belief in the Cross, renders it a sacrament for us—the sign of God in space and time. If we have grasped this, we will say yea to Nature, but yea likewise to its aspirations toward the supernatural, where it attains form and true being. Let us hold marriage as a sacrament, a copy of the great sacrament of the Creation, and restless with the substance of all our endowment, be creative toward eternity. We are not without help, and we are not alone. Strength comes to us in our colloquy with the Word which was in the beginning, and we are allied with the whole communion of the saints, of all those who have become aware of themselves in God. If death tears us asunder, he tears one personality from the other, but he does not tear it away from the Third to which ours, His likenesses, were directed."

The evanescent marriage of husband and wife becomes perfect and full of reality when it strives for likeness to the secret God and creation, or, speaking in the Catholic manner, that of Christ and the Church. And here we touch on a mystical element of marriage which does not possess its like in the history of man, nor is it ever to be surpassed in profundity, strength, and beauty. In a singular manner, it does justice to the dignity of the personalities, to metaphysical discussion of the sexes, and to the best in society. Here the immanent religion of marriage and parenthood is sanctioned and fortified in the objective explanation of world and existence as a concern of God. But the complete secularization of life and the reasons for the inner security of the Catholic Church have at the present time too deeply shaken the religious significance of sexuality and of the family to permit the old revelation to preserve itself as the universally obligatory form.

The culture which cannot endure without the heroic affirmation of the tragic has already been almost consumed by civilization, and the human formed or misformed by it, like a perverted centaur who shamelessly turns upward his animal part, stands shyly before the temples of God, for which the niggardly calculation which has supplanted his shrivelled soul can see no need. What can a sacrament be to him! And where will the religious genius of marriage still have shelter and home when the woman becomes mannish, can no longer be a wife to the husband?

She, the eternal feminine, in deepest proximity to the foundations of life, which moves closer, more narrowly, and therefore more contentedly around the centre of the source of life, and is thereby qualified to assemble and bind the fragmentary qualities in the husband, to solve his problematic element, and to adjust and expiate the fate of his centrifugal God-opposed disposition! How shall we reanimate the spirit of the ritual according to which the parties concluding marriage receive the Cross and Sword on each other's heads bent toward each other, the one as the symbol of their tragic, courageous trust in a higher order than the human, the other as the symbol of the unfailing wrath for every infraction of the law of the Cross?

The German Luther let loose the German demon of chaos on a structure a thousand years old. It is useless to argue with him, for the power of the dissonance which he released in the historic life of Europe is not without the character of a higher mandate. But to perpetuate the chaos, in the name of the hundred Germanic Christian faiths into which Protestantism has broken up Christendom, to throw back the most elementary benefit of culture, sacramental marriage—I know not whether from the terror of man or from desertion by God—into the natural state of the pleasure of lust, and moreover to do so in the name of an evangelistically intensified morality—that is sin against the Holy Ghost. Must it be perpetuated? Could there not be for the coming *una sancta evangelica* [one holy evangel] unification on the Luther of 1519, who was still in control of himself? He confessed to the *mysterium magnum*, the great mystery of holy matrimony, and wrote thus: "Is it not a great thing, that God is Man, that God gives himself to man and is his? . . . Behold, for the sake of marriage, since the union of husband and wife signifies so great a matter, the marital state must enjoy such importance. . . . Therefore a married man should heed this sacrament . . ." Hold by Christ, whom Luther followed, and not by Luther, who called on Christ to follow him; do not shun the truth of the spirit in the ruins of your worn-out Christianity, since all the piety and religion which are built solely on life and experience inevitably fail, and out of the strength of the Lutheran dispensation the might and consecration of the Logos may arise again—and thus may the new cells with which our German chaos is pregnant today help you to the light.

Our task, to prove the holy essence of marriage, is accomplished. Every child knows that it is so pronounced by the Catholic Church; there is no question that no jot will be altered in this pronouncement, but thereon depends the important question of the effective influence of this Church in the future. This leads to depths which are not to be investigated here. One thing is certain: the Catholic affirmation of the tragic, symbolized in the adoration of the Cross; its affirmation of Nature as the foundation of the higher reality of the supernatural to which it aspires and which it symbolizes in the process of the sacraments; its absolute will to the salvation and exaltation of Nature through culture, symbolized in law and dogma—the whole, although it must be modified in form and expression, cannot be abandoned in content and spirit without serious loss to the northern countries. Therein the sacramental marriage stands supreme. It shall be holy, not only for the sake of marriage and of society, but rather prototypically as the source and womb and cherishing of that sacrosanct essence which exists above all things—the daughter and mother of religion.

How the peoples will decide, we do not know. There remains to us for the hour only our confidence in the biblical sage: "*Deus sanabiles fecit nationes*"—"God has made the nations capable of being healed."

Postscript by the Editor

CERTAINLY many of the readers of *The Book of Marriage* will wish to know something of its several contributors. Among these, the creative artists—Thomas Mann, Munich, Poschingerstrasse 1; Jakob Wassermann, Altaussee, Steiermark; Ricarda Huch, Munich, Kaulbachstrasse 35; Princess Lichnowsky, Berlin W. 35, Buchenstrasse 2, and Rabindranath Tagore, Shantiniketan, Bengal, India—surely need no introduction. Paul Ernst, St. Georgen a.d. Stiefing, Steiermark, has written, in addition to many plays, three distinguished critical works concerning the problems of this age, namely: *Die Krisis der deutschen Idealismus* ("The Crisis of German Idealism"), *Den Zusammenbruch des Marxismus* ("The Breakdown of Marxism"), and *Die Zerstörung der Ehe* ("The Destruction of Marriage"—all published at Munich by Georg Müller). Among the men of learning are A. W. Nieuwenhuis, professor of anthropology in the University of Leyden, in Holland; Privy Councillor Professor Leo Frobenius, Frankfurt a. Main, Untermainkai 4, Director of the Institute for Culture Morphology of the same city, the originator of the precepts of a new system of culture and of a completely new organic examination of history as well. His small book *Paideuma* (Frankfurter Sozietäts-Druckerei), which contains its fundamental aspects, should be read by every one. Professor Dr. Richard Wilhelm, of Frankfurt a. Main, Lersnerstrasse 4, the founder and leader of the China Institute of that city, understands China better than any man not only in the West, but even in the Far East as well; and whoever truly wishes to understand the wisdom of China should read Wilhelm's translations of the Chinese classical writings which have appeared under Diederich's imprint, his *Chinesische Lebensweisheit* ("The Chinese Wisdom of Life"—Darmstadt: Reichl) and his *Kungtse* ("Confucius") and *Laotse* ("Lao-Tse"), volumes which have appeared under the imprint of Fr. Frommann. Ernst Kretschmer, author of *Körperbau und Charakter* ("Physical Form and Character"), is professor of psychiatry in Tübingen; Count Thun, Vienna I, Hoher Markt 8, formerly a diplomat, poet, and critic, was until recently editor-in-chief of *Die Europäische Revue.* Havelock Ellis, the world-famous author of many books on love and marriage, lives in London S.W. 9, 14 Dover Mansions, Canterbury Road; Sanitary Officer Dr. Dahlke, who resides in the Buddhist House, Berlin-Frohnau, at Kaiserpark, is the most significant living Buddhist, and his books on Buddhism, published in part by himself and partly under the imprint of Oskar Schloss of Munich, are by far the best which have been written by a Northerner on this problem. Rabbi Dr. Leo Baeck, Berlin W. 62, Burggrafenstrasse 19, is the author of many of the best modern writings on the spirit of the Old Testament, his *Wesen des Judentums* ("Essence of Judaism"—Frankfurt a. Main: J. Kaufmann) being especially commendable. Dr. Joseph Bernhart, Munich, Mauerkirchenstrasse 3, is one of the originators of the religious revival of our age. Dr. von Hattingberg, Munich, Ainmillerstrasse 32, Dr. Maeder, Zürich, Bergstrasse 107, and Dr. Beatrice M. Hinkle, 34 Gramercy Park, New York City, are neurologists and psychoanalysts. The last-named has written what is thus far the best introduction to psychosynthesis, a book entitled *The Re-Creating of the Indi-*

vidual (New York: Harcourt, Brace and Company). Dr. von Kemnitz is likewise a physician, residing in Tutzing, near Munich; and to her valuable pioneer work in the psychology of women many references have already been made in the text. The psychoanalysts—Dr. Jung, of Küssnacht b. Zürich, Seestrasse 228, and Dr. Adler, of Vienna 1, Dominikanerbastei 10—are, as everybody knows, the heads of whole schools. The former is the founder of the epoch-making theory of types—one should read especially *Psychologischen Typen* (Zürich: Rascher & Co.; English translation, *Psychological Types,* New York: Harcourt, Brace and Company)—and the propounder of the psychology of the collective unconscious, which proposes the reading of the history of peoples in the spirit of the individual. The "individual psychology" of the latter chiefly outlines a new course for the process of education—one should read his *Theorie und Praxis der Individualpsychologie* ("Theory and Practise of Individual Psychology"—Munich: F. Bergmann). Frau Karlweis, Altaussee, Steiermark, is the wife of Jakob Wassermann; and the Baroness Ungern-Sternberg is professor of philosophy and history in the Chinese University at Shanghai (address in care of Siemens China Company, Shanghai) and a sister of the editor. Her principal book in German is *Der Sinn des Sozialismus* ("The Significance of Socialism"—Darmstadt: Otto Reichl).

Note on the Translation

For the essays in this book by Dr. Beatrice M. Hinkle, Mr. Havelock Ellis, and Sir Rabindranath Tagore, the original MSS. in English have been used. The remainder have been translated from the German as follows: by Therese Duerr (Jung); by Paul Fohr (Dahlke); by William A. Drake and Dr. Walter J. Briggs (Adler, Lichnowsky, Kemnitz, Maeder, Baeck, Bernhart, Ungern-Sternberg, Hattingberg, Kretschmer, and the Postscript); and the others by W. H. Hilton-Brown under the personal supervision of Count Hermann Keyserling.